D0397527

The Sum of Our Dreams

Also by Louis P. Masur

Lincoln's Last Speech: Wartime Reconstruction and the Crisis of Reunion

Lincoln's Hundred Days: The Emancipation Proclamation and the War for the Union

The Civil War: A Concise History

Runaway Dream: Born to Run and Bruce Springsteen's American Vision

The Soiling of Old Glory: The Story of a Photograph that Shocked America

Autumn Glory: Baseball's First World Series

1831: Year of Eclipse

Rites of Execution: Capital Punishment and the Transformation of American Culture, 1776–1865

The Sum of Our Dreams

A CONCISE HISTORY OF AMERICA

Louis P. Masur

OXFORD
UNIVERSITY PRESS

OXFORD
UNIVERSITY PRESS

Oxford University Press is a department of the University of Oxford. It furthers
the University's objective of excellence in research, scholarship, and education
by publishing worldwide. Oxford is a registered trade mark of Oxford University
Press in the UK and certain other countries.

Published in the United States of America by Oxford University Press
198 Madison Avenue, New York, NY 10016, United States of America.

© Louis P. Masur 2020

CIP data is on file at the Library of Congress
ISBN 978-0-19-069257-5

1 3 5 7 9 8 6 4 2

Printed by Sheridan Books, Inc., United States of America

To Jani
Ben and Rachel
Sophie and Garrett
and my grandson,
Evan Saul Jaffe

The United States themselves are essentially the greatest poem.

—Walt Whitman

American history is longer, larger, more various, more beautiful and more terrible than anything anyone has ever said about it.

—James Baldwin

CONTENTS

LIST OF IMAGES

PROLOGUE: "LAND OF HOPE AND DREAMS"

A MERICA WAS MADE FOR DREAMING. It offered escape and it offered opportunity. For some who colonized it, this New Found Land promised religious freedom. For others, it afforded ownership of property and, eventually, slaves. Conquest was part of the enterprise right from the start. Only a few of those who arrived in the early days of settlement saw the indigenous population as having any rights, and warfare marked the first centuries as surely as disease. Over time, a common purpose emerged, sturdy enough to declare independence and create a new form of government. The United States became a land of dreams.

A Frenchman was among the first to examine the conditions that allowed Americans to forge a collective identity. J. Hector St. John de Crèvecoeur, a soldier and adventurer, arrived in New York in 1759 and farmed a parcel of land in Orange County, New York, near Goshen. His book *Letters from an American Farmer* (1782) made him a minor celebrity. Crèvecoeur asked a question that has resonated across time: "What, then, is the American, this new man?" His answer stressed equality and the possibility of enrichment. "The rich and the poor are not so far removed from each other as they are in Europe," he declared. The immigrant "looks around and sees many a prosperous person who but a few years before was as poor as himself." In America, anyone could succeed.[1]

In time, these elements formed part of what we now refer to as the American Dream. The phrase is credited to James Truslow Adams, a banker turned historian with no relation to the presidential

Adamses, who used the term repeatedly in his book *The Epic of America*, published in 1931 during the Depression. Adams defined it as "the dream of a better, richer, and happier life for all our citizens of every rank." Whether that dream is obtainable, and how access to it has changed over time, is the central theme of American history.[2]

Equal opportunity—"for all our citizens"—lies at the core of the American Dream, and it is linked to other fundamental principles such as freedom and democracy. These words have also been fraught and contested across generations. Americans have invoked them time and again during wrangles over domestic reforms and foreign involvement and, once, in the Civil War, on actual battlefields. Celebrated for their "individualism" (a word coined by another Frenchman, Alexis de Tocqueville), Americans have continuously debated the place of government in their lives. Whether invoking Abraham Lincoln's "Government of the People" or Ronald Reagan's "Government Is the Problem," citizens have fought over what it is they want their government to do, and not do, over how dreams can best be achieved and who should achieve them.

The struggles over these American ideals ground this history of the United States. An earlier example of the genre, Allan Nevins and Henry Steele Commager's *A Pocket History of the United States*, was first published during World War II. Revised and expanded editions in the decades that followed sold more than two million copies. One reader in particular illustrates the potential impact of such a work. On tour in Europe in 1981, Bruce Springsteen, who had dropped out of community college to pursue his rock 'n' roll dream, announced from a stage in Rotterdam that in reading *A Pocket History of the United States* "I found out where I came from and how I ended up where I was and how easy it is to be a victim of things you don't even know exist."

Thirty years later, Springsteen was promoting an album featuring a song called "Land of Hope and Dreams." His life's work, he said, had been about "judging the distance between American reality and the American dream."[3]

Judging that distance also informs this book. To do so means narrating the central developments and dramas of American history. Each chapter covers a distinct period of time and is divided into five sections that address some of the key events of the times. For example, the era of the 1920s–1940s is separated into sections on Prohibition, the Depression, the Dust Bowl, the New Deal, and World War II. Treating any of these topics in fewer than ten pages means streamlining them. My objective is not to overwhelm readers but to engage them. My goal is to provide a foundation of knowledge on which readers can base further exploration of American history. This book is about the sum of our dreams, not their conclusion.

All histories have a point of view and readers would be right to be curious about mine. I have been teaching American history for more than three decades and thinking about writing a one-volume narrative of the United States—and about how to address all of it, the reprehensible and the redemptive—for nearly as long. Some readers may dislike my emphasis on the underside of American history— racism, violence, and corruption. Other readers may wince at my unabashed admiration for the American experiment—freedom, democracy, and opportunity. I hope all can agree that Americans need to learn more about their nation's history.

The title of this book comes from a speech Barack Obama delivered in 2007 in Bettendorf, Iowa. A candidate for president, Obama emphasized what united Americans, not what divided them. Americans, he said, "share a faith in simple dreams. A job with wages that can support a family. Health care that we can count on and afford. A retirement that is dignified and secure. Education and opportunity for our kids. Common hopes. American dreams." They inspired his grandparents, and his father-in-law, and his mother. Visions of a better life for ourselves, and even better lives for our children, went to the heart of them. As he concluded his speech, he rose to his theme: "every American has the right to pursue their dreams. . . . America is the sum of our dreams."[4]

Plural, not singular. The many, not the one. Difference, not unanimity. This is the American story, one that has featured clashes between groups with divergent dreams as often as it has forged agreement on shared ones. Arguments about the role of government or the meaning of freedom expose major fault lines and at times the tremors have convulsed the nation. "America is a constant work in progress," Obama said on March 7, 2015, the fiftieth anniversary of the Selma to Montgomery civil rights march. Lincoln understood that as well. What he proclaimed at the start of the Civil War holds true throughout American history: "the struggle of today, is not altogether for today—it is for a vast future also."[5]

CHAPTER 1

To Plant and to Conquer

I N THE BEGINNING, AMERICA OFFERED a vision. In *Inducements Toward the Liking of the Voyage Intended Towards Virginia* (1585), Richard Hayklut the Elder, a member of Parliament who promoted English colonization of North America, provided these reasons for settlement: "To plant Christian religion. To trafficke. To conquer. Or, to doe all three." Some colonists came for faith; others to seek fortune. For many, North America offered escape from persecution, prison, or poverty. The land they settled was far from uninhabited, and they knew it. In 1600, millions of people lived between the Atlantic Ocean and the Mississippi River. But Europeans discounted indigenous peoples in their idea of America as virgin land, a wilderness onto which one could project anything. "In the beginning all the world was America," wrote John Locke in 1689. During the seventeenth century, approximately 160,000 English people traveled to the British mainland colonies in often harrowing journeys across the Atlantic that could last two to four months. It would take time, but eventually these colonists would transform themselves from British subjects into Americans.[1]

Virginia and Southern Colonies

In 1585, John White, a London illustrator, joined an expedition to establish an English colony in America. White's purpose was neither evangelical nor commercial. It was artistic, even anthropological. White was commissioned to "draw to life" the inhabitants he encountered. He landed at Roanoke Island, in present-day North Carolina, and completed dozens of watercolors of Algonquin people.

After White returned to England, Sir Walter Raleigh (who held a royal charter from Queen Elizabeth to explore and colonize non-Christian lands) asked him to organize another expedition and named him governor. Supplies began to dwindle for the more than one hundred colonists, and conflict with native tribes put the enterprise at risk. White sailed for England to gather supplies, but on his return five years later, delayed because of conflict with Spain and the defeat of the Spanish Armada, no sign was left of the settlement.

White's original watercolors became the basis for engravings by Theodore de Bry that accompanied the illustrated edition of Thomas Harriot's *A Brief and True Report of the New Found Land of Virginia*, published in 1590. A mathematician and navigation expert, Harriot had been central to Raleigh's colonization plans. A comparison of a White watercolor and de Bry's engraving illustrates the vision of America presented in the promotional literature that sought to persuade Englishmen to migrate. White's original is a plain, unadorned drawing that shows two Algonquians squatting before a plate of deer meat they are eating. In de Bry's version, the Algonquins have been Europeanized. The man is muscular and the woman enticing. They no longer squat, as White had observed, but sit in European fashion. The simple meal has been transformed into a feast with water gourd, fish, maize, and a clam or scallop shell. A horizon line has been added: Here is a vast land of plenitude.

In 1607, the Virginia Company, with a charter from King James (Elizabeth had died in 1603), celebrated as some 104 settlers landed at Jamestown peninsula and established the first permanent English settlement in North America. (Spain established the first permanent European settlement along the Atlantic coast at St. Augustine, in what is now Florida, in 1565; the French founded Quebec in 1608. The histories of New Spain and New France follow their own trajectories; the focus here is only on English colonization). They were all men—gentlemen and laborers. The following year, the first women arrived, wives of husbands already settled as well as servants and maids.

It is remarkable that the settlement survived. Drought, famine, and disease killed many, as did hostilities with the Powhatan. Matters improved for a brief period when Captain John Smith arranged for trade with the Indians, but in 1609 he returned to England for treatment of injuries caused by a gunpowder explosion and the Powhatans, threatened by the arrival of hundreds of new settlers,

Figure 1.1 John White, Watercolor of Indian Man and Woman Eating (1585–1586). British Museum.

cut off trade and laid siege. Having chosen a poor location for an English colonial outpost, only 60 of 300 colonists survived the winter of 1609–1610. Although the arrival of supply ships saved Jamestown, still it seemed colonists preferred not to work or plant. "He that will not work shall not eat," John Smith had admonished. In May 1611, a new governor observed that the people were at "their daily and usuall works, bowling in the streets."[2]

The story that Pocahontas, the daughter of Chief Powhatan, intervened to save John Smith is almost certainly an invention created by the captain. Colonists kidnapped her in 1613. She converted to Christianity and in 1614 married John Rolfe, a tobacco planter. The plant may have saved the settlement from disease, famine, sloth, and Indian incursions. Rolfe experimented with tobacco seeds and the settlers soon found a product that smoked "pleasant, sweet and strong," and also could compete in English markets with tobacco from Spain. The cash crop came to dominate the economy and over the next century spread across Virginia. In need of labor for

Figure 1.2 Theodore de Bry, "Their Sitting at Meate" (1590). John Carter Brown Library.

the explosive growth of tobacco planting, a legal grant of land to settlers, known as a headright, offered colonists who paid their own way fifty acres of land. Wealthy individuals would amass vast tracts by paying the way of the poor. Tobacco led to the creation of port towns where warehouses stored the hogsheads of tobacco ready for ship-ment across the Atlantic.[3]

Tobacco cultivation required labor. Indentured servants, who agreed to work for four to seven years in return for passage, food, clothing, and shelter, filled the need at first. Between 1630 and 1680, three-quarters of the immigrants to Virginia (more than 50,000 people, mostly men) were indentured servants. Virginia's elites grew increasingly anxious over the behavior of servants and those who had been released from their indentures. The General Assembly convened in 1619 "to establish one equal and uniform government over all Virginia" and regulated servants' freedom and movement. In time, they even passed an act "against fornication." The assembly also tried to legislate against mistreatment of servants.

Over the course of the seventeenth century, servitude for whites coexisted with slavery for Africans and eventually disappeared. An English privateer brought the first Africans to Virginia in 1619, and colonists most likely treated them as indentured servants. In 1650, some 300 Africans lived in Virginia. While slavery was not yet codified into law, it is clear that African and European servants were treated differently and some African servants were considered slaves. Starting in the 1660s, the assembly passed slave laws that addressed "whether children got by an Englishman upon a Negro woman should be slave or free" (children would follow the mother's status), and declared that baptism "doth not alter the condition of the person as to his bondage."[4]

Colonists embraced slavery for a variety of reasons: a decline in the number of available indentured servants; the success of European entrepreneurs using slave labor to produce sugar in the Caribbean; the expansion of labor-intensive tobacco growth; and a belief in racial superiority. An Act Concerning Servants and Slaves, passed by the General Assembly in 1705, provided that all nonwhites and non-Christians brought into the country (except for Turks and Moors) "shall be accounted and be slaves." The act also provided for harsh punishment for slaves who committed crimes or ran away. In his *History and Present State of Virginia* (1705), Robert Beverly, clerk of the House of Burgesses, made clear the new reality: "Slaves are the Negroes, and their Posterity follow . . . the condition of the Mother." By 1750, slaves from West Africa constituted more than 40 percent of the population in Virginia.[5]

The transition to racial slavery served another purpose: It helped unify wealthy and poor whites. As the colony grew in the 1660s and 1670s, and settlers moved west toward the Piedmont, the area between the Atlantic Ocean and the Appalachian Mountains, they sought protection from Governor William Berkeley and allies in the East. The governor, however, refused to battle the Indians on behalf of the poor farmers and frontiersmen. Nathaniel Bacon, a wealthy Cambridge-educated planter, had arrived in Virginia in

1674, and was almost immediately appointed to the Governor's Council. Ignoring the governor, a kinsman through marriage, Bacon organized an attack on the frontier tribes. On July 30, 1676, he issued a Declaration of the People of Virginia that condemned the governor as corrupt, denounced excessive taxation, and demanded protection against "many invasions, robberies, and murders committed upon us." The outraged rebels—poor whites and blacks who had found common cause—even attacked Jamestown. Berkeley fled for safety. The rebellion came to an end only with Bacon's sudden death from the "Bloodie flux," probably dysentery. Berkeley hanged twenty-three rebels for treason. The prospect of such biracial cooperation caused social elites as much anxiety as anything and served as another factor in the codifying of slavery.[6]

Slavery's entrenchment came even more quickly in neighboring Maryland. Established in 1632, Maryland was founded by Cecil Calvert as a refuge for British Catholics in an age of religious persecution. The colony was named after King Charles's wife, Queen Henrietta Maria, who was Catholic. More Protestants than Catholics, however, settled the colony, and Anglicans battled Catholics for control of government. In 1649, the Maryland Assembly passed the Maryland Toleration Act to allow Catholics to practice their religion. After the execution of King Charles in that same year and the outbreak of the English Civil War, however, the law was revoked. With the Glorious Revolution of 1688, in which the Catholic King James II was deposed, Protestants gained complete control of Maryland and banned Catholic worship.

Both Catholics and Protestants participated in tobacco cultivation, and Maryland, like neighboring Virginia, moved swiftly from indentured servants to enslaved Africans. The first slaves arrived at St. Mary's City in 1642. In 1664, the assembly passed an act that established that all slaves would serve for life. Conversion to Christianity would not free them. The white population of Maryland grew from 25,000 in 1700 to 100,000 in 1750, by which point there were more than 40,000 slaves in the colony. The assembly also passed a law that barred masters from freeing their slaves. Some of the enslaved tried to escape, and the assembly issued various laws for tracking down and punishing recaptured runaway slaves.

North and South Carolina grew more slowly than Virginia and Maryland. They began as a single entity, the Province of Carolina, which was run by proprietors who held a charter from Charles II. Religious and political battles roiled north and south (in Cary's rebellion in 1711 the governor, Thomas Cary, refused to relinquish his position to British administrator Edward Hyde), and in 1712 they divided into distinct territories and eventually became separate royal colonies. By 1750, North Carolina had a white population of 53,000 and a black population of nearly 20,000, whereas South Carolina claimed 25,000 whites and 39,000 blacks. The presence of a black majority in South Carolina would shape politics there and elsewhere for decades to come. Rice was to South Carolina as tobacco was to Virginia, and planters relied on slaves for their knowledge of rice cultivation, which was commonplace in West Africa. Charleston, therefore, became the port of entry for hundreds of thousands of enslaved West Africans.

As elsewhere in the South, east-west divisions in the Carolinas formed as coastal planters owned slaves and upcountry Appalachian subsistence farmers did not. Differences of religion, wealth, and education, not to mention geography, separated those in the backcountry from those on the coast, though fear of Indians and blacks kept their interests united. In 1739, a slave rebellion near the Stono River led to the killing of more than forty whites and burning of plantations. The captured slaves were executed and the colonists mounted their severed heads on pikes as a warning to others.

Unlike Virginia, North Carolina, and South Carolina, Georgia's founding was based on the vision of one man, James Oglethorpe, a Member of Parliament and a social reformer. In 1732, Oglethorpe won a charter for a new colony with the idea of providing an alternative to the horrors of debtor prison. Led by Oglethorpe, some forty English families established a settlement near present-day Savannah. Oglethorpe's vision did not include rum or slavery, and he had the trustees ban both. "If we allow slaves," he wrote, "we act against the very Principles by which we associated together, which was to relieve the distressed." Over time, self-interest overcame principle as settlers believed that slave labor would make the fledgling colony more successful. In 1751, the House of Commons adopted new legislation that permitted slavery in Georgia. White South Carolinian slaveholders flooded into the region, and between 1750 and 1775 Georgia's slave population expanded from 500 to some 18,000. Oglethorpe did not witness the turn to slavery. Following a series of military campaigns against the Spanish, who sought to invade the English colonies, Oglethorpe had left Georgia for good and returned to England in 1743. He lived until 1785, long enough to meet with John Adams, minister to the Court of St. James for the newly founded republic, and express his "great esteem and regard for America."[7]

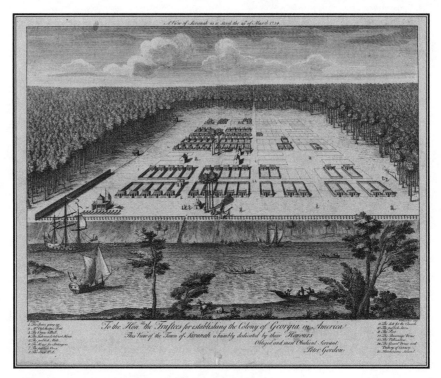

Figure 1.3 *A View of the Savannah* (1734). Library of Congress.

Massachusetts and New England Colonies

The immigrants we call "Pilgrims" broke from the Anglican Church completely, were persecuted for their practices, and, as separatists, traveled first to Holland before embarking on a journey to America in 1620 aboard the *Mayflower*. The Puritans (a term of derision first used in the 1560s and applied to Pilgrims as well) also wanted a reformed and purified church and migrated by the hundreds in 1630, and in the thousands in the following decade. Pilgrim Plymouth Colony and Puritan Massachusetts Bay Colony, their differences always more abstract than real, merged in 1691.

Aboard the *Mayflower*, which took sixty-six days to cross the Atlantic and carried just over one hundred passengers, forty-one men signed a compact and agreed to "Covenant and Combine ourselves together into a Civil Body Politic." One of the signers, William Bradford, would serve as governor and first historian of Plymouth. Tragically, his wife, Dorothy, fell overboard and drowned while the men were still exploring the area for a place to settle. By the summer of 1621, more than half the settlers had perished. Bradford's story, as told in *Of Plymouth Plantation* (1651), extolled the courage and faith of the Pilgrim fathers who crossed a vast ocean and entered a "hideous and desolate wilderness, full of wild beasts and wild men" and out of it created a covenanted community. That "desolate wilderness" was a result of Plymouth being depopulated by epidemic disease among the Indians (perhaps leptospirosis, a disease caused by contamination from rodents that arrived on European ships). Those "wild men," the Wampanoag, helped the settlers survive. With the aid of Squanto, an Indian who spoke some English because he had been abducted in 1614 by a trader and spent time in England, the groups agreed to a formal treaty of mutual aid and defense. Squanto lived among the settlers and taught them how to grow corn. He proved indispensable to Bradford, who recorded Squanto's death in 1622 as a "great loss."[8]

While Bradford led Plymouth colony, John Winthrop, an affluent lawyer, led Massachusetts Bay Colony. The seal of the Massachusetts Bay Company, which financed the colony, showed an Indian holding an arrow pointed down and saying, "come over and help us." In 1630, Winthrop delivered a lay sermon on the *Arbella* to the colonists titled "A Modell of Christian Charity." Winthrop appealed to the need for community and selflessness: "We must bear one another's burdens. We must not look only on our own things, but also on the things of our brethren." The stakes for New England were high: "we must consider that we shall be as a city upon a hill. The eyes of all people are upon us. So that if we shall deal falsely with our God in this work we have undertaken, and so cause Him to withdraw his present help from us, we shall be made a story and a by-word through the world." City on a hill: visible but exposed, exceptional but isolated. John F. Kennedy, Ronald Reagan, and Barack Obama would each invoke the phrase to define the American experiment.[9]

All communities of faith face the dilemma of how to deal with the unfaithful. Bradford discovered that Reverend John Lyford had been writing letters back to England that undermined the separatist movement, those who had broken away completely from the Church of England, and that the reason Lyford had first come to Plymouth was because he had "defiled" a congregant before her marriage. Trembling at the "deceitfulness and desperate wickedness of man's heart," Bradford banished Lyford, who settled in Virginia.[10]

Lyford was a reprobate. Thomas Morton might as well have been a heathen. He arrived in 1624, rejected the religious strictures of Plymouth, and started his own community, called Merrymount.

Colonists engaged in sexual relations with Algonquin women and spent time in drunken revelry and merriment. Come May 1, they would hold a party and erect an eighty-foot maypole. Morton's actions scandalized the Pilgrims. Bradford denounced them as dissolute and profane, "the beastly practices of ye mad Bacchanalians." Morton was repeatedly banished, but he kept returning and was arrested each time. While awaiting trial in Boston for sedition, his health deteriorated. He was granted clemency and died in 1647.[11]

Morton was a religious outsider. Massachusetts Bay Puritans also faced controversy over religious orthodoxy from insiders, from members of the community. As Calvinists, all Puritans believed in predestination, original sin, and innate depravity, but they disagreed over how one was saved. The Covenant of Grace held that only God's grace, a mystical experience of the spirit, granted salvation. Conduct and effort did not matter. Believing that moral behavior was a sign of salvation inched toward a Covenant of Works. This was Anne Hutchinson's critique of the clergy when she arrived in 1634 with her husband and ten children (her oldest son arrived the year before).

Hutchinson had followed her minister John Cotton to Boston, and she soon developed a following of her own for weekly meetings held in her home. Hutchinson denounced the clergy for offering a doctrine of works. She insisted that outward signs of behavior bore no relation to salvation, a proposition that scandalized orthodox ministers, who charged that Hutchinson was an Antinomian, someone who believed that faith alone assured salvation. That a woman would dare to preach only added to the clergy's hostility. She was tried for defaming the ministers. John Winthrop condemned the meetings she held as a "thing not tolerable nor comely in the sight of God, nor fitting for your sex." Hutchinson refused to give way. "Now having seen him which is invisible, I fear not what man can do unto me," she testified.

The General Court found her guilty and banished her. Hutchinson resettled in Providence Plantations, begun only a few years earlier by Roger Williams, another heterodox thinker who had left Massachusetts in 1636 and founded Rhode Island and organized the first Baptist Church in America. In his many writings, Williams argued for separation of church and state and, in *The Bloody Tenant of Persecution for Conscience Sake* (1644), used the phrase "wall of separation." He also defended Indian rights to their land, arguing that the King could not deed what was not his to give, and he admired the way Narragansett tribes lived.

Others, too, faced banishment in the aftermath of the Hutchinson affair. John Wheelwright was banished for defending Hutchinson (his sister-in-law) and helped found New Hampshire. In contrast, Thomas Hooker settled Connecticut in 1636 (and received an official charter in 1662). Hooker had arrived on the same ship as John Cotton, but disagreed with Cotton's preaching. Believing that people could take actions to prepare for conversion, he also participated in the prosecution of Anne Hutchinson.[12]

If the government of God could be severe and dogmatic, the government of man proved flexible and even democratic. In a sermon delivered in Hartford in 1638, Hooker declared, "The foundation of authority is laid, firstly, in the free consent of people." The people would choose who governed them by electing representatives. The Fundamental Orders of Connecticut, adopted by the General Court in 1639, following a model already established in Massachusetts, created a basis for government, and enumerated individual rights.[13]

The 1641 Massachusetts Body of Liberties provided a legal code that included freedom of speech, right to assembly and petition, and right to trial by jury. The Body of Liberties also legalized slavery in Massachusetts, and although slavery in New England never accounted for much in terms of percentage of population (a few percent in Massachusetts and Connecticut and perhaps as much as 10 percent in Rhode Island, though much higher in cities such as Boston and New London), the institution had an impact on all aspects of the economy. The enslaved worked in households, held various skilled jobs, and supported the lives of ministers and merchants, among others. More broadly, the region was deeply invested in slavery. Many merchants made their fortune through the shipping industry and by provisioning the West Indies, where slaves were being imported from Africa to cultivate cane and produce sugar and where the mortality rate reached 50 percent. Peter Faneuil, for example, owned five slaves and made his fortune not only in trade for tobacco, rum, and molasses, but also through direct involvement in the slave trade. He gave the hall named after him to the city of Boston. Before it gained the nickname of "Cradle of Liberty," Boston's slaves were bought and sold next to Faneuil Hall.

Though colonists enjoyed elected government and individual rights, these should not be mistaken for secularism: these were theocratic governments in which only white male church members participated. To become a full church member, a congregant had to show signs of a saving faith through a conversion experience. As the decades passed, church membership posed a problem, as many had been baptized yet few showed signs of a conversion experience. Their children, therefore, could not be baptized. The so-called Half-way Covenant, adopted in 1662, allowed for the children and grandchildren of church members who had not demonstrated a saving faith to be baptized. The Half-way Covenant did nothing to curb the anxiety over spiritual declension—a belief that the children and grandchildren did not share the sense of piety, providence, and mission that motivated the first generation. For example, preach as they might against the sin of fornication, ministers faced the reality that it was prevalent. In Plymouth, between 1633 and 1691, based on marriage and birth records, approximately 11 percent of married couples engaged in premarital sex. During that period the courts tried sixty-five cases of fornication before marriage. This is not to say the founding generation was chaste. They nonetheless lamented the behavior of succeeding generations even as they participated in worldly commerce and trade that helped accelerate their perception of decline.

One way to purify the community was to cast out Satan. Winthrop declared that the devil had deluded Anne Hutchinson, and anxiety over the devil's presence, which emerged time and again in the seventeenth century, reached frenzied proportions during the Salem witchcraft trials of 1692. The hysteria began in January 1692, when two girls, the daughter and niece of Reverend Samuel Parris, started to behave strangely. They screamed and howled, said they were being bitten, and acted as if they were flying. Others also became afflicted. Soon, three people were accused of being witches, Sarah Good, Sarah Osborne, and Tituba, a West Indian slave. Accusations spread to others and prosecutions and trials began in June. Yet without a confession, how could it be determined if the devil possessed someone? Courts relied on various signs, including spectral evidence—a belief that the spirit of someone could appear even while that person's body was elsewhere. Executions for witchcraft began in June and continued until September. Good was hanged, Osborne died in jail awaiting trial, and Tituba, by confessing to witchcraft, escaped prosecution.

By the time the trials ended, Salem had hanged nineteen people, including five men. Others perished in prison. Some escaped. Giles Corey, eighty-one years old, refused to plead and died from pressing, the placing of heavy stones on his body in an attempt to force him to declare guilt or innocence. The events in Salem have been variously interpreted as a battle between neighbors vying over property; a conflict between rural Salem Village and commercial

Salem town; an episode of psychological hysteria led by young girls rebelling against parental authority and dreading their future role as wives and mothers; or a response to anxiety over outsiders (one accuser said the devil had "taken the shape of a black man whispering in her ear") and the traumatic events of Indian wars. It did not take long for regrets to set in. Cotton Mather, who played a crucial role in condemning the witches, expressed remorse. A few years later a Salem judge, Samuel Sewall, apologized, and in 1711 the colony compensated some of the survivors and the families of the deceased.[14]

By then, the seventeenth-century wars between colonists and Indians had largely concluded. Between 1636 and 1638, English colonists and their Narragansett and Mohegan allies decimated the Pequot. Settlers set fire to a Pequot village near the Mystic River in modern-day Connecticut, blocked the exits, and shot anyone trying to escape. King Philip's War nearly forty years later proved more deadly and inverted alliances from 1637. In 1675, the surviving Pequots joined with the colonists against the Narragansett. Metacom, who had taken the English name Philip, launched an assault after three Wampanoags were hanged in Plymouth Colony. His sister-in-law, Weetamoo, played a critical role in trying to protect tribal lands and, as leader of a branch of the Wampanoags, help her people survive. The war spread across New England, with more than half of the towns and villages facing raids. It is estimated that more than 2,500 colonists died. Natives lost far more, perhaps 5,000 killed or dead from disease and another 1,000 sold into slavery.

In 1689, another war erupted in Europe and America, King William's War, the first of several colonial wars that pitted the English against the French with Indian allies fighting on both sides. The Wabanakis allied with the French. Even when that war ended, other conflicts followed. In 1704, an Indian raid on Deerfield in western Massachusetts led to dozens of deaths and the capture of more than one hundred colonists, who were marched to Canada. Some were ransomed, but others chose to remain with their captors. Captivity narratives became a popular literary genre as readers hungered for true tales of life among the Indians. In *The Redeemed Captive Returning to Zion* (1707), John Williams, a Deerfield minister, related how he remained steadfast in his faith and avoided sacrilegious behavior. "I should sooner choose death than to sin against God," he proclaimed. No narrative was more influential or successful than Mary Rowlandson's. Captured during King Philips's War and held for eleven weeks before being ransomed in 1676, she published *The*

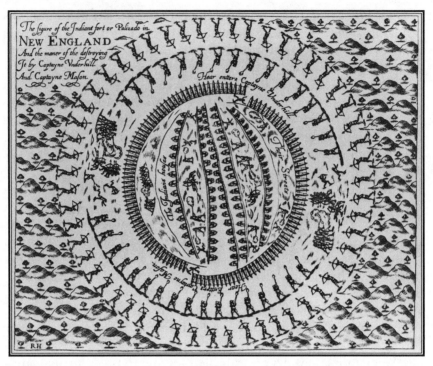

Figure 1.4 *The Figure of the Indians' Fort or Palizado in New England* (1638). Library of Congress.

Sovereignty and Goodness of God (1682). Readers on both sides of the Atlantic were enthralled by the story of her captivity and restoration.[15]

Orthodoxy waxed and waned in Massachusetts and New England. By 1750, the population of New England exceeded 300,000 people. Boston claimed 15,000 residents. The colonies were thriving, and new ideas were pushing against Puritan pieties. Isaac Newton's *Principia* (1687) established universal laws of motion and gravitation and ushered in a scientific revolution. John Locke's *Essay on Human Understanding* (1690) argued that all people were born blank slates (*tabula rasa*) and therefore environment, not predestination, determined their fates. One could make oneself into what one wanted to be, and newly established colonial colleges in Cambridge and New Haven, though begun as seminaries to train clergy, helped spread these beliefs.

Ministers on both sides of the Atlantic fought back against rationalism and the Enlightenment. A religious revival, originating in England and called the Great Awakening in America, swept New England and the Middle Colonies in the 1730s and 1740s. Jonathan

Edwards, a pastor at Northampton (and John Williams's nephew), became a leading figure in the Great Awakening. He terrified his congregants to inspire conversion. In his sermon "Sinners in the Hands of an Angry God" (1741), Edwards compared the parishioners to a spider held over the pit of hell by God. Edwards threatened that only solemn worship kept them from being cast into the flames. Faith was a matter of emotion, not reason. In 1758, Edwards accepted the presidency of the evangelically minded College of New Jersey (later named Princeton University) and died from complications after taking a smallpox inoculation. Edwards is buried in Princeton next to his grandson, the New York politician Aaron Burr.

New York and Middle Colonies

It was New Amsterdam before it became New York. Dutch merchants and traders, seizing on a report written by the English explorer Henry Hudson, who in 1609 explored the narrows and the river that now bears his name, began settling the region in 1613. In 1624 New Netherland became a province of the Dutch republic, and New Amsterdam, on the lower tip of Manhattan Island, served as its center of government. The Dutch acquired the land from the Lenape for sixty guilders worth of goods (myth has placed this at $24, but the price was closer to $1,000). For the next forty years, the settlement grew, part of that time under the direction of the Dutch West India Company. Its location at the mouth of a river that ran to Beverwijck (renamed Albany) provided a lucrative opportunity to trade with native tribes for beaver pelts. A sawmill for timber was erected as well. Large farms that grew corn, wheat, flax, and vegetables soon emerged.

Under Peter Stuyvesant, the director-general from 1647 to 1664, the colony developed. Like the Puritans in New England, Stuyvesant, a member of the Dutch Reformed Church, had little tolerance for religious freedom. He would not allow the Lutherans to organize a church, he opposed the entry of Jewish refugees from Brazil, and he ordered the public torture of a Quaker minister. In 1657, residents of Flushing protested and issued a remonstrance: "We desire therefore in this case not to judge least [i.e., lest] we be judged, neither to condemn least we be condemned, but rather let every man stand and fall to his own Master." The Dutch West India Company overruled Stuyvesant and ordered him to "allow every one to have his own belief."[16]

In 1664, the English seized the colony and rechristened the area New York (after the Duke of York). The Dutch relinquished their claim following the second Anglo-Dutch War (1665–1667). New York was probably the most polyglot place in North America. In addition to the Dutch and English, there were Germans, French (mainly Huguenots), Swedes, and Finns. There were also enslaved Africans. Newcomers spoke at least sixteen languages. Lutherans, Presbyterians, Congregationalists, Jews, and Quakers were among the religious groups. In the eighteenth century, English clergyman Andrew Burnaby commented that the Middle Colonies were "composed of people of different nations, different manners, different religions, and different languages." He doubted whether they could ever unite for a single purpose.[17]

In 1674, the Duke of York named Edmund Andros to the position of Royal Governor. Andros, a military hero in the English war with the Dutch, made himself obnoxious to colonists by repeatedly trying to expand his jurisdiction and by strictly enforcing taxes. If New Yorkers mistrusted him, New Englanders reviled him for trading guns to the Indians during King Philip's War. The crown recalled him in 1681. Five years later he returned as Governor of the Dominion of New England, which was expanded in 1688 to include New York and East and West Jersey (united as New Jersey in 1702). Colonists resented Andros, who made the Church of England the official religion, seized public land, and raised taxes. After news of the overthrow of James II in the Glorious Revolution of 1688 reached America, colonists in Boston arrested Andros and held him for ten months before sending him back to England. There was rebellion in New York as well. Jacob Leisler, a wealthy merchant who represented the interests of shopkeepers and farmers, led a revolt and installed himself as acting lieutenant governor. Leisler ended the rebellion when the crown commissioned a new governor, who arrived in 1691 and promptly arrested Leisler for treason and had him tried and executed.

Although political stability may have returned, economic growth led to new anxieties, especially over slavery, which was deeply embedded in the colony from the start. In New Amsterdam, slaves labored on farms and in construction. The wall of the fort that ran along Wall Street was built by slaves, many of whom learned to speak Dutch. In various ways, whether through shipbuilding or commerce, British New York tied itself to the Atlantic slave trade. Forty-one percent of the city's households contained slaves, exceeded in colonial America only by Charleston, South Carolina. Laws forbade slaves from leaving their master's houses without permission and those born to a slave mother were slaves for life, even if baptized.

On April 6, 1712, a group of slaves in New York gathered in protest against the law limiting their movement and set fire to a building. They then attacked white colonists, killing nine and injuring others. The slave revolt unleashed the worst fears of the white population in a city that was 20 percent enslaved. Authorities called out the militia and authorities arrested dozens of blacks. The courts convicted twenty-one blacks who allegedly participated in the revolt. Some were burned to death.

Nearly thirty years later, after a series of fires swept across the city, colonists believed that they had uncovered a conspiracy among slaves and free blacks, in concert with poor whites, to burn down New York and murder slaveholders. Hysteria swept the city and trials were quickly held. Judge Daniel Horsmanden gave credence to the testimony of a sixteen-year-old indentured servant named Mary Burton, and at the trials some slaves confessed and implicated others. Authorities arrested 160 blacks and 21 whites, executed 17 blacks and 4 whites by hanging, burned 13 blacks at the stake and banished dozens of others to the Caribbean. Other factors fed the New York Conspiracy of 1741, including economic distress and the fear of a Spanish invasion to burn the city and install Catholicism. In the end, Horsmanden wrote, "We have not been able entirely to unravel the Mystery of this Iniquity; for 'twas a dark Design, and the Veil is in some Measure still upon it!"[18]

Slavery was also a part of colonial life elsewhere in the middle colonies. New Jersey contained about 4,000 slaves in 1738 and would be the last Northern state to abolish the institution when it passed a gradual abolition law in 1804; slavery remained legal in Delaware until the Thirteenth Amendment was ratified in December 1865.

In 1780, during the War of Independence, Pennsylvania became the first state to abolish slavery. Pennsylvania began as a haven for the Quakers, the Society of Friends, who formed in the seventeenth century and rejected religious rituals and creeds in favor of simplicity and inner truth. They would come to oppose slavery, but not at first. Indeed William Penn, who received a charter from King Charles II in 1681 to settle the new colony, owned slaves. Penn had been expelled from Oxford for refusing to accept Anglicanism and was jailed several times for advocating Quaker religious doctrines. Pennsylvania, named after his father, who died in 1670, served in Penn's words as "a holy experiment" where religious freedom would be paramount. Penn lived in the new colony from 1682 to 1684, and then returned from 1699 to 1701. Upon arriving the first time, he is believed to have signed a treaty of perpetual friendship with the Lenni Lenape. Virginia had Pocahontas, Massachusetts had Squanto, and Pennsylvania had the Lenni Lenape as a critical part of its origins story.

Pennsylvania became a haven not only for Quakers, but also for any group that did not adhere to Anglican orthodoxy—Huguenot, Mennonite, Amish, Lutheran, and Moravian. In time, colonists would build Presbyterian and Episcopal churches. Many Germans and Scots-Irish settled in the colony, which grew from 11,000 in 1690 to 120,000 in 1750. Colonists flooded into the rich farmlands beyond Philadelphia that produced corn, wheat, and rye. They also developed Philadelphia, which had more than 2,000 people by 1700 and more than 12,000 by 1750. Philadelphia grew into an important commercial center (by 1790, it was second only to New York) and became the center of the American Enlightenment thanks to its most prominent citizen, Benjamin Franklin.

Born in Cotton Mather's Boston in 1706, Franklin was the youngest son of the youngest son, which meant dim prospects. He was apprenticed to his brother in a printing shop. Seeking freedom and broader horizons, in 1723, at age seventeen, he ran away to Philadelphia. Still, Puritan Boston had left its mark as Franklin developed a *Plan of Conduct* (1726) that emphasized industry and temperance. In Philadelphia, Franklin published the *Pennsylvania Gazette* and formed the Junto (from the Spanish for "meeting"), a club devoted to learning and mutual improvement. He served as postmaster, founded numerous cultural institutions, including the first circulating library, and invented everything from a stove to bifocals to swim fins. His experiments with lightning showed it to be a form of electricity and made him the most famous American in the world. In 1754, he organized a meeting in Albany, New York, of delegates from New England and the Mid-Atlantic to discuss a plan of union. For the occasion he drew a political cartoon that showed a snake divided into pieces, with each piece identified as a colony, and the caption read "Join, or Die." Ultimately, delegates rejected the plan, and Franklin condemned the provincial outlook and suspicion between the colonies that prevented unified action for their common good.

Native Americans

In the Southern, Middle, and New England colonies, contact and conflict with Indians shaped colonization. Indians may have been incorporated into America's mythos of origin, but they also became a people the colonists sought to contain and conquer. Very few outside of a vocal minority of Pennsylvania Quakers shared Roger Williams's view that Indians had rights to the land and to life. William Bradford had declared the land "vast and unpeopled"; it was anything but. One estimate posits that in 1492 a native population of between seven and ten million people lived in North America above the Rio Grande. The Eastern Woodlands included the Iroquois Confederacy, Abenakis, Shawnees, Delawares, Micmacs, Mahicans, Narragansett, and Pequots. The Southeast Indians included the Powhatans, Catawbas, Cherokees, Creeks, Seminole, Natchez, Choctaws, and Chickasaws. There were also Southwest Pueblos, Navajo, Zunis, and Hopis. Add to the diversity the Plains Indians, Pacific peoples, and Arctic peoples. The English settlers who first arrived in the seventeenth century were not the first Europeans eastern native tribes had ever seen. At various times explorers, missionaries, traders, and trappers had made their presence known. From the moment Columbus made contact, disease proved to be the most virulent enemy of native peoples, who had no immunity to smallpox, measles, and influenza. "The people began to die very fast," wrote Thomas Harriot in 1585 after visiting Indian villages in coastal North Carolina.[19]

Native people lived in complex, hierarchical societies generally ruled by a chief or sachem. Across most of eastern North America, men hunted, fished, cleared fields, gathered, and prepared for war with other tribes. The women performed all other agricultural work; they also cooked, collected water, constructed housing, and made clothing and pottery. Women also exercised political power, participating in decisions whether to go to war and what to do with captives. From New England to Virginia, those who spoke Algonquian languages believed in Manitou, a transcendent life force and personal spirit, often envisioned in a dream. Some tribes undoubtedly believed in what missionaries came to translate as the Great Spirit and told various creation stories. Language differences meant that most tribes could no more understand one another than they could a European immigrant, though trade across linguistic boundaries allowed for communication.

Long before the colonies banded together, some Indians had. The Iroquois Confederacy consisted of the Mohawk, Oneida, Onondaga, Cayuga, and Seneca and, after 1722, the Tuscarora. The English referred to them as the Six Nations. The Iroquois General Council approved laws and actions that required unanimous consent. Wampum, or beads made from shells, played a critical role in the lives of the Iroquois who used it for various purposes: as gifts, to establish identity, record events, and to make peace. With the population decimated from disease following contact, warfare, which had mainly been a part of a mourning ritual whereby captives would be taken to replace lost tribal members, took on economic and geopolitical motivations. The Iroquois battled the French and traded with the English under what was known as the Covenant Chain. The Mohawk declared that chain broken in 1753 and ended up siding with the British during the American Revolution.

It is impossible to know exactly what the Indians thought of the Englishmen whom they first encountered, except that the newcomers smelled bad and could not survive without their help. In the seventeenth century, from Virginia to Massachusetts, Native Americans taught colonists how to live off the land and served as interpreters and guides. Trade grew, with Indians receiving weapons, tools, utensils, and various other European goods in return for food, deerskins, and furs. Many Indians became Christianized and studied the Bible, which missionary John Eliot translated into Algonquian in 1663. And many colonists adopted Indian ways of hunting and dress, with some choosing to join Native societies after being taken captive. Eunice Williams, the daughter of Deerfield minister John Williams, who wrote of his redemption from captivity, remained with the Mohawks and married. In his *New English Canaan* (1637), Thomas Morton praised the Indians who, "According to humane reason, guided only by the light of nature, these people leade the more happy and freer life, being voyde of care, which torments the mindes of so many Christians: They are not delighted in baubles, but in usefull things."[20]

Colonial appetite for land, and the way in which colonists transformed the landscape from forests into farms, shocked Indians, who had also seen the introduction of strange new plants, fruits, and domesticated animals. Conflicts over colonial expansion led quickly to explosions of violence on both sides. In 1622, Powhatan's brother Opechancanough attacked the Virginians and killed nearly 350 colonists. One colonist responded with a plan "to bringe in the Indians into subiection w[th]out makinge an utter exterpation of them."[21]

In trade with colonists, no item proved more transformative to Indians than rum, which contributed to the decline of native peoples in eastern America. Alcohol was central to the life of colonists, and most of them drank beer, ale, rum, or hard cider every day. One estimate suggests that colonists imbibed three pints of distilled beverages per week. If drinking did not, for the most part, fundamentally alter the day-to-day behavior of colonists, Indians, it seemed, reacted differently to alcohol, at least to European eyes. Franklin would recall a scene at Carlisle, Pennsylvania, when rum was given out following the signing of an Indian treaty: "they were all drunk Men and Women, quarrelling and fighting, Their dark-colour'd Bodies, half-naked, seen only by the gloomy Light of the Bonfire, running after and beating one another with Firebrands, accompanied by their horrid Yellings." Franklin thought it resembled his idea of hell.[22]

Franklin was not the first to offer the stereotype of the drunken Indian. While colonists saw Indian drinking as leading to barbarity and savagery, behavior that further justified attempts to Christianize the natives, Indians drank for specific reasons. Alcohol became part of religious and hospitality rituals and was used in ceremonies for mourning the dead. Drunkenness, Indians believed, conferred power by altering perception. Nonetheless, the rum trade undoubtedly disordered Indian life and led to violence both within and outside the community. Colonial legislators passed laws banning the trade. As early as 1654, in New Netherland, an act stated that "many Indians are daily seen and found intoxicated, and being drunk and fuddled, commit many and grave acts of violence." Try as they might, legislators could not stop the trade in alcohol and Indian consumption gave colonists further reason to view Indians as inferior and uncivilized.[23]

In colonial America, the colonists also enslaved the Indians and profited from the Indian slave trade. Long before the settlers arrived, some Indian tribes held other Indians in slavery. This was not based on race. Rather it was a part of native warfare and diplomacy. In some cases, colonists took Indians as captives of war, yet they enslaved them not to integrate them into colonial society, but to keep them as servants. Indeed, before the gradual shift to African slave labor in the early eighteenth century, there were more enslaved Indians than Africans in America. In the aftermath of the Pequot War, colonists distributed captives for their personal use. They shipped others to the Caribbean. According to one estimate, between 1670 and 1715, South Carolinians exported more Indians into slavery from Charleston than they imported Africans. In the South, early experiments with Indian slavery ended after war with the Yamasee between 1715 and 1717, a war that nearly obliterated South Carolina's nonnative inhabitants. In time, Native Americans, most notably the Cherokee in the Southeast, began to hold Africans in slavery.

Indian resistance to enslavement contributed to Pontiac's War, which exploded on the frontier in 1763. Two Indian slaves had murdered their master, a British trader, and the British commander in North America, Jeffrey Amherst, ordered them executed. The British had taken over the Great Lakes and Ohio Valley region, formerly controlled by the French, and Amherst intended to make it clear that the native tribes would be subjects of British dominion. In response to the execution, numerous tribes across the region communicated with one another. Other resentments festered as well, as Amherst cut off some trade and the giving of gifts to native tribes. Ottawa leader Chief Pontiac led a series of surprise attacks in which the Indians recaptured British forts and launched raids into Pennsylvania, Maryland, and Virginia.

Amherst had no intentions of allowing the Indians to wreak havoc and was nothing if not ruthless. He suggested sending blankets infected with smallpox to the forts in order to cause an epidemic. "Could it not be contrived to send the small pox among the disaffected tribes of Indians," he wrote in a letter. "We must, on this occasion, Use Every Stratagem in our power to Reduce them." He wanted to "Extirpate this Execrable race," and may have followed through with the distribution of two smallpox-infected blankets at Fort Pitt, which led to an outbreak among nearby Delaware and Shawnee Indians.[24]

Numerous tribes across several regions participated in the war: the Ottawa, Ojibwe, and Huron from the Great Lakes; the Miami, Wea, and Kickapoo from eastern Illinois territory; and the Delaware and Shawnee from the Ohio region. It was not only British policies that motivated them. Spiritual leaders such as Neolin, the Delaware Prophet, preached the rejection of European influences and trade for goods. He called for a return to traditional Native practices and the purification of body and soul. Corn, not alcohol, would sustain health, and only separation from all things European would preserve life. A Creek Indian would lament, "we have been used so long to wrap up our Children as soon as they are born in Goods procured of the white People, that we cannot do without it."[25]

In May 1763, Pontiac led an attempt to take Fort Detroit and after failing to do so laid siege through July. Other tribes took a series of smaller forts on Lake Erie and in Michigan, Indiana, and Pennsylvania. Natives ritually scalped many of those they took captive. Indians also laid siege to Fort Pitt in Pennsylvania and launched raids into western Pennsylvania. Angry over the violence and dismayed at the lack of protection provided by the colonial government, some settlers took it upon themselves to fight back. In December a group from Paxton attacked and murdered a group of peaceful, Christian Conestoga Indians near Lancaster. The governor issued warrants for their arrest, but colonists, living far from Philadelphia, the seat of the colony's government, refused to cooperate. Dismayed by the lack of protection provided by the legislature, a larger assemblage of backcountry residents then marched on Philadelphia. Franklin was among those who convinced the Paxton party to back down. Franklin, for one, lamented indiscriminate attitudes toward Natives. He denounced revenge against all Indians for an injury committed by one person just as he would not kill all "freckled red-haired men" should someone with those characteristics cause his family harm. Despite his entreaties, violence between settlers and Indians on the frontier would continue, as would political tensions between the backcountry and the seaboard.[26]

Angered by the continued uprising, the British government recalled General Amherst and replaced him with Thomas Gage, who promptly launched two expeditions to subdue the Indians. Beginning in 1764, a series of treaties with different tribes eventually brought the conflict to a close. Pontiac agreed to a treaty on July 25, 1766. The Indians had not been defeated, though neither had they won. The British would recognize certain land rights of Indians, but the horrific violence of conquest (murder, scalping, germ warfare, even reported episodes of cannibalism) would annihilate all distinctions.

Seven Years' War

Pontiac's war had followed directly from the Seven Years' War (also called the French and Indian War) that lasted from 1756 to 1763. The war, a global confrontation between Great Britain and France, began in the interior of North America, where the claims of the British, who had moved inward from the Atlantic, and the French, who had laid claim to the Mississippi Valley, came into conflict. The governor of Virginia, concerned about the encroachment of the French in the Ohio Territory, sent a force to warn them away. A young colonel, George Washington, commanded the mission. The French ignored his entreaties and Washington returned with a force that included a contingent of Indians. After a raid on the French, Washington retreated and constructed a stockade that he named Fort Necessity. The French sent troops from newly constructed Fort Duquesne, near what is now Pittsburgh, and attacked on July 3, 1754. On July 4, Washington surrendered.

The following year, the British dispatched General Edward Braddock and two regiments to the colonies with orders to take Fort Duquesne. At the Monongahela River, the French and their Indian allies attacked Braddock's forces, which included Virginia militia led by Washington. Although vastly outnumbering the French, Braddock's forces were defeated and the general killed. In the aftermath Washington found fault with the British regulars ("[They] broke and run as sheep before the hounds"), but not the Virginia militiamen, many of whom died.[27]

In 1756, Great Britain declared war on France, and a conflict that began in colonial North America spread to Europe, Africa, India, and Spain. In London, William Pitt took over as minister responsible for North American affairs. A brilliant orator, he was an ambitious, nettlesome politician with little regard for the day-to-day affairs of the House of Commons. He and the prime minister, the Duke of Newcastle, despised one another. Pitt understood the provincial situation better than anyone, and his new policies, which allowed colonial assemblies to raise their own troops and eased the financial burdens of war, made him popular in the colonies. In 1766, he would describe Americans as "the sons, not the bastards, of England."

The first victories of the war belonged to the French, who captured Fort Oswego on Lake Ontario, Fort William Henry on Lake George, and defended Fort Carillon (later Fort Ticonderoga) on Lake Champlain. At Fort William Henry, in August 1757, the Indian allies of the French slaughtered nearly two hundred Anglo-Americans who had surrendered. The Abenaki and Nipissing took hundreds captive. Louis-Joseph de Montcalm, the French commander, helped negotiate for the prisoners' return. He understood that terms of surrender had to be inviolate and he feared revenge on the part of the British if they were not. A year later, in July 1758, he defended Fort Carillon against a force of more than 15,000 men, four times his numbers.

Montcalm barely had time to celebrate before learning of the success of British and provincial troops at Louisbourg, a fortress that guarded the St. Lawrence River and protected Quebec. The British laid siege and, after seven weeks, during which British mortars damaged ships and buildings and set much of the city ablaze, the French surrendered. As Montcalm had feared, the horrors of Fort William Henry would be revisited on the French and their allies as a group of Massachusetts soldiers killed more than one hundred French regulars and scalped two Indians. "We cut them [Indians] to pieces whenever we found them," wrote General James Wolfe, "in return for a thousand acts of cruelty and barbarity."[28]

Wolfe may have hated the Indians ("the most contemptible canaille upon earth," he said), but the British understood the importance of peace with those tribes not fighting alongside the French. In October 1758, colonial governors of Pennsylvania and New Jersey signed a treaty at Easton, Pennsylvania, with some 500 representatives from thirteen Indian nations, including the Iroquois and Delaware. In return for land they had previously ceded, the tribes promised not to ally with the French.

While peace was being established with the Delaware, British troops tried again to take Fort Duquesne. Led by General John Forbes, a Scottish doctor who was so ill that at one point he was carried on a sheet strung between two horses, the force included 2,700 Pennsylvanians and 1,600 Virginians again under Washington. The challenging campaign required the construction of a new road, an endeavor Washington opposed. The French, suffering from low rations and loss of Native allies after the Treaty of Easton, decided to burn the fort and retreat. Control of the important intersection of the Ohio and Allegheny belonged to the British. Washington, disappointed not to receive a commission as a British offer, resigned his command and returned to Mt. Vernon.

British success continued with victories at Fort Niagara, Fort Ticonderoga, and Fort Wagner. The British now controlled the frontier and soon would conquer Canada. In September 1759, they waged battle for Quebec. Wolfe found a way to lead his troops up a narrow path and mass on the west side of the city's walls. Montcalm, shocked by the sight of thousands of soldiers set up in a line across the Plains of Abraham, ordered an attack. In the ensuing battle, the French scattered in disarray and both Wolfe and Montcalm received fatal wounds. A year later, Montreal fell and the war in North America was effectively over.

In the Treaty of Paris in 1763, the French surrendered to the British all possessions east of the Mississippi, except for New Orleans, and guaranteed navigation of the Mississippi River. Great Britain also secured Canada, several West Indian islands, and Senegal. The Paris Peace was followed independently with the Royal Proclamation of 1763 by which King George III, crowned in 1760, sought to organize the British Empire. The proclamation, in the aftermath of Pontiac's rebellion, declared lands west of the Appalachians closed to colonial

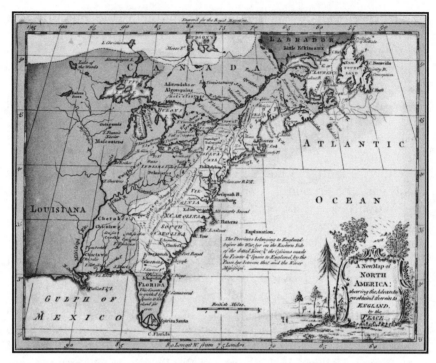

Figure 1.5 *A New Map of North America, Shewing the Advantages Obtained Therein to England by the Peace* (1764). Library of Congress.

survey and settlement so that the Indians "shall not be molested or disturbed." That guarantee would quickly be breached.

The Seven Years' War had a profound effect on the colonists. Thousands had served alongside British regulars and the victory, they believed, belonged as much to them as to the redcoats. The colonists identified as Englishmen and felt proud to be part of the British Empire. Indeed, Ben Franklin thought the British should conquer all of Canada and told Lord Kames "not merely as I am a Colonist, but as I am a Briton. I have long been of Opinion, that the Foundations of the future Grandeur and Stability of the British Empire, lie in America."[29]

Military service had an opposite effect as well. The discipline imposed by British officers on British regulars seemed cruel to colonists who had their own ideas about just punishment. British soldiers condescended to the colonists who in turn thought the skill and sophistication of the regulars overblown. What they knew was that, as provincials, they had organized their own troops and contributed to the triumph of the Crown. They expected their efforts to be acknowledged, even rewarded.

Instead, the ministry sought new ways to raise money to help pay for the expensive global conflict that had just concluded and for the stationing of troops in British North America. The ministry decided to crack down on smuggling and enforce the customs duties to which Parliament was entitled. They also decided to impose new taxes on the colonists. The American Duties Act of 1764 (which colonists called the Sugar Act) placed duties on items such as Madeira wine, which the colonists imported tax-free from Portugal. Parliament also expanded the number of royal officials and gave them new powers of enforcement. With these actions, the ministry seemed not to have given colonial assemblies, soldiers, and citizens any credit in helping to win the war. Instead, the British government felt they had triumphed despite the participation of the colonists, rather than because of it, and the time had arrived for British America to contribute financially to the cost of empire.

Led by merchants and planters who would be most affected by the new taxes, and who found themselves in the war's aftermath deep in debt (unable to profit from tobacco sales, Washington owed more than 2,000 pounds, nearly $400,000 today), assemblies and individuals in America protested. In Boston, a group of merchants expressed dismay over British interference with their right to self-government. If trade was taxed now, what next—land? And while colonists had not questioned the right of Parliament to tax imports— or what they would have thought of as external taxes—direct taxes, internal taxes on goods produced and consumed in the colonies, were an entirely different matter. The colonists had understood, since the founding of the House of Burgesses in Virginia in 1619, that they had complete control over their own domestic affairs. These new taxes violated "our British privileges," and by agreeing to being taxed without suitable representation in the body that lays them "are we not reduced from the character of free subjects to the miserable state of tributary slaves"[30]

That was 1764. Within a decade, these British subjects would think of themselves as Americans more united by common interest and destiny than divided by colony. At times, however, those differences trumped all else. For example, in his will, Lewis Morris, former chief justice of the New York Supreme Court and governor of New Jersey, stated that his son, Gouverneur, should get the best education possible in England or America except "that he never be sent for that purpose to the colony of Connecticut, lest he should imbibe in his youth that low craft and cunning so incident to the people of that Country." His son ended up going to King's College—later Columbia—in New York instead of Yale.[31]

Settlers in North America had always viewed their colony as their country and their country as part of the British Empire. A separate sense of American identity and nationhood that erased colonial boundaries and transatlantic fealty emerged only over time. In assessing the rising protests against Parliament and King, John Adams viewed each colony as run by its own mechanism. "Remember," he wrote to a friend in June 1776, "you can't make thirteen Clocks, Strike precisely alike, at the same Second." With the Seven Years' War, the erasure of difference had begun and soon the bells would toll for a portion of the British Empire.[32]

CHAPTER 2

If Men Were Angels

ONE OCTOGENARIAN WRITING TO ANOTHER, on February 15, 1825, Thomas Jefferson wished John Adams "nights of rest . . . and days of tranquility." Together they had once helped create a nation. They had also waged furious battle against each other as the leaders of opposing political parties that held distinct visions of American government and growth. Jefferson had been Adams's vice president, but Adams fled Washington, DC, early in the morning on the day of Jefferson's inauguration. In retirement, they rekindled their friendship and watched as the United States entered another war against Great Britain, this time in an attempt to assert national sovereignty. They lived long enough to see slavery emerge as the central issue in American politics. Jefferson could never solve the problem of slavery, for himself or the nation. At times, he supported a plan of gradual emancipation, keyed to education and expatriation. He knew slavery was wrong. "I tremble for my country when I reflect that God is just and his justice cannot sleep forever," he wrote. But he did not believe whites and blacks could live peaceably together. He never freed his slaves, except those he fathered with his slave Sally Hemings. Challenged in 1814 to lead Virginia to abolish slavery, he demurred by pleading that "this enterprise is for the young." "We have the wolf by the ear," he wrote in 1820, "and we can neither hold him, nor safely let him go. Justice is in one scale, and self-preservation in the other."[1]

Revolution

"We hold these truths to be self-evident, that all men are created equal, that they are endowed by their Creator with certain unalieniable Rights, that among these are Life, Liberty, and the pursuit of Happiness." It is perhaps the most felicitous sentence ever written. By 1776, American colonists were ready to declare independence from Great Britain. The Continental Congress appointed John Adams, Thomas Jefferson, Benjamin Franklin, Robert Livingston, and Roger Sherman to prepare a draft Declaration, and the committee decided Thomas Jefferson should write it. Adams later recalled that they chose Jefferson because of his "reputation for literature, science, and a happy talent at composition." Adams recalled that Jefferson was not an orator ("during the whole Time I satt with him in Congress, I never heard him utter three Sentences together"), but he praised his writings as "remarkable for their peculiar felicity of expression."[2]

Looking back from 1776, it is easy to identify the "long train of abuses" that Jefferson enumerated in the Declaration and see them as leading inexorably to revolution. The Sugar Act of 1764 and the Stamp Act of 1765, as we have seen, passed by Parliament in an attempt to raise revenue and alleviate the costs of defending the colonies, led to protests against extralegal taxes imposed without acquiescence since the colonists had no representation in London. "The Parliament of Great Britain hath no more right to put their hands into my pocket, without my consent, than I have to put my hands into yours for money," George Washington explained to a friend. A group that called itself the Sons of Liberty emerged to protest the Stamp Act. Their actions against those associated with collecting the new taxes included burning effigies and houses and tarring and feathering taxmen.[3]

Parliament repealed the Stamp Act, but declared it had the right to govern the colonies. In 1767 it passed the Townshend Duties, which imposed taxes on such essential items as tea, paper, glass, lead, and paint, and created new enforcement mechanisms. Colonists responded with actions—boycotts and riots—and, as important, words. Numerous pamphleteers began to articulate the political philosophy behind rebellion and the rationale for a revolt against monarchical government. In his *Letters from a Farmer In Pennsylvania* (1767–1768), for example, John Dickinson legitimized resistance by force to any attempt to "annihilate the liberties of the governed."[4]

The British sent troops to Boston and, on March 5, 1770, soldiers fired into a crowd and killed five people. One of the first casualties was Crispus Attucks, a black sailor. Paul Revere quickly issued an inflammatory engraving of *The Bloody Massacre* that helped fuel anti-British feeling. The British condemned the colonists as spoiled, unappreciative children. In the war of perception, however, the insurgent sons of liberty seemed to have every right to rebel against their oppressive mother country.

In reaction to the Tea Act, which exempted the East India Company from import duties and gave it a monopoly on all tea sold

Figure 2.1 Paul Revere, *The Bloody Massacre* (1770). American Antiquarian Society.

in America, a group of colonists disguised as Indians dumped more than 92,000 pounds of tea worth more than £9,000 into Boston Harbor on December 16, 1773. (The value today is estimated at $1.7 million). Parliament responded with the Coercive Acts— called Intolerable Acts by the patriots—that closed Boston port and stripped Massachusetts of self-government. Virginia's Richard Henry Lee called the acts "a most wicked System for destroying the liberty of America." Banding together, colonists formed the first Continental Congress, which met in Philadelphia in September 1774.[5]

American independence began before it was declared. In Massachusetts, a rebel provisional government had been formed and British troops arrived to destroy the militia's arms and supplies stored in Concord. On April 19, 1775, at the North Bridge in Concord, militia fired on soldiers. British forces withdrew. Half a century later, Ralph Waldo Emerson would memorialize the event in a poem, calling it "the shot heard round the world."

Two months after the battle at Concord, a Second Continental Congress appointed George Washington commander-in-chief of the Continental Army. It did so just in time. The next day, on June 17, Sir William Howe and his army attacked colonists who had occupied the high ground at Breed's Hill. Despite sustaining heavy casualties, the British took the ground at what would come to be known as the Battle of Bunker Hill. The world's greatest army might not so easily defeat the outnumbered colonists, who had the advantage of a huge territory that British forces would have to invade and conquer far from their home base.

In George Washington, the patriots chose a tested military leader and a man for whom public character was everything. If it remains difficult to remove the mask to get at the person, it is because Washington, who stood an imposing six foot two, concealed his ambitions and desires behind a stern, stoic exterior. He was forty-four in 1776, three years older than Adams, eleven years older than Jefferson, nineteen years older than James Madison, and twenty-three years older than Alexander Hamilton. He was the founding father who refereed the rivalry among the founding brothers. Born into the Virginia slaveholding gentry, Washington had minimal formal schooling and cared little for philosophical debates. After his experience in the Seven Years' War, in which he had horses shot out from under him and bullets pierced his coat, he married Martha Custis, a wealthy widow with two surviving children, and led a respected, patrician life. When he appeared in May at the Continental Congress, he arrived in uniform. In 1777, Henry Knox wrote, "The people of

America look up to you as their Father, and into your hands they entrust their all."[6]

While Washington was in Cambridge organizing the Continental Army against 10,000 British forces camped in Boston, a pamphlet that made the case for revolution became a sensation. "A new method of thinking hath arisen," announced Thomas Paine in *Common Sense* (1776). Paine had arrived from England only two years earlier. A writer and editor, he helped persuade the reluctant that rebellion against the king was both just and inevitable, and as much a scientific law as a political principle. "Every thing that is right or natural pleads for separation," he wrote. Until *Common Sense*, the colonists' dismay had been with Parliament, not the king. Most colonists did not want to leave the British Empire, they merely wanted the rights of Englishmen. By directly challenging the tyrannical power of the king, Paine helped turn a rebellion into a revolution for self-rule and self-government. "The cause of America," he declared, "is in a great measure the cause of all mankind."[7]

Not everyone was convinced. Of a white population of some two million inhabitants, perhaps one-fifth remained loyal to the crown. Many of these were older, wealthier families, though many backcountry farmers also opposed independence. Royal officials and Anglican clergymen stayed loyal, and some colonies, such as New York, had a greater proportion of loyalists than others. While many merchants and planters supported the patriot cause, so too did mechanics and laborers, people from the lower or middling classes of colonial society. Thus the revolution served as a civil war between patriots and loyalists and contained aspects of a class war between common people and aristocrats. It also carried the seeds of a different war for liberty—slaves in Massachusetts petitioned the legislature for freedom based on sharing "in Common with all other men a Natural and Unaliable Right to that freedom which the Grat Parent of the Unavers hath Bestowed equalley on all menkind."[8]

The Declaration of Independence listed the patriots' grievances with the king and placed the rationale for separation on universal grounds: "the laws of nature and nature's God" demanded it. On July 9, 1776, George Washington, now in New York, read the Declaration to the troops. The next month, the first major battle of the war erupted when a 20,000-man force under General Howe crossed from Staten Island to Long Island. Washington evacuated to Manhattan and from there to New Jersey. He had 23,000 men, most were raw recruits from various militia who were ill-prepared to face British Army regulars. After the debacle, the numbers declined rapidly as men deserted and refused to re-enlist. John Adams offered a cogent assessment: "our Generals were out generalled." Washington somewhat redeemed himself with a surprise nighttime attack across the Delaware River on December 25 that enabled him to take Trenton. Washington would lose many more battles than he would win. His strategy was one based on attrition, to last long enough to wear down British public opinion.[9]

In October 1777, American spirits lifted with the surrender of nearly 6,000 British regulars and German mercenaries to General Horatio Gates at Saratoga, New York. The victory had profound consequences. It led the French to enter the war on the American side (they would contribute some 12,000 soldiers, a fleet, and the Marquis de Lafayette, who had offered his services in June). And it contributed to the British decision to evacuate Philadelphia and concentrate its forces in New York.

The encouraging results of Saratoga were offset by the misery Washington's army suffered at Valley Forge in the winter of 1777–1778. Soldiers endured harsh conditions and inadequate housing. Disease and starvation ravaged the 11,000 men (and 500 women and children). Washington feared that, unless something was done, "this Army must dissolve." A congressional committee visited, and supplies began to flow. In the end, nearly 2,000 men perished and Washington bristled at the criticism he received.[10]

The Continental Army emerged from Valley Forge hungry for action and fought the British to a stalemate at Monmouth, New Jersey. Over the next few years, the British decided to shift their focus from the mid-Atlantic to the Southern colonies. They captured Savannah and attacked Charleston. Lord Cornwallis faced Nathaniel Greene, who divided his troops and made use of the vast terrain to exhaust the opposition. At the Battle of Guilford Courthouse, fought on March 15, 1781, the British won the day, yet paid a heavy price. Cornwallis headed for Virginia, where he would encounter Washington, who had marched 7,000 American and French soldiers to Yorktown. The arrival of the French fleet in Chesapeake Bay kept the British fleet from resupplying the Redcoats and on October 19, 1781, Cornwallis surrendered. The war was effectively over. Nearly two years later with the signing of the Treaty of Paris on September 3, 1783, Britain acknowledged the United States to be "free sovereign and independent."

In the end, 25,000 Americans died (nearly 1 percent of the population) during the War of Independence and as many were wounded. While some blacks fought for the patriots, others joined the British cause as loyalists. In November 1775, Lord Dunmore, the Royal Governor of Virginia, issued a proclamation that offered freedom to slaves who agreed to fight for the British. Indians fought on both sides. The Revolution divided the Iroquois Confederacy. The Mohawks, Seneca, Cayuga, and Onondagas supported the British, and the Oneidas and Tuscaroras assisted the Americans. In the South, the Cherokee sided with the British. The Treaty of Paris ignored Britain's Indian allies and awarded British territorial claims to the United States, which continued to expand across native lands.

Victory meant far more than separation from Great Britain. In 1818, John Adams asked, "What do we mean by the American Revolution?" It was not the military struggle for independence, he answered. Rather, long before the war, "the Revolution was in the minds and hearts of the people . . . this radical change in the principles, opinions, sentiments, and affections of the people, was the real American Revolution." America already was a land that promised equality and opportunity. Now it needed a government that allowed its citizens to rise in the world.[11]

Constitution

Whatever else it was, the American Revolution was a revolt against monarchical authority. As the revolutionary generation would soon discover, it was easier to dismantle one form of government than to create another. Within a week of the Declaration of Independence, the Continental Congress considered a draft of the Articles of Confederation by which the thirteen states would be bound in "Perpetual Union." They entered into "a league of friendship," and each state retained "its sovereignty, freedom, and independence, and every power, jurisdiction, and right, which is not by this Confederation expressly delegated to the United States, in Congress assembled." The powers expressly delegated to the Confederation government included the power to declare war, conduct foreign relations, and coin and borrow money. A common treasury would defray the costs of war and advance the general welfare. Each state had one vote and could be represented by no fewer than two and no more than seven delegates. The Confederation could not tax, regulate commerce or foreign trade, enforce laws, or administer justice. Acts of Congress required nine of thirteen votes to pass. Any amendment to the articles required unanimity.

In November 1777, Congress sent the articles to the states for ratification, which was completed in 1781. Perhaps the most important accomplishment of the Confederation government was to persuade states to relinquish their claims to western and north-western lands, establish a Public Land Survey whereby settlers could purchase land, and create protocols for the addition of new states. From the start, the expansion of slavery was an issue. Under the Northwest Ordinance of 1787, which organized the lands west of the Appalachians, slavery would not be allowed in any new states carved out of this territory.

The problems of a weak central government manifested themselves during the war and after. The Confederation could request money from the states, but the states, preoccupied with local concerns, did not comply in full, and sometimes not at all. States competed against one another and often adopted policies that hurt other states. James Madison, who would soon lead the attempt to revise the articles, expressed his exasperation in a letter to Jefferson in 1786: "The States are every day giving proofs that separate regulations are more likely to set them by the ears, than to obtain the common object."[12]

Debt became the biggest problem. There was no uniform currency and states issued whatever money they wanted, leading to high inflation and a lack of credit. For example, at the war's start, three dollars in Congressional bills was worth one dollar in silver. By 1781, the ratio had ballooned to 147:1. An impost plan proposed in 1781 would have given the Confederation government a permanent source of revenue with a 5 percent ad valorem tax on imported goods. Rhode Island voted against the amendment as an infringement on states' rights, thus blocking the measure, which required unanimity.

The impotence of the Confederation government in the face of state power made so-called nationalists nervous, and none more so than Alexander Hamilton. Born in the British West Indies, Hamilton wrote a letter in 1769, when he was fourteen years old, that reveals a great deal about the man he would become: "My Ambition is prevalent. . . . I wish there was a war." He arrived in the colonies in 1772 and found an environment well suited to an ambitious young man. He attended King's College and joined a volunteer militia company. Commissioned as a captain, he distinguished himself and came to the notice of George Washington, who made him an aide de camp. On leaving the army following victory at Yorktown, Hamilton studied law and returned to New York to start a practice that included defending colonists who had remained faithful to the crown whose property had been confiscated.[13]

In 1781, Hamilton wrote a lengthy letter (he knew no other kind, it seemed) to the financier Robert Morris. In it he complained that even if "future measures of Congress would be dictated by the most perfect wisdom and public spirit there would be still a necessity for a change in the forms of our administration to give a new spring and current to the passions and hopes of the people." Hamilton believed in a strong executive ("An administration by single men was essential to the proper management of the affairs of this country"), and he was writing to Morris to suggest a financial plan to help the fledgling nation, one that included a managed national debt.[14]

Five years later, Hamilton's dismay with the weak Articles of Confederation led him to Annapolis, where twelve delegates, including James Madison, met to discuss the problem of state taxes on trade. In their report, submitted to Congress, which was meeting in Philadelphia, they called for a constitutional convention to gather in 1787. Adding urgency was rebellion in western Massachusetts, as indebted farmers around Springfield, led by Daniel Shays, began shutting down courts after their petitions to the state government in Boston for debt relief went unanswered. The rebels believed they were continuing the tradition of protest that had led to revolution against England, only this time the remote authority unfairly taxing them and foreclosing on their mortgages was located in Boston, not London. Government forces, led by Benjamin Lincoln, a former major general in the Continental Army, moved west and put down the rebellion. The unrest added to the anxiety that the new American nation was too fragile to survive and that a new form of government was needed. Only weeks after Shays' rebellion, Congress called for a convention to meet in Philadelphia to consider revising the Articles of Confederation.

Pursuant to that call, fifty-five men labored in Philadelphia from May 25 to September 17, 1787, supposedly to revise the articles but in fact to draft a new constitution. They included Madison, Hamilton, Washington (elected president of the convention), and Ben Franklin. (Adams was in England and Jefferson in France.) If these men favored a strong national government, other delegates remained devoted advocates of states and individual rights advocates: George Mason of Virginia, Elbridge Gerry of Massachusetts, and John Lansing and Robert Yates, the two other delegates from New York. Rhode Island refused to send delegates. Patrick Henry of Virginia stayed away because he "smelt a rat."[15]

The delegates represented the political and economic elite of America. Most of them had some training as lawyers and experience in politics. Nearly half of them owned slaves. Their average age was forty-two, at a time when life expectancy was approximately thirty-six. Their disagreements centered mostly on the different interests of large and small states with respect to representation. While delegates proposed several plans, the final document created an executive branch and a bicameral legislature, with the number of house representatives apportioned by population (with slaves among those counting as three-fifths "of all other persons") and the senate with an equal number per state. The federal government gained the power to collect taxes, coin money, regulate commerce, and administer justice. "We the people," begins the preamble. The delegates created a republican form of government that vested power in the people who elected representatives and that sought to balance monarchical (executive) and democratic (legislative) tendencies.

The proposed constitution had to be ratified and almost immediately writers began to publish essays for and against ratification. Opponents came to be known as the anti-Federalists. They held onto the belief that the people were virtuous and government could not be trusted because it was prone to corruption. They critiqued specific aspects of the plan. For example, the senate, in the view of one, would lead to a "permanent ARISTOCRACY." They feared the executive would devolve into tyranny. They viewed the Constitution as an assault on liberty and demanded a bill of rights. One writer hoped the proposed government would be rejected and the people would "rise superior to the most formidable conspiracy against the liberties of a free and enlightened nation, that the world has ever witnessed."[16]

Those who supported ratification called themselves Federalists, and the papers written by Hamilton, Madison, and John Jay, under the pseudonym Publius, made the case for a stronger, more energetic government with the power to raise revenue. Hamilton wrote fifty-one of the eighty-five essays. In Federalist 51, Madison explained why government was necessary, and in doing so he offered a political philosophy that questioned the virtue of the people and defended the need for government oversight. "If men were angels," he wrote, "no government would be necessary. If angels were to govern men, neither external nor internal controls on government would be necessary. In framing a government which is to be administered by men over men, the great difficulty lies in this: you must first enable the government to control the governed; and in the next place oblige it to control itself."[17]

Experience had shown that Americans would not subordinate self-interest to the public good, would not forgo debt for independence, and would not avoid vice for frugality. Federalist 10 explained that faction was inevitable in a republic and the key was to control its effects. If the new nation were to survive, it needed a government to control the governed.

Nine states were needed to ratify the Constitution. The process began in December 1787. Given the turmoil of Shays' rebellion, which further inflamed suspicion of executive authority, the vote in Massachusetts was the most deeply contested. By a vote of 187–168 it became the sixth state to ratify. On June 21, 1788, New Hampshire became the ninth state (57–47) and then Virginia and New York fell into line with votes of 89–79 and 30–27, respectively. Rhode Island did not ratify the Constitution until May 1790, more than a year after the inauguration of George Washington.

The promise of a "bill of rights" made ratification palatable to some anti-Federalists. Writing from France in 1787, Jefferson told Madison that he did not like "the omission of a bill of rights providing clearly & without the aid of sophisms for freedom of religion, freedom of the press, protection against standing armies, restriction against monopolies, the eternal & unremitting force of the habeas corpus laws, and trials by jury in all matters of fact triable by the laws of the land and not by the law of Nations." Congress declared that ten states had ratified the Bill of Rights, the first ten amendments to the Constitution, by December 15, 1791.[18]

Ben Franklin's presence at the convention drew stares of admiration. "He is eighty-two," wrote a delegate from Georgia, but "possesses an activity of mind equal to a youth of twenty-five years of age." There was no greater American of the eighteenth century, at least prior to George Washington. Printer, inventor, philosopher, Franklin left posterity a memoir in which he explained that success was open to all: that rags to riches could be obtained by following the path of industry, frugality, temperance, and order, among other virtues. Franklin did not invent the idea of upward mobility, but he lived it and became its most zealous proselyte. He wrote his son in 1771 that he had "emerg'd from the Poverty and Obscurity in which I was born & bred, to a State of Affluence & some Degree of Reputation in the World." In his autobiography, he would reveal how he did it by maintaining public appearance; private reality was another matter. Thus Franklin suggested that the youth of America avoid sexual indulgence, yet he often engaged in "intrigues with low Women that fell in my Way." No matter. In America it was one's public persona that mattered.[19]

Toward the end of life, Franklin, who had once owned slaves, spoke out against slavery and became president of the Pennsylvania Society for Promoting the Abolition of Slavery. Starting in the 1750s, Pennsylvania Quakers, led by John Woolman and Anthony Benezet, began organizing against slavery and the slave trade. Franklin joined the cause, and a year before his death in 1790 he wrote that the "luminous and benign spirit of liberty" must be extended to the enslaved, but so, too, must attention be paid to the needs of the emancipated which, he urged, "must become a branch of our national policy." The Constitution did not use the word "slave" and alluded to the institution in only three places, one of which was a clause requiring the return of fugitive slaves. In time, the debate over whether it was a proslavery document would animate a generation of abolitionists.[20]

Franklin said little during the Constitutional Convention, though at one point he suggested a morning prayer, his deism notwithstanding. In the end, he supported the Constitution "with all its faults, if they are such." In a final speech, he acknowledged that at times his opinions about government had changed and that he respected the judgment of other delegates. No one could predict. In 1789, Franklin wrote in French to the scientist Jean-Baptiste Leroy: "Our new Constitution is now established, and has an appearance that promises permanency; but, in this world, nothing can be said to be certain, except death and taxes."[21]

Political Parties

Out of the cauldron of the debate over ratification, the Federalists and anti-Federalists hardened into opposing political parties, the Federalists and the Democratic-Republicans. Such parties generated enormous anxiety in the early American republic. Political philosophy had taught that where the people ruled, factionalism, by which one group promoted its own interests instead of the common good, could lead to the republic's destruction. Even as the founders identified with parties, they continued to denounce them. "If I could not go to heaven but with a party, I would not go there at all," asserted Jefferson.[22]

The political parties took form out of the policy battles in George Washington's administration, and in particular from the rivalry between Alexander Hamilton, the secretary of treasury, and Thomas Jefferson, the secretary of state. Jefferson would later write,

"It was impossible for two men to be of more opposite principles." Hamilton and the Federalists favored a strong, powerful, energetic national government, promoted commercial policies such as taxation and tariffs, represented the interests of bankers, merchants, and manufacturers, and tended to prefer British pomp and privilege. By contrast, Jefferson and the Democratic-Republicans favored limited government interference, opposed national, centralizing monetary policies, championed the independent farmer and landholder, and leaned toward French sophistication and socialability and away from the British (who Jefferson called "rich, proud, hectoring, swearing, squibbing, carnivorous animals").[23]

Federalists and Democratic-Republicans battled over Hamilton's plan to fund and assume the debt of the various states, a plan that gave the national government power over the states and created a national debt, something terrifying to the Democratic-Republicans, who believed, according to Jefferson, that debt led to corruption and prepared "fit tools for the designs of ambition." In 1790, Democratic-Republicans agreed not to oppose the plan in return for relocating the government from New York to the banks of the Potomac. At least this way, the Virginia Democratic-Republicans Jefferson and Madison could literally keep an eye on the affairs of state. They also opposed Hamilton's idea for a national bank, designed to expand the money supply, provide credit, and collect revenue. Opponents feared the creation of a "monied aristocracy," who would exploit debtors and engage in unchecked speculation. Despite entreaties from his fellow Virginians to veto the bill, Washington signed it.[24]

Jefferson resigned from office in 1793, though not before writing Washington to condemn Hamilton. "His system flowed from principles adverse to liberty, and was calculated to undermine and demolish the republic," he asserted. Hamilton, not one to remain silent, complained about Jefferson: "I have long seen a formed party in the Legislature, under his auspices, bent upon my subversion." Jefferson's views, thought Hamilton, were "subversive of the principles of good government and dangerous to the union, peace, and happiness of the Country." What the two men did not say about each other, opposition newspapers said about each party. The *Gazette of the United States,* under the editorship of John Fenno, served the interests of the Federalist administration. Jefferson denounced it in May 1791 as a "paper of pure Toryism, disseminating the doctrines of monarchy, aristocracy, and the exclusion of the influence of the people." He and Madison encouraged Philip Freneau, a poet and writer, to start the *National Gazette* as a Democratic-Republican paper.

Other party papers emerged and both sides engaged in vituperative and ad hominem attacks. It was in the papers that citizens first read rumors of Hamilton's affair with Maria Reynolds, a married woman, and Jefferson's relationship with Sally Hemings, his slave.[25]

Party factionalism and political vitriol were not the only signs of the dangers facing the new American republic. In August 1793, residents of Philadelphia, then the nation's capital, began falling ill with fever, chills, headache, nausea, and vomiting. Death came quickly and the number of fatalities began to soar. Yellow fever had taken hold of the city and between August and November thousands died, as many as 5,000 in a population of 50,000. Doctors referred to it as "bilious remitting fever" and "malignant fever," and had little idea what caused it or how best to treat it. (Not until the 1880s would physicians identify mosquitoes as the source of the viral infection.) Some thought it was connected in some way to foreign commerce— perhaps a pile of rotting coffee beans left on the dock—or to the habits of the poor who lived close to the wharves where the disease first appeared. Others viewed it in divine terms, a pestilence set upon a nation that had strayed from probity and virtue. Benjamin Rush, America's leading physician, treated the disease with bleeding and purging, which only served to speed many to their death.

Federal government officials and state legislators fled. The wealthy sought safety in the countryside. "Every body, who can, is flying from the city, and the panic of the country people is likely to add famine to the disease," noted Jefferson. The free black community, led by Richard Allen and Absalom Jones, founders of the African Methodist Episcopal Church, remained and heroically served as nurses and gravediggers, though in the aftermath they would be falsely accused of profiting from the epidemic. Stores and coffee houses closed, and even some churches. Only one of the four newspapers continued to publish. Wherever one looked, it seemed "a total dissolution of the bonds of society," as Jefferson wrote to Madison, was underway. Corruption, decay, and dissolution seemed to be the fate of the republic; the disease was as much moral and political as it was medical and physical.[26]

The following year, the Whiskey Rebellion provided further evidence of the ill health of the body politic. Farmers in western Pennsylvania protested a seemingly innocuous tax that the Federalists imposed on distilled spirits. They condemned the tax as unfair, unconstitutional, and reminiscent of what remote Parliamentary authorities had enacted before the Revolution. In July 1794, rebels set fire to the house of the tax collector and tarred and feathered an inspector. Resistance had turned to rebellion, and the federal government raised a militia of some 13,000 men to put down the insurrection. George Washington squeezed into his old uniform and personally led the troops west. Rebels would rise to defend liberty against the forces of order. "Their liberty they will maintain / They fought for't, and they'll fight again," wrote one poet and believer in the cause. Government forces put down the rebellion. The actions of the whiskey rebels highlighted the tensions between Federalists and Democratic-Republicans (as president, Jefferson would repeal the tax), as well as between eastern elites and frontier farmers and settlers. Within the next decade, Pennsylvania's state capital was relocated from Philadelphia to Harrisburg and New York's from New York City to Albany, in part to make government more responsive to the needs of those moving toward the interior.[27]

The show of force demonstrated that, for now at least, the government would endure. The nation passed through another vulnerable moment with the peaceful transition of power from Washington to John Adams, who defeated Jefferson in the election of 1796. Under the terms of the Electoral College (the Twelfth Amendment would change it), Jefferson, as the second-place finisher, became vice president. Thus, political enmity seeped into governance, like blood mixing with water. "Politics & party hatreds destroy the happiness of every being here," wrote Jefferson to his daughter Martha.[28]

Adams's administration was preoccupied with foreign affairs, especially the threat of a war with France, where the effects of the Revolution blazed in full force. Adams rebuffed Hamilton's martial desires (the two Federalists despised each other, evidence that political hatred was not just between parties) and avoided war. He also signed the Naturalization Act and Alien and Sedition Acts (1798), which increased the residency requirement period required for immigrants to become citizens from five to fourteen years, authorized deportation or imprisonment of aliens who supposedly posed a danger to the United States, and forbade any "false, scandalous, or malicious" speech or writing against the president or Congress. Horrified Democratic-Republicans signed resolutions denouncing the acts as "impolitic, unjust, and a disgrace to the American name." Jefferson would label the Adams administration an "Anglican, monarchical, aristocratical party," a "reign of witches."[29]

Representative Matthew Lyon of Vermont, for one, would not tolerate Federalist haughtiness without a fight. Lyon had come to America from Ireland as an indentured servant in 1765. He joined the Continental Army and was eventually dishonorably discharged. In January 1798, he was overheard saying that with a good printing press he could weaken the Federalist hold over Connecticut. Roger Griswold, a Connecticut congressman, responded that if Lyon tried to enter the state he had better be wearing his wooden sword, a jibe at the dishonorable discharge. Lyon spat in Griswold's face, earning him the nickname "The Spitting Lyon." A month later, Griswold smacked Lyon over the head with a hickory stick and Lyon grabbed fire tongs and thrust them at Griswold. All of this took place on the floor of the House. Federalists kept their eye on the "Beast of Vermont," and later that year he was imprisoned for sedition after accusing President Adams of having "an unbounded thirst for ridiculous pomp, foolish adulation, and selfish avarice." Voters in Vermont reelected him from jail.[30]

Lyon would have the last laugh with his reelection in 1798 and in the election of 1800, which pitted John Adams and Charles Pinckney against Jefferson and Aaron Burr. The campaign reached hysterical heights of vituperation. The Federalists warned that if

Figure 2.2 *Congressional Pugilists* (1798). Library of Congress.

Jefferson were elected, "murder, robbery, rape, adultery, and incest will all be openly taught and practiced, the air will be rent with the cries of the distressed, the soil will be soaked with blood, and the nation black with crimes." Adams was denounced for his "disgusting egotism, the distempered jealousy, and the ungovernable indiscretion of . . . [his] temper." And this issued from his fellow Federalist Alexander Hamilton.[31]

Electors cast separate votes for president and vice president, and as they came in over a period of months, Jefferson and Burr ended up tied with 73 electoral votes each. The House, with each of the 16 states having one vote, would decide the election. Nine votes were needed to win and on the first ballot Jefferson had 8, Burr 6, and two states, Maryland and Vermont, with representatives evenly splitting the vote, had no result. It remained this way for 35 ballots. On the thirty-sixth ballot, Maryland and Vermont (with Lyon casting the state's deciding vote) went for Jefferson, and Delaware and South Carolina went from Burr's column to no result. (After being heavily lobbied, James Bayard, Delaware's lone congressman, switched). With ten states in his column, Jefferson was elected.

In his inaugural address, Jefferson proclaimed, "We are all Republicans, we are all Federalists." The sentiment only applied when faced with defending the union. Still, his election was more than a peaceful transfer of power between two bitterly opposed political parties. He would later describe it as the "revolution of 1800 . . . as real a revolution in the principles of our government as that of 76 was in its form." Jefferson's administration quickly repealed Federalist policies such as the Naturalization Act and an excise tax on whiskey, and sought to reduce the national debt. Jefferson also refused to recognize the last-minute appointment of Federalist judges by Adams. This eventually led to the Supreme Court case of *Marbury v. Madison* (1803), in which Chief Justice John Marshall, a Federalist appointed by Adams, established the principle of judicial review by declaring part of the Judiciary Act of 1789 unconstitutional. William Marbury, a Maryland businessman, was one of many judicial nominations made by John Adams as his term expired. Jefferson's administration refused to deliver the commissions and Marbury filed suit against Secretary of State James Madison. Marshall found that although Marbury was entitled to the commission, he could not issue an order for him to receive it. The Federalists lost their eleventh-hour appointments, but achieved something much more valuable—the Supreme Court's power to overturn laws passed by democratic majorities. Marshall would go on to write a number of other opinions that greatly expanded the power of the central government.[32]

For much of his two terms, events forced Jefferson to focus more on events abroad than home. He defended the nation against attacks from Barbary corsairs and labored to stop the seizure of American ships and seamen by the British, who were locked in battle with Napoleon. Even his domestic actions had in mind reigning over the American continent. In 1803, he purchased the Louisiana Territory from France, and the following year he sent Lewis and Clark on an exploratory mission that would lead them to the Pacific after eighteen months and 4,000 miles. By the time mounting Anglo-American tensions led to war, Jefferson had retired to Monticello. He died on July 4, 1826, fifty years after the Declaration of Independence. Adams too died that day. His last words were "Thomas Jefferson survives."

War of 1812

New Englanders denounced the War of 1812 as "Mr. Madison's War," but it also belonged to Thomas Jefferson. In many ways, the War of 1812 marked a culmination of the Revolution as, once again, Americans battled Great Britain, this time over issues of trade, freedom of the seas, and the security of the frontier. American ship owners had been profiting from Britain's war with Napoleon and the merchant marine's registered tonnage grew from 558,000 tons in 1802 to 981,000 in 1810. Anxious about losing its maritime supremacy, and seeking to limit neutral nations trade with France, in 1807 Britain instituted a series of decrees, known as Orders in Council, that established a blockade on trade with continental Europe. Napoleon responded with his own measure, the Milan Decree, which declared that any ship submitting to the English blockade would be denationalized and considered English property. Caught in the middle, American merchants found their ships being seized by both nations.

Americans denounced these measures as a violation of neutral rights and an infringement on national sovereignty. Abstract economic policies paled in comparison to overt military action. In June 1807, the British warship HMS *Leopard*, looking for sailors who had deserted, stopped and boarded the USS *Chesapeake* and removed four seamen. British impressment of sailors had been taking place for years, but this went farther. Americans, eager to show that the Revolution forever liberated them as British subjects, wanted war. Jefferson wrote in July, "Never, since the battle of Lexington have

I seen this country in such a state of exasperation as at present: and even that did not produce such unanimity."[33]

Jefferson and Congress responded with the Non-Importation Act, followed by several Embargo Acts in 1807 and 1808, which prohibited foreign trade. The hope was that by refusing to send goods across the Atlantic, the United States would force Great Britain and France to agree to free trade. Secretary of State Madison believed, "we send necessaries to her [Great Britain]. She sends superfluities to us." It would do Americans good to forego some luxuries in order to further secure economic freedom as well as freedom of the seas as a neutral nation. Whatever the intentions, the embargo proved disastrous for Americans. Exports fell from $108 million to $22 million. American merchants, especially in Federalist New England, resisted by smuggling goods. In response, Jefferson expanded the power of the federal government to administer and enforce the law. In the end, the legislation did nothing to secure free trade for the United States and did much to damage the economy and inflame sectional tensions.[34]

Dismay with British actions continued to blaze, fanned by newly elected members of Congress, dubbed the "War Hawks," who favored military action. Foremost among them were the thirty-four-year-old Henry Clay of Kentucky, who was promptly elected speaker, and the twenty-nine-year-old John C. Calhoun of South Carolina. Whatever united them in 1812 would soon vanish and for nearly four decades the two would stand opposed to one another on the issues of union, states' rights, national growth, and slavery. The proponents of war were especially outraged to learn that the Indians along the frontier carried weapons provided by the British.

Settlement on the frontier and conflict with Indian tribes deeply troubled Americans. As part of the Treaty of Paris, Britain ceded lands in the Ohio Valley, where Americans engaged in a series of battles with native tribes, ultimately driving them farther northwest into Indiana. Tecumseh, a young Shawnee leader, participated in these frontier battles, which ended with the Battle of Fallen Timbers in 1794. The following year, the tribes surrendered their lands in the Ohio Valley by signing the Treaty of Greenville.

In the first decade of the nineteenth century, the Shawnee experienced a revival in which they sought to purify themselves of Anglo-American influence and return to traditional beliefs and practices. In Indiana they established Prophetstown, named for Tenkswatawa, Tecumseh's brother and the Shawnee prophet who inspired the revival. Tecumseh now took the lead in opposing the ongoing acquisition of native lands, especially after William Henry Harrison, governor of the Indiana Territory, negotiated a treaty at Fort Wayne that Tecumseh viewed as unjust and illegal.

Tecumseh and Harrison met in 1810 and again in 1811. The first meeting nearly led to war when Harrison rejected all demands to adjust the Fort Wayne treaty. After the second meeting, Tecumseh left Indiana on a mission to recruit members of what were known as the five civilized tribes to band together in opposition to encroachment upon Indian lands. While Tecumseh was away, his brother took it upon himself to make war against Harrison, who marched with 1,000 men toward Prophetstown. On November 7, 1811, Tenkswatawa attacked and in the aftermath of the Battle of Tippecanoe (named for the nearby river) the Indian confederacy was disrupted and Harrison, despite losing more men than the Indians, claimed a major victory that he would one day ride to the White House.

The War Hawks blamed the British for fomenting Indian insurrection in the territories. With Americans feeling besieged both east and west, on the ocean and the frontier, Madison felt he had to seek a declaration of war against Great Britain. In his message to Congress on June 1, 1812, he warned that "the conduct of her Government presents a series of acts hostile to the United States as an independent and neutral nation." Britain's Orders in Council had created a "sweeping system of blockades" that had destroyed neutral trade. Furthermore, "the warfare just renewed by the savages on one of our extensive frontiers" could be tied to British relations with the Indians. Madison concluded that Britain was in a state of war against the United States.[35]

The vote went 79–49 in the House and 19–13 in the Senate, the closest vote on a declaration of war in American history. Ironically, two days prior to the vote, the British announced that they would suspend the obnoxious Orders in Council; whether American knowledge of this would have changed the outcome is impossible to say. Numerous state legislatures adopted antiwar resolutions. In New Jersey, for example, the general assembly declared that "the war with Great Britain, in which the present administration has plunged the United States, was inexpedient, ill-timed, and most dangerously impolitic."[36]

For the most part, Federalists opposed the war and Democratic-Republicans supported it. The conflict between anti- and prowar factions turned violent in Baltimore. When a Federalist newspaper denounced Madison's war message, a crowd descended on the publisher Alexander Contee Hanson's office and destroyed the printing press. The next month, a mob attacked Hanson's new quarters and two assailants were killed. After he was moved to the city jail for safekeeping, a mob again attacked. One of Hanson's defenders was killed and nearly a dozen others were severely wounded, including Henry "Light Horse Harry" Lee, Revolutionary War officer and Robert E. Lee's father. Hanson was "dreadfully beaten, trampled on, and pitched for dead down the high flight of stairs in front of the gaol." It took the militia to put an end to the mob violence.[37]

Having entered into an unpopular war, Madison would now have to lead an unprepared nation into fighting one. The US Army had about 7,000 troops; the navy boasted only sixteen vessels. By comparison, the British had a quarter-million men in the regular army and more than 600 warships on active duty. Nonetheless, American commanders planned to take the battle to the British on the open seas and across the Canadian border.

Remarkably, American naval vessels scored some early successes, much to the stupefaction of the British. On August 19, 1812, the USS *Constitution* defeated HMS *Guerriere*. "Never before in the history of the world did an English frigate strike to an American," wrote the mortified editor of the *London Times*. In late October, the *USS United States* captured HMS *Macedonian* and sailed it into Newport Harbor. The success of the US Navy, as well as the hundreds of privateers who captured British merchant vessels, helped assure Madison's reelection and led Congress to authorize the building of new ships. A popular cartoon printed in the aftermath of the defeat of the British warship *Boxer* by the American frigate *Enterprise* showed a symbol of the United States bloodying King George III and proclaiming, "I'll let you know we are an Enterprizeing Nation, and ready to meet you with equal force any day."[38]

News from the Atlantic, however, could not offset failures on the Canadian frontier. The British attacked first, capturing major forts, as well as Detroit, in the summer of 1812, thus giving them control of the Michigan Territory. Tecumseh fought beside Major-General Sir Isaac Brock in these British victories. (Both men would die in battle, first Brock and a year later Tecumseh.) The Americans burned York, the capital of Upper Canada (later renamed Toronto) and then abandoned the town. Americans had some success at Fort George on the Niagara River, but eventually evacuated the position. The final invasion of Upper Canada came in July 1814, when Americans seized Fort Erie. By November, however, they had abandoned the campaign.

Figure 2.3 *A Boxing Match* (1813). Library of Congress.

Borders, of course, are crossed in two directions, and in 1814 the British invaded the United States. British forces held the Maine coast (it would be returned under the terms of the Treaty of Ghent) and their invasion aimed at New York City was stopped at Plattsburgh. On August 24, 1814, the British entered Washington, DC, after a victory at Bladensburg, Maryland. Politicians and citizens fled. Dolley Madison saved some of the White House silver. The White House doorkeeper and a gardener retrieved Gilbert Stuart's portrait of Washington. Only hours after the building emptied, the British commander dined on the meal that had been prepared for the president by Paul Jennings, Madison's slave. (In 1847, Daniel Webster purchased Jennings's freedom for $120 and allowed him to work off the debt at $8 a month.) In retaliation for the burning of public buildings in York, the British torched the presidential mansion, the Capitol, and other government structures.[39]

As Washington burned, peace negotiations had begun in Ghent. The American delegation included John Quincy Adams, Henry Clay, and Albert Gallatin. The Americans were willing to end the war with a return to the way things were before it started; the British sought to keep what they had gained and demanded concessions regarding navigation rights and protection of native lands, which would serve as a buffer with Canada. Talks dragged on and the war continued. On September 13, the British bombarded Fort McHenry in Baltimore Harbor. The next morning, resilient soldiers raised an American flag. Francis Scott Key, who witnessed the bombardment, wrote a poem that was set to a tune that became the "Star-Spangled Banner" (made the national anthem in 1931).

On Christmas Eve, with the British relenting on their claims because of their greater concerns about Napoleon, negotiators agreed to a treaty that ratified the status quo antebellum. Lands were returned; issues of freedom of the seas and impressment were left unaddressed; and there was agreement to restore to Indians their lands, but no enforcement mechanism.

It took weeks for news of the treaty to reach the United States. The war had begun after the Orders in Council had been rescinded, and it ended before a final battle gave Americans cause for celebration and created a new national hero. In January 1815, British forces sought to take New Orleans. Despite superiority in numbers and experience, they came up against Major General Andrew Jackson, who had been held as a prisoner during the Revolutionary War and carried a hatred for the British the rest of his life. Jackson successfully defended the city with a ragtag collection of regular army, militia, volunteers, and even pirates, and became a symbol of American democracy and vigor. News of the victory, recalled one witness, "came upon the country like a clap of thunder in the clear azure vault of the firmament."[40]

Victory made heroes of the Democratic-Republicans and villains of the Federalists, who had opposed the war and even met in convention in Hartford from December 15, 1814, to January 5, 1815, to air their grievances over such topics as the embargo and the three-fifths clause that gave Southerners additional political power. Twenty-six delegates from the five New England states met in secret and even discussed secession. In their final report they condemned the Democratic-Republicans for entangling the country in "an unjust and ruinous war." The timing could not have been worse for the Federalists as news of New Orleans and peace, linked in American minds, led to a new nationalism and patriotism that left the party of Adams and Hamilton hopelessly discredited.[41]

The war expanded the nation's control over the continent and contributed to the destruction of America's first political party. It also left Native Americans more vulnerable after the war than they had been before. However glorious the victory, in only three years, some 15,000 soldiers, sailors, and marines had perished. By comparison, the Revolutionary War lasted eight years and claimed 25,000 lives. Within a decade, American politicians articulated a doctrine whereby the United States would not allow European powers to colonize or wage war in the Americas. The United States would remain neutral in European affairs and expected Europe to stay out of American affairs. These principles would come to be known as the Monroe Doctrine, after James Monroe's Message to Congress on December 2, 1823, in which he declared, "American continents, by the free and independent condition which they have assumed and maintain, are henceforth not to be considered as subjects for future colonization by any European powers" and doing so would be viewed as "the manifestation of an unfriendly disposition toward the United States." With peace at hand, and spheres of influence established, attention could again turn to national growth.[42]

Missouri Compromise

At the War of 1812's conclusion, the United States consisted of eighteen states and five territories. Between 1816 and 1819, Indiana, Mississippi, Illinois, and Alabama entered. Also in 1819, the United States acquired Florida from the Spanish and the territory, organized in 1822, would become a state in 1845. Of the twenty-two states, eleven were free and eleven were slave. Slavery had always been just below the surface of national and local politics, but it was not yet the vortex of discourse. The Federalists had made an issue of the problem of representation through the three-fifths clause. The British during the war welcomed slaves who made their way to British vessels and promised them freedom. In Illinois and Indiana, pro- and antislavery factions jostled, and while Illinois drafted a free state constitution it also imposed stringent measures to discourage blacks from immigrating to the state. By 1804, all northern states had passed acts of gradual emancipation, although most of these acts applied only to children of slaves once they reached a certain age. (Massachusetts and Vermont abolished slavery immediately.)

Learning of Virginia legislator Charles Fenton Mercer's efforts to revive interest in African colonization, Robert Finley, a Presbyterian minister who directed the Princeton Theological School and was anxious about the presence of blacks in America, embraced the idea and took the lead in organizing the founding meeting of the American Colonization Society, which was devoted to settling free blacks abroad. Politicians from Henry Clay to Abraham Lincoln supported its efforts. The colony of Liberia ultimately received more than 12,000 blacks, its capital Monrovia named after President James Monroe. Post-revolutionary ideas about liberty and anxiety over slavery (a rebellion was organized by Denmark Vesey, a Caribbean-born freed slave in Charleston in 1822, leading to his martyrdom) led to increased opposition to slavery North and South. Indeed, through the 1820s there were more antislavery societies in the latter than in the former.

Nonetheless, gradualist antislavery sentiment was nothing like the immediatist abolitionist fervor that emerged in the 1830s. In 1820, there were 1.5 million enslaved persons in the South, out of a population of 4.5 million. Total population in the United States was nearly 10 million and New York and New Jersey still contained thousands of slaves. About one-third of white southern families owned slaves. Most slaveholders were farmers who possessed very few bondsmen. By 1860, less than 1 percent of slaveholders owned more than fifty slaves. Those several thousand plantation owners held disproportionate political power and gave rise to the myth of the Old South as a land of aristocratic planters. More than half of all slaves were owned by those who possessed twenty or more, the number that distinguished a plantation from a farm. In 1820, most Southerners viewed slavery as a "necessary evil," an inherited way of life, indispensable to southern agriculture and maintaining white supremacy, a paternalist institution in which slaveholders cared for those seen as incapable of caring for themselves.

For the enslaved, the institution offered little hope. To be sure there were some benevolent masters. The "peculiar institution," however, did not recognize any rights for the enslaved. "The power of the master must be absolute, to render submission of the slave perfect," wrote Judge Thomas Ruffin in *State v. Mann*, a North Carolina case decided in 1829. The institution differed in the Upper South, where crops were more diversified, slaves constituted a smaller percentage of the population, and there were a greater number of free blacks, from the Lower South, where there were large cotton plantations, as well as sugar and rice, and the slave population generally exceeded 40 percent of the overall population. There was an outright black majority in South Carolina and Mississippi. The internal domestic slave trade carried more than a million slaves from the Upper to the Lower South. In Alabama, Mississippi, and Louisiana, the slave population increased 27 percent per decade. The enslaved tried in various ways to resist the brutality of the institution: slowing down as they labored, breaking tools, feigning illness, temporarily running away, practicing a religion that offered hopes of deliverance, risking taking a spouse and having children knowing that the whims of the master could separate them at any point, forever. Some thousands of slaves, particularly in the Upper South, managed to escape through the use of secret networks that entered the public imagination as the Underground Railroad in the 1840s. For most slaves there would be no deliverance and they would live with the constant threat of violence, rape, and death.[43]

If Southern antislavery sentiment offered a check on the brutality of slavery, the revitalization of cotton ended any amelioration. Eli Whitney's gin, patented in 1794, allowed for the easy cleaning of cotton, removing the seeds from the boll. As a result, a laborer's production escalated from one pound per day to fifty. It also made the cultivation of short-staple cotton feasible, cotton that could be grown throughout the Lower and Middle South. Cotton production fueled a consumer revolution and fed Northern and British textile mills. It led both to the increase in the number of slaves and expansion westward as planters looked for fertile ground in which to grow the crop. "Instead of an evil," John C. Calhoun told the Senate in 1837, slavery was "a positive good," both for the economy and the enslaved as well. "Cotton is king," declared James Henry Hammond of South Carolina in 1858.[44]

Although the Missouri Territory, carved out of the Louisiana Purchase, was unsuited for cotton production, slaveholders had settled the area and by 1820 some 10,000 slaves resided there. When a statehood bill came before Congress in 1819, it seemed that Missouri would be admitted as a slave state with little controversy. James Tallmadge, a Democratic-Republican representative from Poughkeepsie, New York, had different ideas. On February 13, he introduced an amendment that barred the further introduction of slavery into Missouri and provided for the freedom of the children of slaves when they reached age twenty-five. Tallmadge's motives were unclear. It seemed unlikely the amendment would help his political chances in New York. Probably the proposal issued from his dismay over the unequal representation given Southerners as a result of the three-fifths clause and his personal dislike of slavery.

Whatever his motivations, Tallmadge's amendment unleashed a furious debate in the House. One Southerner minced no words when he said, "I perceive a brother's sword crimsoned with a brother's blood . . . if Congress persist in the determination to impose the restrictions contemplated." For their part, antislavery representatives insisted that the amendment presented an opportunity to "prevent the growth of a sin which sits heavy on the soul of every one of us." The vote on the amendment exposed a sectional division that would persist for decades to come and lead eventually to the Civil War. The first clause prohibiting slaves from entering Missouri in the future passed 87–76, with Northerners voting 86–10 in favor and Southerners 66–1 against. The second clause, providing for gradual emancipation of slaves born in Missouri, passed 82–78, with Northerners voting 80–15 in favor and Southerners 63–2 against. The Senate rejected both clauses of the amendment: 22–6 and 31–7. The Fifteenth Congress expired in March 1819 without the issue of Missouri being resolved.[45]

When the Sixteenth Congress convened the following December, Maine's application for admission as a free state came before the body. Southerners announced they would not vote to admit Maine unless Missouri was admitted as a slave state. Thus, the fate of the two states became linked. Newly elected House Speaker Henry Clay argued that if a condition could be applied to the admission of Missouri, so too could one be applied to the admission of Maine. The Senate approved a Maine-Missouri compromise bill, proposed by Illinois Senator Jesse B. Thomas, that admitted Maine as a free state and Missouri as a slave state, opened Arkansas Territory (which included much of today's state of Oklahoma) to settlement by slaveholders, and banned slavery from the rest of the Louisiana Territory north of 36 degrees, 30 minutes North latitude. The House agreed 90–87 to remove the restriction on slavery in Missouri and voted 134–42 to exclude slavery from the remainder of the Louisiana Purchase. President Monroe sought advice from James Madison, who told the president that he thought the exclusion of slavery was unconstitutional, but that it was justified to sign the bill if "the injury threatened to the nation" was greater from vetoing than approving. Monroe signed the bill on March 6, 1820.[46]

Ceding authority over slavery in the territories created anxiety among some Southerners who opposed any sort of interference with the institution. Others sought to allay fears by pointing out that the compromise only applied to a territory and that Congress could legislate as it saw fit at the time of statehood. This was the belief of Tennessee Senator John Eaton, who informed Andrew Jackson that the compromise "preserved peace dissipated angry feelings, & dispelled appearances which seemed dark & horrible & threat[en]ing to the interest &harmony of the nation."[47]

While the Missouri Compromise preoccupied Congress, everyday Americans worried about their survival as an economic panic swept the nation in 1819. Demand for staples abroad declined and prices plummeted some 30 percent between 1818 and 1821.

Businesses folded and unemployment spiked. State banks, which had engaged in speculative, inflationary practices, began to foreclose on farms. The Second Bank of the United States exacerbated the crisis, first by expanding and then by tightening credit. John C. Calhoun lamented to John Quincy Adams that "there has been within these two years an immense revolution of fortunes in every part of the Union: enormous numbers of persons utterly ruined; multitudes in deep distress; and a general mass disaffection to the government."[48]

The Panic of 1819 hit North and South equally hard, but the debate over the Missouri Compromise unleashed sectional tensions that had remained relatively muted until then. During the debates, Congressmen first used the term Mason-Dixon line (a line surveyed in the 1760s to resolve a border dispute between Pennsylvania and Maryland) to denote the dividing line between free and slave states east of the Ohio River. Henry Clay observed in 1820 that "the words civil war and disunion are uttered almost without emotion." Thomas Jefferson expressed his anxieties in an April 1820 letter to John Holmes, a Massachusetts representative who supported compromise: "But this momentous question, like a fire bell in the night, awakened and filled me with terror. I considered it at once as the knell of the Union. It is hushed, indeed, for the moment. But this is a reprieve only, not a final sentence."

Jefferson saw little hope for the nation. He knew well the truth of what his friend Madison had posited more than thirty years earlier: men were not angels and while government was necessary, it could not solve the nation's most intractable problems. He ended the letter: "I regret that I am now to die in the belief that the useless sacrifice of themselves, by the generation of '76, to acquire self-government and happiness to their country, is to be thrown away by the unwise and unworthy passions of their sons, and that my only consolation is to be that I live not to weep over it."[49]

CHAPTER 3

Empire of Liberty

T HE COUNTRY WAS IN MOTION. The expansion of democracy offered wider opportunities for some Americans,
and the nation's physical enlargement provided new routes
of development, conquest, and escape. An English visitor remarked,
"Old America seems to be breaking up, and moving westward." That
was in 1817, long before moving west meant Oregon and California.
It may have been that the Union itself showed signs of splintering
into pieces. Andrew Jackson would try to hold it together, but his
actions would also unleash uncontrollable passions. Described as a
"roaring, rollicking, game-cocking, horse-racing, card-playing, mis-
chievous fellow," Jackson was the first president not from Virginia
or Massachusetts, the first from the frontier, and the first of humble
origins, born in 1767 in a log cabin in the Carolinas. There were
indeed forces at work no one could contain. Evangelical minister
Lyman Beecher warned against the dangers arising from "our vast
extent of territory, our numerous and increasing population, from
diversity of local interests, the power of selfishness, and the fury of
sectional jealousy and hate." In 1846, at the start of the Mexican
War, Herman Melville wrote to his brother that "something great is
impending . . . 'A little spark kindleth a great fire.' "[1]

Nullification

Andrew Jackson deplored nullification, the doctrine that a state could
interpose itself and declare an act of Congress unconstitutional.

"Assert that a state may declare acts passed by Congress inoperative and void," he said, "and revolution with all its attendant evils in the end must be looked for and expected." The issue was not states' rights—no one, he affirmed, had a higher respect and regard for the rights of states than he. The issue was observing the rights of states without threatening the Union.[2]

Many Americans loved Jackson. He had been denied the presidency in 1824 in what many voters thought was a corrupt bargain where Henry Clay gave his support to John Quincy Adams, supposedly in return for being appointed secretary of state. Jackson became a symbol for the age. He was tall and lean (6 foot 1 and 140 pounds). His nickname, "Old Hickory," spoke to his toughness. The story spread how he refused to shine the boots of a British officer when he was a prisoner and suffered blows for his intransigence. Everyone knew of his duel with Charles Dickinson in 1806, when he took a bullet in the chest yet stood firm, leveled his pistol, and then killed his opponent. The man of courage was also a man of providence. In 1835, he survived an assassination attempt when Richard Lawrence, angered over losing his job, pulled not one but two pistols and both misfired. The odds of this happening were so improbable that Jackson's opponents became convinced that the president must have set it up as a stunt to gain political support.

Perhaps nothing endeared him more to an electorate whose own backgrounds were neither wealthy nor Eastern than his appearance at Harvard in 1833. The university invited the president to receive an honorary degree. John Quincy Adams was apoplectic. He wrote Josiah Quincy, the university's president and his cousin, that he would not attend and watch his alma mater disgrace itself by "conferring her highest literary honors upon a barbarian who could not write a sentence of grammar and hardly spell his own name." Jackson was expected to give a speech in Latin. Boston's Brahmins snickered, waiting for the moment. Jackson rose and said, "E pluribus unum, my friends, sine qua non," and sat down. The populist president had shown America's social elite.[3]

New England's Whigs were not amused. The Whig Party had begun to emerge out of the collapsed Federalist party and the short-lived anti-Masonic party, which opposed the secret Freemason fraternal organization. The Whig party coalesced around a set of principles articulated by Henry Clay and known as the "American System": support for internal improvements, tariffs to promote local industries such as textiles, and a Bank of the United States. Guided by these principles, states embarked on massive road, turnpike, and canal projects. Transportation underwent a revolution, especially with the development of the steam engine, which Robert Fulton put to use in 1807 when the *Clermont* carried passengers round trip between New York and Albany in sixty-two hours. The Erie Canal, which spanned more than 350 miles and was completed in 1825, connected New York Harbor to the Great Lakes and earned New York the nickname "empire state." Steamboats and canals paled in comparison to the epidemic of "Rail-Road Mania," as railroad lines such as the Baltimore and Ohio lay hundreds of miles of iron tracks. Commentators marveled at how this new form of travel "annihilated time and space by its celerity."[4]

Jackson's era ushered in an age of democracy, a word anathema to many of the founders, who feared "democratical despotism." In his final letter, written on July 10, 1804, the day before his duel with Aaron Burr, Alexander Hamilton lamented the destruction of the nation from "our real Disease; which is Democracy."[5]

In the first decades of the century, however, democracy flourished. States removed property and tax requirements for voting (itself an expression of the fear of pure democracy) and established universal white manhood suffrage (at the same time, the legislature in New York increased property requirements for free blacks). Moreover, political parties became entrenched. If Jefferson's generation feared the factionalism embodied by parties, Jackson's generation turned political parties into well-financed and organized entities driven to mobilize supporters. Newspapers proliferated and became party organs, and politicians used rallies and nominating conventions to marshal supporters, whether Democrats (evolved from the Democratic-Republican Party of Jefferson and Madison), who favored limited government and westward expansion, or Whigs, who favored an energetic federal government and investments in industry. Voter turnout in elections soared, at times approaching 80 percent. When Alexis de Tocqueville visited America in 1831 and returned to France to write a book about his experiences he could think of only one suitable title for the work: *Democracy in America.*[6]

Tocqueville offered a trenchant account of the American character. In searching for the right word to describe what he encountered he coined a new one: "individualism." America, he thought, presented "the spectacle of a society marching along all alone, without guide or support, by the sole fact of the cooperation of individual wills." The American, he observed, was "devoured by the longing to make his fortune; it is the passion of his life; he has no memory that attaches him to one place more than another, no inveterate habits, no spirit of routine; he is the daily witness of the swiftest changes of fortune, and is less afraid than any other inhabitants of the globe to risk what he has gained in the hope of a better future."[7]

Tocqueville feared for the survival of the republic precisely because there seemed to be no central government strong enough to hold the enterprise together. "The Union," he realized, "has never shown so much weakness as on the celebrated issue of the tariff." From the start, the idea of a tariff to protect American industries aroused constitutional and political controversy. As early as 1790, one proponent of free trade thought a tariff would lead to "dissolution of the Union." For Southerners, tariffs on imported goods favored northern industry over southern agriculture and raised the price of consumer goods purchased in the region. Moreover, southern planters feared that English manufacturers would retaliate and reduce their imports of cotton. The price of cotton had been plummeting—from thirty-one cents per pound in 1818 to eight cents in 1831. Southerners denounced the Tariff of 1828 as an abomination. In addition to the explicit question of economics there was an implicit one as well: if the federal government had the power to impose taxes, might they not also claim the power to attack slavery?[8]

Southern anxiety over slavery was especially acute in the aftermath of Nat Turner's rebellion. In August 1831, Turner, fueled by prophetic visions, led a slave rebellion in Southampton, Virginia, that resulted in the massacre of dozens of whites. Southerners blamed northern abolitionists for inciting the slaves to rebel, and many states passed laws banning "incendiary literature" from the mails. Jackson, a slaveholder, asked Congress to prohibit the circulation of abolitionist material in the South. Slavery had to be protected. "There cannot be a durable republican government without slavery," declared John C. Calhoun.[9]

Calhoun, who was Jackson's vice president, not only staunchly defended slavery, he articulated and promoted a doctrine of nullification. Educated at Yale, and a nationalist during the War of 1812, Calhoun later became a zealous states' rights advocate. In his *South Carolina Exposition and Protest* (1828), published anonymously, though everyone knew Calhoun was the author, he argued that the tariff stole southern wealth and acted "to corrupt the government and destroy the liberties of the country." An unchecked majority led to despotism and the only check was "the constitutional rights of the states to interpose in order to protect their powers." Interposition and nullification were the same. According to Calhoun, a state could nullify an act of Congress as unconstitutional and, if Congress did not retract or revise the objectionable legislation, the state could then leave the union. On November 24, 1832, the South Carolina legislature adopted an Ordinance of Nullification that declared the tariff null and void and not binding upon the state.[10]

Numerous politicians denounced nullification as an "absurdity" and a "heresy." None other than James Madison, eighty years of age, wrote that the Constitution "cannot be altered or annulled at the will of the States individually." Thinking back to 1787, he lamented, "Who could, at that day, have foreseen some of the comments on the Constitution advanced at the present." As for those who quoted as precedent his and Jefferson's Virginia and Kentucky resolutions of 1798, issued in response to the Alien and Sedition Acts and arguing for the rights of states to nullify unconstitutional federal laws, Madison sought to rescue the resolutions from being misconstrued. Jefferson never "asserted a right in a single State to arrest the execution of an Act of Congress." Rather, the plural "states" had always been used.[11]

The only opinion that mattered was Jackson's, and some Southerners held high hopes that the president would support their states' rights stand. After all, he had waged war on the Bank of the United States (which was championed by the Whigs) as unconstitutional and inimical to the interests of the states. He denounced the bank for concentrating power in the hands of a few men who exercised the power to create and destroy wealth, for allowing foreigners to own its stock, and for strengthening the national government at the expense of state governments. Besides, he said in his first annual message, it failed at its stated goal of "establishing a uniform and sound currency." The battle with the bank became personal for Jackson: "The Bank is trying to kill me," he told Martin Van Buren, "but I will kill it." True to his word, he vetoed the bill to recharter the institution and justified it on grounds that "government authority should not be centralized in institutions such as the Bank of the United States, but rather consists in leaving individuals and States as much as possible to themselves." Opponents called Jackson's veto message "a manifesto of anarchy." A popular cartoon showed him as a king who wielded the power of the veto and trampled on the Constitution.[12]

If Southerners thought that Jackson's veto message, emphasizing state prerogatives over the federal government, would lead him to support nullification, they were in for a surprise. When it came to the growth of the nation, Jackson was a nationalist—he had previously supported protective tariffs. He endorsed a reduction of the tariff to

Figure 3.1 *King Andrew the First*
(ca. 1833). Library of Congress.

ease economic conditions in South Carolina, and while he opposed
"all encroachments upon the legitimate sphere of state sovereignty,"
he would defend the preservation of the nation at all costs. "If they
attempt disunion," Jackson said of the nullifiers, "it must be because
they wish it, and have only indulged in their vituperations against the
Tariff for the purpose of covertly accomplishing their ends."[13]

On December 10, 1832, Jackson issued his Nullification
Proclamation. He would not stand for the actions of South
Carolina: "the power to annul a law of the United States, assumed by
one State, incompatible with the existence of the Union, contradicted
expressly by the letter of the Constitution, unauthorized by its spirit,
inconsistent with every principle on which it was founded, and destructive of the great object for which it was formed," did not exist.
"Disunion by armed force is treason," he thundered, and the military hero threatened to use whatever means necessary to save the
country. Congress lowered the tariff in 1833 and also passed a Force
Bill that authorized the government to use federal troops to enforce
compliance with tariff laws. South Carolina acquiesced to the new

tariff, though promptly nullified the Force Bill. For now, the Union was saved. When South Carolina seceded nearly thirty years later, Abraham Lincoln chose to place Andrew Jackson's portrait on his office wall.[14]

Revival

Democratization applied to religion as well as politics. The First Amendment to the Constitution reads that Congress "shall make no law respecting an establishment of religion, or prohibiting the free exercise thereof," and in the late eighteenth century states moved away from established denominations. Thomas Jefferson articulated the principles of disestablishment and freedom of religion as clearly as anyone in a letter written to the Danbury Baptists in 1802: "Believing with you that religion is a matter which lies solely between man and his God, that he owes account to none other for his faith or his worship, that the legitimate powers of government reach actions only, and not opinions, I contemplate with sovereign reverence that act of the whole American people which declared that their legislature should 'make no law respecting an establishment of religion, or prohibiting the free exercise thereof,' thus building a wall of separation between church and State."[15]

The Baptists were just one of many denominations that proliferated in a period of evangelical revival that would sweep the United States in the first half of the nineteenth century. The Second Great Awakening, as it was known, took place on the frontier as well as in cities and was characterized by huge outdoor meetings led by charismatic ministers who traveled the circuit rather than being tied to any one congregation. Most important of all was the theology that underpinned the revival: free moral agency. In democratic America, one could choose to be saved.

Charles Grandison Finney was the most famous evangelical minister of the era. Each wave of religious enthusiasm in America has produced a leading evangelist, whether George Whitfield in the 1740s, Dwight Moody in the 1880s, Billy Sunday in the 1920s, Billy Graham in the 1950s, or Jerry Falwell in the 1970s. In the 1830s, Finney galvanized audiences. Born in 1792 in western New York, an area that would come to be known as "the burned-over district," scorched by the fires of evangelical enthusiasm, Finney studied law. One day, walking in the woods, he looked about him and decided to give himself to God. Due in court the next morning, he told his client he could not represent him because "I have a retainer from the Lord Jesus Christ to plead his cause."[16]

Finney's earliest success came in Rochester, New York. Revivals seemed particularly successful in those places experiencing the social transformation brought on by economic development and growing population. Finney preached three evenings a week and three times on Sunday. When his deeply set, piercing blue eyes fixed on you, it was hard to turn away. His voice, clear and shrill, pierced the congregation. Sinners whom he heard were particularly anxious about their souls were seated in the front, on benches that came to be known as "anxious seats," so Finney could preach directly at them. By the time he left Rochester, more than 800 residents had converted and joined the church.

It is ironic, of course, that the solution to the problem of individualism was the individualist act of choosing salvation over sin. Evangelical Christianity rejected the Calvinist ideas of innate depravity and original sin. Rather, people were free to choose their fate, to renounce evil, and to embrace the kingdom of God. Finney often used a parable that described a man in a rowboat drifting toward the precipice of Niagara Falls unaware of the danger. From

Figure 3.2 *Camp Meeting* (ca. 1829). Library of Congress.

shore someone shouts "STOP!" The man is awakened and he turns toward safety. Finney was the one shouting from shore, awakening congregants to the imminent danger toward which they were rowing.

Many of Finney's converts were middle-class white women. Through religion these women codified their role in the home as keepers of morality and virtue and educators of the children. If the men tumbled through the corrupting public sphere to work, women would make the private sphere of the home sacred. And from that place they would evangelize and transform society. Catherine Beecher, the daughter of Lyman Beecher, a leading Presbyterian minister, became one of the foremost advocates for education. Her *Treatise on Domestic Economy* (1842) guided women in their duties at home. Beecher wrote of "the superiority of women" and their role in preserving democratic institutions. She called for domestic education and physical exercise, and saw how American women could overcome difficulties peculiar to them. If the home became the fulcrum of life for all middle-class whites, the slaves' lack of a home became one reason to oppose the institution as immoral and unjust. Frederick Douglass made a point of this in his memoir, *Narrative of the Life of Frederick Douglass* (1845), when he described the miserable, barren, isolated conditions under which his grandmother had lived. And Catherine Beecher's sister Harriet would make homes the center of her novel *Uncle Tom's Cabin* (1852), gushing at one point about runaway slave George Harris: "This, indeed, was a home,—home,—a word that George had never yet known a meaning for; and a belief in God, and trust in his providence, began to encircle his heart."[17]

From their home base, Christian women began their assault on social evils. They condemned poverty, drunkenness, prison conditions, and slavery, and agitated for educational reform and women's rights. Many men joined their wives in these endeavors, and the career of the professional reformer came into existence, an activist who made a living off of reform, whether the abolitionist William Lloyd Garrison or the prison reformer Charles Spear. In reform, America's tendencies toward association, first recognized by Alexis de Tocqueville in *Democracy in America* as the nation's cure for its individualistic tendencies, came to the fore. Activists formed scores of reform and benevolent associations: the American Anti-Slavery Society, American Society, American Peace Society, Children's Aid Society, Moral Reform Society, Society for the Prevention of Pauperism, and the Magdalen Society, devoted to stamping out prostitution. Religion and free agency taught that the world could be perfected, and eager Americans sought to prove it.

Perhaps no reform movement was more widespread than the temperance movement. Of course, moralists had always warned about the evils of alcohol. In 1673, Increase Mather published "Woe to Drunkards: Two Sermons Testifying against the Sin of Drunkenness." Mather was concerned with peoples' souls. While salvation of the individual mattered deeply in the 1830s and 1840s, preservation of family and society weighed as heavily. One reason for the renewed attention to alcohol was an increase in consumption to six gallons per capita annually. Exclude women and children, and it is conceivable that most males drank as much as half a pint a day. The increase was driven in part by the movement west of farmers who converted grain into alcohol and flooded the eastern markets. The expansion of drinking combined with evangelical fervor and the expansion of poverty among many urban Americans led to cries for moderation and abstinence. By 1833, the American Temperance Society had more than 6,000 branches. If these groups contained mainly middle-class Americans, another group, the Washingtonians, had half a million working-class members. Popular literature and melodrama scared people in to abstinence. In the novel *Ten Nights in a Bar-Room and What I Saw There* (1854), for example, Timothy Shay Arthur described scenes of violence and illness. "Rum and ruin. Are they not cause and effect?" asks a character. By the 1850s a number of states prohibited the sale of alcohol.

As with all reforms, temperance would wax and wane. Many saw it as an assault on Irish immigrants (more than 500,000 in the late 1840s) who celebrated a culture of drink, and as an attempt on the part of business owners to impose new rules of discipline for their workers. Whatever the motivations, temperance reform spoke to the desire to create a more peaceful, harmonious society.[18]

If most reformers worked within society to effect change, many others looked outside. Dreams of perfection led some to seek alternatives to the jangle of competitive, capitalistic life by forming new societies based on utopian principles. Utopias formed like so many bubbles in a bath: New Harmony, Oneida, Fruitlands, Shakers, Nashoba, Hopedale. Mormonism also emerged in this era and can be seen as another attempt to create a utopian community based on new principles. Some of these utopias featured communal ownership of property. Most focused on reformist Christian principles. Some had a spiritualist or a health element—vegetarianism for example. Many expressed a desire for remaking sexual relations. The Oneida community supported free love (they called it "complex marriage") and male continence. Its founder, John Humphrey Noyes, took responsibility for indoctrinating teenagers into sex. Mormons practiced polygamy; the Shakers celibacy. While some of these experiments lasted only a year or two, others, such as Hopedale and Oneida, persevered for decades, and the Mormon religion, emerging out of the same cauldron of perfectionist desires, flourished and continues to play a prominent role in American society.

Brook Farm, a transcendentalist community in West Roxbury, near Boston, attracted the attention of New England writers, reformers, and intellectuals. Founded in 1841 by George Ripley, a Harvard-educated Unitarian minister turned reformer, the experiment attracted the leading denizens of Concord and its surrounds, including Margaret Fuller, Nathaniel Hawthorne, and Elizabeth Peabody. The idea was simple enough: buy a farm, work it, and cultivate it collectively as a community. "Each of us wishes to be enriched with the power of the other, be it manual, intellectual, or moral," wrote one member. Hawthorne was at first so enthused he signed his letters "ploughman." In short order, his enthusiasm would wane (community, he thought, was overrated; he preferred to focus on writing alone rather than laboring together). After leaving Brook Farm, he wrote *The Blithedale Romance* (1852), a novel that exposed the fallacies of the utopian ideal.[19]

From the start, Ralph Waldo Emerson stayed away. Emerson was the leading transcendentalist of the day, the chief philosopher of a movement to reject the past and inherited forms of worship and instead establish an original relationship to the universe. Emerson denounced his Unitarian religion as "corpse cold," and argued that society debilitated and dissected men into pieces to do its bidding. Instead, he preached the power of nature to restore one's moral clarity. His most famous essay, "Self-Reliance," advised nonconformity, going it alone, and living fast by one's principles. Of course, he made good money lecturing around the country to audiences eager to hear his message while continuing to work hard. "Do your work and I shall know you," he advised, an apothegm that might keep people searching where they were rather than moving on. A bolder version appears in his diary: "do your thing and I shall know you." Emerson rejected the myriad social reforms of the day ("are they my poor," he asked?) and he rejected an invitation to join Brook Farm. He confided in his journal, "I do not wish to remove from my present prison to a prison a little larger."[20]

The dean of individualism, Emerson had a difficult time lending his voice to the reforms of the day. He admitted in "Self-Reliance" that he sometimes donated money to social causes, but he called it a "wicked dollar" that he wished he had the strength to withhold. He spoke out against slavery, but never much farther than from the comforts of his Concord study. One social cause that did gain his attention and support was opposition to the efforts being made to remove the Cherokee from their homeland in the Southeast. Emerson delivered speeches and wrote a public letter to President Martin Van Buren. In the end, however, the entire experience dragged him down, "like dead cats around one's neck." The religious, spiritual, revivalist impulses of the era would do much to remake America, but none of it would suffice to save the Cherokee.[21]

Removal

With Andrew Jackson as president, the fate of the Indians in the Southeast became more tenuous. Jackson had made his name (and his wealth) fighting the Creeks in 1813 and the Seminoles in 1817. He adopted a Creek orphan named Lyncoya, yet he never changed his belief that it was the Indians'—all Indians— intention "to comit murder with impunity." Like many American political leaders, Jackson believed that the Indians must convert to Christianity and submit to the laws of the states in which they resided; he refused to acknowledge their existence as independent nations. In 1789, Secretary of War Henry Knox talked of "civilizing and Christianizing the Indians." The Treaty of New York in 1790 recognized southeastern tribes' rights to their land. It also marked the beginnings of an official policy of assimilation whereby the tribes would surrender their identities as hunters and instead become "herdsmen and cultivators." Settlers continued to invade Indian lands and do battle against them. Knox wrote to George Washington that tribes were becoming extinct and he feared "in a short period, the idea of an Indian on this side of the Mississippi will only be found in the page of the historian."[22]

One of the bitter ironies of the story of the Cherokee is that they had embraced the "civilization" program. One visitor noted that "they adopt in part the costume of Europeans; they have schools, and churches, and printing press among them." No amount of assimilation, however, protected them from the encroachment of the states. Indeed, Jackson proclaimed that the Cherokee had doomed themselves to "weakness and decay" and an inability to ward off transgressors. Just as some advocates of colonization at the time were encouraging free blacks to leave the nation for Liberia, Jackson thought Indians should voluntarily immigrate to the area west of Mississippi.[23]

That they could do so was a result of the Louisiana Purchase. Jefferson saw expansion as central to the American mission and to counteracting the power of the British. In 1780, he called for an "Empire of Liberty," the spread of nascent American ideals to new, fertile areas. Other forces motivated him as well. Both Federalists and Democratic-Republicans agreed that only through expansion ("extend the sphere," Madison wrote in Federalist 10) could the nation escape the baneful effects of faction. They also believed that population growth would outrace subsistence and so the only way to avert what Madison saw as the misery that would result from population growth was to take advantage of what Jefferson viewed as "the singular circumstance of immense extent of rich and un-cultivated land." Although his constitutional authority to do so was dubious, Jefferson leapt at the chance to purchase some 828,000 square miles from the French in 1803 for a price just over $11 million. The Purchase nearly doubled the size of the United States. It removed the French presence from North America and it furnished the territory over which the expansion of slavery would become contested and to which the Indians would be forced to move.[24]

Removal became the official policy of the US government in 1830, when Democrats introduced a bill, the Indian Removal Act, that authorized the president to provide land west of the Mississippi for Southeastern Indians in exchange for tribal property in the Southeast. Congress would appropriate $500,000 for resettlement. Opponents of the measure denounced removal on historical, constitutional, and moral grounds. The government would be abrogating fourteen treaties signed with the Cherokee that guaranteed the tribe "the remainder of their country forever." Furthermore, the Cherokee Nation was a state as articulated by Article IV, Section 3 of the Constitution ("no new State shall be formed or erected within the Jurisdiction of any other State.") "Removal is a soft word," observed Massachusetts Congressman Edward Everett, "and words are delusive." Removal was not voluntary but compulsory and would lead to expulsion of some 15,000 Cherokee from their homeland. In conclusion, Everett appealed to the conscience of his fellow legislators, pointing out that they were going to take families, "who live as we do in houses, work as we do in the field or the workshop, at the plough and the loom, who are governed as we are by laws, who raise their children to school, and who attend themselves to the ministry of the Christian faith, to march them from their homes, and put them down in a remote, unexplored desert."[25]

Despite the entreaties of opponents like Everett, the Indian Removal Act passed the Senate by a vote of 28–19 and the House by a vote of 103–97. Antipathy to Indians, states' rights advocacy, and the desire for riches trumped all other concerns. Jackson called the act "true philanthropy," and compared forcing the Indians to leave behind their ancestral homelands to what American forefathers had done to better their condition. The president, Congress, and the states aligned against the Cherokee whose leader, John Ross, decided that their only hope was to bring their case to the US Supreme Court.

In Ross, the Cherokee had a formidable spokesman. Born to a mixed-Cherokee woman and Scottish father, he learned English at an early age. In addition to becoming a successful businessman (Ross's Landing would serve as the original settlement in Chattanooga, Tennessee), he worked as an Indian agent and representative of the Cherokee Nation to negotiate treaties in Washington. He was elected principal chief of the Cherokee, who had established a tripartite constitutional government. With the passage of the Indian Removal Act, Ross took the advice of Whig leaders such as Henry Clay and Daniel Webster, who supported the Cherokee cause and recommended they enlist William Wirt as their attorney. The attorney general under James Monroe, Wirt was one of the most distinguished lawyers in the nation. "Your case is a great and urgent one," he told Ross.[26]

In March 1831, the Supreme Court heard arguments in *Cherokee Nation v. Georgia*. The State of Georgia refused to participate, insulted to be asked to become a party before the Supreme Court "with a few savages." Chief Justice John Marshall would not let Georgia's intransigence stop the proceedings. Seventy-five and showing signs of anguish after the recent death of his wife, Marshall had served as chief justice since 1801. During his tenure, he established the principle of judicial review, bolstered the idea of federal supremacy, and issued rulings that generally strengthened economic competition and growth.

Wirt delivered a long and passionate argument that sought to establish that the Cherokee were an independent foreign nation who controlled their borders and had fixed boundaries, were ruled by laws and government, and were parties to treaties that recognized their rights as nation. With the darkness of late day descending on the chamber, Wirt concluded: "They are here in the last extremity, and with them must perish forever the honor of the American name. . . . 'Remember the Cherokee nation' will be answer enough to the proudest boasts we can ever make."[27]

Although the Cherokee plight moved Marshall, the Court's majority ruled that the Cherokee could not "with strict accuracy, be denominated foreign nations." Ultimately, the Cherokee, he said, were neither a foreign state nor a subject tribe but a "domestic, dependent nation" and therefore the Court did not have jurisdiction. Concurrent opinions displayed less respect. William Johnson laughed off the idea of the Cherokee as a nation; instead they were "wandering hordes." Marshall, however, was uneasy with the procedural ruling against the Cherokee, and he encouraged Joseph Story and Smith Thompson to file a dissent. They argued that the Cherokee were a foreign state and that the Court held jurisdiction under various articles of the Constitution dealing with treaties and commerce. Marshall signaled to the Cherokee to bring a case that involved specific laws, not abstract principles. Privately, Joseph Story told his wife, "I feel, as an American, disgraced by our gross violation of the public faith towards them."[28]

Marshall had a second chance to rule a year later in *Worcester v. Georgia*. Georgia authorities arrested Samuel Worcester, a thirty-three-year-old Congregationalist missionary, for violating a new state law that prohibited whites from residing in Indian Territory. The law was intended to keep sympathetic whites from supporting the growing Cherokee resistance movement. Authorities convicted Worcester and sentenced him to prison. He and several other missionaries appealed to the Supreme Court. This time Marshall ruled that the Cherokee Nation "is a distinct community, occupying its own territory, with boundaries accurately described, in which the laws of Georgia can have no force, and which the citizens of Georgia have no right to enter but with the assent of the Cherokee themselves."[29]

The decision eventually helped free Worcester, but it did not help the Cherokee. Jackson reportedly said, "John Marshall has made his decision, now let him enforce it." He gloated that the ruling "has fell still-born"; it would not stop efforts to remove the Indians from their land. The Cherokee themselves became divided. One faction believed that removal was inevitable and formed the Treaty Party, which supported making a deal with the US government to cede their lands. Led by Major Ridge, his son John, Elias Boudinot, and Stand Waite, the men agreed in 1835 to the Treaty of New Echota by which they surrendered claims to land east of the Mississippi for land west of the river in Indian Territory. Chief Ross's National Party, which comprised a majority, protested that they had not approved of the treaty. The Senate ratified it by one vote. The Ridges and Boudinot paid with their lives, assassinated by members of the Ross faction for their apostasy. Waite survived and ended up joining with the Confederacy during the Civil War. He served as a brigadier general and on June 23, 1865, became the last Confederate leader to surrender, more than three months after Robert E. Lee. Ross had sided with the Union.

With the treaty ratified, removal of the Cherokee began in earnest in 1838. Under General Winfield Scott, an armed force removed some 16,000 Cherokee to military posts and camps across Georgia, Tennessee, and Alabama. Hundreds died from dysentery and cholera during a summer heat wave in 1838. From those internment camps began a thousand-mile march to Oklahoma in multiple detachments of approximately 1,000 people each. On the trail west, the heat and drought of summer turned to the ice and blizzards of winter. John Ross's wife, Quatie, died after giving her blanket to a child in a snowstorm. In camps and on the trail, Indians perished by the thousands, from hunger, disease, brutality, and despair. A solider recalled that the Indians "had to sleep in the wagons and on the ground without fire. And I have known as many as twenty-two of them to die in one night of pneumonia due to ill treatment, cold, and exposure." A missionary who accompanied the Cherokee asked, "For what crime then was this whole nation doomed to this perpetual death? This almost unheard of suffering? Simply because they would not agree to a principle which would be at once death of their national existence?" "The trail of the exiles was a trail of death," recalled one soldier. The Cherokee came to call it a trail of tears.[30]

Mexican-American War

South of Oklahoma Territory, Jefferson's "empire of liberty" continued to expand as a fledgling Texas republic took shape. Throughout the 1820s and 1830s, settlers from the southern United States had moved into Mexico, bringing their slaves with them. Although Mexico at first welcomed the immigrants, in short order they outnumbered the native-born in the area they settled. Tensions between invading Texians (as they called themselves) and Mexicans grew over a number of issues: slaveholding, religion, race, and taxation. In 1829, Mexico abolished slavery, forbade future immigration, and raised taxes. When Santa Anna, the hero of Mexican independence, began expanding and centralizing his power, American settlers in the province of Texas moved toward independence. Led by Stephen A. Austin, who in 1825 had brought some 300 families to settle the colony he had established, Texians formed an army and, starting in October 1835, battled the Mexican regulars in a series of campaigns that lasted through the following year. One Texas newspaper alleged one reason for the rebellion: Mexico was attempting to "give liberty to our slaves, and to make slaves of ourselves."[31]

In March 1836, delegates to a convention held at Washington-on-the-Brazos adopted a Declaration of Independence modeled on the one signed nearly sixty years earlier. Rebellion was justified "when a government has ceased to protect the lives, liberty and property of the people, from whom its legitimate powers are derived, and for the advancement of whose happiness it was instituted."[32]

As the document was being signed, the Alamo in San Antonio was under siege. Santa Anna's forces had crossed the Nueces River into Texas Territory in February and attacked the Alamo on February 23. Led by James Bowie, William Travis, and Davy Crockett, some 200 men defended the mission. (Crockett was already a frontier legend and a member of Congress. He had told his constituents that if reelected he would serve them faithfully; if not "they might go to hell, and I will go to Texas"). On March 6, the Mexican army overtook the fortress. Outgunned and outnumbered, the Texians refused to surrender and almost all were killed, their bodies burned in the aftermath. Several weeks later, at Goliad, Santa Anna executed more than 300 prisoners. The following month, however, the general was defeated at the Battle of San Jacinto. Cries of "Remember the Alamo," and "Remember Goliad," led to calls for Santa Anna's execution. Santa Anna would survive and, in time, again face the Americans. Texians had won independence and for the next ten years would exist as an independent republic.[33]

On his last day in office, Andrew Jackson recognized Texas independence and diplomatic relations began in March 1837. Talk of annexation percolated from the start, but the discussions also raised concerns about the extension of slavery and political stability in the United States. John Tyler made expansionism the centerpiece of his policy when he assumed the presidency following William Henry Harrison's death from pneumonia only four weeks after his inauguration in March 1841. A Tyler-Texas treaty would have admitted Texas as a territory. Anti-annexation forces rallied, however, and the Senate voted against it, with Whigs opposed 27–1 and Democrats in favor 15–8. Tyler was not finished, and before leaving office he offered Texas annexation based on a joint congressional resolution that passed on a sectional majority vote.

With a popular vote of 49.5 percent, Democrat James K. Polk narrowly defeated Henry Clay in the election of 1844. Polk, from Tennessee, was a favorite of Jackson's, but he was not a natural politician. Stern and sullen, he spoke poorly, had no sense of humor, and botched any attempt to tell a story. Yet he transformed himself into a formidable leader. In his inaugural address, he made clear his view that Texas was an "independent power" free to pursue its destiny. Enlarging the nation, he said, was to "extend the dominions of peace over additional territories and increasing millions."[34]

Texans acted quickly and a convention held on July 4, 1845, approved the resolution of annexation. Tired of the ongoing opposition to annexation, Democratic columnist and editor John O'Sullivan crafted a justification for American expansionism that would become fundamental to any vision of American identity. "Texas is now ours," he declared, "and it is now time for opposition . . . to cease." Annexing Texas, he avowed, provided "the fulfillment of our manifest destiny to overspread the continent allotted by Providence for the free development of our yearly multiplying millions." The phrase "manifest destiny" captured the American sense of mission in the nation's march across the continent. It became a justification for hemispheric conquests and the spread of the "empire of liberty." New land would help provide opportunity and protect democracy, and democracy, with or without slavery, would expand.[35]

Mexico had its own ideas and did not accept Texas's claim that its southern border was the Rio Grande, more than 100 miles south of the Nueces. Polk tried to purchase the disputed territory (as well as New Mexico Territory and California) and was rebuffed. American troops under Zachary Taylor had massed at the Nueces River. When they moved toward the Rio Grande and established camp near Matamoras, Mexican cavalry fired upon them. This gave Polk what he needed. In a message delivered to Congress he claimed that, "after reiterated menaces, Mexico has passed the boundary of the United States, has invaded our territory and shed American blood upon the American soil. She has proclaimed that hostilities have commenced, and that the two nations are now at war." Two days later Congress declared war.[36]

The claim outraged Whigs. Polk, they charged, had manufactured a war to acquire territory and secure the spread of slavery. Polk's statements, declared the *American Whig Review*, were "calculated to mislead the popular mind, and to imbue it with false impressions." He had "extorted from Congress a declaration of war that was nothing but evidence of American aggression and rapacity."

Emerson predicted in May 1846, "the United States will conquer Mexico, but it will be as the man swallows the arsenic, which brings him down in turn. Mexico will poison us."[37]

Northern legislators found the inflammatory rhetoric of American blood having been shed on American soil especially galling. On December 27, 1847, freshman congressman Abraham Lincoln offered a series of resolutions that demanded to know the exact "spot" on which American blood was shed and whether it "was or was not our own soil." (War supporters derisively nicknamed him "Spotty Lincoln.") In a speech delivered on January 12, 1848, Lincoln insisted on facts, not deception and distortion. As was his lawyerly way, he reviewed all the evidence and found it wanting. "The soil was not ours," he would later write. He concluded that Polk was a "bewildered, confounded, and miserably perplexed man" who knows that "the blood of this war, like the blood of Abel, is crying to Heaven against him."[38]

By the time of Lincoln's "Spot Resolutions," the war was well underway. It was the first war in an age of changing communication and newspapers played a key role in shaping public opinion. Dozens of correspondents covered the campaigns and using steamship, railroad, and the ever-expanding telegraph, often beat military reports back to Washington. Polk learned of one victory from a headline in the *Baltimore Sun*. Mexico also served as a training ground for future Civil War generals, such as Robert E. Lee, James Longstreet, Stonewall Jackson, Ulysses S. Grant, William T. Sherman, and George B. McClellan. And although eclipsed by what would come fifteen years later, the casualty rate of nearly 17 percent (most from disease) shocked Americans.

Americans fought the war on several fronts, including campaigns in Texas, California, and New Mexico. In Northern Mexico, Zachary Taylor (known as "Old Rough and Ready") faced off against Santa Anna, who had returned to Mexico a hero in 1837 after having lost a leg fighting against the French. The Battles of Monterrey and Buena Vista revealed the power of American artillery against superior numbers. At Buena Vista, Jefferson Davis and the Mississippi rifles distinguished themselves. Killed at the battle was Colonel Henry Clay Jr., a West Point graduate whose father had opposed the war. Two months later, at the Battle of Cerro Gordo, members of the Fourth Illinois Infantry captured Santa Anna's cork prosthetic leg.

In Southern Mexico, General Winfield Scott, whose career began in the War of 1812, where he had earned the nickname "Old Fuss and Feathers," moved toward Mexico City. The US Navy helped his army take Vera Cruz in late March 1847. Over the next six months, Scott, with a force outnumbered by perhaps three to one, conducted a remarkable campaign that culminated with the capture of Mexico City in mid-September. He also took measures intended to prevent volunteer troops from assaulting Mexican women and plundering wealth, or acting on racial and anti-Catholic prejudices, He was only partially successful. "The majority of the Volunteers sent here are a disgrace to the nation," wrote the correspondent for the *Charleston Mercury.*[39]

The two nations agreed to peace on February 2, 1848. Under the terms of the Treaty of Guadalupe Hidalgo, the Rio Grande was established as the southern boundary of Texas and the United States acquired California and New Mexico Territory, expanding the nation by some 525,000 square miles. The United States agreed to pay $15 million and assume some debts owed to Americans. Mexicans and Indians living in those newly acquired areas were allowed to resettle or become American citizens. Most chose the latter. Some Americans still wanted more. Sam Houston opposed the treaty. "Now the Mexicans are no better than the Indians," he declared, "and I see no reason why we should not go on in the same course now, and take their land."[40]

The war was over. Denunciation of it continued, however. The Whigs had opposed the war, and some Democrats did as well. Even John L. O'Sullivan, whose doctrine of manifest destiny helped justify the conflict, expressed his opposition to anything but peaceful expansion. Writing more than thirty years later, Ulysses S. Grant concluded, "I do not think there was ever a more wicked war than that waged by the United States on Mexico."[41]

Of all the writings the war spawned, none became more prominent over time than one by Henry David Thoreau. Thoreau came from Concord, the center of transcendentalism, and returned there after attending Harvard. He wanted to teach and ended up living with Emerson for a few years. After his brother died from tetanus, Thoreau turned to writing, lecturing, and traveling in the region. He also embraced abolitionism. Between 1845 and 1847, Thoreau spent time at a house that he built at Walden Pond, on land leased from Emerson. In 1854, he published *Walden,* a book about the experience. Few paid it any attention, but over time, Thoreau became synonymous with naturalism and environmentalism, celebrating the power and wonder of nature.

Thoreau was also a political activist. In July 1846, as he was walking back to town from Walden Pond, the town constable stopped

Thoreau and said he owed poll taxes that he had not submitted for several years. Thoreau refused to pay because he would not contribute to a government that was prosecuting an unjust, immoral war designed to expand slavery. He declined an offer from the constable to loan him the money. Thoreau was jailed for refusing to pay his taxes. Someone, likely his aunt, paid the debt, and the constable released Thoreau the next day.

Thoreau's act led to his lecture on the subject and his essay "Civil Disobedience" (originally published as "Resistance to Civil Government" in 1849). For Thoreau, excessive government posed a danger. In the opening paragraph he wrote: "The government itself, which is only the mode which the people have chosen to execute their will, is equally liable to be abused and perverted before the people can act through it. Witness the present Mexican war, the work of comparatively a few individuals using the standing government as their tool; for, in the outset, the people would not have consented to this measure." He did not want to abolish government—he was no anarchist—but asked for "a better government." It was the responsibility of the citizens to protest and resist the evils of government: "Let your life be a counter-friction to stop the machine," he advised. He encouraged people not to pay their taxes to support corrupt government and should they end up in jail so be it: "the true place for a just man is also a prison." In time, Thoreau's essay would influence a generation of activists throughout the world, and civil disobedience would become a hallmark of the civil rights movement in the 1950s and 1960s, as well as to the opposition to the Vietnam War.[42]

During the 1850s, Thoreau traveled through New England and began delivering a lecture on "Walking, or the Wild." It was published after his death from tuberculosis in 1862. Thoreau declared, "Eastward I go only by force; but westward I go free. . . . I must walk toward Oregon, and not toward Europe. And that way the nation is moving." Thoreau sought wildness and wilderness, the forest not the field. The principles of manifest destiny that Thoreau vehemently opposed provided the very territory that offered him the freedom he so desired.[43]

Westward the Course of Empire

Thoreau was right that the nation was moving west. Polk's inaugural address in March 1845 had not only made clear his intention of annexing Texas; he also insisted that "our title to the country of Oregon is clear and unquestionable." Only weeks after Congress declared war on Mexico, a new treaty with Great Britain gave the United States control of the Oregon Territory up to the 49th parallel. Long before then, traders, trappers, missionaries, and migrants had begun to blaze a path toward the Pacific. In 1843, a wagon train of a thousand completed a passable route to lead settlers to the Willamette Valley.

The Oregon Trail started in Independence, Missouri, and ran across the Great Plains, Rocky Mountains, and Great Basin. Fort Laramie in Wyoming and Fort Hall in present-day Idaho (then the eastern part of the Oregon territory) were key stopping points. During the 1840s thousands contracted "Oregon Fever." Books and articles did what promotional literature had always done: provided a utopian vision of a rich and fertile land. Thousands journeyed west in teams of covered wagons. Not everyone caught the fever—Abraham Lincoln turned down an offer to serve as territorial governor—but many did, and guidebooks advised them on clothes, food, equipment, wagons, animals, and route. They also warned about the challenges of crossing as a group. Lansford Hastings's *Emigrants' Guide to Oregon and California* (1845) noted, "We had proceeded only a few days travel, from our native land of order and security, when the 'American character' was fully exhibited. All appeared to be determined to govern, but not to be governed."[44]

If Oregon fever burned, California fever eventually blazed. Those headed to Oregon and California generally followed the same trail, until splitting at Fort Hall. There was also the Mormon Trail, which took shape in 1846 when Brigham Young led the trek that would bring church members to Fort Laramie and from there to Salt Lake City. The Sierra Nevada Mountains posed a challenge to overland migrants headed to California. In 1846 the Donner party became trapped in the snowbound mountains and only forty-six of eighty-seven travelers survived, some through acts of cannibalism. Even the famed explorer and soldier John C. Fremont, known as "Pathfinder," found himself trapped in the Sierras and lost a third of his party.

The year 1846 would prove pivotal in other ways. American immigrants in Alta California staged a rebellion against Mexican authorities and proclaimed a California republic, represented by a flag with a grizzly bear. It lasted several weeks before being subsumed by federal forces under the command of Fremont, who had won a series of military victories. From the start, California offered a vision of heaven on earth. "If man were to ask of God a climate," wrote one traveler, "he would ask just such an one as that of California."[45]

Whether headed to Oregon, California, or Salt Lake, pioneers faced similar challenges. The 2,000-mile trek could take anywhere from four to six months, and preparation for the journey began a year before departure. Supplies would weigh more than 2,000 pounds and cost more than $200. Either mules (a team of cost $600) or oxen (a team of eight cost $200) pulled the wagons. Emigrants traveled in caravans and before departing wrote up agreements to govern behavior on the frontier. Leaders were elected and rules created. Some caravans would split up because of dissention. Others would face the hardships of terrible storms or the spread of cholera, which would leave many buried along the side of the trail in shallow graves. Sarah Royce dreaded falling ill with her husband and leaving their children orphaned, "among strangers, in a land of orphans." One in ten did not survive the journey.[46]

Indians posed less of a threat than the historical imagination suggests. To be sure, hundreds of Indians and pioneers died in skirmishes. Most Indians, however, were more interested in trading and preparing for warfare against other tribes than in attacking the caravans. Indeed, one missionary noted that "emigrants and Indians meet, it appears, for the purpose of affording mutual aid." Indians provided advice on routes and migrants hired them to help them navigate dangerous river crossings. Of course, where there is commerce there is deception. Indians would sometimes steal a horse then sell it back to the pioneer. It worked both ways, as pioneers would unload tattered and worn-out clothing on Indians eager for these items. As the numbers of migrants on the overland trails increased, Indians started to assert their rights and demand tribute payment or bridge tolls from the caravans, which were exploiting native resources by killing buffalo and other game. The Commissioner of Indian Affairs observed that "no people, probably, are more tenacious of what they consider their rights than the Indians."[47]

After 1848, neither the journey's hardship nor Indian rights would get in the way of tens of thousands who headed west. Gold had been discovered in California. Indeed, the numbers that embarked on the overland trail over the Sierra Nevada in 1849 alone eclipsed the number of migrants between 1841 and 1848 on the Oregon, California, and Mormon trails combined. Many others came by water routes and from all over the world, including Latin America, China, and Australia. News of gold also brought thousands south from the Oregon Territory, whose proximity allowed them to arrive first after word of the discovery by James Wilson Marshall at John Sutter's Mill near Sacramento in January 1848 began to spread. In

December 1848, nearly a year later, President Polk confirmed the rumors: "The accounts of abundance of gold are of such an extraordinary character as would scarcely command belief were they not corroborated by the authentic reports of officers in the public service." The following year, more than 80,000 Forty-Niners arrived and began mining. Almost overnight San Francisco became a major metropolis.[48]

The gold was no hoax. For the first few years, miners pulled tens of millions of dollars' worth from the ground. William Tecumseh Sherman reported that "no capital is required to obtain this gold, as the laboring man wants nothing but his pick, shovel, and tin pan, with which to dig and wash the gravel." Surface gold, such as what Marshall found, disappeared quickly and miners turned to hydraulic methods that plumbed deeper deposits (and caused vast environmental damage.) As it became more competitive and difficult to unearth gold, racial and ethnic tensions intensified. Violence against Indians and Californians of Mexican descent was rampant. The government denied African Americans and Native Americans civil rights, and a law passed in 1850 allowed the use of Indians as forced labor. The Chinese especially, with their odd customs and non-Christian beliefs, became objects of bigotry. A Foreign Miner's License Law imposed a monthly tax that contributed to destitution. Like blacks and Indians, the Chinese could not testify in court. In 1854, the California Supreme Court called them "a race of people whom nature has marked as inferior, and who are incapable of progress or intellectual development beyond a certain point." There may have been no more polyglot place in America than San Francisco in the 1850s. A rough kind of harmony reigned, though only as long as the wealth held out.[49]

None of the hard reality and disappointed hopes eclipsed the vision expressed in numerous images, most notably Emanuel Leutze's painting *Westward the Course of Empire Takes Its Way*. Leutze, who had come to America from Germany as a child, left to study painting as a young man in Dusseldorf and returned to open a studio in New York in 1859. He had established his reputation with *Washington Crossing the Delaware* (1851), which he painted in Germany using American tourists and students as his models.

In 1861, Congress commissioned Leutze to paint a mural for the Capitol building that celebrated the westward movement. The painting shows a wagon train of pioneers just as they cross the Sierra Nevada and climb a ridge to view the golden land of California and the Pacific Ocean. The panoramic vignette on the border below

Figure 3.3 Emanuel Leutze, *Westward the Course of Empire Takes Its Way* (mural study, 1861). Smithsonian American Art Museum.

shows San Francisco Bay. The darkness in the east gives way to the light emanating from the west, and the viewer's eye is drawn to the pioneer standing atop the outcropping in the distance being handed an American flag by another.

On the rock pinnacle below is a family, the father in raccoon cap pointing out the Promised Land to his wife with infant. She prays as their son, the young American whose future is bright, stands at the precipice. On the left, an old trapper guide in buckskin shows the way as men with axes work to clear the ground ahead. One migrant, helping a woman climb, has a fiddle on his back while another helps someone who has been wounded. At the center is a smiling black youth holding a mule that bears another woman and child, evocative of the Madonna. A boy riding an ox carries Indian arrows and a bow. In the mural, the ornamental border is as revealing as the image itself. The title of the painting is written in arabesque across the top. Portraits of early explorers William Clark and Daniel Boone are included. The American eagle shields the symbols of union and liberty, and the Indians are reduced to the margins of the painting.

Leutze completed the work in 1862. He had imagined an image that would perhaps help inspire and unify the nation during the Civil War. Nathaniel Hawthorne read it that way. The mural is "full of energy, hope, progress, irrepressible movement onward, all represented in a momentary pause of triumph; and it was most cheering to feel its good augury at this dismal time, when our country might seem to have arrived at such a deadly standstill." It is unclear whether Leutze, or Hawthorne for that matter, realized that the manifest destiny and westward migration celebrated in the painting had helped deliver the very conflict that now threatened to destroy the expanding American empire.[50]

CHAPTER 4

A Higher Law

N O ONE COULD HAVE PREDICTED that Harriet Beecher Stowe would write *Uncle Tom's Cabin*, a book read by people in parlors and palaces that further polarized a nation where barely six months went by without a calamitous event that left many wondering whether the United States would remain intact or disintegrate into civil war. At age forty, she had previously written only a few trifling stories. Her religious beliefs—her father was minister Lyman Beecher—prepared her to feel inordinate sympathy for the downtrodden, and the signs of discord and disunion politicized her along with millions of others. Stowe later claimed that she had not so much written the novel as taken dictation from God: "It all came before me in visions, one after another, and I put them down in words."

Published in 1852, after first appearing as a serial the previous year in *The National Era*, a leading antislavery newspaper, *Uncle Tom's Cabin* sold 10,000 copies in the first week. Presses were kept running around the clock, and by the end of the year 300,000 books were sold. Readers in England purchased more than a million copies. German, French, Spanish, Italian, Danish, and Portuguese editions quickly appeared. It was said to have sold more copies than any work other than the Bible in the nineteenth century. "It is impossible to extricate oneself from the questions in which our age is involved," Ralph Waldo Emerson would write. "You can no more keep out of politics than out of the frost."[1]

Compromise of 1850

Again, the nation was in trouble. New territory meant new states. And new states meant that the vexed question of slavery and representation would arise anew. California was prepared to enter the Union as free. However, that would upset the balance of free and slave states (fifteen each), a prospect abhorred by Southerners. They desired parts of the Mexican cession to enter as slave states. A majority of Northerners opposed introducing slavery into the territories and stood by the policy embodied by the Wilmot Proviso, which passed the House but was defeated in the Senate in 1846. David Wilmot, a Democratic Pennsylvania congressman, had added a proviso to an appropriations bill that would have banned slavery in any territory acquired from Mexico. Southerners would have no part of it. Voting in Congress became increasingly sectionalized, the fragile balance of Northern and Southern Whigs and Democrats breaking down. Rhetoric escalated. One Southerner thought that if Northerners prevailed the Capitol should be set on fire. Another turned words into actions. During the debate, Senator Henry Foote of Mississippi pulled a pistol on Senator Thomas Hart Benton of Missouri. (Foote would prove no less intransigent as a member of the Confederate Congress during the Civil War, when he denounced cabinet member Judah P. Benjamin, who was Jewish, as "Judas Iscariot Benjamin.")

Henry Clay offered a compromise and, in the first months of 1850, Clay, Calhoun, and Webster, the leading statesmen of the era, rose to speak on the problem of slavery in the territories. Clay was nearing the end of a remarkable career in the House and Senate, a career that left him short of the presidency (he ran five times), yet made him the most influential Whig of the era. His faith in manufacturing, tariffs, banking, and internal improvements offered a road map for American progress. Clay was Abraham Lincoln's "beau ideal of a statesman." He had previously engineered compromises during times of crisis and was now prepared to do so again.

The compromise resolutions would admit California as a free state, organize Utah and New Mexico Territory without restriction on slavery, settle a boundary dispute between Texas and New Mexico, abolish the slave trade in Washington, DC, and amend the Fugitive Slave Act of 1793 to strengthen it.

Clay spoke on February 5 and 6 to defend the measures. At seventy-three years old, he remained one of the Senate's great orators. Words alone did not matter as much as the delivery. Congressman John Wentworth recalled "the varied intonations of his ever-pleasing voice, or of seeing his gesticulations, his rising upon his toes, his stamp of the foot, his march down the aisles until his long fingers would almost touch the president's desk, and his backward tread to his seat, all the while speaking; his shake of the head, his dangling hair."[2]

Clay expressed his concern over the danger that the nation faced and blamed it on "the violence and intemperance of party spirit." Clay declared that his proposed compromise sought to settle the political controversies over slavery. He despaired to consider "what a spectacle should we present to the contemplation of astonished mankind . . . if the two portions of this Confederacy should unhappily be involved in civil war." He asked members to put aside abstract constitutional questions and focus on both parties getting what they desired without setting any precedents. Clay, a slaveholder, also defended slavery and denounced as "unneighborly" Northern laws that did not allow masters to bring their slaves with them. Late on the second day, Clay pressed on despite repeated calls for adjournment. He warned that there was no right to secession and concluded that without compromise "war and the dissolution of the Union are identical and inevitable." He ended by saying he would not survive to "behold the sad and heart-rending spectacle" of the dissolution of the Union. He was right. Two years later he was gone.[3]

Clay's longtime political opponent John C. Calhoun teetered closer to the grave. Indeed, he was so ill that John Murray Mason of Virginia read his speech as the senator, weak and emaciated, rested at his desk wrapped in flannels. Anyone who knew him at the height of his vigor would have been startled. The English traveler Harriet Martineau described him as "a cast-iron man, who looks as if he had never been born, and never could be extinguished." Calhoun had served as a congressman, secretary of war under James Monroe, and vice president under John Quincy Adams and Andrew Jackson. He ended his career as a senator from South Carolina. He had begun as a supporter of strong national government and protective tariffs, but he spent the final two decades of his life crafting the doctrine of nullification and supporting states' rights and slavery. It was Calhoun who in 1837 defended slavery as a positive good. In that same speech, he proclaimed concession and compromise on the issue of slavery to be fatal.[4]

He began on March 4 by restating his belief that "the agitation of the subject of slavery would, if not prevented by some timely and effective measure, end in disunion." Calhoun denounced the shattering of political equilibrium and argued that over the decades the

North had systemically increased its power over the South. To make the case, Calhoun had to ignore that for most of the era the White House had been occupied by Democrats, and slaveholders at that. Whatever the cause, whether in the settlement of new territories or the raising of revenue through taxes, the North had amassed power and wealth. As a result, what was once a federal republic had mutated into a consolidated national democracy in which the North held absolute power and the South had to sacrifice its interests to it. In addition, an abolition movement had gained prominence and strength since the 1830s. If nothing was done to arrest this movement, Calhoun argued, "the South will be forced to choose between abolition and secession." How could the Union be saved, he asked? Not by Clay's proposed plan, which left the South with little of its honor intact. California, he argued, was not a state and therefore could not be admitted to the Union; Congress had no power over slavery in the territories. "The South asks for justice, simple justice, and less she ought not to take," he concluded. "She has no compromise to offer but the Constitution, and no concession or surrender to make."[5]

At the end of the South Carolinian's speech, Daniel Webster rose to express his satisfaction that Calhoun was in attendance and wished him a speedy recovery. Webster also gave notice of his intention to speak on Clay's proposed measures. It was said of him "to have seen Daniel Webster once was to have seen him always." One congressman recalled, "I have never heard that anybody was mistaken for him, or looked like him . . . there was his ever blue coat, white cravat, and buff vest, his massive and over-hanging brow, his raven hair, dark and deep-set eye, portly form and erect gait." Lawyer and politician, Webster was considered the greatest orator of the day, and nationalists still lauded him for his famous reply to Senator Robert Hayne in 1830 during the nullification crisis: "liberty and union, now and forever, one and inseparable."[6]

Still vigorous at age sixty-eight, Webster spoke on March 7 for nearly four hours. His opening line immediately rang iconic: "I wish to speak today, not as a Massachusetts man, nor as a Northern man, but as an American." He supported compromise and shocked his Northern antislavery constituents by defending Southern slaveholders as honest and well-meaning in their opinions. Slavery was a reality and Webster suggested that Americans learn to live with it. He said he would not vote to exclude slavery from New Mexico, and he supported all measures necessary for the recapture of fugitive slaves. He finished by denouncing the absurdity of the idea of "peaceable secession," and asked if secession were to occur "What is to remain American? What am I to be—an American no longer?"[7]

Moderates praised Webster's speech as patriotic. Many New Englanders, however, would never forgive his apostasy. One writer denounced the spirit of the speech even more than the doctrine. Webster "went down upon the knees of his soul, and paid base homage to his own and his country's irreconcilable foes." The poet John Greenleaf Whittier offered an epitaph:

> All else is gone; from those great eyes
> The soul has fled:
> When faith is lost, when honor dies,
> The man is dead.

Webster would resign from the Senate four months later and serve as secretary of state until his death in October 1852, four months after Clay. The "Great Triumvirate" of Clay, Calhoun, and Webster was no more.[8]

On March 11, a new voice was heard. William H. Seward had been elected to the Senate from New York, where he had earlier served two terms as governor. A generation younger than the other speakers, he listened as the political giants of the age spoke and then he delivered his maiden speech. Few paid attention. Some senators, such as Webster, came and went. Others dozed. Seward's monotone delivery did not help, and the galleries soon emptied of spectators. The speech, however, would prove to be a lightning bolt, and tens of thousands of copies were soon being circulated.

Seward opposed any compromise on slavery and denounced legislative compromises as "radically wrong and essentially vicious." A free California was not worth the surrender of liberty elsewhere, and the recapture of fugitive slaves was "unjust, unconstitutional, and immoral." Seward warmed to the point for which the speech would be remembered. The Constitution provides the authority for government "but there is a higher law than the Constitution." No Christian nation could establish slavery. It was axiomatic that all men are created equal and have rights to life, liberty, and the pursuit of happiness. Seward declared emancipation inevitable: "you cannot roll back the tide of social progress." He did not fear disunion. "I know only one country and one sovereign," he concluded. "The United States of America and the American people."[9]

It was a stunning speech, more radical than the moderate politician who delivered it. The *Southern Literary Messenger* mocked Seward as his "Holiness" and marveled that he could so easily surrender the oath of office he took to uphold the Constitution. Southerners denounced the speech as "monstrous and diabolical." Horace Greeley, the influential antislavery editor of the *New York Tribune*, predicted that Seward's speech "will live longer, be read with a more hearty admiration, and exert a more potential and pervading influence on the national mind and character than any other speech of the session."[10]

Seward's "Higher Law" speech, however provocative, did nothing to prevent compromise. Another relative newcomer to the political scene, Stephen Douglas of Illinois, stepped in to shepherd the proposals through. A staunch Democrat, he had first been elected to Congress in 1843 at age twenty-nine. His debates with Lincoln lay in the future, though he had courted Mary Todd and lost to Lincoln in that contest. Clay had tried for months to get the compromise measures passed as a bundle, but only a minority of senators supported a package deal that included elements they opposed.

After the exhausted and frustrated Clay departed Washington for Kentucky, Douglas took over. He assembled various coalitions to pass each measure separately. It helped his efforts that during the negotiations President Zachary Taylor, who wanted California and New Mexico admitted as states, died and was replaced by Millard Fillmore, who was amenable to compromise. The bills passed without the opponents on each side having to vote for measures that went against the interest of their region. For the most part, Northern Democrats joined with upper-South Whigs to deliver the necessary votes. For the moment, a crisis was averted.

Nonetheless, sectional controversy was destined to increase, not diminish. The disunionists of the lower South would continue to call for secession conventions, and an increasing number of Northerners opposed to slavery would continue to fill the corridors of power in Washington. Opposition to slavery had been raging for decades. Ironically, the Fugitive Slave Act, perhaps the least controversial of the separate bills that constituted the Compromise of 1850, helped galvanize the abolitionist movement and radicalize even those who held the most tepid antislavery views.

Abolition

One actual and one fictional fugitive slave helped change everything. On May 24, 1854, Anthony Burns, a twenty-year-old black man working in a clothing store on Brattle Street in Boston, was arrested and charged with being a fugitive slave. Ever since the passage of the Fugitive Slave Act, blacks in the Northeast found themselves in danger of being scooped up by federal marshals and tried as runaways in response to an affidavit from an alleged owner. There were thousands of fugitive slaves in the North and many more free blacks who could falsely be claimed as someone's property.

Under the terms of the Fugitive Slave Act, everyday citizens had to assist in the apprehension of runaway slaves or face criminal prosecution. Federal marshals would enforce the law and bring accused runaway slaves before a federal commissioner, who would consider testimony only from the alleged owner, who did not have to appear in person. Accused runaway slaves could not testify. Commissioners who found in favor of the claimant would be paid $10 as compared to only $5 if he found insufficient proof.

The Fugitive Slave Act was designed to placate slaveholders who bristled at the proliferation of personal liberty laws in the North that held no person could be brought into a state and held as a slave. The Supreme Court in 1842 in *Prigg v. Pennsylvania* had ruled Pennsylvania's liberty law unconstitutional. In response, the various Northern states passed new laws that forbade state officials from participating in the capture of runaway slaves. Rather than reduce conflict, the act instead further polarized North and South. Northerners saw a slave power conspiracy at work; Southerners railed against abolitionist refusal to enforce federal law.

There were more than 300 runaway slave cases in the 1850s. In Boston alone, prominent cases included Shadrach Minkins, who was freed from a courtroom by an antislavery crowd and fled to Canada, and Thomas Sims, who was tried and transported back to Georgia. After Burns was arrested, an interracial crowd stormed the courthouse to try and free the captive. "Rescue him," "Bring him out," they demanded. Authorities restored order, though not before a US marshal was killed. In a hearing, Burns was found to be the property of Charles F. Suttle. Abolitionists offered to purchase Burns's freedom. Wanting to make a point that federal law supported slaveholders, Suttle rejected the offer. On June 2, with thousands lining the streets of Boston from the courthouse to the custom house, and with federal troops in place to prevent any rescue efforts, marshals marched Burns to a ship and returned him to slavery. (The following year, a group raised funds and purchased Burns's freedom. He returned to New England and eventually moved to Canada where he died in 1862).[11]

The reaction in Boston and throughout the North was instantaneous. Vigilance committees vowed to prevent any further rendition and antigovernment sentiment spread as many Northerners embraced the doctrine of a higher law. Amos Adams Lawrence, a prominent merchant turned social activist, best summarized the effects of the Burns case: "I put my face in my hands and wept . . . I could do nothing less. We went to bed one night old-fashioned, conservative, Compromise Union Whigs & waked up stark mad Abolitionists."[12]

Abolitionist William Lloyd Garrison was among those who were outraged. At a rally sponsored by the Massachusetts Anti-Slavery Society on July 4, 1854, Garrison produced a copy of the Fugitive Slave Act and set it on fire. He then took out a copy of the Constitution. As it burned, he shouted, "So perish all compromises with Tyranny!"[13]

Inflammatory acts and words were nothing new to Garrison. Ever since January 1, 1831, when he published the inaugural issue of the *Liberator*, Garrison had defined the radical abolitionist position. Like many Americans, he had previously favored gradual emancipation: the passage of laws that would eventually free the

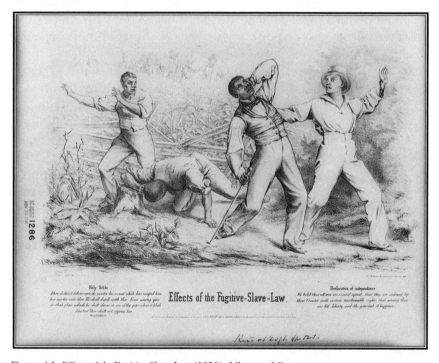

Figure 4.1 *Effects of the Fugitive Slave Law* (1850). Library of Congress.

children of those who were enslaved. It was by such means that the Northern states, after the American Revolution, had eliminated slavery. Garrison came to understand that slavery and slaveholding were sins, channeling the powerful evangelical impulses of the day, he insisted that a sin such as slavery must be stopped not gradually, but immediately: "I *will be* as harsh as truth, and as uncompromising as justice. On this subject, I do not wish to think, or speak, or write, with moderation. . . . I am in earnest—I will not equivocate—I will not excuse—I will not retreat a single inch—and I will be heard."[14]

For more than twenty years, Garrison had remained true to his word. Not wanting to endanger their economic dealings with the South, conservative Northerners threatened the abolitionist. At one point, some southern-oriented businessmen even dragged Garrison through the streets of New York with a noose around his neck. The American Anti-Slavery Society, which Garrison helped found, continued to grow, and many others devoted themselves to the cause of immediate abolition.

If Garrison mistrusted working through the political system, there were others who disagreed and took a different approach. In 1840, a third political party, the Liberty Party, ran a candidate for president and did so for the next five presidential elections. In 1844, James G. Birney, a renegade former slaveholder, captured 2 percent of the vote. More important was the election of antislavery candidates to Congress, many of them as Conscience Whigs. In the aftermath of the compromise of 1850, and with antislavery politics becoming increasingly sectionalized, the Whig Party began to disintegrate. Some Whigs joined a nativist movement, known as the Know Nothings, and consolidated into the American Party, which was anti-immigrant and anti-Catholic. After the election of 1852, when the Whigs ran Mexican War hero Winfield Scott as president and lost decisively, one Whig congressman declared the party is "dead—dead—dead."[15]

Out of a coalition of different groups and interests (primarily Conscience Whigs and Free-Soil Democrats) the Republican Party emerged in 1854. The party fused various antislavery political factions into a platform for keeping slavery out of the territories, defending wage labor, and opposing slavery. Republicans promoted the free market economy. Its Northern and Midwestern supporters were professionals, skilled laborers, and farmers, whose access to transportation networks had helped them profit from a burgeoning capitalist economy. The Republican Party initially included an anti-immigrant strain. Lincoln, for one, denounced nativism. "I am not a Know-Nothing," he said. "How can any one who abhors the oppression of negroes, be in favor of degrading classes of white people?"[16]

The abolitionist movement not only made slavery into a cultural and political issue, it also inspired women to enter public discourse. The antislavery and women's rights movements developed hand-in-hand. Women filled the ranks of antislavery societies and organized petition campaigns. Congress became so saturated with antislavery petitions that antagonized Southern proslavery representatives (more than 130,000 in 1837–38 alone), the body passed a rule that automatically tabled such petitions. Congressman John Quincy Adams called himself gagged, and the so-called gag rule lasted until 1844.

Lydia Maria Child never felt gagged. Born in Medford, Massachusetts, in 1802, she wrote fiction, poetry, and domestic advice manuals. She advocated for black rights, women's rights, and Native American rights, both in her fiction and through antislavery tracts. Her *Appeal in Favor of that Class of Americans Called Africans* (1833) argued for immediate, uncompensated emancipation. In *The Duty of Disobedience to the Fugitive Slave Act* (1860), she began her appeal to the legislators of Massachusetts by disclaiming any need to apologize because a woman was addressing them. She lambasted the legislators for adhering to the act and, instead of protecting liberty, taking "as your motto, Obedience to tyrants is your highest law."[17]

Many others insisted on a higher duty of obedience than to the law. Charles Beecher told his congregation, "If a fugitive claim your help on his journey, break the law and give it to him." Harriet Beecher Stowe agreed with her brother, and she helped not by aiding an actual runaway slave but by creating a fictional one, Eliza Harris. Rich with sentimentality and emotion, as well as with romantic ideals about racial harmony, *Uncle Tom's Cabin* reached out to Northern, middle-class, evangelical, female readers. It called for the immediate renunciation of sin, made salvation a reality, the Bible a guide, and spoke to mothers by making home and the unbreakable love of child the benchmarks of a Christian life.[18]

In a chapter titled "The Mother's Struggle," Stowe spoke directly to the reader after the slave Eliza, learning that she was to be sold, ran off: "If it were your Harry, mother, or your Willie, that were going to be torn from you by the brutal trader, tomorrow morning,— if you had seen the man, and heard that the papers were signed and delivered, and you had only from twelve o'clock till morning to make good your escape,—how fast could you walk?"

Stowe turned what was an abstraction for most of its readers—slavery—into an assault upon the family and the soul, upon faith and salvation. Still, her portrait was always a mosaic, never a simple story of struggle. Little Eva, the sweet daughter of a slaveholder, would die seeing only goodness in people, white or black; Uncle Tom would be martyred at the hands of Simon Legree, a Northerner who abused alcohol. There was evil in the system of slavery and Stowe argued that it was an evil that beset the entire nation: "But who, sir, makes the trader? Who is most to blame? The enlightened, cultivated, intelligent man who supports the system of which the trader is the inevitable result, or the poor trader himself?"

Stowe's novel fortified antislavery feeling and despair over the national sin of slavery—while compelling proponents to intensify their already robust defense of the institution. A literary countermovement emerged: anti-Tom novels that sought to offset the claims of Stowe's fiction by showing slaves as content, denouncing the treatment of free blacks in the North, and portraying slaveholders as good Christians. They didn't ring as true as Stowe's fiction. The importance of *Uncle Tom's Cabin* may be not as a work of romance buttressed by facts, but as a work of realism encased in romance. Pressed to provide evidence for her depictions, Stowe published *A Key to Uncle Tom's Cabin* in 1853. It focuses on the characters in the novel and provides testimony from newspapers, slave narratives, letters, and other sources to support its portrayal of slavery. Stowe argued that *Uncle Tom's Cabin* was constructed of "a mosaic of facts." On June 16, 1862, as he was moving toward the decision to issue an Emancipation Proclamation, Lincoln borrowed *The Key to Uncle Tom's Cabin* from the Library of Congress.[19]

Bleeding Kansas

Daniel Webster's apostasy was nothing compared to Stephen Douglas's. After passage of the Kansas-Nebraska Act that he shepherded through Congress on May 30, 1854, hostile crowds greeted him wherever he traveled. He would recall that he was so hated "I could travel from Boston to Chicago by the light of my own [burning] effigy."[20]

The Kansas-Nebraska Act organized the unorganized portion of the Louisiana Purchase, up to the Canadian border. Nebraska Territory encompassed much more than the current state of Nebraska. And the entire area was above the Missouri Compromise line, which demarcated free from slave territory. Southerners would not endorse any bill that excluded slavery. With the support of President Franklin Pierce, the bill repudiated the Missouri Compromise in favor of the doctrine of "popular sovereignty," under which a territory's residents would decide whether slavery was permitted. The phrase sounded democratic, yet it would prove to be the undoing of any equilibrium that had been established by the Compromise of 1850. Joshua Giddings, Salmon P. Chase, Charles Sumner, and several others minced no words in condemning the act as "a gross violation of a sacred pledge; as a criminal betrayal of precious rights" in that it would turn it into "a dreary region of despotism, inhabited by masters and slaves."[21]

Douglas was vilified. Southerners felt invigorated. Northerners viewed the act as continued evidence of a slave power conspiracy to spread bondage across the nation. At Peoria on October 16, 1854, Lincoln responded directly to Douglas, who had spoken for three hours, and denounced the repeal of the Missouri Compromise. Letting slavery into Kansas and Nebraska was "wrong for it would allow it to spread everywhere . . . where men can be found inclined to take it." He also denounced "the monstrous injustice of slavery." He confessed not to know what to do about the institution except to end it through some form of gradual emancipation. Nonetheless, he declared, "If the negro is a man, why then my ancient faith teaches me that 'all men are created equal'; and that there can be no moral right in connection with one man's making a slave of another."[22]

The speeches of 1854 did nothing to slow the rush of settlers into Nebraska Territory. Even before the act was passed, Eli Thayer of Massachusetts formed the Massachusetts Emigrant Aid Company to promote the settlement of the West. The company helped some 650 emigrants in 1854 and more than a thousand the following year. Fearing an influx of Northern antislavery settlers, Missourians on the Kansas border formed regulator groups to challenge the emigrants. Proslavery and Free-Soil settlers raced to Kansas. Free Soilers settled in Topeka and Lawrence (named after Amos Lawrence) whereas proslavery forces were concentrated in Leavenworth and Atchison (named after proslavery Missouri Senator David Rice Atchison). It looked as if Kansas would serve as surrogate for a war between antislavery and proslavery forces. William Seward, for one, welcomed it: "We will engage in competition for the virgin soil of Kansas, and God give the victory to the side which is stronger in numbers as it is in right."[23]

A proslavery territorial legislature was elected in March 1855. Missourians outnumbered New Englanders in racing to become "residents" in time to vote. Many of the proslavery voters who streamed across the border were not residents at all and crossed only to swing the election. Afterward, the territorial governor invalidated some of the results as fraudulent. Still, proslavery forces held a majority. The legislature took draconian actions to protect slavery, passing laws that made it a capital crime to aid a fugitive slave and excluding persons opposed to holding slaves from juries. They also expelled several antislavery legislators.

To counter the power of the proslavery legislature, Free State delegates met in Topeka and drafted a state constitution that banned slavery. The document also forbade the entry of free blacks into the state. They passed the constitution, but Congress did not accept it and President Pierce denounced it. The proslavery legislature gathered at Lecompton in September 1857 and framed a competing constitution that would make Kansas a slave state. Voters were asked to choose in a referendum. Many legitimate voters refused to participate, and thousands of fraudulent votes were cast. Although Pierce supported the Lecompton constitution, the House of Representatives eventually rejected it, as did Kansas voters in 1858 when they were again given chance to vote, this time in an honest election.

The constitutional battle was not the only one being fought. Democratic Senator David Atchison of Missouri spoke of his desire

Figure 4.2 *Forcing Slavery Down the Throat of a Free Soiler* (1856). Library of Congress.

"to kill every God-damned abolitionist in the Territory." In contrast, Jim Lane, a congressman from Indiana and future senator from Kansas, earned the nickname "the Grim Chieftain" for his relentless warfare against proslavery forces.[24]

In 1855 and 1856, Lane helped lead the defense of Lawrence, which came under assault from proslavery activists. His efforts could not prevent the sacking of the city on May 21, 1856, when a posse of almost a thousand Southerners destroyed antislavery presses, burned the Free State Hotel, and looted the town. Kansas had become "Bleeding Kansas," a phrase popularized by Horace Greeley in the *New York Tribune*. The Emigrant Aid Society made a plea for rifles and Massachusetts responded. Henry Ward Beecher, a leading Congregationalist minister and a brother of Harriet Beecher Stowe, supported sending Sharps rifles to Kansas. One crate, marked "books," contained weapons; the rifles came to be known as "Beecher's bibles."

The violence in Kansas found its way to Washington. On May 19, Senator Charles Sumner spoke on "The Crime Against Kansas." A graduate of Harvard College and Harvard Law School, Sumner became known as a remarkable orator. Tall and broad, with brown hair streaked with gray and deep-set blue eyes, he attracted attention. One English visitor called him "a man whom you would notice amongst other men." In response to the Mexican War, he became a Free-Soil advocate and was elected senator in 1851. In 1852 he spoke passionately on a motion to repeal the Fugitive Slave Act and declared "Freedom National, Slavery Sectional." Now he prepared to lecture the Senate and the nation on what was taking place in Kansas, and he minced no words as he spoke for five hours over two days.[25]

The battle over Kansas, he warned, "threatens to scatter from its folds civil war." The crime of proslavery forces was nothing less than the "rape of a virgin Territory, compelling it to the hateful embrace of Slavery." Sumner denounced the crime and also identified the criminals. He singled out Senator Douglas and Senator Andrew Butler of South Carolina. Calling Douglas "the squire of Slavery," he saw him as Sancho Panza to Butler's Don Quixote. He asserted that Butler had chosen as mistress "the harlot Slavery." He predicted that if Kansas was not admitted as a free state, and the sanctity of free soil preserved, the conflict would become a national one.[26]

Several days later, while Sumner was working at his desk in the Senate chamber, Preston Brooks, a South Carolina representative, and Andrew Butler's cousin, approached him. He denounced Sumner's speech as a libel on South Carolina and, without warning, lifted his hard rubber cane and began beating Sumner with it. He believed he was vindicating the honor of his cousin whom Sumner had derided in his speech. Sumner struggled to rise from his desk but his legs were trapped under it. The blows kept coming until Brooks's cane broke. Sumner was left bloodied and only partly conscious. He would not be able to return to the Senate for three years. The Massachusetts Legislature reelected him in 1857 and kept his seat empty as a symbol of Southern barbarism. Brooks was censured (an attempt to expel him failed). He resigned his seat and then was reelected in a special election.

In the South, Brooks became a hero for defending Southern honor against Northern abolitionists. "Every Southern man is delighted," Brooks wrote. "The fragments of the stick are begged for as *sacred* relics." In tribute, Brooks received dozens of canes, one of them inscribed "hit him again." The *Charleston Mercury* applauded the action: "Sumner was well and elegantly whipped, and he richly deserved it." Brooks would not get to enjoy his celebrity for long—he died suddenly in January 1857.[27]

If many Southerners applauded the action, most Northerners condemned it in the harshest terms. Violence on the frontier in Kansas was one thing. Bloodshed in the Senate was quite another. Denouncing the assault on Sumner as a "national outrage," Republicans rallied to condemn the act as emblematic of the evils of slavery and the intentions of the Southerners to use violence to curtail debate. "The mouths of the representatives of the North are to be closed by the use of bowie-knives, bludgeons, and revolvers," wrote the *Boston Atlas*. Here, mocked Northern papers, was "Southern Chivalry." Under that title, an influential print circulated showing Sumner with pen in hand being brutally assaulted. Northern editorials viewed the attack as evidence of the continuing degradation of the North at the hands of the slave South, which would continue to use violence to get its way because "the youth trained to knock down his human chattels for 'insolence'—that is, for any sort of resistance to his good pleasure—will thereafter knock down and beat other human beings who thwart his wishes."[28]

With the sacking of Lawrence and the beating of Sumner, proslavery forces had so far instigated the violence. On the night of May 24, in response to the proslavery assault on Lawrence, a group of abolitionists sought revenge. John Brown, a businessman turned radical abolitionist, led them. Raised in Ohio, Brown moved to Springfield, Massachusetts, in 1846. He believed in the use of violent means to oppose the evils of slavery and in response to the Fugitive

Slave Act formed the League of Gileadites, a militant group named for the biblical Gilead who led an assault that kept the Israelites free. The League consisted of forty-four black men and women and its purpose was to forcibly resist anyone seeking to recover a fugitive slave. Brown immersed himself in the black community, even choosing to worship at the black church. Upon meeting him, one former slave said Brown acted as if "his own soul had been pierced with the iron of slavery."[29]

In 1855, Brown moved to Kansas, where several of his sons had settled. He was ready to engage in the battle to make Kansas a free state and to avenge the violence the border ruffians from Missouri perpetrated against antislavery settlers. In response to the sacking of Lawrence, Brown and a band of men that included his sons murdered five men with broadswords in what would come to be known at the Pottawatomie Massacre. In the aftermath, Kansas continued to bleed. The actual number of killings (probably fewer than 200) was less significant than the publicity they attracted and the recognition that Kansas had become proxy for a war between proslavery and antislavery forces that could turn national. The state entered the Union as a free state on January 29, 1861. In August 1863, Lawrence would again be the scene of violence as guerrillas led by W. C. Quantrill murdered more than 150 people and burned the city.

Dred Scott

Chief Justice Roger B. Taney seemed to believe that the Supreme Court could resolve the enmity and violence that threatened to tear apart the nation. Taney had succeeded John Marshall as chief justice in 1836. Many Whigs opposed him. Daniel Webster denounced him as a "political hack" who would sully the Supreme Court. Taney, a Maryland lawyer and attorney general, was a devout Jacksonian Democrat, a Catholic, and a supporter of gradual emancipation who had freed the slaves he inherited from his family. Tall and slightly stoop-shouldered, "a gaunt, ungainly man," one visitor observed, Taney had an effective courtroom style of speaking clearly and simply. "That infernal apostolic manner of his," complained one rival, "there is no replying to."[30]

The Taney Court had dodged political questions previously (in *Luther v. Borden* the Court ruled it was up to the president and Congress to enforce the constitutional clause that guaranteed a republican form of government to every state). Now, however, with a new Fugitive Slave Act in force, and the issue dividing the nation, it seemed like an apt time to rule on the status of slaves who accompanied their owners into free territories. Besides, Democratic presidents had appointed eight of the nine justices, and five of the nine came from slave states. Justice John McLean, nominated by Andrew Jackson in 1829, and by this point a Whig and Free Soiler in sympathies, wrote to a friend in November 1855, "Next winter, a case will be before the Court, which involves the right of a slaveholder to bring his slaves into a free State for any purpose whatever."[31]

The trail that brought Dred Scott's case before the Supreme Court was long and serpentine. It began in 1834 when Dr. John Emerson, an Army surgeon, brought Scott from Missouri to Illinois and then, two years later, to Wisconsin Territory. Scott married another slave Emerson had purchased and had a daughter who was born on a steamboat north of the Missouri state line. Emerson returned to Missouri. On his death in 1843, he left his property in trust to his wife, who soon departed for Massachusetts and left Scott with Taylor Blow, the son of the master who had sold Scott to Emerson. While Blow's motives are unclear, he brought Scott to a law firm to bring suit for his freedom, claiming that Scott's residence in free territory under the terms of the Missouri Compromise had made him free. Mrs. Emerson defended the suit, in all likelihood because if the court found that Scott was held illegally, she would be responsible for twelve years of wages.[32]

Scott initially lost the case, then won on retrial in circuit court. On appeal, the Missouri Supreme Court ruled against him. Mrs. Emerson, who had remarried, transferred ownership of Scott to her brother John F. Sanford (forever misspelled as Sandford in the case, *Dred Scott v. Sandford*), who was a citizen of New York. Federal courts had jurisdiction over cases between residents of different states and a new suit was brought. The federal circuit court ruled against Scott, a decision that was appealed to the Supreme Court. The case was first argued in February 1856 and held over for re-argument, which took place in May.

The Court issued its decision on March 6, 1857, two days after the inauguration of President James Buchanan, who had been secretly lobbying the justices to make a sweeping ruling that resolved the question of slavery in the territories. Buchanan had owed his election to the South (he carried fourteen of fifteen slave states and only five free states) and put pressure on Justice Robert Grier, a Democrat and fellow Pennsylvanian, to join the five Southern justices so that the decision would not appear sectional. The final ruling had the six justices agreeing with Taney's decision, one (Samuel Nelson of New York) agreeing with the ruling, but not with the chief justice's precise reasoning, and two, John McLean of Ohio and Benjamin Curtis of Massachusetts, dissenting.

The Court could have avoided the larger political questions of the constitutionality of the Missouri Compromise and black citizenship by refusing jurisdiction or upholding the circuit court ruling that Scott had been a sojourner in Illinois and Wisconsin Territory, not a resident, and therefore remained a slave. Instead, Taney saw this as an opportunity to offer a definitive opinion on the constitutionality of the Missouri Compromise and the citizenship of blacks.

The Court offered a sweeping ruling that left Dred Scott a slave and went a step further. Taney wrote that blacks "had for more than a century before been regarded as beings of an inferior order, and altogether unfit to associate with the white race, either in social or political relations; and so far inferior, that they had no rights which the white man was bound to respect; and that the negro might justly and lawfully be reduced to slavery for his benefit." Blacks were not citizens and therefore did not have the right to sue. As for residence in a free state making him free, Missouri state law continued to apply. Furthermore, Congress had no power to deprive citizens of their right to take their property wherever they desired. Therefore, the Missouri Compromise was unconstitutional.

In his dissent, Curtis spoke of birthright citizenship ("a natural born citizen"), a principle that would be enshrined in the Fourteenth Amendment to the Constitution. He argued that the laws enacted by Congress with respect to the territories were constitutionally binding. Where slavery existed, municipal law created it and the laws of Illinois and Wisconsin Territory forbade slavery. He believed the circuit court decision should be overturned. McLean, too, dissented from Taney's ruling about the status of blacks in society, arguing that treating them outside the polity was not a matter of law, but one of taste.

Responses to the decision fractured along party lines. Democrats rejoiced and viewed the decision as putting an end to the sectionalism being caused by antislavery sentiment. "This decision in the Dred Scott case must be a finality, so far as the federal legislation on the institution of slavery is concerned," declared the *Richmond Enquirer*. Anticipating Republican reaction to the decision, the *Cleveland Plain Dealer* concluded, "No man is justifiable in advocating a 'higher law'—it is treason against the cornerstone of republican institutions." The decision, predicted the editor, "will give the country rest on this vexed and unprofitable question of slavery extension." He was mistaken.[33]

The case put the fledgling Republican Party in a difficult spot. It not only undercut the fundamental principles of Free Soil and free men upon which the party was formed, it placed Republicans in the position of having to oppose a Supreme Court decision, just as some of them had been resisting the Fugitive Slave Act. According to Southerners and northern Democrats, this made them into the firebrands and disunionists. One Democrat crowed that the decision "utterly demolishes the whole black republican platform and stamps it as directly antagonistical to the constitution."[34]

Oppose it Republicans did. The key to doing so stemmed from the belief that the court had ruled on issues that were not before it. Since the circuit court was found to lack jurisdiction because Scott was not a citizen, any further decision was extrajudicial, or obiter dictum. The *New York Tribune* insisted, "The decision, we need hardly say, is entitled to just as much moral weight as would be the judgment of a majority of those congregated in any Washington bar-room."[35]

In a speech in Springfield, Illinois, in June 1857, Lincoln expressed surprise that Senator Douglas attacked the Republicans for resisting the decision. No one had tried to rescue Dred Scott, he stressed. Indeed, the Blow family had freed Scott two months after the decision. He worked in St. Louis as a porter and died a free man only a year later. Republicans would work to overrule the decision, but "we offer no resistance to it."[36]

The case was a recurrent theme in the two men's series of debates across Illinois in 1858. Lincoln pointed out that Douglas had once praised Andrew Jackson for ignoring the Supreme Court decision that the Bank of the United States was constitutional when he vetoed its recharter. He warned voters that the *Dred Scott* decision threatened to make slavery a national institution. Douglas was more interested in votes than doctrines and he played to the crowd's basest instinct. Lincoln, he said, wants blacks to be citizens. "Do you," he asked the people in the first debate at Ottawa, "desire to turn this beautiful state into a free negro colony?" Douglas reminded his audience that Lincoln opposed a decision of the Supreme Court. Lincoln responded that he could not understand why, despite Douglas's own contradictions with respect to judicial decisions, the senator continued to support the decision: "But I cannot shake Judge Douglas's teeth loose from the Dred Scott decision. Like some obstinate animal (I mean no disrespect), that will hang on when he has once got his teeth fixed, you may cut off a leg, or you may tear away an arm, still he will not relax his hold."[37]

Douglas continued to defend the decision, and Republicans and abolitionists continued to denounce it, perhaps none more powerfully than Frederick Douglass. Enslaved in Maryland, Douglass escaped to New York in 1838 and then settled in New Bedford, Massachusetts. He became active as an abolitionist speaker and writer. In 1845 he published *Narrative of the Life of Frederick Douglass: An American Slave*. The slave narrative was already a well-established literary genre, so much so that white authors would take advantage of the public's interest and produce bogus narratives. There was nothing bogus about Douglass's account, which sold thousands of copies. Douglass exposed Northern readers to the harsh truth of slavery: how slaveholders broke up families and beat slaves mercilessly; how slaves sang out of misery, not happiness as proslavery ideologues insisted; how the enslaved were kept from practicing their own religion; and, most important, how slaveholders denied the enslaved education because literacy, Douglass came to learn, was the key to freedom. Douglass overheard his master tell his mistress that teaching a slave to read "would forever unfit him to be a slave." Those words; he recalled, "sank deep into my heart, stirred up sentiments within that lay slumbering, and called into existence an entirely new train of thought. . . . I now understood what had been to me a most perplexing difficulty—to wit, the white man's power to enslave the black man. It was a grand achievement, and I prized it highly. From that moment, I understood the pathway from slavery to freedom."[38]

After two years in Ireland and Britain, where he gave numerous lectures before large, enthusiastic antislavery audiences, Douglass was freed when two English female abolitionists purchased him from his owner, Hugh Auld, for $711.66. On his return to America, he moved to Rochester, New York, and started the *North Star*, an abolitionist paper, embraced other causes, including women's rights, and devoted his life to abolition and social reform. He lived until 1895 and was the most photographed American figure of the nineteenth century.

In 1857, Douglass spoke against the *Dred Scott* decision. The Supreme Court decision notwithstanding, he held high hopes for the future. He predicted, "This very attempt to blot out forever the hopes of an enslaved people may be one necessary link in the chain of events preparatory to the downfall and complete overthrow of the whole slave system."[39]

Figure 4.3 *Reynolds Political Map* (1856). Library of Congress.

The event they looked toward was shifting political fortunes. "The remedy is . . . the ballot box," argued the *Chicago Tribune*. "Let the next president be Republican, and 1860 will mark an era kindred with that of 1776." At least one abolitionist had a very different idea of the meaning of 1776. Rather than a political upheaval, he sought a violent revolution.[40]

John Brown's Raid

Frederick Douglass first met John Brown in 1847. Decades later he recalled a person "who was lean, strong, and sinewy." "His eyes were bluish-gray," remembered Douglass, "and in conversation they were full of light and fire."[41]

That meeting occurred before the Compromise of 1850, the Fugitive Slave Act, the violence on the Kansas frontier and in the US Senate, and the *Dred Scott* decision. That was before Brown grew an

Old Testament beard and conceived a plan of leading an insurrection among the slaves of Virginia and establishing an independent republic. Brown's hatred of slavery was fueled by a religious fanaticism that led him to believe that only bloodshed could expiate the sin of slavery and provide redemption. "Without shedding of blood, there can be no remission of such a sin," said the Bible and to that Brown added, in what would turn out to be his final letter, "the crimes of this *guilty land; will* never be purged *away;* but with Blood."[42]

Between 1856 and 1859, Brown traveled between Kansas and the Northeast, where he sought to raise money and recruit volunteers for his scheme to invade the South and lead a slave insurrection. One night in May 1858, he met with Franklin Sanborn, a twenty-six-year-old Harvard graduate and the secretary for the Massachusetts State Kansas Committee. Like so many educated young New England men, he was smitten with transcendentalist idealism and Free-Soil politics, both of which made him susceptible to Brown's entreaties. Others also provided help, including ministers Theodore Parker and Thomas Wentworth Higginson, the physician Samuel Gridley Howe, and the wealthy abolitionists Gerrit Smith and George Luther Stearns. Together they would be known as the "Secret Six," who financed Brown's plan to raid the armory at Harpers Ferry and use the confiscated weapons to launch a marauding slave insurrection. Others also greeted Brown: Amos Lawrence, William Lloyd Garrison, Ralph Waldo Emerson, and Henry David Thoreau. At a meeting with Charles Sumner, the senator showed Brown the bloodstained coat from Brooks's attack. The agitator gazed upon it as he would a martyr's Christian relic.

In January 1858, Brown lived for a month in Rochester at Frederick Douglass's home and drafted a provisional constitution for the State of Virginia, one that would respect the rights of black men despite what the Supreme Court had declared. By the fall, Brown was preparing to strike, and Douglass visited him in Chambersburg, Pennsylvania. Implored to join in the attack, Douglass demurred and returned home. Afterward, he would flee to Canada. Many other black activists also supported Brown, including Harriet Tubman, Martin Delaney, and Lewis Hayden.[43]

Brown launched his raid on the evening of October 16, 1859. His band consisted of twenty-one men. Five were black, including Shields Green, an escaped slave from South Carolina, whom Douglass had brought with him to Chambersburg. Three of Brown's sons also joined the raiding party. They began by taking hostages, including Lewis Washington, great-grandnephew of George Washington. In the evening, Brown occupied the federal armory at Harpers Ferry. Militia rushed to the scene and a sporadic battle was fought. Late in the day, US Marines under the command of Robert E. Lee arrived. Brown refused to surrender and the marines stormed the engine house where the raiders were gathered. Lieutenant Israel Greene used his ceremonial dress sword to strike Brown over the head and stab at his breast. The blunt weapon did not penetrate, and Brown survived. Troops killed ten members of his party. Those captured would be tried for treason.

Brown's trial began on October 25. Because of his wounds, he laid on a cot in the courtroom, often with his eyes closed. He was found guilty of treason, for conspiring to foment an insurrection, and murder in the first degree. On November 2, the trial's sixth day, Brown spoke: "Now, if it is deemed necessary that I should forfeit my life for the furtherance of the ends of justice, and mingle my blood further with the blood of my children and with the blood of millions in this slave country whose rights are disregarded by wicked, cruel, and unjust enactments, I say let it be done."[44]

On December 2, the State of Virginia executed Brown. He had no minister present and he said nothing. According to one witness, Major Thomas Jackson of the Virginia Military Institute, soon to be known to history as "Stonewall" Jackson, Brown wore carpet slippers, white socks, black pants, coat, and hat. He met his end "with un-flinching firmness." His body was allowed to dangle for forty-five minutes. On December 16, four more men were hanged in Charles Town; finally, on March 16, two who had escaped and were later captured followed their compatriots to the gallows.[45]

Northern reaction to Brown's execution appalled some Americans nearly as much as the raid itself. Throughout New England, abolitionists transformed the zealot from a murderous madman into a martyr. Many denounced Brown's scheme as fa-natical, deluded, and misguided. At the same time, however, they praised his convictions and conscientiousness. Many pleaded that Brown's life should be spared. Thoreau argued that Brown must be seen as a man of faith, not an ideologue; a Puritan not a politi-cian. Lydia Maria Child's correspondence with John Brown became public. She told Brown that although she was a pacifist, "I admire your courage, moral and physical. I reverence you for the humanity which tempered your zeal. I sympathize with you in your cruel be-reavement, your sufferings, and your wrongs. In brief, I love you and bless you." In a lecture on "Courage," Emerson proclaimed that Brown was as a "new saint awaiting his martyrdom, and who, if he shall suffer, will make the gallows glorious like the cross." The conservative lawyer George Templeton Strong saw this coming. "I'm not sure the South can afford to hang him," to give fanaticism a martyr, he wrote in his diary, "though he plainly deserves it. . . . His name may be a word of power for the next half century"[46]

Abolitionist hosannas for Brown enraged Southerners. Northerners had resisted the Fugitive Slave Act. They had denied slaveholders their rights in the territories. They had condemned the Dred Scott decision. Now they endorsed armed invasion. "It is useless to disguise the fact, that the entire North and Northwest are hopelessly abolitionized," wrote the Wilmington, North Carolina, *Daily Herald*. In response to Brown, the South unified and prepared for disunion. If the Anthony Burns case transformed Northern opinion, John Brown's raid radicalized Southern sentiment.[47]

Democrats tied Brown's actions to Republican Party principles, to Seward's "higher law." "Such is the ripening of the black republican harvest," warned the *Illinois State Register*. Stephen Douglas declared that Harpers Ferry was "the natural, logical, inevitable result of the doctrines and teachings of the Republican Party." Lincoln proclaimed at an address he gave at Cooper Union in New York in February 1860, "John Brown was no Republican," and many other Republicans echoed the sentiment. Southerners, however, did not see it that way and, as a result, the election of a Republican the following year would prove cataclysmic. "To elect Lincoln is to vote old John Brown a saint," warned the Democratic *Pennsylvania Statesman*. Ironically, Brown detested the Republican Party because of its refusal to oppose slavery where it existed. Upon his election, Lincoln would reassure the slave states precisely of this, but it was too late.[48]

In the raid's aftermath, the Secret Six feared for their lives. Gerrit Smith was so distraught he confined himself to the New York State Lunatic Asylum for two months; Howe and Stearns fled to Canada; Parker was in Florence where, in May 1860, he died of tuberculosis; Sanborn also headed to Canada and, on one occasion, federal marshals tried to arrest him and a Concord crowd saved him. Only Higginson remained in plain sight and continued to defend Brown. During the war he would serve as a colonel of a black regiment.

The Raleigh, North Carolina, *Register* concluded, the affair at Harpers Ferry "marks a new and most important era in our country's history. It will bring to an immediate solution the question as to whether the Union can be preserved, and the right of the South to hold property in slaves be maintained. This is the issue to be tried now. The trial can no longer be deferred."[49]

Osborne P. Anderson, a black abolitionist who participated in the raid and escaped, agreed, but saw it from an opposing view. In 1861, he published *A Voice from Harper's Ferry*, in which he defended Brown ("A Puritan of the most exalted type") and the actions he had taken. Anderson concluded, "John Brown did not only capture and hold Harper's Ferry for twenty hours, but he held the whole South. He . . . dug the mine and laid the train which will eventually dissolve the union between Freedom and Slavery."[50]

Going into battle later that year, thousands of Union soldiers would sing "John's Brown Body lies a-moldering in the grave / his soul is marching on."

CHAPTER 5

Government of the People

T HROUGH ALL THE DEATH AND suffering, Abraham Lincoln maintained a sense of humor that helped leaven his melancholic tendencies. On his return from Gettysburg, after delivering an address that received mixed reviews, he contracted varioloid, a form of smallpox, and was confined to bed. Having put up with endless entreaties and requests, he said, "I've got something now that I can give to everybody"

Lincoln understood that the Civil War required a new way of thinking. "The dogmas of the quiet past, are inadequate to the stormy present," he declared on December 1, 1862, in an address to Congress. After eighteen months, the war showed no sign of relenting. Different approaches were needed to win what he had called a "People's contest" and preserve the nation. Thinking of future judgments, he believed that "*We* cannot escape history . . . we will be remembered in spite of ourselves." He therefore began considering measures that once were unthinkable: freeing the slaves, enlisting them in the army, and recommending that some black men be given the right to vote. Lincoln would not be afraid to take dramatic action. Neither would he compromise his vision of a nation whose purpose, he believed, was "to afford all, an unfettered start, and a fair chance, in the race of life."[1]

Secession

Secession, thought Lincoln, was absurd, "an ingenious sophism" and "the essence of anarchy." There could be no constitutional doctrine of secession. The union was perpetual and it preceded the states. Even if the nation resembled only a contract, all parties had to agree to break it. Constitutional means existed to address grievances, Secession was not one of them. Democracy itself was at stake as the states that seceded sought by their actions to overturn the democratic election that had made Lincoln president. "There can be no successful appeal from the ballot to the bullet," he pronounced. Secession was rebellion and rebellion was treason. Lincoln would never relent on this point, referring time and again to the "so-called seceded states." On March 4, 1861, in his inaugural address, he told the seven states that had seceded to that point, "you have no oath registered in Heaven to destroy the government, while I shall have the most solemn one to 'preserve, protect and defend it.' "[2]

Secessionists disagreed. The South Carolina Declaration of Secession adopted on December 24, 1860, argued for state sovereignty and posited that the government was a compact of the states in which the failure of one party to uphold its obligations released the other from the contract. What material part of the agreement had the federal government failed to perform? Specifically, Northern states had refused to enforce the Fugitive Slave Act, which made the federal government responsible for returning runaways, and, generally, the rising opposition to slavery threatened the Southern way of life. At the Virginia secession convention, one representative declared, "The great question which is now uprooting this Government to its foundation—the great question which underlies all our deliberations here, is the question of African slavery."[3]

Lincoln did his best to reassure Southern disunionists. "I have no purpose, directly or indirectly, to interfere with slavery where it exists," he announced. Of course he knew he had no power to do so. Slavery was a state institution governed by state laws, and the federal government could not interfere. His comment did little to soothe Southerners, who wanted not only to protect slavery where it existed but also to retain the opportunity for it to spread to areas where it did not exist, such as to the new territories or via annexation of areas in the Caribbean and Central America. The Mississippi secession declaration denounced the federal government because it denied slavery the "power of extension."[4]

With the results of the election of 1860, the government fell into the hands of the Republican Party. Founded only a few years earlier as an antislavery-extension party, Republicans were committed to Free Soil and Free Labor. They declared the natural condition of the territories to be free. They condemned slave labor and celebrated wage labor. They also revealed a nativist strain fearful of immigrants and outsiders. Lincoln best expressed the highest ideals of the Republican Party and, in so doing, articulated a fundamental principle of the American dream: "the prudent, penniless beginner in the world, labors for wages awhile, saves a surplus with which to buy tools or land, for himself; then labors on his own account another while, and at length hires another new beginner to help him. This, say its advocates, is free labor—the just and generous, and prosperous system, which opens the way for all."[5]

It seemed unlikely in 1859, when Lincoln delivered those remarks, that he stood a chance of being elected president. Gangly and awkward, the Westerner, thought the poet Walt Whitman, "has a face like a hoosier Michael Angelo, so awful ugly it becomes beautiful, with its strange mouth, its deep cut, criss-cross lines, and its doughnut complexion." Born in Kentucky in 1809, Lincoln moved with his family to Indiana in 1816 and then Illinois in 1830. His mother died in 1818 and his father, Thomas, married Sarah Bush Johnston the following year. One of her great gifts was to arrive with a collection of books that allowed Lincoln to use education to make himself. In his first political speech, delivered in 1832, he announced that education was "the most important subject which we as a people can be engaged in."[6]

Lincoln moved to New Salem, Illinois, in 1831 and in 1834 was elected to the General Assembly. He relocated to the new capital of Springfield in 1837 and his law career started to take off. Married in 1842, Lincoln was elected to the US House of Representatives in 1846. Following his one term as a congressman, he withdrew from politics until 1854 when the Kansas-Nebraska Act, which opened the unorganized portion of the Louisiana Purchase to slavery, was passed. The measure reawakened his passion for politics. He recollected in 1859, "I was losing interest in politics, when the repeal of the Missouri Compromise aroused me again."[7]

In the 1858 contest with Stephen Douglas for a seat in the Senate, Lincoln began to gather national attention. He warned, "A house divided against itself cannot stand. I believe this government cannot endure, permanently half *slave* and half *free*." Lincoln and Douglas held seven debates. They made for quite a contrast: Lincoln was 6 foot 4 and lean, whereas Douglas was 5 foot 4 and squat. Lincoln put his self-deprecating humor to good effect. When Douglas accused his opponent of being two-faced, Lincoln responded, "If I had another face do you think I'd wear this one." The legislature chose Douglas, the Little Giant, over Lincoln, Honest Abe.

Ambitious for political success, Lincoln devoted himself to a speech scheduled for New York in February 1860. At Cooper Union, he stunned the New York political elite with a lengthy address that showed that the founding fathers had favored limiting the expansion of slavery, accused the Southerners of abandoning the doctrines of the founders, and inspired fellow Republicans with the conclusion that "right makes might, and in that faith, let us, to the end, dare to do our duty as we understand it."[8]

Talk of Lincoln as the Republican nominee began to circulate, and he privately confessed, "The taste is in my mouth a little." The Republican nominating convention was held in Chicago, which turned out to be an advantage, as did the Democrats' state of disarray. The party would eventually split, with the Northern wing nominating Stephen Douglas and the Southern secessionist wing nominating thirty-nine-year-old John C. Breckinridge of Kentucky, the vice president under James Buchanan. Before the Republicans gathered, a Constitutional Union Party, seeking compromise with the South to save the union, nominated John Bell of Tennessee.[9]

When the Republicans met in Chicago, most observers thought New York senator William Seward would be nominated. Seward had a national reputation and was the candidate of most antislavery activists because of his "Higher Law" speech. The problem with Seward was that he would have trouble winning Pennsylvania (which had its own candidate in Simon Cameron), Indiana, and Illinois, which were crucial to Republican hopes of a victory. Another candidate, Salmon P. Chase of Ohio, did not even have the full support of his state. Lawyer and statesman Edward Bates of Missouri, more conservative than the other candidates, had the backing of the powerful newspaper editor Horace Greeley. He stood little chance, however, of winning the nomination.

Lincoln had an effective team of floor managers at the convention. Fanning out among various state delegations, Lincoln's supporters tried to secure votes for their candidate, but had to operate without offering any promises. "Make no contracts that will bind me," Lincoln directed. He added that he did not endorse Seward's "Higher Law" doctrine. On the first ballot Seward received 173½ votes, Lincoln 102, Bates 48, Chase 49, and Cameron 50½. The nomination required 233 votes. On the third ballot, Ohio switched four votes from Chase to the Illinoisan and Lincoln was nominated.[10]

It was to Lincoln's advantage that he was relatively unknown. It was to the Republicans advantage that the Democrats had split. In the election of 1860, Lincoln carried all of the free states except New Jersey, which divided its electoral vote with Douglas. The only slave states that even offered a Republican ticket were Delaware, Maryland, Kentucky, Missouri, and Virginia, where Lincoln took 1 percent of the vote. With 180 votes in the Electoral College (nearly 60 percent), Lincoln had been elected. In ten of the eleven states that would become the Confederacy, he did not receive a single vote.

Between Lincoln's election and inauguration on March 4, 1861, seven states seceded: South Carolina, Mississippi, Florida, Alabama, Georgia, Louisiana, and Texas. Lincoln reiterated that he had no intention of interfering with slavery where it existed, yet made it clear he would not compromise on the issue of extending slavery. "Stand firm," he privately advised Republicans in Congress. "The tug has to come, & better now, than any time hereafter."[11]

On February 11, 1861, he departed from Springfield and told his neighbors who gathered to wish him farewell, "let us confidently hope that all will yet be well." On the journey to Washington, he spoke of maintaining composure, keeping calm, and taking time. He called himself "an accidental instrument," and suggested in four years, if "you find you have made a mistake, elect a better man next time." He also grew a beard in response to an October letter from an eleven-year-old girl who had told him he would look "a good deal better" with facial hair.[12]

As Lincoln instructed, Republicans united to defeat any compromise measures, most notably a series of constitutional amendments proposed by Kentucky Senator John J. Crittenden that would have recognized and protected slavery where it existed, revived and extended the Missouri Compromise line to the Pacific, forbade Congress to interfere with the interstate slave trade, and abolish slavery in Washington, DC. A final amendment prohibited any future amendments authorizing Congress to interfere with slavery. The vote was 25–23, far short of the required two-thirds majority. At long last, after almost seventy-five years of struggle, the time for compromise had passed.

On March 4, a day that broke blustery but cleared toward afternoon, Lincoln delivered his inaugural address. He tried to convince Southerners that his election posed no threat to slavery. He insisted that secession was unconstitutional and the union perpetual. He also made it clear that he would protect and defend federal property and that should a war begin it would be "in *your* hands, my dissatisfied countrymen, and not in *mine*." He ended on a conciliatory note: "We are not enemies, but friends. We must not be enemies." With the firing on Fort Sumter on April 12, "the momentous issue of civil war" was decided.[13]

Not everyone in the newly formed Confederacy agreed with the action. Secretary of State Robert Tombs warned that it would "strike a hornet's nest. . . . It is unnecessary; it puts us in the wrong; it is fatal." Jefferson Davis, the provisional president who would be elected to a six-year term in early 1862, pursued the evacuation of Fort Sumter by federal forces. Perhaps he thought firing on the fort did not mean war. Senator James Chesnut, of South Carolina, said he would drink all the blood shed as a result of secession. His wife, Mary, heard the boom of cannon on April 12. "I sprang out of bed," she wrote, "And on my knees—prostrate—I prayed as I have never prayed before."[14]

In response to the attack, Lincoln requested 75,000 militia to serve for ninety days. He also called for 42,000 three-year volunteers, enlarged the Army and Navy, and declared a blockade of southern ports. When Congress assembled on July 4, Lincoln requested 400,000 men and $400 million. By December, he expressed his hope that the conflict would not "degenerate into a violent and remorseless revolutionary struggle."[15]

With the attack on Fort Sumter, four additional southern states seceded: Virginia, Arkansas, North Carolina, and Tennessee. The Confederacy would consist of eleven states with a total population of nine million, of which 3.5 million were enslaved persons. By war's end, more than a million white men had fought for the Confederacy. Although outnumbered, outfinanced, and outmobilized by the Union, the Confederacy had the advantage of covering a huge territory (750,000 square miles) with natural obstacles such as mountains and rivers, a territory that would be defended against an invading army by soldiers protecting their homes.

With a population of 22 million, of which 500,000 were enslaved, and an industrial capacity that dwarfed the Confederacy, Unionists felt reasonably certain that the war would be a brief affair once forces were mobilized. But that would take time. At the start, the US Army had only 16,000 soldiers (many of the best military leaders, such as Robert E. Lee, sided with the Confederacy), a limited navy (only forty-two ships in commission), and no clothing or weapons for the newly raised troops. By war's end, more than two million men had fought for the Union.

The war began over the terms of union. In time, however, it would be fought over the question of freedom. And it would also be fought to define the meaning of American democracy.

Civil War

The first major battle of the war took place on July 21 in Virginia at Bull Run, just twenty-seven miles from Washington. The Confederates had moved their capital from Montgomery to Richmond, and the war would be contested on two fronts: in the eastern theater throughout northern Virginia and in the western theater along the Mississippi, Tennessee, and Cumberland rivers. At Bull Run, some Northerners, including many members of Congress, thinking this would be the only contest of the war, traveled to the battlefield to picnic and observe. They were nearly crushed when Confederate forces, able to reinforce because of the slow and disorderly march of some 35,000 Union men from Alexandria, counterattacked and drove the Union army back. The next day Lincoln called for 500,000 troops and brought in George B. McClellan to lead Union forces. The war would be neither brief nor limited.

The Confederates were buoyed. Not only did they have superior generals such as P. G. T. Beauregard, Joseph E. Johnston, and Thomas "Stonewall" Jackson (who earned his nickname at Bull Run), they had Robert E. Lee, who took command of the army in northern Virginia on June 1, 1862. A devout Christian and a slaveholder, Lee was revered by his troops. As a student at West Point, one of Lee's classmates called him "the Marble Man," and the sobriquet captured his lifelong reputation of being noble and moral, if also cold and distant. Lee remained in command throughout the war. By contrast, Lincoln ran through a series of leaders for the Army of the Potomac: McClellan, Ambrose E. Burnside, Joseph Hooker, George G. Meade, and, finally, Ulysses S. Grant. Union generals often overestimated Confederate troop strength or, as at Fredericksburg in December 1862, attacked impregnable positions. They imagined Lee as having preternatural ability. An exasperated Grant once bellowed, "I am heartily tired of hearing about what Lee is going to do. Some of you always seem to think he is suddenly going to turn a double somersault, and land in our rear and on both of our flanks at the same time." Lee, too, came to believe the myth, and it may have been his undoing, leading him to take chances he otherwise may not have.[16]

Confederates had confidence that they would defeat the Union. They believed in their military superiority. At Bull Run, the rebel yell, unleashed in battle, sent Yankees retreating in fear. They also placed their hopes on support from Europe. Southern diplomats were working to persuade England and France to protect their commercial interests in cotton and recognize Confederate independence. Had they done so, the Union could not have prevailed.

On September 17, 1862, in the Battle of Antietam, Union forces under General George McClellan stopped Lee's drive into Maryland. The victory did much to diminish the possible European embrace of the Confederacy. The human toll was unimaginable: more than 23,000 total casualties with more than 3,500 killed. Antietam remains the single bloodiest day in American history. Photographs of the dead appeared soon thereafter at Mathew Brady's gallery on Broadway in New York. One reporter wrote that "Mr. Brady has done something to bring home to us the terrible reality and earnestness of war."[17]

That reality had already become apparent six months earlier in the battle of Shiloh in the western theater, where casualties over two days also numbered more than 23,000. Grant would later recall that the battlefield "was so covered with dead that it would have been possible to walk across the clearing, in any direction, stepping on dead bodies, without a foot touching the ground." The war turned out to be more lethal than anyone had imagined. One reason for this was the shift from smoothbore muskets to rifled barrels that fired bullets called Minie balls, which had greater accuracy and force, shattering bones and causing far greater destruction than traditional musket balls.[18]

By 1863, the Union had stopped the rebels' offensive campaign in the east and had won important victories in the west. The Union Navy under Admiral David Farragut had taken New Orleans in April 1862, and the blockade was becoming increasingly effective. Despite these Union advances, the Confederates had turned back McClellan's Peninsula campaign in the spring of 1862 and had again defeated the Union at Second Bull Run in late August. Under Stonewall Jackson, Confederate forces wreaked havoc in the Shenandoah Valley. At the end of 1862, after the Union's disastrous defeat at Fredericksburg, Robert E. Lee said, "It is well that war is so horrible, or else we should grow too fond of it."

The soldiers fought for many reasons, and for no reason at all. Some soldiers fought for union and some for secession, some fought against slavery and some for it. Some men enlisted because their neighbors did and some enlisted because they received money to do so. Not everyone volunteered. The Confederacy passed a conscription law in April 1862, and the Union followed in March 1863. Though a small percentage of soldiers were drafted, the opportunity in the North to pay $300 for commutation and more for a substitute and in the South to allow slaveholders with more than twenty slaves to avoid service, led to the complaint that it was "a rich man's war but a poor man's fight." Foreigners too served (especially German- and Irish-born), perhaps constituting 25 percent of Union forces and tens of thousands in the Confederacy.

For some households, it was literally a brother's war. In Kentucky, one of John J. Crittenden's sons fought for the Confederacy and another for the Union. Often, soldiers on each side would fraternize while on picket duty, trading goods and news, and then go about the business of shooting at one another. Whatever motivation delivered soldiers to the battlefield, the experience forever changed them. "I look on the carcass of a man now with pretty much such feeling as I would do were it a horse or a hog," acknowledged one. The war took more than 620,000 lives, perhaps as many as 750,000. For every soldier killed in combat, two died from disease. More Americans perished in the Civil War than in all other US wars combined. The percentage of the population that died was between 2 and 2.5 percent. The equivalent in the twenty-first century would be approximately 7 million lives.[19]

Thousands suffered as prisoners of war. Of 194,000 Union prisoners of war, 30,000 died, and of 215,000 Confederate prisoners, 26,000 died. There were atrocities on both sides. Thousands perished from disease and malnutrition at Andersonville prison in Georgia. After the war, Henry Wirz, the prison's Confederate commander in charge, was tried for murder by a military commission and executed. He met his fate, said the *New York Times*, "with quiet, cheerful indifference."[20]

At Gettysburg from July 1 to July 3, 1863, soldiers on both sides showed remarkable courage and heroism. Afterward, as with every battle, it was easy to locate moments that could have turned the outcome either way: Confederate General Richard Ewell's failure on Day 1 to take Cemetery Hill and Culp's Hill; Union Colonel Joshua Chamberlain, Gouverneur Warren, and Strong Vincent saving Little Round Top on Day 2; the charge of the First Minnesota regiment on the afternoon of Day 2 that plugged a hole in the Union line. Men did what they were ordered to do. On Day 3, more than 12,000 Confederate soldiers led by General George Pickett stepped into an open field and led an assault across three-quarter miles of unprotected ground toward an entrenched Union position. Driven back, with casualty rates over 50 percent, Pickett was ordered to rally his division. Pickett replied, "General Lee, I have no division." Confederate forces would never again penetrate this far north.

The war did not end at Gettysburg, though it might have if Meade had pursued Lee in the days following the battle. Nor did it end as a result of Grant's victory at Vicksburg, Mississippi, after a forty-seven-day siege that left Confederate soldiers and townspeople eating slaughtered mules and rats. Jefferson Davis thought, "We are now in the darkest hour of our political existence." In November, Lincoln dedicated Gettysburg cemetery and in his speech defined the war as a struggle for the endurance of the nation, "a new birth

Figure 5.1 Timothy H. O'Sullivan, *Harvest of Death* (1863). Library of Congress.

of freedom," and that "government of the people, by the people, for the people shall not perish from the earth."[21]

In March 1864, Lincoln brought Grant east and put him in command of all Union armies. Born Hiram Ulysses Grant in Point Pleasant, Ohio, in 1822, he became Ulysses when the wrong name was written on his nomination letter to West Point. Compact and muscular, Grant was described by a Union officer as someone who "habitually wears an expression as if he had determined to drive his head through a brick wall, and was about to do it." His initials came to stand for Unconditional Surrender. Toward the end of his life he wrote, "I am a verb instead of a personal pronoun." Under his command, the Army of the Potomac, with 115,000 men, moved against the Army of Northern Virginia, with 65,000 men. William T. Sherman moved against Atlanta. There were auxiliary campaigns in Georgia and Louisiana. Grant's Overland campaign in Virginia from May through June led to what one Confederate called "a Golgotha of horrors." The Wilderness, Spotsylvania, Cold Harbor— brutal, costly battles, yet Grant kept going. He could absorb casualties that Lee could not. Only later in life did he express regret over the assault at Cold Harbor, a loss that cost the Union 7,000 casualties in less than an hour. Critics called Grant a butcher. Northern public opinion increasingly turned against the war, and a peace movement, led by Northern Democrats, gained traction.[22]

In the summer of 1864, Lincoln believed he would not be reelected. The Democrats had nominated George McClellan, whom Lincoln had relieved of command of the Army of Potomac in November 1862. Hoping to win over those Democrats who favored the war, the Republicans, running as the National Union Party, nominated Andrew Johnson of Tennessee for vice president, replacing the incumbent Hannibal Hamlin. As September neared, it appeared that Lincoln would indeed lose. "Our bleeding, bankrupt, almost dying country also longs for peace," wrote Horace Greeley.[23]

And then the war turned. Sherman took Atlanta, Philip Sheridan rampaged through the Shenandoah Valley, and David Farragut steamed into Mobile Bay. The war had long ago stopped being exclusively a war against the enemy armies and had become a war against the Southern people. Sherman made sure of that. "If the people raise a howl against my barbarity and cruelty," he declared, "I will answer that war is war, and not popularity-seeking." After Atlanta, Sherman marched to Savannah and then through the Carolinas and left a 450-mile path of desolation. South Carolina was made to pay the greatest price. One Union private wrote, "Here is where treason began, and, by God, here is where it shall end."[24]

The victories transformed Northern public opinion and Lincoln easily won reelection. He took 55 percent of the popular vote and won the Electoral College 212–21. McClellan captured only Delaware, New Jersey, and Kentucky. The soldiers who voted in the field also overwhelmingly supported Lincoln; he received 78 percent of those soldier votes that were separately tabulated. Lincoln rejoiced: "we cannot have free government without elections; and if the rebellion could force us to forego, or postpone a national election, it might fairly claim to have already conquered and ruined us."[25]

Now it was only a matter of time. Confederate soldiers were running out of food and desertion rates rose sharply. Union forces pressed their advantage in numbers and resources. On April 2, Lee ordered the evacuation of Petersburg and Richmond. On April 9, he met Grant at Appomattox Courthouse and surrendered. The terms were generous. Lee's men were paroled as long as they swore not to take up arms against the United States, and those who had horses were allowed to keep them. Grant gave rations to Lee's starving men. Other Confederate generals surrendered over the following weeks. Four years of war were over and the nation now faced the challenge of reunification.

Lincoln had addressed reunion in his second inaugural, delivered on March 4. He reflected on the providential import of the war—"every drop of blood drawn with the lash, shall be paid by another drawn with the sword"—but also struck a note of forgiveness—"let us judge not that we be not judged." It was in the remarkable final sentence that he sought to set the tone for the future: "With malice toward none; with charity for all; with firmness in the right, as God gives us to see the right, let us strive on to finish the work we are in; to bind up the nation's wounds; to care for him who shall have borne the battle, and for his widow, and his orphan– to do all which may achieve and cherish a just, and lasting peace, among ourselves, and with all nations."[26]

Emancipation

Radical abolitionists and the enslaved hoped the war would end slavery. One activist declared in August 1861: "The only key to victory is a Proclamation of Emancipation." Yet Lincoln would not sign such a decree until January 1, 1863. What took so long?[27]

First, the president did not have the power to act against slavery where it existed. State laws, not federal law, governed slavery. For Lincoln, the battle over slavery was not about where it existed; it was about the territories where it did not yet exist. Lincoln was antislavery, believed that barring slavery's expansion would put it "in the course of ultimate extinction," and said time and again that he wished all men could be free. He also assured Southerners that he recognized he had no constitutional right to interfere with the institution. When Generals John C. Fremont and David Hunter early in the war issued orders freeing the slaves in their districts (Missouri in the one case and three Southern states in the other), Lincoln overturned the orders, saying that if ever such action was to be taken it would be he and not his commanders who did so.

Second, Lincoln worried that any action against slavery would drive the key border states, Maryland, Kentucky, and Missouri, out of the Union. (Delaware posed less concern). "To lose Kentucky," he said, "is nearly the same as to lose the whole game." Lincoln focused on trying to get legislators to adopt plans of compensated gradual emancipation in these states for which Congress pledged to appropriate money to pay for the freedom of the slaves. In his message he made it clear that in doing so the government claimed no right to interfere with slavery in the states.[28]

Finally, white fears of black freedom was an impediment to emancipation. What would be done with 4 million freed slaves? Even the most benevolent Southern whites, having heard proslavery defenses all their lives, thought of the enslaved as either barbaric and savage or docile and childlike. Either way, how would they adjust to freedom? Where would they go? Lincoln, among others, believed for a long time in voluntary colonization, and encouraged free blacks to leave the United States for Africa or Central America. This was just a fantasy. In 1854, Lincoln expressed the dilemma: "If all earthly power were given me, I should not know what to do, as to the existing institution" He realized colonization would be impossible. He despaired over keeping anyone in slavery, but could not imagine what a freedom looked like in which blacks were more than "underlings." As for political and social equality, he confessed, "My own feelings will not admit of this; and if mine would, we well know that those of the great mass of white people will not.[29]

Lincoln as president now had the equivalence of "all earthly power," and as the war progressed he moved gradually, deliberately, inexorably toward issuing an emancipation proclamation. "The pressure, in this direction, is still upon me, and is increasing," he said in July 1862.[30]

One of those pressures came from runaway slaves who took advantage of the dislocations of war and delivered themselves to Union forts and encampments. What to do with them became a policy question. Returning runaway slaves to their masters would only strengthen the Confederate war effort, as slaves aided the army in such non-combatant roles as teamsters and laborers and worked the fields that produced the crops that fed the army and generated revenue. The Union Army decided to confiscate these slaves as contraband of war, and Congress ratified these actions by passing two Confiscation Acts, the first in August 1861 and the second in July 1862.

At the time of the second confiscation act, Lincoln decided to issue an Emancipation Proclamation. He used his authority as commander in chief and, based on military necessity, proclaimed that those slaves in areas in rebellion and not under Union control would be freed. He issued a preliminary emancipation proclamation on September 22, 1862, tying it to the victory at Antietam five days earlier. He announced that on January 1, 1863, one hundred days away, he would issue the final proclamation.

As the day came, anticipation mounted. People gathered in churches and lecture halls in the North, and secretly in slave quarters in the South, and waited for the moment of jubilee to arrive. On signing the decree Lincoln said, "I never in my life felt more certain that I was doing right than I do in signing this paper." The final document differed from the earlier one. Lincoln no longer mentioned any support for colonization and he advised the freedmen not to engage in violence except in self-defense. He added a line in which he called the decree "an act of justice, warranted by the Constitution, upon military necessity."

Like the earlier proclamation, the Emancipation Proclamation freed those slaves in Confederate areas not under control of Union forces. The exceptions were necessary to be consistent with the doctrine of military necessity; slaves could not be emancipated where there was no military necessity, as in parts of Virginia and Louisiana, which were under Union control. The proclamation also did not apply to the four slave states that remained in the Union. In all, it exempted about 800,000 of the 4 million slaves.

The final Emancipation Proclamation did something else as well: it authorized the enlistment of black troops. By war's end, 179,000 black men served in the army and 19,000 in the navy. They contributed significantly to the war effort, working both behind the lines and in combat at such battles as Port Hudson, Milliken's Bend, and Fort Wagner. They also suffered at the hands of Confederates who refused to recognize them as soldiers. At Fort Pillow in Tennessee on April 12, 1864, forces under Confederate General Nathan Bedford Forrest murdered dozens of men after they surrendered, one of several battles in which black troops were massacred. Black soldiers also faced discrimination in the Union Army. Serving in units commanded by white officers, black soldiers received unequal pay and suffered harsher punishments than white soldiers. More than half of the soldiers came from the eleven states that constituted the Confederacy, runaway slaves who enlisted and returned to fight. Frederick Douglass, whose son enlisted in the famous Massachusetts Fifty-Fourth Regiment, best explained the larger significance of black troops: "Once let the black man get upon his person the brass letters, U.S., let him get an eagle on his button, and a musket on his shoulder and bullets in his pocket, there is no power on earth that can deny that he has earned the right to citizenship."[31]

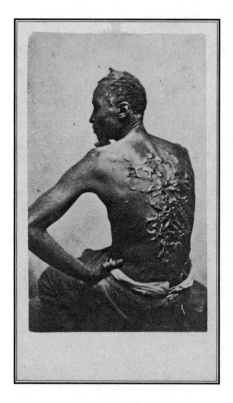

Figure 5.2 *The Scourged Back*
(ca. 1863). Library of Congress.

In 1865, desperate to reverse their fortunes, the Confederate Congress considered offering some adult male slaves their freedom and enlisting them as soldiers. While Robert E. Lee supported the idea, Howell Cobb, a former governor of Georgia, understood that "if slaves will make good soldiers, [then] our whole theory of slavery is wrong." On March 13, Jefferson Davis signed a bill that allowed for the enlistment of slaves. None fought for the Confederacy, however. It was a final, desperate effort for the Confederacy to win its independence.[32]

The Emancipation Proclamation and the enlistment of black troops was only the beginning of the movement toward the abolition of slavery. Lincoln refused to back away despite accusations that he was a dictator who, in freeing the slaves, was perverting the goal of saving the Union and was trying to initiate a race war. He fired back that once the war was over "there will be some black men who can remember that, with silent tongue, and clenched teeth, and steady eye, and well-poised bayonet, they have helped mankind on to this great consummation; while, I fear, there will be some white ones, unable to forget that, with malignant heart, and deceitful speech, they strove to hinder it."[33]

The experience of combat changed some white soldiers' minds about what they were fighting for. Charles Wills enlisted as a private in the Eighth Illinois and rose to be a lieutenant colonel in the 103rd Illinois. In the summer of 1863 he wrote, "How queer. A year ago last January, I didn't like to hear anything of emancipation. Last fall accepted confiscation of rebel's negroes quietly. In January took to emancipation readily, and now believe in arming the negroes." Daniel Sawtelle of the Eighth Maine said he was glad he enlisted because he learned something about slavery that for him, as for many Northerners, had been only an abstraction: "Men that called themselves negro haters a while ago are compelled to say they are better than they thought they were. And why should not some of them (with the same advantage) be our equals."[34]

Lincoln knew the only certain way to end slavery throughout the nation was a constitutional amendment abolishing it. He worried that the Emancipation Proclamation might be litigated and overturned by the courts. In 1864, the Senate passed such an amendment but the House did not. After his reelection, Lincoln dedicated his office to helping secure votes to obtain passage of the amendment. On January 31, 1865, the Thirteenth Amendment to the Constitution passed the House 119–56, just over the two-thirds majority needed. Illinois became the first state to ratify the amendment that prohibited slavery or involuntary servitude. On December 6, 1865, the amendment, with Georgia's ratification, became law.

Emancipation was one matter; freedom was another. How would the enslaved make the transition from slavery to freedom? Not nearly enough attention was given to this momentous issue. Once, when asked what the former slaves would do, Lincoln told a story about hogs in winter who had to root around in the frozen ground for food or else die. Recognizing the problem, one of the last bills Lincoln signed (in March 1865) created the US Bureau of Refugees, Freedmen, and Abandoned Lands, known as the Freedmen's Bureau. The law authorized the bureau for only one year, which reflected misgivings about creating a government agency committed to helping former slaves make the transition to freedom. The Freedmen's Bureau provided food, clothes, medical help, relocation to abandoned lands, and courts to review labor contracts. The bureau also played a role in establishing schools for the freedmen. Lincoln had come to understand that the federal government would have to play a crucial role in supporting the freedmen and providing them with the resources they needed to support themselves.

In what would turn out to be his final speech, delivered on April 11, 1865, Lincoln took a further step. He endorsed the right to vote for literate black men and those who had served in the military. Abolitionists had been pressing for such a right as the only way in a democracy for the freedmen to protect their interests. John Wilkes Booth was among those who heard Lincoln speak, and the idea of black citizenship led him to warn, "That is the last speech he will ever make." Three days later, on Good Friday, Booth followed through on his threat and assassinated the president. In December, Frederick Douglass would note, "Whoever else have cause to mourn the loss of Abraham Lincoln, to the colored people of the country his death is an unspeakable calamity."[35]

Home Fronts

In civil wars, battlefronts and home fronts are often indistinct. Throughout the South, civilians experienced battle directly, heard the boom of cannon, and saw the dead and wounded at their doors. In the North as well, the war was felt in the soldiers leaving home, in the transformation of daily life, in the casualty lists in the daily newspaper, and in vehement discussions of the politics of the conflict.

Dissent was a prominent feature on the Northern home front. In the presidential election of 1864 Stephen Douglas received nearly a million votes outside of the states that had seceded. These Democrats divided into War Democrats and Peace Democrats—those who supported the war but not any effort to tamper with slavery and those who opposed the war regardless of its aims. Many Northern Democratic editors and politicians spoke against the war effort and walked a fine line at times between dissent and sedition. In Ohio, Clement Vallandigham, a former congressman, denounced the war as "wicked, cruel, and unnecessary." He was arrested, tried, and convicted before a military tribunal. Lincoln suspended the prison sentence and banished Vallandigham to the Confederacy.

Northern Democrats denounced Lincoln as a despot for using executive power to suspend habeas corpus and suppress opposition newspapers. The president transferred responsibility for security to the War Department, and during the rebellion authorities arrested at least 15,000 citizens for suspected disloyalty. One of the editors imprisoned was Frank Key Howard, grandson of Francis Scott Key who had written "The Star Spangled Banner." Howard was imprisoned at Fort McHenry, the bombardment of which during the War of 1812 had inspired his grandfather. Lincoln stoutly defended such measures. On his release, Howard published *Fourteen Months in American Bastiles* (1863) and denounced "the unlawful and oppressive acts of Mr. Lincoln." The president defended his actions against all critics. "Must I shoot a simple-minded soldier boy who deserts, while I must not touch a hair of the wily agitator who induces him to desert?" he asked. What he called "the fire in the rear" raged throughout the war.[36]

That fire sparked violence in the North as Democrats fueled strong antidraft feelings. In New York for several days starting on July 13, 1863, riots erupted as Irish workingmen burned the draft office and then turned their anger on the free black population. By the time they were done, a Colored Orphan's Asylum lay in embers and a dozen blacks had been lynched. Police and troops from the Army of the Potomac killed more than 100 rioters before restoring calm.

Riots were not unique to the North. In Richmond, Virginia, in 1863, there was a bread riot. Dismayed by rising prices and the scarcity of food, sickened by the actions of speculators and merchants, women took to the streets crying "Bread or blood." They broke into warehouses, bakeries, and groceries. Order was quickly restored, and forty-four women were arrested. The bread riot exposed the hardship the war was exacting on the home front, and the power of women to do something about it.

Southern white women, in particular, saw their lives transformed by the war. Suddenly, they had to operate farms and supervise plantations, not to mention manage enslaved labor. They also involved themselves however they could in the Confederate war effort, sewing uniforms and cooking for soldiers. Whatever the ideal of Southern white womanhood for the planter classes may have been—the so-called Southern belle of refinement and gentility—the war's devastating economic consequences and loss of life wrenched women out of old roles and into new. The wives of yeomen, non–slave-owning farmers, also saw their lives remade and, as the war progressed, they increasingly urged their husbands and sons to leave the army and return home. One Virginia woman, Lucy Buck, eighteen years old in 1861, summarized the effects of the war on the home front: "we shall never any of us be the same as we have been."[37]

Many Northern women became involved directly in the war effort, particularly through the auspices of the US Sanitary Commission (USSC), a private relief agency that supported sick and wounded soldiers. Women organized volunteer activities and became nurses working in hospitals to care for soldiers. Under the leadership of Dorothea Dix, thousands of women volunteered. Elizabeth Davis, the wife of a Philadelphia merchant, captured the feelings of many when she wrote to a friend, "I know there must be something for me to do in this time of suffering." The USSC also helped organize massive "sanitary fairs" that served both to raise funds for the soldiers and provide entertainment for families—dances, parades, displays, and shows.[38]

The USSC was created in 1861 by the federal government. Starting in 1861, Congress passed a torrent of legislation that would expand the reach of the federal government and transform the nation: the Revenue Act (3 percent tax on annual incomes over $800), the Legal Tender Act (authorized issue of $150 million in US Treasury notes), creation of a Department of Agriculture, the Homestead Act (160 acres of public land to settlers after five years' residence), the Pacific Railroad Act, the Morrill Land Grant Act (sale of public lands to be used for the creation of agricultural and mechanical arts colleges), and National Banking Acts.

In the Union, two-party politics helped unify the Republicans. The presence of the Democrats forced Republicans to articulate their goals and act in concert to advance the war effort at home. In the single-party Confederacy, on the other hand, Jefferson Davis found it much more difficult to build consensus, particularly given the doctrine of states' rights. He could ask states to help, but many governors bristled at any kind of nationalization and refused to accede to the government's requests. For example, Governors Zebulon Vance of North Carolina and Joseph E. Brown of Georgia opposed the administration and resisted conscription and the impressment of crops and supplies. The paradox of trying to create a nation based on the doctrine of states' rights would in the end contribute to the defeat of the Confederacy.

Reconstruction

Ideas about reconstruction date from the war's beginning, not its end. Before secession, some Southerners used the word to describe reconstructing the Constitution to recognize slavery and forbid any interference with it. That was never going to happen, at least not while Lincoln was president. In his first inaugural, Lincoln looked past the conflict and hypothesized, "Suppose you go to war, you cannot fight always; and when, after much loss on both sides, and no gain on either, you cease fighting, the identical old questions, as to terms of intercourse, are again upon you." Of course he could not see in 1861 that in 1865 some of the "identical old questions" would have vanished with the abolition of slavery.[39]

From the start of the war, reconstruction was both an end in itself—preserving the nation as a whole—and a means to that end. Lincoln believed that if he could convince some of the seceded states to organize new state governments, adopt new state constitutions, and elect representatives to Congress, they could be restored and thereby weaken the Confederate effort. He placed special hopes on Louisiana when New Orleans came under Union control in 1862, and pressured state officials to hold a convention to adopt a state constitution that abolished slavery, which was accomplished in 1864. Lincoln went further and wrote privately to Governor Michael Hahn that perhaps the state should consider black suffrage for the educated and those who fought. But delegates rejected giving former slaves the right to vote.

Louisiana's actions were in keeping with Lincoln's Proclamation of Amnesty and Reconstruction, issued on December 8, 1863, only weeks after his return from Gettysburg. Lincoln offered full pardon to rebels (except for government officials, high-ranking military officers, and those who had not treated captured black or white soldiers as prisoners of war) who took an oath of allegiance. Their property, except for slaves, would be restored to them. Furthermore, as soon as 10 percent of those who voted in the state election of 1860 vowed allegiance, a new state government could be established. In addition to Louisiana, Arkansas, and Tennessee began to take steps toward reconstruction.

Congress had alternative ideas and passed the Wade-Davis bill in 1864. It differed from the president's plan by mandating that to initiate the process, 50 percent of those voting in 1860 had to take an oath of future loyalty. It also limited the ballot to those who could take an "ironclad oath" that they had never participated in the rebellion. Lincoln vetoed the bill. Congress would have its revenge in February 1865 when members refused to seat the newly elected representatives from Louisiana.

Part of the tension between the president and Congress was purely procedural and revolved around the question of who had the ultimate authority over reconstruction. Part was more substantive. Radical Republicans such as Charles Sumner and Thaddeus Stevens wanted a fundamental reconstruction of the Confederate states— not merely restoration or reunion. Sumner believed that in leaving the Union these states had committed suicide and Stevens believed they were conquered provinces. They argued that planters should be stripped of their wealth and that the freedmen should receive the right to vote. Lincoln had little patience with their constitutional theories, which he called "a pernicious abstraction." Since secession was illegal, the states had never left the Union. Lincoln had no taste for revenge. "Let them up easy," he said. He was relieved at war's end that Congress was out of session and would not be back until December. It gave him time to bring the case for reconstruction directly to the people.

Lincoln's assassination cut short his opportunity to unify the nation. His successor, Andrew Johnson, was at first praised by the radical Republicans as someone who would have the spine to punish the Southerners for their treason. Johnson had risen from poverty to become a slaveholder who emancipated his slaves and stuck by the Union. He was the only Southern senator not to resign his seat with secession, and Lincoln appointed him military governor of Tennessee. Johnson hated the planter aristocracy, and radical Republicans hoped he would be remorseless toward them. By December 1865, however, it became clear that Johnson's antipathy toward blacks would trump whatever ill feeling he held toward Southern elites. He enjoyed having aristocrats come to him personally to beg for pardon, which he granted in wholesale lots. At year's end, Johnson declared the work of reconstruction over.

Congressional Republicans had a very different idea and refused to seat any of the representatives elected by the Southern states that November. Shockingly, these included former Confederate officials and officers, including Alexander Stephens, whom Georgians sent to the Senate. As vice president of the Confederacy, he had declared that slavery formed its "cornerstone.".

For the next two years, Congress advanced its own plan of reconstruction while battling Johnson. The president vetoed the Freedman's Bureau Act and the Civil Rights Act of 1866, which provided equal rights under the law for all citizens, defined as those born in the United States. Congress in both cases overrode the president's veto. In June 1866, Congress approved the Fourteenth Amendment to the Constitution, which defined citizens as those born or naturalized in the United States and offered equal protection under the laws and due process of law. In July 1868, the amendment was ratified. The next year Congress passed the proposed Fifteenth Amendment, saying that voting rights could not be denied based on color or previous condition of servitude. It was ratified in March 1870. The abolitionist William Lloyd Garrison, who had been pressing for immediate emancipation and equal rights since 1831, marveled at "this wonderful, quiet, sudden transformation of four millions of human beings from . . . the auction-block to the ballot box." Frederick Douglass exclaimed, "At last, at last the black man has a future."[40]

Starting in March 1867, Congress passed a series of four Reconstruction Acts to govern the business of readmitting states to the Union. These acts divided the former Confederacy into military districts and established military courts. They also required states to ratify the Fourteenth Amendment. Tennessee, which had promptly ratified the amendment, was exempted from these acts. Although in 1867 there were only about 15,000 federal troops in the former Confederacy, the presence of these soldiers helped protect the rights of freedmen. They would also loom large in the memories of Southerners who would represent the era of reconstruction as one of unbridled tyranny on the part of Republicans. In June 1868, representatives from seven states were readmitted to Congress.

The Congressional battle with Andrew Johnson reached its peak in February 1868, when the House of Representatives voted 126–47 to impeach him. Tired of Johnson's resistance, Congress in 1867 passed the Tenure of Office Act, which forbade the president from removing an official whose appointment required Senate approval. When Johnson removed Secretary of War Edwin Stanton, who supported Congressional Republicans, the House impeached the president. Johnson's trial before the Senate lasted eleven weeks. His defense argued he could only be impeached for criminal acts for which he could be indicted in court, and the Tenure of Office Act did not apply because Stanton was a holdover from Lincoln's administration. Moderate Republicans, while despairing over Johnson's intransigence on Reconstruction, feared the precedent of conviction, and on May 16 the president was acquitted with one vote to spare.

Johnson may have been neutralized, yet Southern resistance to reconstruction was not. In the immediate aftermath of the war, Southern state legislatures, created under Johnson's reconstruction plan, enacted harsh codes that excluded blacks from juries, stipulated segregation in public accommodations, punished blacks more harshly than whites for certain crimes, and forbade racial intermarriage. Some codes defined vagrancy broadly and allowed for the state to arrest any black man who was unemployed. And some required free blacks to get licenses in order to work in any occupation other than agricultural or domestic labor. All of these were intended to limit black movement and transform free labor into new forms of servitude such as apprenticeships. In Memphis, mobs attacked black soldiers and their families, and burned black churches, schools, and homes. These actions compelled many black citizens to leave Memphis. In New Orleans, a white mob attacked black supporters of an effort to revoke the black codes. Several dozen blacks and three white Republicans were killed. Federal troops had to put down the riot. The local police aided and abetted the rioters, as they had in Memphis. These riots were a major reason Congress passed the Reconstruction Acts. They also further emboldened Southern defiance.

Several states remained to be restored to the Union. When Virginia and Mississippi purged their new state constitutions of disfranchisement provisions, they were readmitted in 1870 along with Texas. Southerners continued to despise Southern Republicans, some of whom were Northerners who had moved South ("carpetbaggers") or Southern Whigs now turned Republican ("scalawags"). Most were blacks, who constituted 80 percent of the Republican voters. In the early 1870s, blacks held about 20 percent of state offices (except in South Carolina where it reached over 50 percent). In total, through the era, some 2,000 blacks served in state and city governments. Nationally, two US senators (Hiram Rhodes Revels and Blanche Bruce from Mississippi) and twenty congressmen were elected. Southern whites would characterize the era of reconstruction as one of "Negro rule." In fact state governments under Republican control were a biracial coalition of politicians who sought to restore economic stability to a region devastated by war and build toward the future.

The Republican state governments did not last long. Violence and other forms of intimidation helped Southern Democrats regain power. Measures disfranchising black voters, such as poll taxes, residency requirements, and literacy tests, helped them to maintain it. By the end of the century these measures became systematic and proved so effective that in Alabama, for example, at the turn of the century more than 180,000 blacks were eligible to vote yet by 1903 fewer than 3,000 were registered.

Even more threatening than legal measures was the constant menace of extralegal violence. The Ku Klux Klan emerged after the war, its ranks filled with former Confederates and planters, and the secret society systemically burned black churches and schools and murdered innocent citizens. The Grand Wizard was none other than Confederate General Nathan Bedford Forrest, who was responsible for the Fort Pillow Massacre during the war. It seemed that Republicans could do little at the local level to reign in the Klan's terrorist activities. In 1870 Congress took action with passage of an Enforcement Act that outlawed conspiracies against citizens exercising their constitutional rights and made interference with voting rights a federal offence. With the passage of a second act in 1871, known as the Ku Klux Klan Act, Congress held hearings and indicted thousands of Klan members. Most charges were dropped, although hundreds of others were fined or received jail sentences.

By 1872, however, with the return to power of Democrats, most state governments had been what Southerners called "redeemed." Ulysses S. Grant swept into the presidency in 1868 with the campaign slogan "Let Us Have Peace." Despite his plea, his first term in office forced him to deal with the violence of ongoing Southern resistance to civil rights. Reelected overwhelmingly four years later, Grant seemed unable to advance the Republican agenda, and his administration struggled against charges of cronyism and corruption. Northern Republicans grew weary of the struggle over reconstruction, now going on for nearly twice as long as the war itself. "Let us have done with Reconstruction," pleaded one New York newspaper in 1870, "the country is tired and sick of it."[41]

For Southern blacks, that meant being left to struggle on their own to give meaning to freedom. In the immediate aftermath of the war, some freedmen left the plantation to experience

Figure 5.3 Thomas Nast, "This Is a White Man's Government," *Harper's Weekly* (1868). Library of Congress.

personal autonomy, to search for lost loved ones, and to seek better opportunities. Without land of their own to farm, or capital for tools and supplies, many of them became locked into sharecropping agreements that left them permanently ensnared in cycles of debt and tenantry that became in effect a new form of bonded labor. Congress passed a Southern Homestead Act in 1866 that put aside forty-six million acres of public land for black families. The land, however, was of poor quality and white-owned lumber companies ended up controlling most of it. A sharecropper said, "Give us our land and we can take care of ourselves, but without land the old massa can hire us or starve us as they please." Thaddeus Stevens called for the confiscation of the land of Southern planter elites to strip "a proud nobility of their bloated estates." Stevens's radical desire to break up the foundation of Southern society would not gain purchase. One Southern lawyer concluded that the former slaves had "freedom in name, but not in fact."[42]

Perhaps the greatest achievement of the Reconstruction Era came from the investment in education. Freedmen's schools emerged across the South, and various Northern aid societies, such as the American Missionary Association and the New England Educational Association, sent teachers, books, and supplies. Northern women in particular traveled South by the thousands to volunteer to teach. Southerners also filled the ranks. In Georgia, for example, of some 600 teachers in the Freedmen's schools during Reconstruction, more that 20 percent were native Georgians, both black and white. A letter from Philena Carkin, a woman from Massachusetts who taught in Charlottesville, Virginia, captures the dedication of both teachers and students: "there have been a good many days when the mud was nearly ankle-deep at our door, and the roads outside of town were in a state impossible to describe. Still the scholars got here in some way." By the end of the century, literacy rates among blacks across the South had increased by 50 percent. Religious, political, and educational leaders also created institutions such as Fisk University, Howard University, Morehouse University, and Hampton Institute, which provided opportunities for African Americans to attend college. In 1894, a year before he died, Frederick Douglass, who had made education the key to freedom in his work published nearly fifty years earlier, gave a speech in support of the Manassas Industrial School. He marveled at the proliferation of such schools in Virginia, "a State so averse in the past to the education of colored people, so as to make it a crime to teach a negro to read," and declared educational institutions "one of the best fruits of the agitation of half a century, and a firm foundation of hope for the future."[43]

The official end of reconstruction came with the election of 1876. Rutherford B. Hayes, Ohio's Republican governor, ran against Samuel J. Tilden, New York's governor. Hayes was a Civil War veteran who had been wounded in battle; Tilden a northern Democrat who lamented Lincoln's use of executive authority. Although often sickly (one writer called him "a life-long invalid"), Tilden campaigned vigorously. After the ballots were counted, he led Hayes by more than 200,000 votes and was one electoral vote short of victory. Chaos ensued with claims and counter-claims of fraud and corruption. The electoral certificates from Florida, Louisiana, and South Carolina, which went for Tilden, were challenged, as was the vote from Oregon, which went for Hayes. With the possibility of another civil war erupting, Congress in January 1877 established a fifteen-member electoral commission to resolve the dispute. By a party-line vote of 8–7, Hayes received the disputed electoral votes and in turn Republicans promised to withdraw all remaining troops from the South. The final three Southern states that were still Republican would now return to Democratic control. In his inaugural address, Hayes advocated protection of the constitutional rights of all. He also stated that local government was the only true self-government.

Reflecting on the era of Civil War and Reconstruction, Mark Twain and Charles Dudley Warner concluded that the years "uprooted institutions that were centuries old, changed the politics of the people, transformed the social life of half the country, and wrought so profoundly upon the entire national character that the influence cannot be measured short of two or three generations." The book in which they made these observations also gave the name to the era that followed. They titled it *The Gilded Age*.[44]

CHAPTER 6

Survival of the Fittest

WALT WHITMAN PUBLISHED *LEAVES OF GRASS* in 1855 and continued to revise the work during his lifetime. In the process he became America's poet. Through the 1890s, newspapers regularly reported on the state of his health. "Walt Whitman Has a Bad Cold," read one headline. Whitman never stopped celebrating the America he heard singing, as he put it. He loved democracy, yet never took it for granted. "It is a word," he wrote, "the real gist of which still sleeps." He sought equality, but witnessed class struggle instead. He desired community, yet encountered unfettered individualism. He loved the West that made America "the continent of glories," but he knew empire could have a corrosive effect on democratic institutions. "Never was there, perhaps, more hollowness at heart than at present, and here in the United States," he wrote in 1871, just as Reconstruction was losing steam and government corruption seemed on the rise. He also celebrated the "intense practical energy, the demand for facts, even the business materialism of the current age." Although he believed in evolution, he submitted to its worst manifestation as social theory when he once claimed that "the nigger, like the injun will be eliminated: it is the law of races." "Do I contradict myself?" he asks in "Song of Myself." "Very well then I contradict myself / (I am large, I contain multitudes)."[1]

Corruption

In 1880, Henry Adams anonymously published *Democracy: An American Novel.* Adams, the grandson and great-grandson of presidents, was one of the era's leading historians. After seven years as a professor at Harvard, he moved to Washington and became a central personality in the intellectual and social life of the city. Later, in *The Education of Henry Adams*, his autobiography written in the form of a novel, he would define politics as "the systematic organization of hatreds." The main character in *Democracy*, Mrs. Madeleine Lee, protests at one point, "Is a respectable government impossible in a democracy? . . . What is to become of us if corruption is allowed to go unchecked?"[2]

Where there is power there is always corruption, and Americans in the decades following the Civil War felt as if they swam in an "ocean of corruption." They had good reason to think so. Scandal after scandal tarnished Ulysses S. Grant's administration. The first major scandal concerned money itself, in this case gold. Jay Gould and James Fisk, railroad developers and financiers, sought to corner the gold market. Gould and Fisk were two of dozens of capitalists and industrialists who emerged in the decades following the Civil War. Jay Cooke, Andrew Carnegie, Henry Clay Frick, and J. P. Morgan were some of the other prominent businessmen who came to be known as "robber barons"—men whose greed knew no bounds and who employed whatever means necessary to defeat their competitors. The description is not entirely fair. These men also advanced industry, helped expand the economy, and used their wealth for philanthropic ends. However one views them, they transformed America in the last half of the nineteenth century.

Gould and Fisk sought to take advantage of Grant's determination to pay down the government debt accrued during the Civil War when it ballooned from $65 million to $2.7 billion. The US Treasury issued $430 million in paper money, called "greenbacks" (for the color of the bills), that was not backed by specie. "To protect the national honor, every dollar of Government indebtedness should be paid in gold," Grant declared in his first inaugural in March 1869. The Treasury Department's weekly gold sales had begun to reduce the debt and also kept down the price of gold. Gould and Fisk bribed an assistant treasurer and gained access to the president through his son-in-law, who was brought in to help influence Grant to stop the sale of gold, which Gould and Fisk had been stockpiling. The two controlled more than $50 million in gold, and by Friday, September

24, 1869, the price had risen from $143 an ounce to $1,602. To break this "gold ring," the Treasury released millions in gold and the price plummeted. So too did the stock market, which fell 20 percent. A congressional investigation cleared Grant, and despite being chased by a mob, Gould and Fisk were financially unscathed. Henry Adams, in his essay "The New York Gold Conspiracy," concluded that Gould and Fisk continued to reign over the Erie Railroad and "no one can say that their power or their credit was sensibly diminished by a shock which for the time prostrated the interests of the country."[3]

Other shocks were to come. In 1872, the public learned that more than a dozen prominent politicians, including Vice President Schuyler Colfax, had accepted discounted shares of stock in Credit Mobilier, a construction company ostensibly independent from the Union Pacific Railroad, but actually created to help defraud the government by charging exorbitant rates to complete work on the transcontinental railroad. The government ended up paying nearly $100 million for work that cost $50 million. A congressional investigation led to the censure of two congressmen, Massachusetts Republican Oakes Ames and New York Democrat James Brooks. The real crime, thought the *New York Tribune,* was not that "these men were bribed or corruptly influenced, but that they betrayed the trust of the people, deceived their constituents, and by their evasions and falsehoods confessed the transaction to be disgraceful."[4]

More scandals followed. Distillers bribed Treasury officials to avoid paying liquor taxes; the secretary of war received kickbacks for awarding licenses to trade on Indian reservations; bribes were paid to obtain lucrative postal contracts; and Congress even passed an act to raise its own salary retroactively. In what was perhaps the most nefarious scandal, Orville Babcock, Grant's private secretary, played a role in planting evidence against someone who was prosecuting a group of corrupt building contractors. Grant dismissed Babcock in 1876. By then the term "Grantism" had entered the lexicon as shorthand for cronyism and corruption. Senator Charles Sumner was disgusted with the president and his effect on the glorious Republican Party, "whose sphere ceases to be republicanism and becomes Grantism; its members cease to be Republicans and become Grant-men. It is no longer a political party, but a personal party." In *The Education of Henry Adams,* Adams quipped, "The progress of evolution from President Washington to President Grant, was alone evidence enough to upset Darwin."[5]

No single party or government monopolized corruption, and the Democrats at the state level drew as much condemnation as the Republicans at the national. One person in particular, William Magear Tweed, or Boss Tweed as he was known, has remained the symbol of corrupt city government practices. Tweed ran Tammany Hall, the Democratic Party political machine, and used his influence to promote the interests of friends and to help get cronies elected to political office in New York. After 1869, Tweed Democrats controlled the state Assembly and Senate, a protégé was governor, and a new charter expanded the power of City Hall. With control over city government, Tweed and his ring used every method possible to defraud the city. In some elections, New York City wards had more voters than residents. It wasn't the ballots that mattered, Tweed said, it was who counted them. Estimates of the amount skimmed range from $30 million to $200 million. Tweed wore a ten-carat diamond stickpin on his shirtfront.

The other side of municipal corruption was that it greased municipal development. New York saw a housing construction boom as well as investment in a transportation system. Developers knew they had to give Tweed his cut. The building of the Brooklyn Bridge across the East River went forward only after Tweed received a carpetbag with $60,000 in it. By 1883, when the Brooklyn Bridge opened, Tweed was out of the picture, having died in jail from pneumonia in 1878. He had been brought down by the reporting of the *New York Times* and the editorial cartoons of Thomas Nast in *Harper's Weekly*. Nast had established himself as an artist during the Civil War and is credited with creating the image of Santa Claus and popularizing the donkey and elephant as symbols of the two political parties. The *New York Times* wrote that he did "more to affect public opinion than a score of writers." Tweed is reported to have said that even though his followers couldn't read the newspapers, "they can't help seeing them damned pictures!" Those pictures lampooned Tweed as a vulture, a corpulent, leering politician whose head was a bag of money, at the center of a ring of men each pointing to the other in answer to the question "who stole the people's money?" Tweed even tried to bribe Nast, but by then his reign was over.[6]

Cronyism and corruption fueled the desire for civil service reform. Under the entrenched spoils system, when the presidency changed from one party to the other, or even from one party faction to another, the victor filled the vast majority of positions with his own loyalists. As much as 50 percent of all federal jobs were patronage positions; and that meant remarkable rates of turnover that often led

Figure 6.1 Thomas Nast, "Who Stole the Peoples Money?" *Harper's Weekly* (1871). Library of Congress.

to unqualified appointees and mass inefficiency in the government. Not surprisingly, the spoils system was increasingly condemned, especially by "good government" types. Grant sought reform and Congress created a Civil Service Commission. Its funding expired in 1874, and Rutherford B. Hayes, whose election in 1876 was tainted by allegations of corruption and bargain-making, sought to make federal positions more meritocratic. He created a cabinet committee to explore new rules for federal employees; had the New York Customs house investigated, much to the chagrin of Roscoe Conkling, a senator from New York and a leader of Republicans who supported the spoils system; and he signed an executive order that forbade federal office-holders from participating in party politics. Of course that was impossible to enforce, and many stalwart Republicans questioned the wisdom of yielding their position of national political power.

The assassination of President James Garfield in 1881 at the Washington railway station by Charles Guiteau altered the landscape for reform. Guiteau, disappointed that he had not received a consular position, shot Garfield, who died not from the bullet lodged in his vertebrae, but the medical care he received afterward (his physicians probed Garfield's body for the bullet using unsterilized instruments and unwashed hands). In 1883, Congress passed the Civil Service Reform Act (called the Pendleton Act after its main sponsor, Senator George Pendleton, a Democrat from Ohio). The act reauthorized the Civil Service Commission, which administered exams for applicants and protected government employees from being fired when administrations changed.

Not everyone supported merit over favoritism, and in the election of 1884 Republicans cast off Chester Arthur, Garfield's successor, for James G. Blaine, former speaker of the house and senator from Maine. Blaine had been a candidate in 1876. His ambitions, however, were derailed in part by his name having been included among those suspected in the Credit Mobilier scandal. Republicans, hoping to keep the Civil War alive as a way to continue to win elections, sought other candidates, including William Tecumseh Sherman, who turned them down, saying he would "account myself a fool, a madman, an ass" to consider it. Blaine's nomination split the Republican Party. E. L. Godkin, editor of the *New York Evening Post*, wrote that Blaine "wallowed in spoils like a rhinoceros in an African pool." Those who bolted included Mark Twain, Carl Schurz, and Henry Adams. They became known as "Mugwumps," an epithet for anyone who left the GOP in favor of the Democratic nominee Grover Cleveland, governor of New York. Blaine's taint was so great that even the revelation that Cleveland had fathered a child out of wedlock did not cost him the election. Republicans chanted, "Ma, ma where's my pa / Gone to the White House, ha, ha, ha," and Democrats responded "Blaine, Blaine, the Continental Liar from the State of Maine."[7]

Cleveland was the first Democrat elected since before the Civil War. The Jeffersonian notion of least government as best government continued to shape the party. Cleveland thought government should get out the way and that the people should be left free to pursue their interests and their welfare. "The lesson should be constantly enforced," he said, "that, though the people support the government, the government should not support the people." Instead, the people must be left free to struggle and compete.[8]

Competition

William Graham Sumner, a professor of political and social science at Yale, was also a Mugwump. His 1883 work *What Social Classes Owe Each Other* argued that no class in society "lies under the duty and burden of fighting the battles of life for any other class." At another point, he used the phrase "struggle for existence." Sumner was echoing the principles of social Darwinism, a philosophy advanced by England's Herbert Spencer, who tried to apply Charles Darwin's theory of natural selection to society. In Spencer's hands, Darwin's phrase "struggle for survival" became "survival of the fittest" and served to undergird such various ideas as laissez-faire capitalism, imperialism, and eugenics. It is no accident that in the late nineteenth century, boxing became the most popular spectator sport in America. In 1889, John L. Sullivan, known as the Boston Strong Boy, fought Jake Kilrain in Mississippi. They clashed using bare knuckles, and the battle, which raged for seventy-five rounds, received national attention. Many of the free libraries Andrew Carnegie funded included a boxing ring.[9]

The struggle between business and labor defined the Gilded Age. This was the era of big business—Standard Oil, Armour meatpacking, and Carnegie steel. It was the era of business tycoons who engaged in shady practices yet became steadfast symbols of the age. Between the Panic of 1873, when the New York Stock Exchange closed for ten days and Jay Cooke's bank failed, and the Panic of 1893, when thousands of businesses and hundreds of banks collapsed and unemployment stood at over 10 percent, the economy prospered. Production tripled and per capita income more than doubled. New technology, whether mechanical reapers on the farm or blast furnaces in the steel mills, increased productivity. The railroads even changed time itself when, at noon on November 18, 1883, they implemented a system of time zones to allow for the coordination of train travel. As the population grew from 40 million in 1870 to 76 million in 1900, the nation became more urbanized: from 26 percent of the population to nearly 40 percent living in towns of 2,500 people or more. It was an era of invention: between 1860 and 1900 the US Patent Office awarded 440,000 patents, twelve times more than all previous decades combined. For someone born in 1830, it must have been difficult to believe that in 1890 they could travel to the Pacific Ocean on a steam-powered train, enter nighttime spaces illuminated by electricity, and speak on a telephone.[10]

What made business expansion possible was the increased power of the corporation, which came to be viewed legally in the 1880s as "a natural person." Under the protection of the Fourteenth Amendment and with the support of the Supreme Court, corporations expanded their control and concentrated their power. Trusts and holding companies emerged, and huge, centralized combinations led to near monopolies in such key industries as oil, steel, tobacco, and rubber. Ironically, for an era that virtually worshipped competition, these conglomerates had the effect of eliminating it. Single corporations could control the market and reap huge profits. They could also control wages.

In the Gilded Age, wage labor became a permanent condition for millions of Americans. It was not supposed to be that way. To work for wages was to be dependent, a "wage slave," that undermined the free labor of the farmer or artisan or producer. The idea, which Lincoln had expressed when he said, "There is no permanent class of hired laborers among us," was to work for a wage for a while, accumulate capital, buy land or tools, and then in turn hire someone else, not to be a wage earner for life. In the late nineteenth century, however, the boundaries became less permeable. "To put a man upon wages is to put him in the position of the dependent," said the *Journal of Social Science* in 1871. One economist warned that the day had arrived when a man "born a laborer, working for hire, [will] never be anything but a laborer."[11]

By 1900, 70 percent of all industrial labor worked for wages for corporations. A new word, "employee," had entered the lexicon. Work became depersonalized, and capitalists, in their effort to increase productivity and decrease costs, introduced piecework and mechanization that led to a decline in skill levels. Workers were paid less and expected to produce more. Managers used stop watches to time their workers and increase efficiency. The capitalists called it "scientific management" and justified their behavior as a "law of competition." In his essay on wealth in 1889, Andrew Carnegie lamented the friction between "the employer and the employed, between capital and labor, between rich and poor." Still, while the law of competition "may be sometimes hard for the individual, it is best for the race, because it insures the survival of the fittest."[12]

"Sometimes hard for the individual" barely hinted at the dangerous conditions and low wages faced by workers who began organizing, campaigning, and striking for their rights. The National Labor Union opposed strikes and instead pressed for legislative changes to improve working conditions, such as an eight-hour workday. By comparison, the Workingmen's Party of the United States, which would morph into the Socialist Labor Party, supported striking workers. When the Baltimore and Ohio Railroad cut wages in 1877, workers in Martinsburg, West Virginia, went on strike. They did more than refuse to work. They not only stopped the trains, they also ripped up rails, tampered with switches, destroyed bridges, and even set trains on fire. The militia was called in and soon railroad workers from New York to Kansas and from Michigan to Texas joined. In Pittsburgh, dozens were killed (strikers, strikebreakers, militia men, cops, bystanders) and buildings were torched. Violence erupted elsewhere and thousands of railroad workers went on strike. The "war between labor and capital has begun in earnest," read an article in the *New Orleans Times*. Americans feared revolution. The strikers were called rioters, a mob bent on mischief. "This insurrection," thought one writer, "presents a state of facts almost as serious as that which prevailed at the outbreak of the Civil War."[13]

The Great Strike of 1877 ended with few gains for the workers, but increased awareness that union organization would be the key to future victory. In its aftermath (President Hayes wrote, "The strikes have been put down by force"), the Knights of Labor, originally a secret organization designed to protect all workers—artisans and farmers in addition to wage earners—saw its influence escalate. By the 1880s, under the leadership of Mayor Terence V. Powderly of Scranton, Pennsylvania, the organization claimed 700,000 members. Although Powderly did not favor strikes, the Knights' support for boycotts, cooperatives, education, and the eight-hour workday made them increasingly popular. Their failure in an 1886 strike against Jay Gould's Union Pacific and Missouri Pacific, in which states used their police power to call out the militia in support of the tycoon, contributed to the Knights' demise.

So, too, the Haymarket Square bombing on May 4, 1886. Following a strike against a McCormick Reaper plant for an eight-hour workday, an outdoor protest in Chicago drew 2,500 people. As police were breaking up the gathering, someone threw a dynamite bomb and the police fired into the crowd. Seven policemen died, as did several protesters. In the aftermath, anti-union sentiment spread, and eight men were tried. These were union organizers, some of whom were self-proclaimed anarchists and socialists and most of whom were not even at the rally. In the end, the state hanged four of them. No one knew who threw the bomb, but journalist John Swinton recognized that it was a "god send to the enemies of the labor movement." Unionism and anarchism became linked and authorities licensed the suppression of radical speech and actions. "There are no good anarchists except dead anarchists," announced the *St. Louis Globe Democrat*.[14]

The corporate and governmental assault on labor did not prevent thousands of strikes and lockouts (when employers refuse to take workers back unless they accept management's terms) from

occurring through the 1880s and 1890s, and a new union emerged
to replace the moribund Knights. The American Federation of Labor
(AFL), formed in 1886, was a national organization that served as an
umbrella for various craft unions that represented skilled workers.
Led by Samuel Gompers, president of the Cigar Makers International
Union Local in New York, the AFL expanded quickly and soon
claimed 500,000 members. Unlike the Knights, the AFL had little
interest in cooperation and collective rights. Gompers focused on
palpable gains in wages and working conditions through collective
bargaining. He argued that reducing the length of the workday
would allow workers to improve themselves and liberate them from
the drudgery of labor. In his 1890 speech, "What Does the Working
Man Want?" Gompers described the cycle of wage slavery: "He is
nothing but a veritable machine. He lives to work instead of working
to live." Workers, he said, needed time, "which brings us from the
lowest condition to the highest civilization." Both business leaders
and union organizers shared this language of evolutionary progress.
Horatio Alger, who wrote popular children's books that forever associated him with the American dream of rags to riches, titled one of
his volumes *Struggling Upward* (1890).[15]

Although within two decades the eight-hour workday had become commonplace, the struggles between capital and labor grew
ever more volatile. The 4,000 steelworkers at Andrew Carnegie's
Homestead works outside of Pittsburgh faced wage cuts and loss of
jobs as management installed open-hearth furnaces that increased
productivity and efficiency. The skilled workers belonged to the
Amalgamated Association of Iron and Steel Workers, a craft union
with 25,000 members nationwide. Carnegie had broken unions
before—in 1888 he locked out workers at the Edgar Thompson
works and brought in Pinkerton guards (a private security force) to
intimidate workers and break the Knights of Labor. And he would try
to break the Amalgamated.

A new contract was to be negotiated in 1892 and everyone knew
a fight was coming. Carnegie left the country for Scotland and placed
Henry Clay Frick in charge. Frick had a fence topped with barbed
wire and fitted with gun openings placed around the mill. Locked-
out workers called it "Fort Frick." When a barge with 300 Pinkertons
tried to land, a battle ensued that resulted in casualties on both sides.
One of the workers killed had been wounded at Gettysburg in 1863.
The Pinkertons retreated and Pennsylvania's governor called in the
militia to defend the strikebreakers. On July 23, Alexander Berkman,
an anarchist unaffiliated with the strikers, entered Frick's office and

fired two shots that hit the business magnate in his ear and neck and stabbed him four times. Frick survived, but the strike and the union did not as public sympathy shifted. Workers labored twelve hours for low wages and faced difficult and dangerous conditions. Death from accidents doubled between 1870 and 1900. A journalist who snuck into Homestead in 1894 described "pits like the mouth of hell" and work that "brutalizes a man."[16]

Like Andrew Carnegie, George Pullman sought to reduce wages and extend working hours. Pullman did more than design and manufacture the railroad sleeping car named after him. He created a company town, Pullman, Illinois, where workers lived. Founded in the early 1880s, the model town had both utopian and dystopian features. Workers on the whole lived better and healthier lives in the town, which featured brick houses, fenced lawns, parks, schools, running water, and a sewer system. "The corporation is everything and everywhere," wrote one journalist. Pullman dictated matters of dress and behavior—only the hotel bar sold alcohol.[17]

The Panic of 1893, a worldwide economic crisis caused by a decline in commodity prices, the failure of numerous railroad companies, and a run on gold, led to massive unemployment, the closing of banks, and the failure of thousands of businesses. When demand for Pullman sleeping cars fell, Pullman slashed wages by nearly 30 percent, but not rents. On May 11, 1894, workers went on strike. The American Railway Union entered the fray and refused to handle Pullman cars nationally. Eugene Debs, who was not yet the socialist leader who would campaign for president, help found the Industrial Workers of the World, and be jailed for sedition during World War I, ran the union. "The strike is the weapon of the oppressed," he wrote in 1888. Although advising restraint, Debs knew the power of his union, and the boycott of Pullman cars led to the paralysis of national railroad traffic.[18]

Across the country, 125,000 workers joined the strike and tied up traffic from Ohio to California. That meant the mails were not being delivered, so the federal government intervened. The attorney general won an injunction by claiming the union had violated the Sherman Anti-Trust Act, passed in 1890 to curtail monopolistic business practices such as Rockefeller's Standard Oil Company as well as railroads, and now applied to labor. President Grover Cleveland ordered federal troops to Chicago. Riots erupted and crowds overturned railroad cars and set fires. More troops arrived and Debs was jailed for violating the injunction. The *New York Times* called him "an enemy of the human race." The strike came to an end, the workers defeated. For Debs the struggle for survival was not over: "the people are aroused . . . and agitation, organization, and unification are to be the future battle cries of men who will not part with their birthrights."[19]

Cooperation

Amid all the struggle and competition, it is little wonder that some envisioned worlds of harmony and cooperation. One of the best-selling works of the era was Edward Bellamy's *Looking Backward*, a utopian novel that imagined a future world in which all the problems of the day were solved. A journalist turned novelist, Bellamy suffered from tuberculosis; the world he foresaw in the future also cured people of illness. Published in 1888, the novel is set in the year 2000. A time-traveler, Julian West, awakes to a world where all social ills have been addressed because of government control and a collectivist spirit. There were no political parties. Women fared as well as men. The nation provided full employment. "Mutual benevolence and disinterestedness" prevailed and the lesson had been learned that "excessive individualism . . . was inconsistent with much public spirit." A dome protected everyone when it rained.[20]

Bellamy's novel touched a nerve. He disavowed the term "socialist." Instead he viewed himself a "nationalist." Nationalist Clubs spread across the land and became politicized. In an address on the first anniversary of the founding of Boston's Nationalist Club, Bellamy warned, "No republic can long exist unless a substantial equality in the wealth of citizens prevails." Bellamy invoked Madison and Hamilton as nationalists. He also argued for women's rights ("put an end to every form of sexual slavery") and black rights. Bellamy's progressive social vision risked encompassing too much and he questioned the wisdom of political involvement. Soon the club's popularity waned as many members decided instead to join a new movement that was gaining traction.

In his speech, Bellamy noted that "the agricultural interests of the country are passing under the yoke of the money power quite as rapidly as the other forms of industry." Buffeted by falling crop prices and lack of affordable credit, and dismayed that neither Republicans nor Democrats were responsive to their needs, farmers banded together to promote their interests. Early organizations were known as the Grange and Patrons of Husbandry (which had over one million members in 1875). In the 1870s Midwestern state legislatures responded to farmers' demands by enacting legislation that regulated the prices railroads charged for storing and transporting agricultural commodities. These state regulatory practices were challenged in court, and in *Munn v. Illinois* (1877) the Supreme Court ruled that states could regulate commerce as a means of protecting the public interest. The federal government also assumed a regulatory function. The Interstate Commerce Act in 1887 and aforementioned Sherman Anti-Trust Act in 1890 prohibited monopolies and attempts to restrain trade.[21]

In the 1880s, farmers began to organize alliances to protect and improve their economic condition. The three most important of these were the National Farmers' Alliance (Southern Alliance), which originated in Texas and spread to much of the South and also had significant support in the Great Plains and the Rocky Mountain states; the identically named National Farmers' Alliance based in Chicago attracted mainly Midwestern farmers; and the Colored Farmers' Alliance, formed in Texas in 1886 and had members in a number of Southern states. These alliances, although independent and varied in their objectives and visions about how to achieve them, sought to defend farmers against declining prices and usurious credit rates. Alliances established their own stores to protect their members from price gouging by landlords and local merchants; they also created their own mills so farmers could get their goods to market less expensively. One of the signature proposals of the alliances was a sub-treasury plan that called for the construction of warehouses by the federal government. Farmers would deposit their crops and receive federal notes for 80 percent of the crop's value in return. The farmers then had a year to sell their crops and pay off the note at 1 percent interest. Under this plan, farmers would be protected from extortion by merchants and could wait for the most propitious time to sell.

When Leonidas Polk, president of the Southern Alliance, testified before the Senate in 1890, he spoke of the crisis of American agriculture in which farmers owned less and less of the total wealth of the country, yet paid an increasingly higher percentage of the taxes. He refuted economists who argued the change was due to "indolence . . . and extravagance" or that it was "God's fault." Rather it resulted from a system of business and taxation that left the farmer in desperate financial straits. Congress did not act on the Sub-Treasury plan.[22]

The demands of the Southern Alliance (now renamed the National Farmers' Alliance and Industrial Union) were embodied in the platform adopted at a meeting in Ocala, Florida, in 1890. In addition to the creation of sub-treasuries, the alliance advocated the abolition of national banks, a graduated income tax, reduction of tariffs, expansion of the money supply, the free coinage of silver, and strong government regulation of railroad and telegraph companies, with government ownership of those industries as a last resort. The Ocala Platform also called for the direct election of US senators by the people instead of state legislatures, which the reformers saw as perpetuating the power and influence of the wealthy.

The alliances did not necessarily begin as political organizations. Meetings served as gathering places and provided an important social outlet. For women, the associations provided relief from the drudgery of everyday life. Women in the Farmer's Alliance could vote and stand for office. They served as lecturers and editors. One Kansas woman was famous for urging farmers to "raise less corn and more hell." Both the Farmer's Alliance and the Colored Alliance promoted self-improvement through education and self-help. Alliance leaders such as Tom Watson of Georgia encouraged biracial cooperation to defeat political elites. "You are kept apart that you may be separately fleeced of your earnings," he explained to farmers, black and white. Increasingly, alliance members won political office: congressmen, senators, governors, and legislators. These Populists, as they called themselves, soon formed the People's Party to contest the two entrenched major parties. Populist state governments were the first to give women the right to vote, Wyoming in 1890 (and as a territory in 1869), Colorado in 1893, and Idaho in 1896.[23]

Meeting in Omaha in 1892, delegates adopted a platform written by Ignatius Donnelly. Born in Pennsylvania, Donnelly moved to Minnesota Territory in 1857, and his skills as a speaker and writer quickly won him election as lieutenant governor and then as a radical Republican member of Congress, where he served from 1863 to 1869. Donnelly then returned to state politics and served in the Minnesota House and Senate. When not advocating populist causes, Donnelly wrote works of fiction and nonfiction, including *The Great Cryptogram* (1888), in which he argued that codes in Shakespeare's work suggested that Francis Bacon was the true author, and *Caesar's Column* (1890), a dystopian novel about class struggle set in the future, where "useless and extravagant luxury" was juxtaposed against the "dreadful homes and working places of the poor." "The luxury of the few; the misery of the many," laments the narrator.[24]

In writing the preamble to the Populist platform, Donnelly summoned all his outrage over a nation "brought to the verge of moral, political, and material ruin." He denounced the power of corporations and a corrupted political process. He lamented the muzzling of newspapers and silencing of public opinion. He despaired over the conditions of labor. "The fruits of the toil of millions," he declared, "are boldly stolen to build up colossal fortunes for a few, unprecedented in the history of mankind. . . . From the same prolific womb of governmental injustice we breed the two great classes— tramps and millionaires."[25]

The party called for public ownership of railroads and telegraphs, a graduated income tax, and the free and unlimited coinage of silver. The Free Silver movement dominated American politics in the era. Farmers and miners in the South, Midwest, and West sought an inflationary monetary policy that favored debtors. The Coinage Act of 1873 had moved the United States to a gold standard, which silver's advocates would later dub "the Crime of '73." Efforts to return to a bimetallic standard succeeded with the passage of the Bland-Allison Act in 1878 (over the veto of Rutherford B. Hayes), which authorized the US Treasury to buy silver and mint silver dollars, although not in sufficient quantities to satisfy inflationists. More legislation followed—in 1890 the Sherman Silver Purchase Act was tied to a new tariff act supported by Republicans. The issue would remain volatile in American politics.

In the presidential election of 1892, Populist candidate James B. Weaver, a former congressman from Iowa who had run in 1880 as the Greenback Party candidate, won more than one million votes and earned electoral votes from six states, including Idaho, Kansas, Colorado, and Nevada. Four years later, the Populist Party united with the Democrats and was subsumed. By then, the Panic of 1893 had devastated the nation. The treasury fell below the minimum gold reserve needed to maintain economic confidence and the price of silver also plummeted. Businesses and banks began to fail. The money supply shrank, interest rates climbed, and unemployment reached 19 percent. Henry Adams wrote, "Men died like flies under the strain, and Boston grew suddenly old, haggard, and thin." Eventually, a private citizen saved the economy. J. P. Morgan, capitalist hero or robber baron depending on one's view, traveled to Washington, met with President Cleveland, and offered to form a syndicate that would purchase treasury bonds with gold. The government remained solvent and confidence was restored. Henry Adams wanted Morgan to run for president.[26]

The election of 1896 found the issue of gold versus silver still very much alive. The election pitted Ohio Governor William McKinley against Nebraska Congressman William Jennings Bryan. McKinley and the Republicans had the support of businessmen, the professional classes, and affluent merchants and farmers in the Northeast and Midwest. Bryan spoke for the working classes and poor farmers in the South, rural areas, and the Rocky Mountain region. At the nominating convention, Bryan gave an electrifying speech in support of silver, proclaiming, famously, that "you shall not press down upon the brow of labor this crown of thorns; you shall not crucify mankind on a cross of gold." Only thirty-six years old, Bryan remains the youngest presidential nominee of a major party. McKinley won the Electoral College and popular vote. In 1900 he signed the Gold Standard Act.[27]

Silver versus gold had its own real financial implications; it also stood as a substitute for labor versus capital, farmers versus railroads, debt versus profit, and a variety of other social and class divisions. The cooperative, populist dream would live on as a fairy tale. In 1900, L. Frank Baum published *The Wonderful Wizard of Oz*, a parable about the struggle to unite farmers (the Scarecrow) and workers (the Tinman) and give them courage (the Cowardly Lion) to take on the capitalist witches of East and West. Oz is a utopia with problems, and Dorothy speaks for the values of home and exposes the bombast of the phony Wizard. Her slippers are silver. They cross the yellow brick road (gold) and alone have the power to return her happily to Kansas. Baum churned out sequels until his death in 1919. In 1939, Hollywood, oblivious to the populist parable, made the slippers ruby; they looked better that way in Technicolor.

Frontiers

Baum found inspiration for his Emerald City in the White City of Chicago's Columbian Exposition in 1893. The exposition covered 600 acres and included pavilions from 46 countries. Exhibits ranged from flowers in the horticultural display to artillery in the Krupp pavilion. An area of the exposition contained brilliant white buildings of stucco and alabaster—a white city—illuminated by electricity at night (Nikola Tesla and George Westinghouse's alternating current beat out Thomas Edison's direct current for the contract). The buildings were shells: gorgeous on the outside, hollow on the inside. By the time it closed toward year's end, 27 million people had made their way to Chicago for the once-in-a-lifetime event. For the exposition, Francis Bellamy, Edward's cousin, a Christian socialist and the editor of the *Youth's Companion*, composed a Pledge of Allegiance to the flag and "the Republic for which it stands" ("under God" would be added in 1954).

Mark Twain was one of the many who made their way to Chicago to see the exposition, but he never made it to the grounds as he took ill and spent his visit convalescing at his hotel. In *The Adventures of Huckleberry Finn* (1884), Huck decides at the end to "light out for the Territory ahead of the rest," to leave behind the conflict and chaos of civilization for the freedom of the frontier. Twain might have been shocked to hear the historian Frederick Jackson Turner declare in a paper read at the exposition that the frontier was closed and that an open line of settlement no longer existed. Turner argued that settling the frontier had helped create American democracy, and he emphasized the qualities of individualism, strength, and perseverance in the American character. In fact, cooperation among settlers mattered as much as individualism. However, it was his assertion that expansion had made America that held greatest sway. In any case, the frontier was now settled and closed; Huck Finn would find no respite there.

It was apt for the exposition to be held in Chicago. Since the fire of 1871 destroyed the city, the middle border of the Midwest had become central to the nation's growth. Indeed, between 1870 and 1900, the mean center of the nation's population moved 121 miles west from Ohio to central Indiana. It was no accident that Ulysses S. Grant, Rutherford B. Hayes, James A. Garfield, Benjamin Harrison, and William McKinley all hailed from Ohio. Since Lincoln had become president, Nevada, Nebraska, Colorado, the Dakotas, Montana, Washington, Idaho, and Wyoming had joined the Union. At the exposition, four territories—Arizona, New Mexico, Oklahoma, and Utah—had pavilions.[28]

In the decades following the Civil War, government had focused on the South. Now it was the frontier West that drew more attention and resources. Making the West safe for railroad building, gold-discovering, and people settling meant waging war against Native tribes, making life for them more unsafe. In some ways, there had never been a halt in the battles against Indians that began well before the American Revolution. Native Americans in Indian Territory did not help themselves by siding for the most part with the Confederacy during the Civil War.

During the Civil War, a US-Dakota War in Minnesota in 1862 led to the largest mass execution in US history as Lincoln signed off on death warrants for thirty-eight warriors (he also commuted the death sentence of 268 others). In Colorado in 1864, the Union

Army, trying to protect gold prospectors, ordered the Cheyenne and Arapaho to relocate. When they refused, the men of the Third Colorado Cavalry under Colonel John Chivington attacked a village under Cheyenne Chief Black Kettle at Sand Creek in eastern Colorado and slaughtered and mutilated dozens of women and children. The Sioux united with the Cheyenne and Arapaho to keep their homelands. Red Cloud warned, "There are now white people all about me. I have but a small spot of land left. The Great Spirit told me to keep it." In December 1866, near Fort Kearney in Montana Territory, Red Cloud and his leading lieutenant Crazy Horse set a trap into which Captain William Fetterman foolishly marched. Fetterman had boasted that "with eighty men I could ride through the Sioux nation." On the Lodge Trail Ridge, Fetterman found himself confronting some 2,000 warriors. His eighty-one men were killed and Fetterman was found with his throat cut and a bullet in his head.[29]

After the Civil War, first William Tecumseh Sherman and then Phil Sheridan took command of the Military Division of the Missouri. Sherman's middle name may have come from an Indian prophet, yet he held no sympathy for the Sioux, against whom, he said, "we must act with vindictive earnestness . . . even to their extermination: men, women, and children." Sheridan gave epigrammatic voice to the justification for annihilation: "the only good Indians I ever saw were dead."[30]

Red Cloud's War in the Powder River country of Wyoming ended with the Treaty of Fort Laramie in 1868. Like so many before it, the treaty did not hold. Told that his people could not trade at Fort Leavenworth and that the army would not abandon Fort Fetterman on the North Platte River and dismayed at the lack of game and the harshness of conditions in the remaining Indian territory, Red Cloud traveled to Washington to meet with President Grant. Red Cloud told Secretary of the Interior Jacob D. Cox, "Our nation is melting away like the snow on the side of the hills where the sun is warm, while your people are like the blades of grass in spring when summer is coming."[31]

Red Cloud and the Oglala Lakota whom he led eventually agreed to deal with US agents, who issued rations and annuities, and to settle on a reservation. Red Cloud may have accepted agency life. Other Lakota tribes did not. Led by chief Sitting Bull and warrior Crazy Horse, the Sioux and Northern Cheyenne allied in battle after gold was discovered in the Black Hills of South Dakota and the government refused to take action against the thousands of prospectors who illegally occupied the territory. In 1876, the US government sought to take ownership of the land.

Several battles were fought in the summer of 1876, none more infamous than the Battle of Little Big Horn on June 25. Lieutenant Colonel George Armstrong Custer, twenty-seven years old, commanded the Seventh Cavalry. He had graduated last in his class from West Point in 1861, but distinguished himself during the Civil War at Gettysburg and throughout Sheridan's Shenandoah Campaign in 1864. Custer set out with 660 men, confidant that the Seventh Cavalry "can whip anything it meets."[32]

Against the advice of a Crow scout, Custer followed common military practice and divided his regiment. And then he divided his five companies. Hundreds of warriors enveloped Custer and his men. Some soldiers tried to surrender. Others committed suicide. Custer was shot in the chest and temple; his brother Tom Custer was killed a few feet away. His youngest brother, Boston, was also killed, along with his brother-in-law and nephew. None of the men of his five companies survived. The battle is often referred to as Custer's Last Stand; it turned out to be the Sioux's last stand as well. In the aftermath, the US government forced the Sioux to cede the Black Hills. Sitting Bull led many Lakota to Canada. Crazy Horse was bayonetted by a guard at Fort Robinson and died September 5, 1877.

The Sioux had been defeated. Crazy Horse had surrendered the previous May, and, at the same time, the Nez Perce found themselves under siege. Bands of Nez Perce who refused to surrender their lands in the Pacific Northwest battled the army in a number of contests before surrendering on October 5, 1877. General O. O. Howard (who chased the Nez Perce on a retreat of 1,700 miles and showed such hesitation that the Indians dubbed him Day After Tomorrow Howard) had promised the Nez Perce that they could return to their reservation. Sherman, however, had them sent to Fort Leavenworth in Kansas. On surrendering, Chief Joseph gave the speech for which he is remembered. "I want to have time to look for my children and see how many of them I can find. Maybe I shall find them among the dead. Hear me, my chiefs, my heart is sick and sad. From where the sun now stands I will fight no more forever."[33]

Like Red Cloud before him, Chief Joseph went to Washington to plead for his people. "Let me be a free man," he implored, "free to travel, free to stop, free to work, free to trade where I choose, free to choose my own teachers, free to follow the religion of my fathers, free to talk, think and act for myself—and I will obey every law or submit to the penalty." He would continue to plead for his people

Figure 6.2 Edward Curtis, *Chief Joseph* (ca. 1903). Library of Congress.

until his death in 1904, having never returned to his homeland in the Wallowa valley of northern Oregon.[34]

More capitulations would follow: Chief Little Wolf of the Northern Cheyenne surrendered in 1879; Sitting Bull returned from Canada and surrendered in 1881; Apache leader Geronimo would surrender, then reject reservation life to continue warfare in the southwest before surrendering for good in 1886. Geronimo was imprisoned at Fort Pickens, Florida, relocated to Mt. Vernon Barracks in Alabama, and in 1894 was transferred to Fort Sill, Oklahoma.

The 1890 events at Wounded Knee Creek on the Pine Ridge Reservation in South Dakota marked an end to the Indian Wars in the West, though fighting continued into the twentieth century. Authorities worried about a spiritual revival among Indians who performed the Ghost Dance. On December 29, 1890, soldiers chased and fired upon a Sioux band led by Chief Big Foot (Spotted Elk). Among the army's weapons was a machine gun. In the end, more than 200 mostly unarmed men, women, and children were killed or wounded. Black Elk recalled in 1932: "When I look back now from this high hill of my old age, I can still see the butchered women and children lying heaped and scattered all along the crooked gulch as plain as when I saw them with eyes still young. And I can see that something else died there in the bloody mud, and was buried in the blizzard. A people's dream died there."[35]

In the late nineteenth century, popular culture turned the tragedy of the wars against Indians into farce. In 1883, William F. Cody, frontier scout and buffalo hunter, opened Buffalo Bill's Wild West. Audiences gathered to witness displays of sharp shooting and tableaux of civilized versus savage life. Dramas were performed, including "Custer's Last Stand." Cody hired Indians to perform and enact savage attacks upon settlers. The moral was always that civilization had won out. Sitting Bull toured for one season and Geronimo joined a competing show. Audiences flocked to see actual Indians in full headdress and war paint. In 1893, Cody was denied permission to perform at the Columbian Exposition, so he staged the show on a lot he leased nearby. More than 300 performances, each drawing an average of 16,000 viewers, were attended by more than 5 million people.

Imperialism

Theodore Roosevelt loved the West. In 1883, the twenty-five-year-old New York assemblyman traveled to the Dakota Territory to hunt buffalo. The herds that once roamed the prairie and sustained Indian society were largely gone, victims of greed and hunting expeditions. The US Army also began indiscriminately killing buffalo, believing that doing so would help defeat the Indians. Millions of hides were shipped east, the meat left to spoil. By 1880, perhaps fewer than 2,000 buffalo remained on the plains.

Roosevelt was not to be denied. He finally tracked a buffalo and shot it, shipping its head back east to hang at his Sagamore Hill home. After his mother and wife died on the same day in 1884, Roosevelt returned to live in the Badlands, where he opened a cattle ranch, continued to hunt, and wrote about the West. An asthmatic child, Roosevelt had always embraced a vigorous life where strength and masculinity trumped all. He lived Darwin's lesson of the struggle for survival—and carried a copy of *Origin of Species* on his bird-viewing journeys. Other races struck him as inferior. In a speech delivered in 1886 he said, "I don't go so far as to think that the only good Indians are the dead Indians, but I believe nine out of every ten are, and I shouldn't like to inquire too closely into the case of the tenth." In

The Winning of the West (1889) he wrote, "The truth is, the Indians never had any real title to the soil."[36]

With the continental United States settled, and Alaska annexed in 1867, some Americans began to look overseas for new conquests. They did so for a variety of reasons: the search for new markets, the belief in Anglo-Saxon racial superiority, missionary zeal, an ardor for spreading American democratic institutions, a diversion from attention on domestic problems, and the desire to become a world power. In 1869, Ulysses S. Grant sought to annex Santo Domingo (in part as a place for free blacks to settle), but the Senate rejected the treaty. In 1893, American businessmen in Hawaii sought to protect their investments in the sugar industry and staged a coup in hopes of encouraging the United States to annex the country. A treaty that came before the Senate expired when President Cleveland objected to it. American attitudes would change, and Hawaii was annexed in 1898 and made a territory in 1900. Sanford Dole, a lawyer who in 1893 had helped depose Queen Liliuokalani, a Hawaiian noble whose reign lasted two years, became governor.

By 1898, some Americans clearly were itching for a war. "I should welcome almost any war," wrote Theodore Roosevelt, "for I think this country needs one." In saying so he was informed by Alfred Thayer Mahan's *The Influence of Sea Power Upon History, 1600–1783* (1890). Mahan argued for imperial ambitions and asserted that nothing was more important than a strong navy with a fleet of warships stationed around the globe. Mahan defended imperialism in terms of national self-interest and balance of power. In his autobiography he wrote, "I am frankly an imperialist, in the sense that I believe that no nation, certainly no great nation, should henceforth maintain the policy of isolation which fitted our early history."[37]

If Mahan provided the rationale, journalists provided the impetus. Joseph Pulitzer's *New York World* and William Randolph Hearst's *New York Journal* published sensationalist stories about the actions of the Spanish against insurgents in Cuba who were seeking independence. Articles describing murder, rape, and pillage of the Cubans, and dastardly treatment of Americans, helped inflame public opinion against the Spanish and edge the United States toward war. Hearst reportedly told one artist who was sending drawings back from Cuba and predicting there would be no war, "you furnish the pictures, and I'll furnish the war."[38]

On February 15, 1898, the battleship *USS Maine* exploded outside Havana Harbor. Hearst and others published reports stating that the Spanish had torpedoed the ship. Whether the cause was a mine or spontaneous combustion (McKinley received a report saying it was an external explosion and various inquiries over the decades reached both conclusions), Americans now had a reason to wage the war they desired. "Remember the Maine!" became a rallying cry. McKinley, the last president to have served in the Civil War, expressed reluctance. Ultimately, on April 11, he asked Congress to declare war. He gave four reasons: a humanitarian obligation "to end the barbarities"; protection of American citizens in Cuba; the right to intervene to protect commerce and trade; and the proximity of Cuba to the United States, which provided additional reason to seek a peaceful neighbor not in the throes of revolution. On April 25, Congress declared war, though not before first adopting the Teller Amendment, proposed by Henry Teller of Colorado, which declared the United States would not annex Cuba but instead leave its governance to its people.

The war lasted four months. John Hay, soon to be secretary of state, wrote in July: "It has been a splendid little war, begun with the highest motives, carried on with magnificent intelligence and spirit, favored by that Fortune which loves the brave." The letter's recipient was Roosevelt, assistant secretary of the navy, who couldn't agree more. Age forty, Roosevelt resigned his position and formed a volunteer company, the First US Volunteer Cavalry Regiment, known as the Rough Riders. At the Battle of San Juan Hill on July 1, he led his men to victory. Two days later, the Spanish Caribbean squadron, attempting to escape Santiago Bay, was destroyed by blockading US naval vessels. Two months earlier, Commodore George Dewey's Asiatic squadron had defeated a Spanish squadron in Manila Bay, and US troops occupied Manila in August 1898.[39]

The possible annexation of the Philippines led to the formation of the Anti-Imperialist League. At its peak, the league enrolled 30,000 members, among them many prominent Americans who cut across political and cultural lines. Carl Schurz, a leading Republican, condemned American imperialism. Humanity, not conquest, he said, should be the purpose of American wars. Expansion to contiguous land was one thing; involvement in the western Pacific, thousands of miles away, where only races suitable to the tropics could thrive, was another. Grover Cleveland, the only Democrat elected president between 1860 and 1912, also opposed annexation of the Philippines as a violation of the fundamental principles of democratic self-government. While some capitalists favored the expansion of markets through territorial acquisitions, Andrew Carnegie, for one, opposed American imperialism, believing that it represented despotism, not democracy, diluted the homogeneity of the Anglo-Saxon nation, opened the nation to attack, and drained resources. Samuel Gompers also used a racial argument to inveigh against imperialism as a threat to American labor: these new territories would open the door to "the hordes of Chinese and semi-savage races." Mark Twain did not share the racial animosities of others. He became a leading opponent of imperialism and served as vice president of the league from 1901 until his death in 1910. "I have read carefully the treaty of Paris," he said, "and I have seen that we do not intend to free, but to subjugate the people of the Philippines. . . . I am opposed to having the eagle put its talons on any other land."[40]

Under the terms of the Treaty of Paris, signed on December 10, 1898, Spain recognized Cuba's independence, ceded Puerto Rico and Guam to the United States, and sold the Philippine islands for $20 million. The Senate debate over ratification lasted until February. Opponents, such as Senator George Frisbie Hoar of Massachusetts, had earlier insisted that acquiring foreign lands "will make us into a vulgar, commonplace empire." Henry Johnson of Indiana was more concerned with tax-free imports flooding American markets and injuring farmers and laborers. Senator Knute Nelson of Minnesota spoke for many when he insisted that the United States had the "duty of extending Christian civilization," and Henry Cabot Lodge of Massachusetts warned that if the treaty was rejected it would

Figure 6.3 "School Begins," *Puck* (1899). Library of Congress.

brand Americans as "a people incapable of great affairs or of taking rank . . . as one of the greatest of the great world powers." Indiana Senator Albert J. Beveridge believed the Philippines would offer "all the profit, all the glory, all the happiness possible to man." On February 6, 1899, the Senate ratified the treaty by a vote of 57–27.[41]

Two days before ratification, an insurrection against US forces began in the Philippines. It was a brutal contest that descended into guerilla war and led to atrocities on both sides. American troops used water torture and massacred women and children; Filipino troops mistreated prisoners and mutilated dead bodies. Mark Twain called the US troops "uniformed assassins." Activist Josephine Shaw Lowell lamented that "not only can no moral good come from such a war, but great moral evil must ensue." And Jane Addams, already gaining fame for her social work in Chicago, emerged as a visible and vocal leader of the Anti-Imperialist League. In an address presented in 1899, she argued that it came down to a choice between "Democracy or Militarism" and reminded listeners and readers that "national events determine our ideals, as much as our ideals determine national events." (Addams would win the Nobel peace prize in 1931.) Filipino civilian deaths ran into the hundreds of thousands. US forces lost 4,200 men and Filipino insurgents more than 20,000. When the war ended in 1902, Congress passed a Philippine Organic Act that, among other provisions, disestablished the Catholic Church. In 1907, even the formerly bullish Theodore Roosevelt conceded, "The Philippines form our heel of Achilles."[42]

In 1899, however, he had no doubts. In a speech delivered in Chicago on April 10, 1899, Roosevelt acknowledged problems in the Philippines but thought it cowardly to shrink from them. America had a responsibility to play its part in "uplifting mankind," especially in a land with so many "half-caste and native Christians, warlike Moslems, and wild pagans" who were unfit for self-government. Responsibility to the Philippines formed only part of the speech, however. Roosevelt sounded the keynote in the opening: "I wish to preach, not the doctrine of ignoble ease, but the doctrine of the strenuous life, the life of toil and effort, of labor and strife." Success, he claimed, came from embracing danger and hardship and trial. Only then could one win a "splendid ultimate triumph."[43]

Struggle, competition, strife, and strength, not ease, laziness, timidity, or cowardice, formed Roosevelt's formula for American triumph and success. The speech became a national sensation. A newspaper editor called him "the coming American of the twentieth century." The GOP nominated him for vice president in 1900 and when McKinley was assassinated on September 6, 1901, Roosevelt became president and served for the first decade of the twentieth century.[44]

In 1904, Roosevelt used the telegraph to officially open the Louisiana Purchase Exposition, informally known as the St. Louis World's Fair. It had been one hundred years since the Louisiana Purchase and the exposition hoped to recreate the success of the Columbian Exposition on a smaller scale. New modes of transportation, including the automobile, were on display. The X-ray machine made its debut at the fair. There was even a wireless telephone, a radiophone created by Alexander Graham Bell.

As a counterpoint to American progress, other exhibits presented examples of uncivilized life: people from the Philippines, Puerto Rico, and Guam were placed on display, exotics to be marveled over, an example of what British poet Rudyard Kipling called "the White Man's Burden." In another exhibit, an Apache village featured Indians who made pottery and bows and arrows. The star attraction was Geronimo. The following year, the aging warrior rode down Pennsylvania Avenue in full headdress for Theodore Roosevelt's inauguration. Geronimo asked the president to allow him to leave Fort Sill and return to his native land in Arizona. Roosevelt denied his request and Geronimo lived out his life in Oklahoma, a farmer, a Christian, a celebrity, and a stranger in his own land.

CHAPTER 7

Land of Promise

I N 1914, CHARLIE CHAPLIN INTRODUCED his screen persona, the Tramp. With baggy pants and tight-fitting coat, small
derby hat, and large floppy shoes, the Tramp was a waddling
contradiction. He was the graceful immigrant, the dignified factory
worker, and the romantic wanderer. Chaplin's Tramp became uni-
versally beloved. He combined pathos and slapstick to emerge from
difficult situations as a hero, the outsider who stood up for fairness
and justice, who battled authoritarianism and the forces of hate. He
spoke to millions of American immigrants and workers in search of
a better life. With World War I, Chaplin, who was British but made
his films in the United States, faced criticism for his pacifist stance.
In 1918 he made a film, *Shoulder Arms,* in which the Tramp finds
himself in the trenches and captures the Kaiser. "It's dangerous at
this time to make fun of the war," warned Hollywood mogul Cecil
B. DeMille. The result was an uproarious success among soldiers and
civilians alike. Decades later, Chaplin would be accused of being un-
American and banned from the country, but Americans saw their
own indomitable spirit in the Tramp.[1]

Immigration

On October 28, 1886, President Grover Cleveland dedicated the
Statue of Liberty. A gift from France in recognition of the country's
alliance with the United States during the American Revolution in
the cause of liberty, the 151-foot statue was shipped from France

in pieces and reassembled in New York. In 1876, at the Centennial Philadelphia Exposition, the disembodied arm holding the torch was exhibited and visitors could buy tickets to climb an internal ladder up to the torch. Funds for the statue's pedestal were slow to accumulate, though a number of auctions helped raise funds. At one of these, Emma Lazarus donated her poem "The New Colossus." It sold for $1,500. Lazarus died in 1887, and in 1903 the words of her sonnet were inscribed on a bronze plaque added to the pedestal. It ends:

> Give me your tired, your poor,
> Your huddled masses yearning to breathe free,
> The wretched refuse of your teeming shore.
> Send these, the homeless, tempest-tost to me,
> I lift my lamp beside the golden door!

Here was a reiteration and reaffirmation of the meaning of America as a land of dreams for all who arrived and as a beacon of light for the world's oppressed.

"Liberty Enlightening the World," the official name of the statue, quickly became a monument to immigration. Between 1880 and 1920, more than 20 million people poured into the United States. In 1882, 789,000 immigrants arrived, the most in one year since 1854, when 427,000 had landed (leading Walt Whitman to describe America as a "teeming nation of nations"), and until 1991, when 1.8 million came. In the first decade of the twentieth century alone, more than 8 million foreigners emigrated, pushing the foreign-born percentage of the American population to an all-time high of 14.7 percent. (After falling to 4.7 percent in 1970, the percentage rose to 12.9 percent in 2010). The majority of these immigrants arrived from Central, Southern, and Eastern Europe—Russia, Austria-Hungary, Poland, Italy, and Greece, for example—and many passed the Statue of Liberty on their way through the processing center at Ellis Island, which opened in 1892 in New York Harbor.

The immigrants who came to the United States were part of a worldwide mass migration from Europe. They were young: only 8 percent were over forty years of age and 16 percent were younger than fifteen. Most came as individuals, prepared to take advantage of the opportunities America provided. Every story was a particular one, yet some generalizations can be made about the reasons for emigrating. People left countries with crowded labor markets and a low standard of living in search of work and higher wages. They left countries convulsed by famine, religious persecution, and political unrest. Push factors such as these were complemented by pull factors: jobs in factories, available tracts of land, and encouragement from those who had already made the journey, not to mention European agents whose job it was to promote emigration. The door might not be golden, as Emma Lazarus suggested, but it was open and inviting. For many immigrants, despite the hardships, America was the Promised Land, a phrase taken from the title of Belarus-born activist Mary Antin's autobiography, which begins, "I was born. I have lived, and I have been made over."[2]

Not everyone stayed, and return migration forms an overlooked part of the overall story. Some immigrants came to make enough money to go back home, and many of them did exactly that. Others discovered that the promise of America was not as advertised. Southern European immigrants often returned to Italy, Slovenia, and Croatia, sometimes at rates of more than 50 percent. Russian Jews were the least likely to return, as were women, who found far greater freedom in America. One immigrant, miserable over dehumanizing factory work and impoverished conditions, wrote, "It would have been better if I had gotten lost; it would have been better if I had drowned at sea; that is how it is in America." He planned to return home.[3]

Immigrants also faced fervent anti-immigration sentiment. Anxiety over Chinese immigration led quickly to restriction and marks the beginning of federal regulation and immigrant exclusion in the late nineteenth century. Thousands of Chinese immigrants arrived in California during the gold rush of 1848, and many of them remained to provide inexpensive labor, building the railroads and opening businesses such as laundries. Anti-Chinese politics in California flourished, fueled by the rhetoric of men such as Denis Kearney, himself an Irish immigrant and a leader of the Workingmen's Party. Kearney described the Chinese as "cheap slaves" who took jobs from natives. "California must be all American or all Chinese," he insisted. Henry George, a social theorist whose book *Poverty and Progress* became a bestseller in the 1880s, denounced the Chinese as "utter heathens, treacherous, sensual, cowardly." "The Chinese Must Go" became an American anthem, and in 1882 Congress passed the Chinese Exclusion Act, which prohibited Chinese laborers, skilled or unskilled, from entering the United States. (Laws prohibiting the Chinese would be extended until 1943.) Senator George Frisbie

Hoar of Massachusetts denounced the act as "nothing less than the legalization of racial discrimination."[4]

Moving beyond the Chinese to new immigrants arriving from Southern and Eastern Europe, a group in Boston in 1894 founded the Immigration Restriction League. Soon branches popped up across the nation. Under the legislative direction of Senator Henry Cabot Lodge, the organization supported a literacy test for admission. Grover Cleveland vetoed one of these bills, calling it "illiberal, narrow, and un-American." The Immigration Restriction League persisted and went beyond literacy. Prescott Hall, a Harvard graduate and one of the league's founders, supported the growing eugenics movement, which proposed more than just anti-immigration legislation: several states passed sterilization laws to prevent immigrants (as well as criminals and those seen as mentally compromised) from having children. "Eugenics," he said, "is encouraging the propagation of the fit, and limiting or preventing the multiplication of the unfit." Anti-immigration legislation culminated in the Immigration Act of 1924, which based a national origins quota on the census of 1890 and reduced quotas established in 1921 for Southern and Eastern European immigrants, maintained a literacy test first enacted in 1917, and excluded Asian immigration entirely.[5]

Opposition to immigration from Southern and Eastern Europe as well as China was fueled not only by anxiety over economic competition and racial prejudice but by a greater concern over the effect of immigrants on American society and democracy. Were these immigrants, as a Joint Congressional Committee on Chinese Immigration put it in 1877, "an indigestible mass in the community, distinct in language, pagan in religion [and] inferior in mental and moral qualities," or could they assimilate and become Americans? So concerned was Congress over this question that in 1907 it convened an immigration commission (known as the Dillingham Commission after its chairman, Republican Senator William P. Dillingham of Vermont). The commission's report was issued four years later. It ran forty-one volumes and included a dictionary of races and people and recommendations for restrictions on immigration.[6]

The assimilation argument in support of immigration was given its catchphrase in a play first performed in 1908 called *The Melting Pot*. Written by Israel Zangwill, the play tells the story of a Jewish immigrant who flees a Russian pogrom and, in America, falls in love with the immigrant daughter of the man responsible for his family's death. At the end, the protagonist exults, "Celt and Latin, Slav and

Teuton, Greek and Syrian,—black and yellow . . . how the great Alchemist melts and fuses them with his purging flame."[7]

Teddy Roosevelt admired the play. A few years later, he gave a speech in which he denounced those who wanted to hold onto their non-American identities. "There is no room in this country for hyphenated Americanism," he declared. Roosevelt's speech came during World War I and he directed it at German Americans as much as anyone else. He insisted on a single American identity unchanged by those melting into it and committed to the idea that "our nation was founded to perpetuate democratic principles."[8]

Others, however, viewed the cultural identities of the immigrants as a virtue and made the case not for assimilation but for pluralism. In "Democracy versus the Melting Pot," Horace Kallen, who had immigrated to the United States in 1887 and studied philosophy at Harvard and Oxford, served as a professor at the University of Wisconsin, and helped found the New School in New York, advocated for cultural pluralism. Pride of origin, he argued, was evidence of Americanization, not a refutation of it. "The most eagerly American of the immigrant groups are also the most autonomous and self-conscious in spirit and culture." In liberating nationality, Americanization made not for assimilation or the creation of a melting pot, but for a vibrant vernacular culture. Life, Kallen said, does not unify, it diversifies. He called the American republic "a democracy of nationalities," and used the metaphor of an orchestra to describe its richness of tone.[9]

Theoretical questions about assimilation versus pluralism revealed little about the actual lives of immigrants. Photographs seemed to provide a different perspective, and none had a greater impact than those by Jacob Riis, who had emigrated from Denmark in 1870. Riis went to work as a police reporter for the *New York Tribune* and scoured the slums and tenements of the Lower East Side, filled with immigrants who lived and worked crowded together in squalid conditions. His articles brought attention to the plight of these immigrants, and he knew photographs might have an even greater effect. He taught himself how to use a camera and took advantage of a new technology, flash powder, which illuminated dark spaces. The result of his efforts was the book *How the Other Half Lives*. Published in 1890, it is the first work to include photographs, rather than re-engravings, in the text.

Riis's work became a sensation. In part because it provided a voyeuristic tour for the affluent classes who could now remotely enter spaces they studiously avoided. More important, his efforts led to

Figure 7.1 Jacob Riis, *Home of an Italian Ragpicker* (1894). Museum of the City of New York.

changes. "Penury and poverty are wedded everywhere to dirt and disease," he wrote. Dismayed by the wretched condition in which more than a million New Yorkers lived, politicians responded by creating a Tenement House Commission that made recommendations on design, safety, and sanitation. Riis's depiction of children who spent their days picking bones and sorting filthy rags led to enforcement of new public health laws and the creation of playgrounds and parks. Riis's text often displayed his own ethnic and racial prejudices (he compared Jews to the Hottentots). He became a leading public lecturer and social reformer, and titled his autobiography *The Making of an American* (1901). His friend Teddy Roosevelt, who as New York's police commissioner in 1895 took a walking tour with Riis and promised to enact reforms, called him "the most useful citizen of New York."[10]

Progressivism

"Useful" was a high compliment from a person more interested in results than abstractions. At Harvard, one of Roosevelt's professors was William James, whose philosophy of pragmatism supported efforts to transform society and politics. James argued that truth was measured by how useful it was to the believer. Pragmatism was a method for approaching the world by which the value of ideas was judged by its "practical cash-value," as apt a metaphor for the age of capital as any. Pragmatism, James argued in his 1906 lecture "What Pragmatism Means," "appears less as a solution, then, than as a program for more work, and more particularly as an indication of the ways in which existing realities may be changed."[11]

Changing existing realities was the essence of progressivism, and it began with a new journalism and literature that sought to expose social ills and evils. Riis's *How the Other Half Lives* was part of an emerging investigative ethos. Much of this work first appeared in magazines such as *Collier's Weekly* and *McClure's Magazine*. Ida Tarbell, the only woman in her graduating class at Allegheny College, wrote a piercing exposé of John D. Rockefeller and the Standard Oil Company; Lincoln Steffens, a New York reporter, investigated corrupt municipal politics in several cities; Ray Stannard Baker, who began his career at the *Chicago News-Record* before joining *McClure's*, interviewed miners who chose not to strike and reported on their struggles. Roosevelt coined a term for these writers: muckrakers, taken from John Bunyan's *Pilgrim's Progress*, in which "the Man with the Muck Rake . . . fixes his eyes with solemn intentness only on that which is vile and debasing."

Although these journalists were influential, it was a work of fiction that generated national outrage by exposing the work conditions under which immigrants labored. Upton Sinclair's *The Jungle* (1906) tells the story of Jurgis Rudkus, a Lithuanian immigrant who works in a slaughterhouse in Chicago's meatpacking district. Sinclair would go on to a prolific career as a writer and as a socialist activist. None of his works, however, had greater impact than the *The Jungle*, which he wrote after spending six months investigating conditions in the stockyards. Sinclair exposed the exploitative labor system that left immigrant workers in poverty and wage slavery—how the company cheated men out of pay, kept speeding up the assembly line, and allowed sick workers to handle the meat. The public, however, focused less on the workers than on the unsanitary conditions. In a typical passage, Sinclair explained, "There were cattle which had been fed on 'whiskey-malt,' the refuse of the breweries, and had become what the men called 'steerly'—which means covered with boils. It was a nasty job killing these, for when you plunged your knife into them they would burst and splash foul-smelling stuff into your face; and when a man's sleeves were smeared with blood, and his hands steeped in it, how was he ever to wipe his face, or to clear his eyes so that he could see?"[12]

The public demanded action. Roosevelt invited Sinclair to the White House and ordered an investigation of the industry. The president's personal dislike of Sinclair (he called him "hysterical, unbalanced, and untruthful") did not prevent him in 1906 from shepherding through the Meat Inspection Act, which authorized federal inspectors to prevent rancid meat from being processed, and the Pure Food and Drug Act, which regulated additives and labeling. Federal regulation became a hallmark of the Progressive Era. As for Sinclair, he lamented, "I aimed at the public's heart and by accident I hit it in the stomach."[13]

Whereas Sinclair focused on working conditions in Chicago, the reformer Jane Addams focused on living conditions. In 1889, she and Ellen Gates Starr opened Hull-House on Chicago's West Side, in the middle of a crowded immigrant neighborhood. Hull-House was part of a transatlantic settlement movement that featured middle-class female residents living and working in poor neighborhoods. The goal was both utopian and practical, nothing less than "to aid in the solution of the social and industrial problems which are engendered by the modern condition of life in a great city." Hull-House provided education, recreation, and charity for those immigrants who lived in the community. Its residents advocated for child labor and safety and health laws as well. While concerned with the urban poor in general, Addams focused on immigrants. In 1908 she founded the Immigrants Protective League, which sought to help new arrivals to the United States locate relatives and jobs. Working against those who would impose restrictions on immigrants and treat them as a cancer, the philanthropists and social workers of Hull-House and the league argued that as a matter of self-respect and humanity, the nation must provide newcomers with "the best possible impression of those who are to be their fellow-citizens." By 1920, hundreds of settlement houses populated cities across the country.[14]

The flip side of overcrowded cities teeming with people living in unsanitary conditions was a growing appreciation for the environment and preservation of natural resources. Conservation became a hallmark of the Progressive moment and Roosevelt's presidency. He created the National Conservation Commission and explained that government must ensure the well-being of the nation, and to destroy its resources would be to "degrade the standard of living or deprive the coming generations of their right to life on this continent." Roosevelt established 230 million acres of public lands, designated numerous national monuments, and signed legislation that created five national parks and wildlife refuges. Environmentalists differed on how best to manage public lands. John Muir, America's leading naturalist and founder of the Sierra Club in 1892, desired preservation, whereas Gifford Pinchot, the first chief of the US Forest Service, advocated conservation. In the end, both approaches gained purchase.[15]

By 1903, when the first World Series was played, a love of the outdoors helped make baseball the national pastime. Roosevelt appreciated how the game promoted "athletic exercise, manly outdoor sports, and healthy muscular amusements." William Howard Taft would become the first sitting president to attend a professional baseball game. More than providing fitness, strength, and healthy competition, the game was celebrated as fundamentally democratic. Although racially segregated, in the stands all social classes were united and the game served as a safety valve to reduce class tensions. In "The United States of Baseball," one writer declared, "base-ball is a government of the people, as well as by the people. . . . Baseball is the melting pot at the boil, the most democratic sport in the world."[16]

Progressives worried about democracy. They focused intently on government reform at all levels. At the municipal level, this led city leaders to strive for Good Government as evidenced by greater efficiency and less corruption. "The issue of city life," said one reformer, "has become one of decent human existence." Mayor Hazen Pingree of Detroit reduced costs and reigned in corruption by renegotiating contracts for such services as sewers and gas. Mayor Tom Johnson of Cleveland established a municipal building code and had the city take over services such as garbage collection and street paving. In Galveston, Texas, which was recovering from the hurricane of 1900 that killed thousands and destroyed the port city, a committee established a new mode of municipal government based on electing commissioners with legislative authority who replaced a mayor and city council. In these ways, municipal reformers undercut the corrupt ward machine politics of an earlier generation and sought to make government both more efficient and more responsive to the electorate.[17]

In the interest of democratizing the political process and expanding the electorate's power, state leaders began to enact reforms. None were more influential than those instituted in Wisconsin, where Robert M. La Follette served as governor from 1901 to 1906. Educated at the University of Wisconsin, La Follette practiced law. After he was offered a bribe to fix a case against former state officials, he devoted himself to weeding out corruption and destroying the state's political machine. When he ran for governor in 1896, a group of Republican Convention delegates accepted bribes to support the machine's choice and deprive La Follette of the nomination. He traveled the state delivering electrifying speeches. One of the most charismatic orators of the day, his full head of hair would whip from side to side and the veins in his neck popped as he denounced corporate power and political corruption aimed at depriving the citizens of their democratic rights. "Let us . . . dedicate ourselves to winning back the independence of this country," he thundered, "to emancipating this generation and throwing off from the neck of the freemen of America, the yoke of the political machine." In 1904, overturning the caucus and convention selection process that had ruled politics, Wisconsin enacted the first open primary in which voters chose who would be the nominee. La Follette also pressed for reforms that came to be known as the Wisconsin Idea: workers compensation and progressive taxation based on income, for example.[18]

In addition to the open primary, other shifts in the political process were instituted. States passed initiative and referendum laws, so proposed legislation could be placed directly on the ballot, and recall, a measure enabling citizens to remove an elected official before term's end. South Dakota led the way in 1898 and, by 1915, twenty-eight states had followed suit. Finally, at the national level, the Seventeenth Amendment, ratified in 1913, provided for the direct election of senators by popular vote as opposed to state legislatures.

Given the advances toward political democracy, it is no surprise that the movement for women's suffrage accelerated in the Progressive Era. Women had been calling for the vote since the Seneca Falls Convention in 1848. That convention, led by Elizabeth Cady Stanton and Lucretia Mott, issued a Declaration of Sentiments modeled on the Declaration of Independence and declared "all men and women are created equal." In the aftermath of the Civil War, suffrage activists were divided over whether to support the Fifteenth Amendment, which gave the right to vote to black men but left women disenfranchised. The groups, led by Stanton, Susan

B. Anthony, and Lucy Stone merged in 1890 and formed the National American Women's Suffrage Association (NAWSA). As president of the association, Carrie Chapman Catt developed a state-by-state strategy to win support for a constitutional amendment. In 1916, Alice Paul broke from the NAWSA and formed the National Woman's Party. Instead of a state-by-state strategy, Paul had been calling for a constitutional amendment. She did so in a massive suffrage march on Washington in 1913 and organized a second one from prison, where she was serving a sentence for picketing at the White House.

A turning point in that battle was the election of 1912. Teddy Roosevelt, who had left office in 1909, making way for fellow Republican William Howard Taft, now returned as the head of the Progressive Party. He gradually came to support women's suffrage (his undergraduate thesis at Harvard was titled "The Practicability of Equalizing Men and Women before the Law"), and women in those states where they could vote (Wyoming, Utah, Colorado, Idaho, Washington, and California) formed Roosevelt Women's Leagues. A total of 1.3 million women of voting age lived in those states and could certainly affect electoral outcomes. A women's suffrage plank was added to the Progressive platform and, at the convention, Jane Addams seconded Roosevelt's nomination. "With a suddenness and force that have left observers gasping," wrote the *New York Herald*, "women have injected themselves into the national campaign this year in a manner never before dreamed of in American politics."[19]

Republicans and Democrats also began to organize women in support of their parties. For example, the Women's Democratic National League was formed. Neither Taft, the Republican candidate, nor Governor Woodrow Wilson of New Jersey, the Democratic candidate, supported suffrage as fully as Roosevelt. Indeed, Wilson privately opposed giving women the right to vote and Taft avoided the issue. Roosevelt won California thanks to the women's vote. Wilson won the election with only 42 percent of the popular vote, but a whopping 435 electoral votes.

Still, the tide toward suffrage had changed for good. State referenda gave women the vote in Kansas, Oregon, and Arizona (though they lost in Wisconsin and Ohio). On June 4, 1919, Congress passed the Nineteenth Amendment, giving women the right to vote. It was ratified on August 18, 1920. Although Wilson, who was born in Virginia and lived in Georgia and South Carolina during much of his youth, eventually supported the amendment, his fellow Southerners did not. His home state did not ratify the amendment until 1952. In

1984, Mississippi became the last state to do so. Black suffragists such as Frances Ellen Watkins Harper and Mary Ann Shad Cary had from the start argued that gender and race could not be separated. White suffragists wrote them out of the movement and proclaimed victory in 1920, but Southern states continued to disfranchise black voters—men and women—and isolate them from political engagement.

Segregation

Wilson was the first Southerner elected president since Zachary Taylor in 1848 and the first Democrat since Grover Cleveland's second term, which ended in 1897. Wilson, a devout Presbyterian, earned a doctoral degree in political science from John Hopkins and shared in the progressive desire to reform corrupt political and economic practices. For example, he signed the Clayton Anti-Trust Act and the Federal Trade Commission Act, which sought to curb harmful business activities. Wilson also oversaw the racial segregation of the federal work force, which had been integrated during Reconstruction. He had won the votes of some black men by promising during the campaign to advance their interests. As president he did anything but. The secretary of the treasury (Wilson's son-in-law) and the postmaster general both segregated their departments; a rule was added requiring photographs to accompany civil service applications as a way of excluding black applicants. When a group of black leaders came to Wilson to protest, he said, "Segregation is not humiliating, but a benefit, and ought to be so regarded by you gentlemen."[20]

Wilson was espousing what had become the law of the land. In 1896, the Supreme Court in *Plessy v. Ferguson* ruled that segregation, separate but equal, was constitutional. The case grew out of a challenge to a Louisiana separate car law that required separate accommodations for black and white passengers on railways. Homer Plessy, a Louisiana Creole who was classified as an octoroon (one-eighth black), and therefore prohibited from riding in a white car, was arrested when he refused to move to a black compartment. His lawyers argued that separate but equal accommodation was unconstitutional and violated civil rights as guaranteed by the Fourteenth Amendment. When Judge John Howard Ferguson ruled against him in criminal court, Plessy's appeal ultimately found its way to the Supreme Court.

By a vote of 7–1, the Court ruled against Plessy. "If the civil and political rights of both races be equal, one cannot be inferior to the other civilly or politically," wrote Justice Henry Billings Brown. "If one race be inferior to the other socially, the Constitution of the United States cannot put them upon the same plane." One Supreme Court justice dissented. John Marshall Harlan of Kentucky, who during the Civil War supported both slavery and the Union, wrote, "Our constitution is color-blind, and neither knows nor tolerates classes among citizens." Harlan's views did not extend to the Chinese. In his powerful dissent he also argued that "there is a race so different from our own that we do not permit those belonging to it to become citizens of the United States. . . . I allude to the Chinese race." In *United States v. Wong Kim Ark* (1898), the Court extended birthright citizenship to the Chinese. Harlan dissented.[21]

How best to challenge segregation and racism divided African American civil rights leaders of the era. Educator Booker T. Washington, who had been born a slave in 1856, assumed a prominent position when, at age twenty-five, he became head of the Tuskegee Institute in Alabama. Washington believed in black self-improvement through the acquisition of skills in manual labor—this was the thrust of the Tuskegee curriculum, what was called "industrial education." He pressed for economic opportunity, not social equality. In 1895, at the Cotton States and Industrial Exposition in Atlanta, Washington delivered what came to be known as the Atlanta Compromise speech. His message to whites and blacks was "cast down your bucket where you are," look around and seek to improve relations with one's neighbors without challenging the status quo. Agitation on the question of social equality, he thought, was folly. Washington declared, "In all things that are purely social we can be as separate as the fingers, yet one as the hand in all things essential to mutual progress." His autobiography, *Up from Slavery* (1901), became a bestseller.[22]

Washington's conciliatory approach to race relations won him support from business titans such as J. P. Morgan and John D. Rockefeller. In 1901, Roosevelt shocked the nation when he invited Washington to dinner at the White House. Privately, Washington sponsored civil rights suits and, in 1915, publicly denounced segregation as unjust, unnecessary, and deleterious to both white and black. By then a new voice and movement had emerged to challenge Washington's positions.

W. E. B. DuBois was twelve years younger than Washington and grew up in Great Barrington, Massachusetts. He graduated from all-black Fisk University in Tennessee and then earned a PhD in sociology—the first African American to receive a Harvard doctorate.

DuBois became a professor at Atlanta University, a black institution, and published books and articles on black life and history. He opposed Washington's belief in racial accommodation and argued that blacks should not settle for the mechanical arts but pursue higher education. DuBois objected to what he saw as Washington's preference for submission and instead called for political power, civil rights, and higher education. "We have no right to sit silently by while the inevitable seeds are sown for a harvest of disaster to our children, black and white," he concluded.[23]

In *The Souls of Black Folk* (1903), DuBois observed that "the problem of the Twentieth Century is the problem of the color line." No one wrote more profoundly or poetically about the dilemma of black identity in America, what he called a state of "double-consciousness": "One ever feels his two-ness, an American, a Negro; two souls, two thoughts, two unreconciled strivings; two warring ideals in one dark body, whose dogged strength alone keeps it from being torn asunder. The history of the American Negro is the history of this strife—this longing to attain self-conscious manhood, to merge his double self into a better and truer self."[24]

DuBois was not alone in his opposition to Washington's Atlanta Compromise. Joined by Boston newspaper editor Monroe Trotter and others at a meeting in Fort Erie, Ontario, in 1905, they launched the Niagara Movement. Its Declaration of Sentiments called for vigilant opposition to the curtailment of political and civil rights and the denial of equal opportunity in economic life and education. The movement lasted only a few years, to be supplanted by the creation of the National Negro Committee in 1909, renamed the following year the National Association for the Advancement of Colored People (NAACP). DuBois served as director of publicity and research and editor of the *Crisis*, the organization's monthly magazine.

One of the founders of the NAACP was Ida B. Wells. Born in Mississippi in 1862, Wells became a journalist and activist whose most important work was to bring to public attention the lynching of blacks in the South and Midwest. In 1892 she published *Southern Horrors: Lynch Law in All Its Phases*. Quoting from Southern newspapers, Wells demonstrated how whites used lynching, often over fabricated accusations of black men having sex with white women, to intimidate blacks, inhibit their advancement, and assert white supremacy. Souvenir postcards with photographs of the lynched, mutilated, and often-burned bodies were circulated widely. To Wells, those who witnessed such horrors and remained mute were as culpable as those doing the lynching. They were accessories "before and after the fact." Activists began an anti-lynching campaign. From the NAACP offices on Fifth Avenue in New York, DuBois displayed a flag that read "A Man Was Lynched Yesterday." In 1918, an anti-lynching bill was introduced in Congress. Southern Democrats in the Senate prevented its passage time and again. Between 1882 and 1968, more than 4,700 people were lynched in the United States. In 2005, the chamber apologized for its failure to act.[25]

White anxiety over black progress and political activism, and a toxic environment in which black men were accused of attacking white women, led to a race riot in Atlanta in 1906. A mob killed dozens of blacks before being dispersed by the militia. And the racial violence was not limited to the South. Two years later, in Springfield, Illinois, after learning that the sheriff had whisked two suspected black criminals out of town, a mob descended on the black neighborhood, burned houses, and lynched two African Americans, including a man in his seventies. According to one report, a rioter yelled, "Lincoln freed you, now we'll show you where you belong." Perhaps the worst racial violence of the century occurred in 1921 in Tulsa, Oklahoma. Frustrated over not being able to lynch a man who had accidentally stepped on a woman's foot in an elevator, yet was accused of rape, white residents attacked the thriving black population who lived in a vibrant area known as Greenwood, nicknamed

Figure 7.2 *A Man Was Lynched Yesterday* (ca. 1936). Library of Congress.

the "black Wall Street of America." They fired upon black defenders, some of them World War I veterans, and looted and burned more than a thousand black homes and businesses. Scores were killed. In the aftermath, thousands of blacks were taken to detention centers. Not a single white rioter was indicted.[26]

Under the unrelenting condition of racial violence and economic exploitation, many black Southerners looked north. Between 1915 and 1918 approximately 500,000 left the South for New York, Pittsburgh, Philadelphia, Detroit, Chicago, and other cities. An additional 700,000 migrated in the 1920s. It was one of the great mass migrations in American history, fueled in part by economic distress in Southern agriculture as a boll weevil infestation ravaged the cotton industry. Another factor, with the curtailment of European immigration, was the need for labor in the North. And of course they fled to escape racial hatred and extralegal violence. "If you thought you might be lynched by mistake," wrote one editor, "would you remain in South Carolina? Ask yourself the question if you dare." The North had become "the land of promise."[27]

Even in the North, blacks could not escape an emerging national vision of Reconstruction as an era characterized by ruthless Republican rule and rapacious blacks running amok, a time when the Ku Klux Klan served as heroic saviors of Southern purity and dignity. Film was still a relatively young medium, and D. W. Griffith's *Birth of a Nation* (1915), based on Thomas Dixon's novel *The Clansman* (1905), invented a new visual language and pioneered techniques that would make movies central to the culture. After a White House screening, Woodrow Wilson apparently declared the film "history written with lightning." It was *Birth of a Nation*, more than any other source, which codified a view of Reconstruction as a crusade against Southern whites and fueled further resentment against blacks. Two years after its release, race riots in East St. Louis, Illinois, left scores of blacks dead.[28]

Monroe Trotter, who broke with the NAACP and created the National Equal Rights League, sought to ban the film from opening in Boston. Trotter and Griffith appeared at a hearing. Moorfield Storey, the first president of the NAACP, testified before the city council that the purpose of the film was "to discredit the Negro all over the country." The mayor allowed it to be shown. Nonviolent protests outside the Tremont Theater, where the film played, led to arrests. A year before, Trotter had met Wilson at the White House. Wilson said he was "insulted" and "offended" by Trotter's tone and ordered him out of the Oval Office. Trotter's offense: he challenged the president on the segregation of federal employees.[29]

Socialism

In 1911, W. E. B. DuBois joined the Socialist Party of America. He was forced to leave after he supported Woodrow Wilson in the election of 1912 (an endorsement he would regret), but his principles remained socialist his whole life. Indeed, in 1961, at age ninety-three, he joined the Communist Party.

In the first decade of the twentieth century, the socialist movement in America flourished. Dismayed by rising inequality between capital and labor and determined to advance social legislation for justice and democracy, voters elected numerous socialists to public office, including two members of Congress, dozens of state legislators, and more than one hundred mayors across thirty-three states. It was an easy step from labor activism and progressivism to socialism, and many took it. When Eugene V. Debs emerged from jail after serving time for his role in the Pullman strike in 1894, he turned to socialism. A decade later he ran for president as a socialist and received more than 400,000 votes, nearly 3 percent of the vote. In 1912, he ran for the third time and received 900,000 votes, 6 percent of the popular vote.

Debs knew well the work of Karl Marx, and his speech at the Socialist Party Convention in Indianapolis in 1904 spoke of class struggle between capitalists and workers and denounced both Republicans and Democrats for representing the capitalist class and supporting "private ownership of the means of production." By contrast, the Socialist Party was a working-class party whose mission was to "defeat capitalism and emancipate all workers from wage slavery."[30]

Unlike Samuel Gompers of the American Federation of Labor, Debs opposed restrictions on immigrants. Socialists, he said, represented the "down-trodden of all the earth" and do not take positions based on expediency or convenience. Debs's international perspective led him to play a role in 1905 in the founding of an international labor union called the Industrial Workers of the World (IWW), whose members were known as Wobblies. Industrial unionism sought to organize all workers in an industry regardless of skill level. At the founding of the IWW, Debs implored unionists to put aside their factions and squabbles and unite under its banner.[31]

The Western Federation of Miners helped form the IWW. The federation had been founded in 1893 and after repeated strikes and confrontations in Colorado and Idaho became one of the most radical and militant labor organizations in the country. One of its leaders was William Dudley Haywood, known as "Big Bill." Born in Utah Territory, Haywood lost vision in his right eye from a childhood accident and went to work in the silver mines. He rose quickly in the union and played a critical role in the Colorado labor strikes of 1903 and 1904. Gold and silver mine operators called in the National Guard, paid by businessmen, not the state. In the end, dozens of strikers were killed. States declared martial law and deported hundreds of union members. Haywood denounced the owners who "did not find the gold, they did not mine the gold, they did not mill the gold, but by some weird alchemy all the gold belonged to them!" Events in Colorado further radicalized him and led to the creation of the IWW. At the organizing convention held in Chicago in 1905, Haywood rose to speak. He looked the part of a leader of miners, described by a contemporary as a large man "with the physical strength of an ox." Haywood declared war: his movement was calling for nothing less than "the emancipation of the working-class from the slave bondage of capitalism."[32]

The ongoing violence between miners and mine owners, which dated to the 1890s, reached a climax in December 1905 when a bomb killed Frank Steunenberg, the former governor of Idaho, as he walked into his house. As governor, Steunenberg had called out troops to suppress strikers and condoned mass arrests and holding suspects without trial. "We have taken the monster by the throat and we are going to choke the life out of it," he declared. Steunenberg's assassination sparked a massive investigation that resulted in the arrest of a former Western Federation of Miners member who, under pressure, named Bill Haywood as one of the conspirators. Extradited from Colorado, Haywood languished in an Idaho jail for eighteen months awaiting trial. While incarcerated, among other activities he read *The Jungle* and ran for governor of Colorado (he won several thousand votes).[33]

Haywood's 1907 trial was a sensation. Newly elected Senator William Borah joined the prosecution team and Clarence Darrow, early in a career that would make him the most famous criminal defense attorney in America, led Haywood's defense. In closing, Darrow spoke for two days. He derided the forced and false confession and mocked the circumstantial evidence. He declared, "I want to say to you gentlemen, Bill Haywood can't die unless you kill him. You must tie the rope. You twelve men of Idaho, the burden will be on you." After deliberating for 19 hours, the jury acquitted Haywood.[34]

Factions are to unions as splinters are to wood, and in 1907 the Western Federation of Miners (WFM), its members disagreeing among themselves as well as with the Wobblies over how to effect change—through politics or strikes, reform or revolution—bolted from the IWW. After his trial, Haywood left the WFM to remain with the IWW and serve as its first chairman. He continued to denounce what he called industrial slavery and proclaimed, "socialism is the future system of industrial society."[35]

Still, socialism never took hold in the United States as it did in Europe, and contemporary commentators wondered why. Even Karl Marx and Friedrich Engels speculated about what made America different: a lack of a feudal tradition; widespread democratic practices; opportunity for social mobility; the availability of land. While the Socialist Party in America won votes and elected officials, it never took root as a lasting social democratic political party as it did in England or France. In 1906, German sociologist Werner Sombart published *Why Is There No Socialism in America?* His answer was that "America is a freer and more egalitarian society than Europe."[36]

Explanations that relied on American exceptionalism failed to consider the efforts made by the government to suppress and destroy the socialist movement. Political leaders and corporate bosses saw socialists as un-American, as foreigners seeking to destroy democracy, as anarchists, syndicalists, communists bent on overturning capitalism and with it the nation. Woodrow Wilson set the tone in his 1915 annual message to Congress: "There are citizens of the United States, I blush to admit, born under other flags but welcomed under our generous naturalization laws to the full freedom and opportunity of America, who have poured the poison of disloyalty into the very arteries of our national life," he told those assembled.[37]

"The poison of disloyalty" was unacceptable at any time, but especially during World War I. Many individuals and groups opposed the United States' entry into war, from Henry Ford to Jane Addams, from the American Union Against Militarism to the Woman's Peace Party. For socialists, it was a war in which capitalists, industrialists, and imperialists would profit on the backs of the laboring classes. In an attempt to suppress opposition, especially from radicals, Congress passed an Espionage Act in 1917 and a Sedition Act in 1918. Under the terms of this legislation, anyone who opposed the draft or the war could be fined and imprisoned. It authorized the postmaster general to ban incendiary material from the mails. In addition, it became a federal offense to use "disloyal, profane, scurrilous, or abusive language" against the government or the Constitution.

No one was more vocal in his opposition than Eugene Debs. In a speech at Canton, Ohio, in June 1918, Debs confidently asserted that socialism was "spreading over the entire face of the earth" and resisting it was to try and "arrest the sunrise on the morrow"; and he denounced war as being waged for "conquest and plunder" in which "the working class carry the burden and furnish the bodies." Although politicians called for Americans to do their patriotic duty, their own "patriotic duty never takes them to the firing line or chucks them into the trenches."[38]

Debs did not explicitly advocate actions to undermine the war effort; he didn't have to. It was enough that he expressed support for those who did. Tried under the Espionage Act, he was convicted and sentenced to ten years in jail. The Supreme Court, in *Debs v. United States*, upheld the conviction and rejected the defense argument that Debs had a First Amendment right to speak his mind. Debs ran for president from prison and won more than 900,000 votes (3.4 percent of the popular vote). In 1921, President Warren G. Harding, a conservative Republican, commuted his sentence.

In 1919, two years before Debs was freed, the Justice Department, under Attorney General A. Mitchell Palmer, launched a series of raids against radicals, anarchists, socialists, and communists. Palmer was reacting to the success of the Bolsheviks in Russia, who had emerged triumphant in the civil war that followed the October Revolution, and the mailing of letter bombs to business and political leaders, including Palmer himself. More than 10,000 people were arrested, with thousands held in detention and hundreds deported. Immigrants, especially from Germany and Russia, became more suspect than ever, and anxiety over the infiltration of communists—a Red Scare—led to a movement for Americanism. Expressions of opposition to the nation would not be tolerated in the aftermath of World War I. One example illustrates the frenzy: In 1919, an immigrant alien in Hammond, Indiana, was gunned down for yelling, "To Hell with the United States!" After deliberating for two minutes, the jury acquitted the assassin. "Run the Reds out from the land whose flag they sully!" demanded the American Legion, a newly formed organization of World War I veterans. Calls to purify the nation through deportation abounded. One writer insisted, "We must remake America. We must purify the source of America's population and keep it pure." Palmer, who had presidential aspirations, said the doctrine he preached was "undiluted one hundred per cent Americans because my platform is, in a word, undiluted Americanism."[39]

Socialist union leaders seemed more un-American than ever, and prior to Palmer's raids, under the Espionage Act of 1917, nearly 150 Wobblies were arrested, including Bill Haywood. The government charged them with interfering with the draft and encouraging desertion through union organizing, which was viewed as undermining the war effort. Haywood was convicted and sentenced to twenty years in jail. While on bail pending his appeal, he fled to Russia where he married, studied the language, and advised Lenin's government. He died in Moscow in 1928 and his ashes were buried at two sites: the Kremlin Wall and Chicago's Haymarket Martyrs' monument.

World War I

Wilson narrowly won reelection in 1916, in part thanks to the slogan "he kept us out of war." The global conflict began in July 1914 when Austria-Hungary declared war on Serbia, followed by Germany declaring war on Russia, whose allies included the French and the British as the result of the 1907 Anglo-Russian Entente. Tens of millions of people became embroiled in the war and millions of soldiers and civilians were killed. The fighting was unlike any that had been seen before. Prolonged trench warfare, massive artillery bombings, the use of machine guns, and the employment of chemical weapons, including mustard and chlorine gas, accelerated the death toll. The Battle of Verdun, for example, lasted nearly all of 1916 and resulted in almost a million casualties. American volunteers drove ambulances, their service honored a decade later in Ernest Hemingway's *A Farewell to Arms* (1929). Teddy Roosevelt, eager for the United States to join the war, praised the American Ambulance Field Service for "helping this nation to save its soul."[40]

Wilson defended American neutrality, in part on the basis of the nation's immigrant history, recognizing that the people of the United States originated from the countries at war and it was natural for them to be sympathetic to one or the other. Under these circumstances, "It will be easy to excite passion and difficult to allay it." He called for Americans to be "impartial in thought, as well as action," yet that became increasingly difficult as German mines and submarines disrupted American transatlantic trade.[41]

On May 7, 1915, German U-boats torpedoed the *Lusitania*, a British passenger liner sailing from New York to Liverpool. More than 1,200 died, including more than 100 Americans. In a speech to naturalized citizens, Wilson said Americans were "too proud to fight." He reminded these new citizens that they must become "thorough Americans. . . . A man who thinks of himself as belonging to a particular national group in America," he said, "has not yet become an American, and the man who goes among you to trade upon your nationality is no worthy son to live under the Stars and Stripes."[42]

In January 1917, British intelligence intercepted and decoded a telegram from Arthur Zimmermann, German foreign secretary, to the German ambassador in Mexico proposing a German-Mexican alliance through which Mexico could regain territory lost to the United States. The outrage shifted the nation to war. On April 2, 1917, Wilson asked Congress for a declaration of war against Germany. "The world must be made safe for democracy," preached Wilson. He claimed no interest in conquest or dominion, just a concern for the rights of mankind. The language of democracy appealed to many, including W. E. B. DuBois, who saw in the war an opportunity for black advancement. "Let us, while this war lasts, forget our special grievances and close our ranks shoulder to shoulder with our own white fellow citizens and the allied nations that are fighting for democracy."[43]

Congress authorized war and quickly passed a Selective Service Act that at first required registration of men ages twenty-one to thirty and, a year later, expanded to men ages eighteen to forty-five. Unlike during the Civil War, substitutes were prohibited; legally, at least, the wealthy could not buy their way out. Some 24 million men registered (23 percent of the population), and more than 2.8 million draftees and 2 million volunteers served. Included among those who registered were nearly 300,000 African Americans, organized in segregated units. Some 500,000 soldiers, about 18 percent, were immigrants who sought to demonstrate their loyalty and win citizenship. Two African Americans and thirteen immigrants from twelve different countries would go on to win the Medal of Honor. Military service, predicted one congressman, "is a melting pot which will . . . break down distinctions of race and class and mold us into a new nation and bring forth the new Americans."[44]

To bolster the draft and American enthusiasm for the war, Wilson signed an executive order creating the Committee on Public Information (CPI). George Creel, a muckraking journalist, led the CPI and understood his role was to furnish "propaganda in the true sense of the word, meaning the 'propagation of faith.'" "We were fighting for ideas and ideals," he later recalled, "and somebody . . . had to say it and keep on saying it until it was believed." Across the United States and in Europe, the CPI used all forms of media to spread a positive message about the war. The CPI understood the power of advertising and public opinion. They tailored a message to promote unambiguous patriotism. The committee issued as many as ten press releases a day, a deluge of curated information with which newspaper editors filled their pages. The CPI also relied on the Espionage and Sedition Acts to make certain that negative accounts of the war effort did not circulate. In addition to written reports, the Division of Pictorial Publicity provided advertisements and posters that helped sell the war to the public. None became more iconic than James Montgomery Flagg's poster of Uncle Sam pointing at the viewer and insisting "I Want You for U.S. Army." Other prints featured Lady Liberty or showed Huns as brutes who threatened female purity. Opponents of the war grasped the danger posed by this vast propaganda machine, dubbed by some the Committee on Public Disinformation. Senator Hiram Warren Johnson of California is credited with observing that "the first casualty of war is truth."[45]

Whatever American soldiers believed, by spring 1918 more than a million of them had landed in France as part of the American Expeditionary Force (AEF) under General John J. Pershing. Born in

Figure 7.3 James Montgomery Flagg, *I Want You* (1917). Library of Congress.

Missouri, Pershing was an indifferent student at West Point. A popular classmate, he was elected class president four consecutive years, graduating in 1886. His military career included action in the Indian Wars on the Great Plains and as the commander of the Tenth Cavalry, a black unit called the Buffalo Soldiers, a name given by Indians. Along the way Pershing acquired the nickname "Black Jack," and led the Tenth Cavalry to Cuba, where he participated in the assault on San Juan Hill. Following the Spanish-American War, Pershing served in the Philippines, where he suppressed uprisings by the Moros, who were Muslim. (He also learned to speak their language and praised the Koran.) Promoted by Roosevelt to brigadier general in 1906, a decade later he was tasked with leading the AEF.

Although American soldiers, called "doughboys" for reasons obscure to us now, first landed in Europe in June 1917, they did not see serious action until spring 1918. What they experienced pricked the balloon of the jingoistic optimism expressed by George M. Cohan's popular tune "Over There," that the Yankees were coming to win the war.

Nearly 50,000 did not come back and more than 200,000 were wounded at battles such as Cantigny, Belleau Wood, Chateau-Thierry, and Saint-Mihiel, where Pershing led half a million men. Only a small percentage of black soldiers were permitted to engage in combat—the majority were relegated to performing service and labor such as unloading ships, digging trenches, and transporting soldiers. Some black soldiers, such as those of the 369th Infantry, the Harlem Hellfighters, did see battle, raising hopes that their service abroad would mitigate prejudice at home.

Although the government censored soldiers' letters home, the terrible realities of war sometimes filtered through. One soldier wrote, "It is hard to tell which way one could go and not find someone shooting at someone else." Under bombardment, Captain Harry Truman wrote to his fiancée, Bess, "My greatest satisfaction is that my legs didn't succeed in carrying me away, although they were very anxious to do it." Another soldier, writing from the trenches, spoke of the constant threat of gas attacks and considered his gas mask "my best friend as does every other man on this front." He told his family, "I'm trying hard to learn how to forget."[46]

Tens of thousands of soldiers who survived the gas and shells succumbed in 1918 to the flu pandemic that ravaged the globe. By the time it passed, influenza had killed more than 600,000 Americans and tens of millions worldwide, somewhere between 3 and 6 percent of the world's population. It affected one-quarter of the US population and one-third of the world population. Even President Wilson was struck with a mild case in the aftermath of the war.

Prior to the flu pandemic, which arrived at war's end, the toxin of prejudice and hate spread through the American home front, and the attack on socialists and communists widened to include German Americans whose loyalty became suspect. Wilson unleashed conspiratorial anxieties in a speech delivered on Flag Day in 1917, when he suggested that Germany infiltrated American communities with spies and conspirators and spread sedition. Most states forbade German language education in schools. Lutheran churches were compelled to switch entirely to English. German newspapers ceased publication and names were changed: the town of East Germantown, Indiana, became Pershing; sauerkraut became liberty cabbage.[47]

The government forced German Americans to register and sent at least two thousand enemy aliens to internment camps in Utah and Georgia. Groups such as the American Protection League and American Defense Society monitored the activities of German Americans. Vigilantism spread. Robert Paul Prager, who arrived in 1905, had the misfortune of being both a socialist and a German American. He was also a patriot who tried to enlist in the navy. Accused of making disloyal comments about the United States and President Wilson to a group of miners, he was lynched by a mob of 500 outside of Collinsville, Illinois, on April 5, 1918. Twelve men, wearing red, white, and blue rosettes in their lapels, were tried for the crime, and acquitted. One jury member said, "Well, I guess nobody can say we aren't loyal now."[48]

Only the end of the war in November 1918 eased the hysteria. In time, the Sedition Act would be repealed (though not the Espionage Act), and in 1919 Wilson commuted the sentences of some 200 people who had been convicted and imprisoned. By then, Wilson was devoting his attention to realizing his vision for peace. If in foreign policy Roosevelt was a realist and a pragmatist, Wilson was an idealist and moralist. On January 8, 1918, he delivered a speech in which he identified the core principles needed to achieve a lasting world peace. Known as the Fourteen Points, Wilson called for open agreements between nations and freedom of trade. Advancing democratic doctrines, he asserted that the people of Austria-Hungary "should be accorded the freest opportunity of autonomous development." Finally, he proclaimed that "a general association of nations must be formed under specific covenants for the purpose of affording mutual guarantees of political independence and territorial integrity to great and small states alike." These points would form the basis for discussions at the Paris Peace Conference that would lead to the Treaty of Versailles in 1919. Wilson's counterparts—Georges Clemenceau of France, David Lloyd George of Great Britain, and Vittorio Orlando of Italy—were skeptical of Wilsonian idealism. Clemenceau remarked, "God gave us his Ten Commandments and we broke them. Wilson gave us his Fourteen Points—we shall see."[49]

The final treaty held Germany responsible for the war and forced the defeated nation to pay reparations. It also included a provision for the creation of a League of Nations. Wilson's glorious moment of international triumph turned to defeat when the US Senate refused to ratify the treaty. Republicans, led by Henry Cabot Lodge, expressed reservations about the League of Nations, especially a provision that would have compelled the United States to enter a war without congressional approval (not coincidentally, Lodge offered fourteen reservations). Some senators opposed the treaty under any circumstances (including Robert La Follette and William Borah). The Senate voted twice, once with Lodge's reservations appended and once without them. Both times the vote fell short of a two-thirds majority. The United States would not join the League of Nations. Instead, Americans would turn isolationist and focus on the domestic and the national. "America's present need," said presidential candidate Warren G. Harding, "is not heroics, but healing; not nostrums, but normalcy; not revolution, but restoration." Americans longed to laugh again.[50]

CHAPTER 8

This New Battle

F RANKLIN DELANO ROOSEVELT WAS THIRTY-NINE
years old when he was stricken with polio. Aristocratic, wealthy,
educated at Harvard College and Columbia Law School, he
seemed to possess everything. He had served in the New York State
Senate and as assistant secretary of the navy under Woodrow Wilson,
and he was the Democratic nominee for vice president in 1920. After
the disease struck in 1921, he withdrew from politics and struggled
to rehabilitate his body. He reemerged in public life several years
later, paralyzed and able to stand only with leg braces and a cane. He
became governor of New York in 1929 and was elected president in
1932, as more than a decade of prohibition against alcohol came to
an end and economic depression and natural disaster convulsed the
nation. In his inaugural address, he told Americans "the only thing
we have to fear is fear itself." He knew so firsthand, and Americans
rewarded his fortitude by reelecting him three times. "If you spent
two years in bed trying to wiggle your big toe, after that anything else
would seem easy."[1]

Prohibition

On January 16, 1919, the Eighteenth Amendment to the
Constitution, which prohibited the manufacture, sale, or transportation of intoxicating beverages, was ratified. Of the forty-eight
states, of which three-fourths, or thirty-six, were needed for ratification, only Connecticut and Rhode Island voted no. Congress

passed the National Prohibition Act over Woodrow Wilson's veto. Known as the Volstead Act, after Representative Andrew Volstead of Minnesota who chaired the judiciary committee, the legislation defined an intoxicating beverage as any drink more than 0.5 percent alcohol by volume. Some exceptions were made, such as wine used in a church services or whiskey prescribed by a physician (leading no doubt to increased religiosity and doctor visits). A special division of the Treasury Department assumed responsibility for enforcement. Penalties included fines and imprisonment. Prohibition went into effect at midnight on January 17, 1920. America had gone dry.

Opposition to alcohol has a long history in the United States. In the early nineteenth century, evangelical ministers and social reformers preached temperance as a cure for myriad social ills. Temperance societies proliferated and some New England states passed what came to be known as a "Maine Law," after that state in 1851 prohibited the sale of alcoholic beverages except for "medicinal, mechanical, or manufacturing purposes."

Women, in particular, became absorbed in temperance work and no group proved more influential than the Women's Christian Temperance Union (WCTU), founded in Ohio in 1873. Led by Frances Willard, an educator and reformer who believed that "women are called to be the saviors of the race," membership of the WCTU grew to hundreds of thousands. They denounced alcohol as an evil that destroyed families and led to poverty and disease. Some activists went beyond words: Carrie Nation, a Kentucky-born temperance reformer who felt called by God to take action, stormed saloons with a hatchet in hand. The organization also embraced a variety of progressive reforms, including women's suffrage, public health, and prison reform. The WCTU pressed for laws banning alcohol and focused especially on German and Italian immigrant communities, where they believed drunkenness was rampant. Willard claimed that "alien illiterates rule our cities today; the saloon is their palace; the toddy stick their scepter."[2]

Willard died in 1898. By then the Anti-Saloon League, founded in 1893 by Protestant clergymen, had embraced Prohibition. With World War I, the league's propaganda efforts led the public to connect beer and breweries with Germans. Drinking alcohol became a form of treason. Posters appeared with soldiers who asked, "Will you back me or back booze?" With politicians arguing that as a result of passage of an income tax amendment in 1913 the federal government was less dependent on liquor taxes, the momentum toward Prohibition accelerated.

No one was a more zealous advocate for Prohibition than the evangelist Billy Sunday. Born in 1862, in Ames, Iowa, William Ashley Sunday lost his father only a few weeks later. At age twelve, his mother sent him and his brother to the Iowa Soldiers' Orphan's Home. Sunday distinguished himself at baseball and, in 1883, he signed with National League champion the Chicago White Stockings. In 1888, he stole seventy-one bases for his new team, the Pittsburgh Pirates. By then, Sunday had experienced a religious conversion and became a devout Presbyterian. Ballplayers were known for drinking, smoking, and gambling. Sunday now avoided all temptations. Still in demand as a ballplayer, in 1891 he rejected a lucrative contract that would have paid him $500 a month and instead joined the YMCA in Chicago for a monthly salary of $83. A few years later, he became a full-time evangelist.

Sunday started small, in rural churches and town halls in Iowa and Illinois. His group of followers soon grew, as did his evangelical ambition. Joined by his wife, Sunday expanded his organization and employed some two dozen staff members. He preached many times a day and his revivals drew vast crowds—70,000 in Boston on one day in 1916 and more than a million during a ten-week crusade. An electrifying speaker, he exemplified the tenets of muscular Christianity. He eyes bulged, his body rocked, he jumped and crouched and slid across the stage. He was "like an addict going cold-turkey," said one observer. Not everyone applauded Sunday's efforts. Conservative clergymen denounced his "extreme sensationalism" and "dancing dervish contortions." Still, even satirist and critic H. L. Mencken felt "a certain respect for the whirling doctor's earnestness, and a keen sense of his personal charm."[3]

No subject aroused him more than alcohol, and he titled his most famous sermon "Get On the Water Wagon." "I am the sworn, eternal, uncompromising enemy of the Liquor Traffic," he began. He denounced the saloon for degrading all aspects of life and refuted the idea that it was needed to lighten tax burdens. Insanity and idiocy, he averred, were the results of alcohol. He claimed that 90 percent of all criminals drank. Castigation, not statistics, was Sunday's currency: "The saloon is the sum of all villainies. It is worse than war, worse than pestilence, worse than famine . . . To license such an incarnate fiend of hell is one of the blackest spots on the American Government."[4]

Religious zeal for Prohibition was part of a fundamentalist resurgence in America that included other goals, such as Bible education in public schools and laws against the teaching of evolution.

Figure 8.1 George Bellows, *Billy Sunday* (1923). National Portrait Gallery.

The trial of John T. Scopes in Tennessee in 1925 pitted prominent defense attorney Clarence Darrow against three-time presidential candidate and biblical literalist William Jennings Bryan and drew national attention. (Scopes was found guilty, Darrow's renown continued to grow, and Bryan died a few days after the trial ended). Religious resurgence also contributed to the rebirth of the Ku Klux Klan in the 1920s; not as the terrorist group of the late 1860s, but as a nationwide middle-class organization joined by millions. Building on Protestant pieties, the Klan sought a purified Americanism that had no place for blacks, Catholics, Jews, immigrants, unionists, socialists, or anyone else who they felt threatened traditional native, white, Protestant values. They also became soldiers in the war on alcohol by positioning themselves as the defenders of law and order and pursuing bootleggers. Klansmen formed part of a citizen army that took it upon itself to enforce the Eighteenth Amendment. At times, the police deputized them to assist in enforcement. According to the *Fiery Cross*, the Klan's Indiana newspaper, "The Klan is going to drive bootlegging forever out of this land."[5]

If moralists supported Prohibition, pluralists opposed it. People condemned the Eighteenth Amendment for various reasons. What tied them together was concern about individual liberties and what they called the "tyrannical power of the Billy Sundays." Numerous anti-Prohibition groups emerged, including the Association Opposed to National Prohibition, the Association Against the Prohibition Amendment, Women's Organization for National Prohibition

Reform, and the United States Brewers Association. Labor unions, whose urban ethnic, working-class communities were targeted by a ban on alcohol, combated Prohibition. A common chorus for Prohibition's opponents was federal government overreach into the private lives of citizens. "A man's home used to be his castle," wrote one editor, but "now it is the United States government's castle and the rights and privileges have been taken away." "Prohibition," declared brewer Adolphus Busch years before it was enacted, "rests on un-American and indefensible interference with the elementary principles of personal liberty."[6]

Making America dry was unrealistic from the start. There were tens of thousands of saloons, networks of economic interests tied to alcohol, and the extraordinary costs of enforcement at the precise moment that the federal government had lost tax revenue. Drinking drifted underground, and speakeasies (unlicensed saloons) and bootlegging (making, selling, and transporting alcohol) became prominent features of a youth culture that featured women who sported bobbed hair and short skirts, and a generation that embraced new forms of dancing and music, such as the Charleston and jazz. These broader cultural shifts only gave further animus to rural, Protestant Prohibitionists, who decried the sins of the flesh. Even worse, the alcohol ban gave rise to gangsters such as Al Capone, Meyer Lansky, Lucky Luciano, Dutch Schultz, and Bugsy Siegel, who captured the public's imagination for their audacious acts and extravagant lifestyles. "I make my money by supplying a public demand," said Al Capone. The money to be made was extraordinary. By one account, in 1926 annual sales of bootlegged liquor neared $3.6 billion, equal to the federal budget.[7]

Prohibition agents, such as Chicago's Elliot Ness, whose group later earned the nickname "The Untouchables" for refusing bribes, did their best, but for every speakeasy and distillery they invaded, dozens of others popped up. At its peak, the Bureau of Prohibition employed some three thousand agents who had responsibility for thousands of miles of shoreline and borders with Canada and Mexico. Many of them ended up taking bribes to look the other way. Juries often proved unwilling to convict anyone charged with violation of the Volstead Act. In New York, for example, 4,000 arrests under a state law led to fewer than 500 indictments and 6 convictions, none of which resulted in jail time.

While per capita consumption of alcohol decreased by as much as 70 percent, Prohibition did not deliver on what its proponents promised. Crime rose rather than diminished; the economy suffered rather than flourished; public health weakened rather than strengthened. Contributors to a national symposium organized to assess five years of Prohibition argued that drunkenness had increased, corruption had spread, and contempt for the rule of law had intensified. A physician saw a surge in mental and nervous disorders. "Stupid and ineffective," concluded one writer. Samuel Harden Church, the president of the Carnegie Institute, called Prohibition "the greatest mistake in the world," and expressed chagrin that "moved by the deep emotions of war," the nation had "indolently permitted a well-organized and enormously financed body composed of zealots, fanatics, and bigots" to enact Prohibition.[8]

The election of 1928 pitted a wet candidate against a dry one. Al Smith, the highly popular governor of New York, promoted progressive policies that brought greater efficiency to the state. He was also ardently and openly opposed to Prohibition. His administration repealed the enforcement statute for the Volstead Act, and he served alcohol to his guests. Smith was also Catholic, and the combination of anti-Eastern, anti-urban bias, Prohibitionist sentiment, and widespread anti-Catholicism cost him the Democratic nomination in 1924. He secured it four years later, the first Catholic ever to do so.

Herbert Hoover, the Republican nominee, hailed from Iowa, was a Quaker, and publicly supported Prohibition as a "great social and economic experiment, noble in motive and far-reaching in purpose." He had made his reputation as an engineer and manager when, as commerce secretary, he organized relief efforts for the disastrous Mississippi Flood of 1927. For many wet Democrats, anti-Catholicism trumped anti-Prohibition. "I'd rather see a saloon on every corner than a Catholic in the White House," said one religious leader. Hoover dominated the election, winning more than 58 percent of the popular vote and taking 444 electoral votes. Traditional Southern Democratic states such as Virginia, North Carolina, Tennessee, and Texas voted Republican. The journalist Frederick William Wile, of the National Broadcasting Company, said that Smith had been defeated by "the three P's: "Prohibition, Prejudice, and Prosperity."[9]

The prosperity of the 1920s seemed widespread. Wages rose for workers and new technologies, such as the assembly line, fueled the emergence of new industries and spurred consumerism. "The chief business of the American people is business," asserted President Calvin Coolidge. The gross national product, adjusted for inflation, grew an average of 4.2 percent a year from 1922 to 1929. In 1927, the Ford Motor Company sold 15 million cars (the US population was about 120 million). Radios became equally ubiquitous: 60 percent of Americans purchased a radio between 1923 and 1930. Movies went from silent to "talkies" when Al Jolson starred in *The Jazz Singer*, and attendance rose with the volume, as more than 50 million people per week jammed the theaters. Jazz itself, what poet Langston Hughes called "the inherent expression of Negro life in America: the eternal tom-tom beating in the Negro soul," emerged as part of the literary and creative ferment that would be called the Harlem Renaissance.[10]

Everything seemed large, loud, and expansive, best represented by Babe Ruth who, in 1927, blasted sixty home runs. Skyscrapers transformed urban life (by 1932, the Chrysler and Empire State Buildings in New York would be completed), and greater verticality was achieved by the burgeoning airplane industry, given a transformative boost in 1927 when Charles A. Lindbergh made a solo transatlantic flight from New York to Paris and became a national hero.

If the working and middle class did well, the wealthy did even better. Income tax rates fell, and a bull market brought healthy returns to investors. The stock market kept climbing, jumping in one year from 200 to 300 points. All of this received religious sanctification in Bruce Barton's *The Man Nobody Knows* (1925), a bestselling work that recast Jesus as the founder of modern business. Only rural America failed to share in the prosperity as farm prices fell and foreclosures ballooned.

The roaring prosperity came to a resounding crash on October 24 ("Black Thursday") and October 29, 1929 ("Black Tuesday"), when the stock market lost nearly 25 percent of its value. Financial ruin marked the death knell for Prohibition. In the election of 1932, Franklin D. Roosevelt claimed victory with repeal of the Eighteenth Amendment written into the Democratic platform. Few believed repeal could be achieved: a handful of dry politicians could stop it, dry states would not ratify it, and some feared that if one amendment could be repealed, why not others (for example, the income tax amendment). One of the original sponsors of the Eighteenth Amendment expressed confidence that there was as much chance for repeal as there was "for a hummingbird to fly to the planet Mars with the Washington Monument tied to its tail."[11]

Some prominent drys, however, transformed into wets (for example, John D. Rockefeller Jr.), and some politicians reversed their votes (of 22 senators who had voted for the Eighteenth Amendment in 1919 and still served, 17 voted for repeal). State legislatures were sidestepped for special ratification conventions. On December 5,

1933, the Twenty-First Amendment was ratified, and Prohibition ended. In March, before passage, Roosevelt had signed an act that legalized the sale of beverages with an alcohol content of 3.2 percent. After doing so, he said, "I think this would be a good time for a beer."[12]

Depression

Statistics are not stories, yet they suggest stories. The stock market's Dow Jones Industrial Average fell from a peak of 381 in September 1929 to a low of 41 in July 1932. The gross national product plummeted from 104 billion in 1929 to 56 billion in 1933. Unemployment soared from 3.2 percent to a peak of nearly 25 percent in 1933. In Harlem, it reached twice that. Forty percent of all farms in Mississippi were up for auction in 1933. The fertility rate (children born to women age 15–44) dropped 20 percent. Suicide rates climbed from 12.1 per 100,000 to 18.1 in 1929 and remained at 15.4 throughout the 1930s.

Events as widespread and cataclysmic as the Great Depression have many causes. Its origins rested in the aftermath of World War I. Global trade became more restricted and new tariffs restrained the flow of goods. The Smoot-Hawley tariff, passed in 1930 in the aftermath of the stock market crash, only worsened matters by reducing trade. After World War I, the United States had become a creditor nation, but restrictive trade policies meant other countries could sell fewer goods and not repay their debt to the American banks from which they had borrowed. Domestically, Americans took advantage of easy credit at high interest rates (up to 30 percent) to finance their changing lifestyles as the economy grew and incomes increased across the 1920s. "Every free-born American has a right to name his own necessities," declared one advertising magazine in 1926. In 1928, however, the Federal Reserve (created in 1913) tightened available credit and increased the interest rate charged by banks for borrowing. Deflation ensued and the Fed failed to increase the money supply. As foreign nations and American citizens found it increasingly difficult to borrow and to pay debts, the economy began to sputter. At the same time, people became enamored with the stock market. Investors purchased stocks on margin, with borrowed money, and banks faced enormous financial risk when stock prices plummeted. In 1930, some 700 banks failed; in 1933, as many as 4,000 closed. Depositors lost billions of dollars, their savings gone. Joseph P. Kennedy, who sold off his portfolio weeks before the crash, supposedly said he knew the time to get out had come when the shoeshine boy gave him a stock tip.[13]

It fell to Herbert Hoover to do something about the spiraling crisis. If we are to believe Calvin Coolidge, in whose cabinet Hoover had served, the prospects were not good. "That man has offered me unsolicited advice for six years, all of it bad," lamented Coolidge. Hoover approached the crisis with an overriding belief in self-help, volunteerism, and community cooperation—not in relief efforts spearheaded by the federal government. His President's Organization of Unemployment Relief furnished funds only to relief agencies, not directly to the people. He opposed a congressional bill that would have provided food to drought victims. He helped defeat a Federal Emergency Relief Bill. The severity of the Depression eventually forced him to yield on his principles and form the Reconstruction Finance Corporation, through which the federal government would try to rescue banks. He also endorsed the Emergency Relief and Construction Act, which provided money for a limited number of public works projects. These measures came only in 1932, an election year. Most Americans probably agreed with one Democrat who said, "With all due regard to his unusual abilities, the fact remains that he has proved the most inept, the most ill-suited man who has filled the Presidential chair in fifty years."[14]

During Hoover's presidency, impoverished Americans demanded more, and they let the president know it. The homeless constructed shantytowns, dubbed "Hoovervilles" by a Democratic politician, a name that stuck. Newspapers used as a shield against the elements became "Hoover blankets," and pants pockets turned inside out to show they were empty were "Hoover flags." Cars pulled by horses because the owner could not afford gas became known as "Hoover wagons." One of the largest Hoovervilles was established in Washington, DC, on the Anacostia Flats. The novelist John Dos Passos described the shantytown as "built out of old newspapers, cardboard boxes, packing crates, bits of tin or tarpaper roofing, old shutters, every kind of cockeyed makeshift shelter from the rain scraped together out of the city dump."[15]

The thousands who crowded into the Washington Hooverville, which came to be known as Camp Marks (after the benevolent police captain in charge of the precinct), were unemployed veterans of World War I who journeyed to the Capitol to demand adjusted compensation for their service. Those who had fought overseas during the war had received less salary than those exempted from the draft because they worked in essential defense industries. Although opponents derided these veterans for wanting a bonus, in 1924 Congress passed a bill over Calvin Coolidge's veto. The veterans demanded payment and, after a new bonus bill was tabled, marched on Washington by the thousands, arriving in May 1932 from all over the country by bus, train, truck, jalopy, and on foot. The bonus marchers, known as the Bonus Expeditionary Force (a reminder of the American Expeditionary Force in which they had served) had arrived.

The Bonus Army made Hoover's administration nervous. Camp Marks became a city of 20,000, complete with street names, newspapers, a library, barbershop, and entertainment. Walter Waters, a former army sergeant who led the Bonus Army and had started his march from Portland, Oregon, made certain that communists or agitators did not infiltrate the group and sully their efforts. His rules were "no panhandling, no liquor, no radical talk." Waters held trials and expelled agitators, though the government seized on the appearance of a radical element to discredit them. J. Edgar Hoover, the young head of the Federal Bureau of Investigation, sought to connect the Bonus Army to communism and others followed suit. Herbert Hoover supported a Justice Department report that found an "extraordinary proportion of criminal, Communist, and nonveteran elements amongst the marchers."[16]

On June 15, 1932, the House passed a veteran's bonus bill (Representative Edward Eslick of Tennessee, an impassioned supporter, died of a heart attack while delivering a speech on the floor of the House of Representatives; thousands of veterans marched in his funeral procession). The Senate, however, rejected it. The administration feared a violent uprising and decided to close down the camp. On July 28, Army Chief of Staff Douglas MacArthur moved in with mounted cavalry followed by tanks (under the command of George S. Patton) and armed infantrymen. They drove off the protesting members of the Bonus Army. MacArthur exceeded orders and attacked Camp Marks on Anacostia Flats with tear gas. He then burned the camp to the ground. The violent images of the military assaulting World War I veterans shocked millions who saw newsreels in the movie theaters and booed the sight of MacArthur and his troops. Hoover's defeat in the election only four months away seemed assured.

One noteworthy feature of the Bonus Army camp was that it was desegregated, and this, too, undoubtedly made it seem to some like a radical experiment. Roy Wilkins, writing for the *Crisis*, reported, "For years, the U.S. Army had argued that General Jim Crow was its proper commander, but the Bonus marchers gave lie to the notion that Black and white soldiers—ex-soldiers in their case—couldn't live together."[17]

Black veterans suffered more severely than others; however harshly the Depression hit whites, it devastated blacks. African Americans endured unemployment rates that reached 50 percent, were paid as much as 30 percent less than white employees and were the first to be fired and last to be hired. A new labor union, the Congress of Industrial Organizations, espoused a racially egalitarian rhetoric that was absent from the competing American Federation of Labor, and while this led to some opportunities, particularly in the steel industry, egalitarian unionism fell short of ameliorating the condition of black workers. The union movement overall received a boost from the Norris-LaGuardia Act of 1932, which banned yellow-dog contracts, in which employees were forced to agree not to join a union, and barred court injunctions against nonviolent protests. This proved vital for minorities who used boycotts as a weapon against discriminatory hiring practices.

Politically, African Americans began to drift toward the Democratic Party, to "turning the picture of Lincoln to the wall." In the election of 1932, Roosevelt won 23 percent of the black vote; in 1936, he received 71 percent. Although Roosevelt refused to support anti-lynching legislation for fear of losing Southern support, he accepted the counsel of a Black Cabinet—the term coined by educator and philanthropist Mary McLeod Bethune—that advised the president and Eleanor Roosevelt, a staunch civil rights advocate, on policy issues.[18]

Tensions for the black community remained high through the 1930s. In the South, nine black teenagers were accused of raping two white women on a freight train. The trials of these Scottsboro boys, named for the Alabama city where the case was first heard, spanned the decade and ended in prison sentences for some of them. In the North, Harlem exploded in a riot after a sixteen-year-old boy was accused of stealing a penknife and people swarmed the store after rumors spread that police had beaten the suspect.

Regardless of the desperation, two black men came to symbolize endurance and democracy for all Americans. At the Berlin Olympics in 1936, with Adolf Hitler looking on, Jesse Owens won four gold medals (Jewish athletes were not allowed to participate), and at Yankee Stadium in 1938, Joe Louis knocked out German Max Schmeling to win the heavyweight championship of the world. Louis later wrote, "White Americans—even while some of them were lynching black people in the South—were depending on me to K.O. a German." In the depths of the Depression, Owens and Louis gave all Americans something to celebrate.[19]

Dust Bowl

First came the drought, then the dust. While the lack of rain spanned the nation, it was especially severe in the Midwest and the Southern Plains (Kansas, Oklahoma, Colorado, New Mexico, Texas) where once-fertile soil cracked and turned barren. The temperatures were suffocating. In the summer of 1934, it reached 115 in Iowa and 118 in Nebraska. Thousands died. With the drought and the heat came the dust storms, blizzards of black particles that covered 100 million acres and blew east from the Southern Plains. In the middle of the day, the storms blackened the skies and dust penetrated every crevice of body and home. It killed cattle, horses, poultry, and sometimes people. Several inches of the most fertile topsoil simply blew away. For some it seemed as if Armageddon had arrived. Woody Guthrie, who in 1940 wrote "This Land Is Your Land" as a response to Irving Berlin's patriotic "God Bless America," penned many ballads about the Dust Bowl crisis. "The Great Dust Storm" told the story of Black Sunday, April 14, 1935, the day of the most destructive dust storm in American history, which thrust more than 300,000 tons of topsoil into the air: "It fell across our city like a curtain / of black rolled down, / we thought it as our judgment, we thought / it was our doom."

The Dust Bowl was a natural disaster manufactured by humans. It resulted from the expansion of farms and destruction of the short grass that literally held soil in the ground. In twenty-two High Plains counties in 1890, there were 5,762 farms, with an average size of 256 acres. In 1910, there were 11,422 farms that averaged 520 acres. By 1930, the average was 813 acres. Pastures gave way to crops, primarily wheat, and huge motorized tractors were used to break up the sod. A documentary produced by the government in 1936 was titled "The Plow That Broke the Plains." Agribusiness had arrived and millions of naked acres lay exposed to the burning sun. When the winds came, the transformed ecology of the region meant there was nothing to hold the soil in place.[20]

In accepting the Democratic nomination in 1932, Roosevelt had pledged "a new deal for the American people," and part of that New Deal included programs intended to benefit farmers. The Agricultural Adjustment Act paid farmers to limit their production in the hope of helping to raise prices; the Farm Credit Administration offered loans; in response to Black Sunday, Roosevelt issued an executive order to create the Resettlement Administration, which would help tenant farmers relocate to more productive land. Those stricken by the dust storms needed more. "You gave us beer," they told the president, "now give us water." "That beer part was easy," said the president. In June 1934, Congress granted Roosevelt's request for $525 million in drought relief.[21]

Roosevelt's administration also made strides toward conservation. The Department of the Interior created the Soil Erosion Service and the Soil Conservation and Domestic Allotment Act (1936), which provided millions of dollars for emergency listing—a lister cut deep corduroy furrows into the earth and prevented erosion. The Taylor Grazing Act (1934) regulated grazing on public land. The government also established the Civilian Conservation Corps (CCC), a public relief work program that ran from 1933 to 1942 and employed millions of young men in various projects including erosion and flood control, forestry, transportation, construction, and beautification. Workers received $30 a month and were required to send home $25. The CCC camps were segregated. More than half of those employed came from rural areas. Residents of the Plains took note. Roosevelt's opponent in 1936 was Alf Landon, governor of Kansas, a bastion of Republicanism, yet Roosevelt carried the state with 54 percent of the vote and swept Colorado with 60 percent, Oklahoma with 67 percent, and Texas with 87 percent.

No amount of government aid could offset the ruination of farms and homes that turned the Plains into what one journalist called "this withering land of misery." For tens of thousands, only the highways west offered hope. In the 1930s, some 2.5 million people abandoned the Plains. Many headed for California with dreams of good-paying work picking fruits and vegetables in the brilliant sunshine. Hundreds of thousands fled Oklahoma and Arkansas for the San Joaquin Valley. Roosevelt's administration understood the need to document the suffering. Doing so might help make his New Deal programs palatable to an American public that was skeptical of handouts from the federal government and thought of relief as moral weakness.[22]

The documentary photography program began when the Resettlement Administration hired a group of photographers to fan out to different regions with orders to shoot various kinds of scenes: people, homes, landscapes. Folded into the Farm Security Administration (FSA), the project generated tens of thousands of images and gave work to a talented group of photographers that included Arthur Rothstein, Dorothea Lange, Walker Evans, Carl Mydans, and Marion Post Wolcott. Images would be selected and sent to newspapers and magazines, including two new magazines, *Life* and *Look*, which reached millions of people and told stories through photo essays.

The work of the FSA photographers was not without controversy and Roosevelt's Republican opponents waited for an opportunity to accuse him of spreading propaganda. One prominent incident involved a photo of a bleached steer skull, its eye sockets facing the viewer, sitting upon barren cracked earth in the South Dakota Badlands. Taken by Arthur Rothstein in 1936, the image circulated widely through the Associated Press. Reporters for the *Fargo Forum* discovered several different images with the same skull. Rothstein explained that he had found the skull, then moved it for compositional purposes and that doing so did not exaggerate the severe drought conditions. Roosevelt's critics exploded, claiming "the principal socialistic experiment of the New Deal" had faked the evidence.[23]

No matter how much critics of the New Deal nitpicked specific images, the mounting visual evidence supported what nearly everyone knew: Americans were suffering and something had to be done. No photograph of the Depression had greater impact than one taken by Dorothea Lange, who was born in Hoboken, New Jersey, and studied photography at Columbia University before moving to California. In 1936, Lange was taking pictures of migratory farm laborers. Outside of Nipomo, California, she passed a sign that said "Pea Pickers Camp," turned her car around, and starting shooting pictures of a mother and her children sitting in a lean-to tent. Lange took five photographs and the final one became iconic. Titled "Migrant Mother," it shows a mother with a baby and two children who look away from the camera. The mother's face is etched with worry and anxiety, and also reveals quiet strength and determination. Here was a Madonna and child image that humanized American suffering. "Look into Her Eyes," read the headline of one of the many newspapers that reproduced the image.

Forty years later, a reporter found the migrant mother living in Modesto, California. Florence Owens Thompson had survived the Depression. Like so many others, her story began in Oklahoma, from which she migrated with her husband and children to California.

Of all the Okies, however, it was not a family of actual migrants who symbolized the era, but a family of fictional ones. John Steinbeck wrote *The Grapes of Wrath* in a four-month burst between June and

Figure 8.2 Dorothea Lange, *Migrant Mother* (1936). Library of Congress.

October 1938. Born and educated in California, Steinbeck had his first critical successes with *In Dubious Battle* (1936) and *Of Mice and Men* (1937), works that revealed Steinbeck's abiding interest in politics and the lives of people on the margins. He first addressed the plight of the Okie migrants in a series of journalistic articles, "The Harvest Gypsies," published in the *San Francisco News*. He soon turned to fiction and wrote the opening sentence of the novel: "To the red country and part of the gray country of Oklahoma, the last rains came gently, and they did not cut the scarred earth."

Grapes of Wrath tells the story of the Joad family. They are forced to pack their belongings and head west to what they believe will be a Promised Land, but which turns out to be troubled Eden, where migrant workers are beaten and exploited by farm owners. It is a story of struggle and survival, a spiritual narrative of American exodus, a meditation on the common people who made America great and the forces of greed that corrupted fairness and justice. At the story's center is ex-convict Tom Joad, who on his journey with his grandparents, parents, siblings, and friend Jim Casey, a lapsed preacher (his initials left little subtlety about his symbolic identity), finds his moral compass.

In a climactic scene, made indelible by Henry Fonda who played Tom Joad in the movie version released in 1940, a year after the novel was published, Tom tells his Ma that he knows "a fella ain't no good alone," and that he will devote his life to others: "wherever they's a fight so hungry people can eat, I'll be there. Wherever they's a cop beatin' up a guy, I'll be there . . . I'll be in the way guys yell when they're mad an' I'll be in the way kids laugh when they're hungry an' they know supper's ready. An' when our folks eat the stuff they raise an' lie in the houses they build—why I'll be there."[24]

The book became a bestseller. Steinbeck won a Pulitzer Prize and, in 1962, received a Nobel Prize. In the final scene Tom's sister, Rose of Sharon, whose child was stillborn, breast-feeds a starving dying man. Steinbeck's editors wanted it changed. He refused. "The giving of the breast has no more sentiment than the giving of a piece of bread," he responded." *Grapes of Wrath* generated controversy. Even as a congressional committee investigated labor practices at migrant farms, Oklahoma Congressman Lyle Boren denounced the book as "a lie, a black, infernal creation of a twisted, distorted mind." Some communities banned it. People tried to discredit the novel in terms of both message and craft. Most found the story irresistible. Eleanor Roosevelt explained the novel's power: "the horrors of the picture . . . made you dread . . . to begin the next chapter, and yet you cannot lay the book down or even skip a page." Steinbeck lamented that the hysteria surrounding *Grapes of Wrath* made him into "a public domain." He was pleased, however, that critics, for the most part, saluted the book as "a fiery document of protest and compassion," as one put it, "a book that must be read."[25]

New Deal

Roosevelt visited the Dust Bowl region only once. He arrived in Amarillo, Texas, on July 11, 1938. People had come to expect miracles from him and he obliged: as he spoke, it started to rain. When he had accepted the presidential nomination at the Democratic National Convention in Chicago on July 2, 1932, he had resolved to "resume the country's interrupted march along the path of real progress, of real justice, of real equality for all of our citizens, great and small." He called the work ahead "this new battle," in which the Democrats must be a party not for the "favored few," as the Republicans would have it, but "of the greatest good to the greatest number of our citizens."[26]

Roosevelt did not disappoint. He would coin the term "the hundred days" to refer to the proliferation of legislation that poured forth in the first months of his presidency, a benchmark applied to all presidents since. Inaugurated on March 4, 1933, two days later he closed the American banking system (a bank holiday he called it) and on March 9 he signed the Emergency Banking Act through which the Federal Reserve issued currency and the government provided insurance for deposits (formalized by the Federal Deposit Insurance Corporation, chartered in 1935). To regulate the unrestrained actions of brokers and control insider trading, the Securities and Exchange Commission was created in 1934.

Before banks reopened on March 13, 1933, Roosevelt took to the airwaves to speak directly to Americans in the first of a series of radio addresses that would come to be known as Fireside Chats. He addressed the audience as "my friends." He explained clearly what action he had taken, why it was taken, and what was coming next. He offered a tutorial on banking. He reassured listeners that there was nothing radical in what the government was doing. He concluded, "You people must have faith; you must not be stampeded by rumors or guesses. Let us unite in banishing fear. We have provided the machinery to restore our financial system; it is up to you to support and make it work."[27]

Legislation continued to issue at a breathless pace during those first hundred days and beyond. Having propped up financial institutions and policies (the Gold Reserve Act of 1934 outlawed private possession of gold and fixed the price at $35 dollars per troy ounce, which led foreign nations to trade gold for cash), other measures provided some form of direct relief to struggling Americans. The Federal Emergency Relief Act gave grants and loans to states to provide unemployment relief by encouraging the creation of any kind of job so people would not feel useless. While critics mocked these workers as subsidized broom sweepers, Harry Hopkins, a gaunt, chain-smoking, disheveled social worker from the Midwest, whom Roosevelt put in charge of the agency, understood the importance of self-worth and became a leading apostle of the New Deal. He soon ran the short-lived Civil Works Administration, which provided construction jobs to 4 million people. Hopkins recognized that most people could not comprehend the scope of the problem of unemployment, which disproportionately affected the young, women, the uneducated, the unskilled, minorities, and the elderly. "You can pity six men," he said, "but you can't get stirred up over six million." Hopkins stayed stirred up.[28]

In the first hundred days, the administration also focused on the problems faced by rural America and farmers. The Tennessee Valley Authority, a public corporation, provided hydroelectric power and economic development to a region that encompassed seven states and had been devastated by the Depression. The Agricultural Adjustment Act paid farmers not to grow crops such as wheat, corn, and cotton (whose price had plummeted from 28.8 cents per pound in 1918 to 17.9 cents in 1928 and collapsed to 5.66 cents in 1931), and provided subsidies to plow under some 10 million acres of cotton and slaughter some 6 million piglets to prevent further glutting of the market. The contradiction of destroying food when people were going hungry did not go unnoticed. It was, observed one farm leader, "an utterly idiotic situation, and one which makes a laughing stock of our genius as a people."[29]

The final major piece of legislation passed during the hundred days was the National Industrial Recovery Act (NIRA). The bill authorized federal regulation of hours and wages in industry and included a provision that guaranteed the collective bargaining right of workers. Union leaders were overjoyed; the United Mine Workers contributed $500,000 to Roosevelt's reelection campaign. Businessmen and proponents of laissez-faire capitalism opposed the proliferation of codes and regulations created by the National Recovery Administration, which was tasked with overseeing the process. In 1935, in *Schechter Poultry Corp. v. United States*, the Supreme Court ruled that the codes of fair competition required by the act were unconstitutional, one of many judicial decisions that would aggravate the president.

The NIRA also created the Public Works Administration (PWA) and gave it a budget of $3.3 billion through which private firms hired people to engage in major construction projects such as bridges, tunnels, dams, and airports, as well as highways and schools. Projects included the Lincoln Tunnel, Grand Coulee Dam, and Los Angeles Airport. Secretary of the Interior Harold L. Ickes ran the PWA. He began his political career as a Progressive Republican from Chicago and quickly became a key figure in the Roosevelt administration. His strong support for civil rights led him to end segregation in the cafeteria and rest rooms of his department, and through his efforts renowned African American contralto Marian Anderson performed before a crowd of 75,000 at the Lincoln Memorial in 1939 after the

Daughters of the American Revolution had denied her permission to sing at Constitution Hall.

Nicknamed "Honest Harold," Ickes was famously frugal and fearful of corruption. As a result, he did not authorize sufficient spending to boost the economy. Regardless of how much was spent, critics denounced the government's actions as communism. Roosevelt explained that the government was not taking control over farming and industry. It was, instead, entering into a partnership for the purpose of better planning. His defense, however, did little to assuage critics. Groups such as the American Liberty League united New Deal opponents aggrieved over what they saw as state centralization and an attack on individual liberty and private property. A conservative manifesto issued in 1937 defended states' rights and free enterprise, opposed deficit spending, and called for reduced taxes.

The most far-reaching criticism of the New Deal, however, came not from conservative Republicans and Democrats who had opposed it from the start, but supporters who felt the New Deal did not go far enough. In 1934, Ickes noted in his diary that Roosevelt "would have to move further to the left in order to hold the country" because that seemed where the people wanted to go. That same year, Upton Sinclair won the Democratic nomination for governor of California on a program called End Poverty in California (EPIC). Caricatured as "a socialist interloper," he lost the election. Another radical proposal came from Francis Townsend, an obscure California physician, who called for the government to make monthly payments of $200 to people age sixty and over on the condition that they spend it within thirty days. So-called Townsend Clubs sprouted across America and 25 million Americans signed Townsend petitions that called for an Old Age Revolving Pension.[30]

Two figures, one a politician and the other a priest, rode anti–New Deal populism to national prominence. In 1928, Huey Long became governor of Louisiana on a platform of "everyman is a king, but no one wears a crown." Two years later he was elected to the Senate. An early supporter of Roosevelt (he helped deliver the South in the election of 1932), he chastised the president for not being radical enough. Long gave a radio address on February 23, 1934, in which he announced a program entitled Share Our Wealth. Invoking the Declaration of Independence and the Bible, he questioned why there were those "born to inherit $10,000,000,000" whereas "another child was to be born to inherit nothing." He made appealing promises to suffering Americans. He would cap personal fortunes, redistribute confiscated wealth, and raise money through progressive income taxes. His program also called for free college education, veterans' benefits, and pensions for people over sixty. He promised every American family $5,000. The math did not add up. Demagogues triumph through rhetoric, not reality. (Walter Lippmann wrote, "This is not water for the thirsty, but a mirage.") Share Our Wealth Societies formed and attracted millions of members. On September 8, 1935, one month after he announced his candidacy for president, Long was assassinated by the son-in-law of a judge he was trying to oust. His challenge to Roosevelt had been brought to a premature end.[31]

When Roosevelt received the news of Long's death, Father Charles Coughlin was visiting him at Hyde Park. Coughlin was vastly popular. In 1926, he had begun broadcasting from his parish in Royal Oak, Michigan. He denounced anti-Catholicism and cross-burnings by the Ku Klux Klan. His radio program went national and attracted millions of listeners who were spellbound by what one writer called "one of the great speaking voices of the twentieth century," a voice "made for promises." Father Coughlin attacked communism and saw Roosevelt as the only barrier between the preservation of democracy and a violent revolution from below (he coined the phrase "Roosevelt or Ruin"). Coughlin came to believe the New Deal did not go far enough. He founded the National Union for Social Justice and attacked Roosevelt's support of capitalism. He advocated nationalization and redistribution of wealth. His popularity was such that he received thousands of letters each day. As the 1930s advanced, Coughlin sympathized with fascism and delivered anti-Semitic tirades that blamed Jewish bankers for starting the financial crisis and conspiring for world conquest. His magazine *Social Justice* published *The Protocols of the Elders of Zion*, a forgery that purported to reveal Jewish plans for world domination. When the United States entered World War II, which Coughlin opposed, the Church forced him to suspend his broadcasts.[32]

Whether his critics' popularity moved Roosevelt toward more radical measures or he gravitated toward them as a natural extension of his initial efforts to end the Depression, the administration launched a new series of initiatives in 1935–1936, usually referred to as the Second New Deal. The Works Progress Administration, with an appropriation of $4.9 billion and headed by Harry Hopkins, put the government in the business of directly hiring people, as opposed to giving grants and loans to state and local agencies. Art, music, theater, and writing projects all received funding. The National Labor Relations Act (also known as the Wagner Act) guaranteed the right to collective bargaining and established the National Labor

Relations Board to adjudicate labor unrest and unfair labor practices. The Wealth Tax Act raised taxes on higher income levels (79 percent on income over $5 million, which applied to one person, John D. Rockefeller). The Social Security Act, through taxes on wages and payrolls, provided pensions to the aged as well as unemployment insurance and benefits for child welfare.

Roosevelt became increasingly dismayed by the actions of the Supreme Court, which, in a series of 5–4 votes, ruled numerous provisions of the New Deal to be unconstitutional. Concerned that this new legislation would face a similar fate, Roosevelt tried to reform the Court (his critics called it "court packing") by adding new justices who would give him a more favorable hearing. The bill to do so stalled, and Chief Justice Charles Evan Hughes managed to forge a majority that ruled the National Labor Relations Act and the Social Security Act were constitutional. In 1940, a seventy-six-year-old woman from Vermont received the first Social Security check. It was for $41.30.

Whatever else it did, Roosevelt's New Deal had laid the foundation for a limited welfare state wherein the federal government assumed some responsibility for the social and economic well-being of its citizens, especially the aged, children, skilled workers, and the unemployed. (The New Deal applied less equally to women and African Americans than to white men.) The movement away from private charity, self-help, and states' rights would continue to provoke opposition, just as others hoped to expand the possibilities of what the federal government could do for its citizens.

In 1937, as the nation faced another economic downturn, and as Roosevelt battled to win support for his new legislation, Ickes observed, "The President is showing the strain that he has been through. He looks all of 15 years older since he was inaugurated in 1933. I don't see how anyone could stand the strain he has been under." With the German invasion of Poland on September 1, 1939, that strain would increase.[33]

World War II

On November 16, 1938, Roosevelt received a telegram signed by thirty-six writers, including John Steinbeck. In the aftermath of Kristallnacht, a systematic pogrom against Jewish synagogues, stores, hospitals, and homes in Nazi Germany, the writers informed Roosevelt "it is deeply immoral for the American people to continue having economic relations with a government that avowedly uses mass murder to solve its economic problems." Although preoccupied with domestic matters, Americans had been warily following events in Europe from the time Adolf Hitler became chancellor in 1933 and then fuhrer the following year. In 1936, German troops occupied the Rhineland, in violation of several treaties that demilitarized the area; Benito Mussolini's Italian forces took Ethiopia. Earlier in the decade Japan had invaded and occupied Manchuria. German military forces continued to mobilize and occupied the Sudetenland in 1938 and the remainder of Czechoslovakia in March 1939. With Germany's invasion of Poland in September, Britain, France, New Zealand, Australia, and Canada declared war on Germany. In 1941, Hitler's invasion of Russia brought the Soviet Union into the anti-Nazi coalition.

As the conflict escalated, the United States officially remained neutral. Between 1935 and 1939, Congress passed several Neutrality Acts, which placed an embargo on arms trade and forbade loans to belligerents. The Neutrality Act of 1939, issued once war in Europe had been declared, allowed for arms trade with Great Britain and France as long as those countries adhered to a policy of cash-and-carry: recipients had to arrange transportation and pay cash. Roosevelt spoke to Americans on September 3, 1939, and reminded them "This nation will remain a neutral nation, but I cannot ask that every American remain neutral in thought as well. Even a neutral has a right to take account of facts. Even a neutral cannot be asked to close his mind or his conscience." On November 4, 1939, Roosevelt issued a Proclamation of Neutrality.[34]

Roosevelt was no isolationist, but many others in the United States were. Conclusions reached in 1936 by a congressional committee led by Republican Senator Gerald Nye suggested that American entry into World War I was unnecessary and fueled by profit-seeking bankers and corporations, especially munitions manufacturers. A broad coalition of pacifists and isolationists advocated nonintervention. These included New Deal opponent Republican Robert Taft and New Deal supporter Robert M. LaFollette Jr., who had succeeded his father as a senator in 1925. Senator Burton Wheeler, Democrat of Montana, a zealous isolationist, sought to investigate interventionists in the motion picture industry, many of whose leaders were Jewish. Radicals such as socialist Norman Thomas helped organize the Keep America Out of War Congress, a group that demanded "jobs at home and not through death on the battlefield."[35]

Among the celebrities who preached nonintervention, Charles A. Lindbergh insisted in 1937 that "the destiny of this country does not call for our involvement in European wars." He became a leading spokesman for the America First Committee (AFC), founded in 1940. At its peak, the AFC boasted hundreds of chapters and hundreds of thousands of members (two-thirds of whom came from the Midwest). Lindbergh, though, went beyond a call for making America stronger and not providing aid. He supported Germany and was sympathetic to the Nazi regime. In one speech, he accused the Jews of posing the "greatest danger to this country" in their control over film, newspapers, radio, and even the US government itself. Roosevelt was so disgusted he told Henry Morgenthau, "I am convinced Lindbergh is a Nazi."[36]

Many others argued that support for Great Britain was essential, especially after France surrendered to Germany in June 1940. Roosevelt's speeches and actions slowly maneuvered the United States toward intervention, although in the campaign for an unprecedented third term as president in 1940 he promised parents "your boys are not going to be sent into any foreign wars." On December 29, 1940, in a Fireside Chat delivered two months after the Axis powers of Germany, Italy, and Japan signed a Tripartite Pact, Roosevelt warned, "Never before since Jamestown and Plymouth Rock has our American civilization been in such danger as now." Roosevelt refused to deny the danger of a situation in which, should the Axis powers succeed, "All of us, in all the Americas, would be living at the point of a gun." There could be no appeasement. It fell to the United States to help arm the British. "We must be the great arsenal of democracy."[37]

The president had spoken to the people; next he spoke to Congress. In his State of the Union address in January 1941, Roosevelt envisioned a new world order based not on tyranny, but "upon four essential human freedoms": freedom of speech, freedom of worship, freedom from want, and freedom from fear. "Freedom," he declared, "means the supremacy of human rights everywhere." Roosevelt had defined the world war that, soon enough, would involve the United States.[38]

In March 1941, American policy shifted with the adoption of Lend-Lease, whereby the United States supplied Great Britain with whatever it needed to defend itself and would worry about being repaid only after the conflict was over. Roosevelt used the analogy of lending one's neighbor a garden hose if their house was on fire. Opponents added an amendment forbidding American warships from escorting the merchant ships. Roosevelt nonetheless authorized expanded Atlantic patrols. Inevitably this led to incidents with German U-boats, most notably on October 31, 1941, when a German submarine sank the destroyer *USS Reuben James.*

War with Germany was all but declared when events in the Pacific ended American neutrality. On December 7, 1941, Japanese warplanes launched a surprise attack against the American naval base at Pearl Harbor in Hawaii. Much of the American fleet was damaged or destroyed (the Pacific Fleet's three aircraft carriers were at sea and thus spared destruction), and more than 2,000 Americans were killed. The next day, Roosevelt called December 7 "a date which will live in infamy," and the United States declared war on Japan. Declaration of war with Germany came on December 11, following Hitler's declaration of war against the United States. The noninterventionists grew silent and largely disappeared. "No matter how long it may take us to overcome this premeditated invasion," Roosevelt declared, "the American people in their righteous might will win through to absolute victory."[39]

That victory would take nearly four years. A peacetime draft, the first in US history, had been instituted on September 16, 1940, for all men between the ages of twenty-one and forty-five. The draft began the process of transforming one of the smallest armies in the world, with fewer than 200,000 active-duty soldiers, into a force of 8.3 million active-duty soldiers and a total of 12 million military personnel in May 1945. Over the course of the war, 16 million men served, more than one-third of whom were volunteers. Nearly one million African Americans served in segregated units and more than 500,000 Jews. Half a million women volunteered. Seventy-three percent of US forces served overseas. Total casualties exceeded one million, out of which an estimated 291,000 were killed in action.

British Prime Minister Winston Churchill rushed to Washington to meet with Roosevelt, establish a Combined Chiefs of Staff, and confirm a military strategy whereby Germany (which threatened both London and Moscow) would remain the prime enemy target. Aside from the ongoing warfare in the Atlantic, which brought German U-boats near the East Coast of the United States to attack shipping, Americans first saw action in the Pacific theater. On April 18, 1942, sixteen B-25 bombers took off from the *USS Hornet,* stationed more than 600 miles from Japan, and made the first bombing raids on Tokyo. It was a one-way trip led by Lieutenant Colonel James Doolittle who, along with most of his men, bailed out over China as their planes ran out of fuel.

Doolittle's raid bolstered American morale. It also led the Japanese to focus attention on Midway, an atoll northwest of the

Hawaiian Islands. American intelligence intercepted and cracked Japanese cypher messages that revealed Midway as the target; Admiral Chester Nimitz had his forces reinforced and ready. In a naval battle in June 1942, the American fleet of seven carriers, whose presence was unknown to the Japanese commander, launched aircraft that decimated the Japanese fleet, sinking four carriers and one cruiser. The United States now had naval supremacy in the Pacific and Japan was on the defensive.

Following Midway, US forces in the Pacific, under the command of Douglas MacArthur, who had been called out of retirement at age sixty, settled on a strategy of island-hopping to wage war against the Japanese. At Guadalcanal, savage, at times hand-to-hand combat raged for six months. Tarawa, Saipan, and other islands followed. MacArthur, who had been forced to flee the Philippines in April 1942 when the Japanese took them over, vowed to return. He had left behind 10,000 American POWs who would be starved and tortured on an eighty-mile forced trek that would come to be known at the Bataan Death March. He kept his promise in October 1944, after the Battle of Leyte Gulf. Photos showed him, defiant, determined, and steely-eyed, as he waded through the waters toward land, both at Leyte and Luzon.

Another photograph became the defining image of the war in the Pacific. At Iwo Jima, on February 23, 1945, Joe Rosenthal snapped six US marines raising the American flag atop Mount Suribachi. The photo was not staged, but because it was the second flag hoisted that day many people believed it was. A perfect image of faceless men working in unison to raise the flag that fills an empty sky, the photo became a symbol of American patriotism and heroism. Only three of the six flag-raisers survived the battle. One of them, Ira Hayes, was a Pima Indian; one Marine who died, Michael Strank, was an immigrant from Slovakia.

As US forces were making their way across the Pacific, the government at home forced thousands of Japanese Americans to relocate to internment camps. Just days after the attack on Pearl Harbor, the FBI began detaining thousands of aliens from Japan, Germany, and Italy. A presidential proclamation in January 1942 forced all aliens to register with the Department of Justice. On February 19, 1942, Roosevelt signed executive order 9066, which gave the War Department authority to create military exclusion zones. More than 100,000 Japanese aliens and American citizens of Japanese descent were taken from their homes on the West Coast and placed in camps such as Manzanar in California and Poston in

Figure 8.3 Joe Rosenthal, *American Marines Raising American Flag on Mount Suribachi* (1945). Library of Congress.

Arizona. Vitriol poured forth against the Japanese, who were seen as disloyal and potential saboteurs. "We want to keep this a white man's country," announced Idaho's attorney general. On December 18, 1944, the Supreme Court, in *Korematsu v. United States*, upheld the constitutionality of removal by a 6–3 decision. Several thousand Americans of German and Italian descent were also sent to relocation camps.[40]

The Office of War Information (OWI), established in June 1942, controlled the flow of information about the war and created propaganda to support government actions and inspire patriotism. This included documentaries such as *Japanese Relocation*, which defended internment as democratic. The office provided Hollywood with a manual stating that films should emphasize the war as a battle of democracy against fascism (*Casablanca*, which premiered in November 1942, fit the bill and won the Academy Award). It was a war against racism as well, and the OWI published a pamphlet on "Negroes and the War" that featured Sergeant Joe Louis, who "is now a champion in an army of champions." The OWI also promoted the work of women, as millions of female workers entered defense industries to help build the planes, ships, and weapons vital to the war effort. Dubbed "Rosie the Riveter," posters showed a woman in a work shirt and bandana flexing her muscle with the caption "We Can Do It."[41]

OWI censors forbade the showing of any images of American war dead until September 1943, when they permitted *Life* to print a photograph titled "Dead Americans at Buna Beach." The editors wrote, "The American people ought to be able to see their own boys as they fall in battle."[42]

Buna Beach was part of the Pacific campaign that began in November 1942. That month, the Allies' Europe First strategy took shape in the fight for North Africa, commanded by Dwight D. Eisenhower. Born in 1890 in Texas, Eisenhower was raised in Abilene, Kansas. In 1915, he graduated from West Point where he played football (he did not make the baseball team, calling this "one of the greatest disappointments of my life"). Despite desiring assignment in France during World War I, his only service had been on the home front. In 1935, he accompanied Douglas MacArthur to the Philippines where he gained valuable administrative experience and came to resent MacArthur's egotism and jealousy.[43]

Appointed Supreme Allied Commander after victory in North Africa in May 1943, Eisenhower led the planning for the assault on Europe, which began with the campaign in Sicily and the Italian mainland. At the same time, the Royal Air Force and US Army Air Force began around-the-clock bombing designed to hit such strategic targets in Germany as oil refineries, factories, and railroad tracks. It spilled over into attacks against civilian populations. A strike on Berlin on February 3, 1945, resulted in 25,000 civilian deaths; ten days later a firestorm ignited by the bombing of Dresden killed 35,000.

By then, Allied troops had begun the liberation of Western Europe. The extensive and costly Italian campaign (more than 43,000 casualties at the Battle of Anzio alone) concluded with the Allies entering Rome on June 4, 1944. Two days later, on June 6, 1944, D-Day, 156,000 soldiers, including 73,000 Americans, landed at Normandy. Allied commanders had divided the landing zones into five beachheads named Omaha and Utah (where Americans would land), Juno (Canadian forces), and Gold and Sword (British forces). Soldiers at Omaha faced entrenched German troops firing machine guns from cliffs above. Americans suffered more than 2,000 casualties at Omaha. Allied forces now had a foothold from which to begin their drive across Europe.

In August 1944, Allied forces liberated Paris. At year's end came the Battle of the Bulge (named for a bulge in Allied lines formed by attacking German forces), fought between December 16, 1944, and January 25, 1945, in the Ardennes region of eastern Belgium. More than 400,000 Germans faced more than 600,000 Americans, who suffered 70,000 casualties. George Patton distinguished himself by disengaging three tank divisions and wheeling north to relieve trapped troops at the surrounded town of Bastogne. (The commander there had responded to a German demand for surrender with one word: "Nuts!") In March 1945, US troops crossed the Rhine. Soviet troops, relentlessly pressing the Germans from the east, took Warsaw in January 1945 and Vienna four months later. On April 29, 1945, US soldiers of the Forty-Second Infantry liberated more than 30,000 survivors at Dachau concentration camp. The next day, Hitler committed suicide. Germany surrendered in May 7, 1945.

Roosevelt did not live to see it. He had easily won reelection in 1944, his fourth term, despite evidence of ill health and an aggressive opponent, Governor Thomas E. Dewey of New York, who campaigned against the New Deal. Harry Truman, a Missouri moderate, had replaced Vice President Henry Wallace, seen as too liberal by the conservative wing of the Democratic Party. In February 1945, Roosevelt had attended a conference at Yalta, in the Crimea, where he met with Churchill and Joseph Stalin to decide on principles for postwar reorganization of Europe and the holding of free elections, a promise Stalin would not keep. Upon his return, the president looked frail and traveled to Warm Springs, Georgia, where he had been going since the 1920s for treatment of the effects of his polio. He was hoping to participate in the founding conference for the United Nations, to be held in April in San Francisco. On April 12, he died of a cerebral hemorrhage.

To prevent the loss of more American lives and to end the war against Japan, Truman ordered atomic bombs dropped on Hiroshima (August 6) and Nagasaki (August 9). More than 100,000 Japanese were killed as the world entered the atomic age. Japan surrendered on August 14. Many have viewed dropping the bombs as an atrocity, dismissing the argument that without doing so an invasion of Japan would have been necessary to end the war. America had become the world's greatest military and industrial power and took the lead in forging a postwar peace based on international cooperation. On August 16, 1945, Churchill rose before the House of Commons and declared, "The United States stand at this moment at the summit of the world."[44]

CHAPTER 9

Blowin' in the Wind

T HE REVEREND MARTIN LUTHER KING JR. was in jail, again. He had been incarcerated more than two dozen times and, in 1967, he returned to jail in Birmingham, Alabama, where he had been imprisoned four years earlier. From writings smuggled out on scraps of newspaper, he published "Letter from a Birmingham Jail," in which he defended nonviolent disobedience and called on all clergy and white moderates to support civil rights. Now back behind bars, King received a telegram from Muhammad Ali that expressed hope the minister was comfortable and not suffering. In February 1964, at age twenty-two, Ali had become heavyweight champion of the world. Born Cassius Clay, he joined the Nation of Islam and changed his name. Clay, he said, was his slave name. Confident and handsome, Ali proclaimed, "I am the greatest . . . I am the prettiest thing that ever lived." King recognized that Ali was an idol to many young people. In 1967, the champ refused to be drafted and faced his own jail time for filing as a conscientious objector to the Vietnam War. "I am America," he declared. "I am the part you won't recognize. But get used to me. Black, confident, cocky; my name, not yours; my religion, not yours; my goals, my own; get used to me."[1]

Consumerism

Following World War II, with so many veterans returning home, marrying, and having children, the birth rate in the United States exploded. Between 1950 and 1960, the population increased from 151 million to 180 million, a growth rate of 19 percent. In 1954, there were more than 4 million births, a first for the country. As a result of this baby boom, as it was termed, by 1965 four out of ten Americans were younger than twenty years old. The impact of the population growth was felt all the more acutely because the birth rate had declined during the Depression. Americans had weathered the hard times, helped win a war, and now started families at a moment of remarkable prosperity.

The US economy grew dramatically in the 1950s. Unemployment dropped below 5 percent. The GNP rose by 37 percent, from $353 billion in 1950 to $487 billion in 1960. Average salaries ballooned: a factory worker went from making $2,793 in 1947 to $4,230 in 1957. For a physician, the raise was even greater: from $10,700 to $22,100. With increased income came increased purchasing power, which also meant ramped up industrial production. In 1952, the United States supplied more than 60 percent of the world's manufactured goods. Americans bought homes (a quarter of all homes in 1960 had been built the previous decade), cars (80 percent of American families had at least one car), and televisions, a new technology. In 1947, there were 44,000 television sets in homes; by 1950 there were more than 9 million and by 1960 over 65 million. Nearly every home owned at least one.[2]

One of the causes of all this was the GI Bill, officially the Serviceman's Readjustment Act, signed by President Roosevelt in 1944. Promoted by members of the American Legion, who sought to avoid the problems faced by World War I veterans, the bill emerged in anticipation of some 15 million armed services members entering the economy after war's end. It offered federal aid for education, homeownership, and unemployment protection. The tuition benefit transformed American education, as more than 8 million veterans took advantage of the provision: the number of degrees awarded by colleges and universities doubled between 1950 and 1960. The bill also contributed to a wave of home-buying that accelerated suburbanization; by 1960, one-third of the population had moved to suburbs, which did not exist in 1950. With no down payment required and low interest rates, veterans accounted for 20 percent of all new homes purchased after the war. The bill, however, proved far less successful as an engine of geographic upward mobility for black veterans, who were routinely denied mortgages and prevented from moving into white suburbs because of racially restrictive covenants.[3]

Figure 9.1 Frank Martin, *Family Time* (1958). Hulton Archive/Getty Images.

Typical of the postwar boom in restrictive suburban housing were Levittowns, a series of developments built on Long Island and in New Jersey and Pennsylvania. Developer William Levitt, who had served in the US Navy during the war, mass-produced affordable Cape Cod–style homes on vast subdivided tracts of land outside of cities. The houses sold for about $8,000 and provided far more than a place to live. The towns became centers of a suburban lifestyle, made possible by the construction of new highways (abetted by the Federal Highway Act of 1956, which led to the construction of more than 40,000 miles of interstate highways), and they were hotbeds of mass consumerism. The creation of indoor shopping malls furthered the expansion of consumer culture. When Southdale opened in Edina, Minnesota, in 1954, journalists celebrated it as "a pleasure dome with parking." A cover story in *Time* magazine in 1950 read, "For Sale: A New Way of Life."[4]

Although that new way of life did not incorporate everyone, Levittown soon represented a durable vision of American existence in the 1950s: the suburban nuclear family with working husband, domestic wife, two-car garage, absorbed with television and encouraged by mass-market advertising to purchase items such as refrigerators, vacuum cleaners, and washing machines. By the 1960s, they did so in a new way—by using credit cards. Of course, as with all clichés, this is only a partial truth. For example, during the decade, more than 5 million women entered the workforce. Levittowners, said sociologist Herbert Gans, although "not a numerical majority . . . represent the major constituency of the largest and most powerful economic and political institutions in America—the favored customers and voters whom these seek to attract and satify."[5]

Those voters elected Dwight D. Eisenhower as president in 1952. Twice he trounced Adlai Stevenson, a progressive Democrat whose intellectual demeanor and oratorical skills some found appealing. The majority of people, however, saw in Eisenhower not only a war hero but also someone who could oversee American prosperity and protect the nation against the threat of communism. "I Like Ike" served as his campaign slogan and, for the first time, television commercials played a key role in swaying voters, especially women, whom Eisenhower's campaign cultivated. A New York advertising firm transformed the stiff, wooden Eisenhower into a likeable and effective speaker by producing a series of one-minute ads called "Eisenhower Answers America." Referring to his wife, Eisenhower would say, "My Mamie gets after me about the high cost of living. It's another reason why I say 'It's time for a change.'" Another ad introduced Eisenhower as a leader "out of the heartland of America," and showed footage of the landing on D-Day. Stevenson complained that a choice of presidential candidates was being reduced to a consumer survey—"this isn't Ivory soap versus Palmolive." What he failed to understand was that politics and consumerism had become inseparable. In 1952, Eisenhower won with more than 55 percent of the vote and, despite having suffered a heart attack in 1955, increased his margin in 1956 to more than 57 percent.[6]

After his heart attack, Eisenhower called the Reverend Billy Graham, who had become a close confidant of the president and the leading evangelist of a new era of religious revivalism. Church membership had expanded from 40 percent in 1940 to 69 percent in 1960. "In God We Trust" became the nation's official motto in 1956 and began appearing on US currency the following year. On television, the Bishop Fulton J. Sheen hosted *The Catholic Hour*. Norman Vincent Peale, pastor of the Reformed Church in America, published *The Power of Positive Thinking* (1952), a work whose message rhymed with the times. No one had greater impact than Billy Graham, whose crusades attracted hundreds of thousands of people. He became known as "America's Pastor." Like Charles Grandison Finney and Billy Sunday before him, Graham was a charismatic figure whose theology encouraged all denominations to renounce sin and return to God. "Belief exhilarates people," he said, "doubt depresses them." He believed in a saving faith and in American values. He denounced communism and opposed the growing civil rights movement. He remained a counselor to presidents up to and including Barack Obama. Harry Truman called him "one of those counterfeits." Millions, however, embraced his ministry.[7]

Not everyone shared in the prosperity and piety of the era. In 1959, more than 20 percent of families lived in poverty. More than one in four children were below the poverty line. The majority of these families lived in rural America, and black families had nearly twice the poverty rate of white families. The revelation of widespread poverty shocked readers of Michael Harrington's bestseller *The Other America* (1962). Harrington, a political scientist and a founder of the Democratic Socialists of America, sought to make poverty visible and explained that the poor—farmers, workers, minorities, the aged— were entrapped in cycles of need that left them as "internal aliens" in the nation. "I want to tell every well-fed and optimistic American that it is intolerable that so many millions should be maimed in body and in spirit when it is not necessary that they should be," wrote Harrington. The book was instrumental in President Lyndon Johnson's decision to declare a "war on poverty," and through measures such as Medicaid, Head Start, subsidized housing, and food stamps, the poverty rate was cut in half by 1973, to 11 percent.[8]

The reality of poverty amid so much comfort only hinted at the deeper struggles faced by everyday people for whom the American dream of success and upward mobility turned out to be hollow. No one dissected this more powerfully than Arthur Miller in his play *Death of a Salesman* (1949). Willy Loman, an aging traveling salesman, hopes to gain a desk job in the central office after decades of service to his company. But the sales game has changed, and he is fired by the boss's son, who Willy had helped name when he was born. Willy cannot understand what went wrong. Why hasn't he thrived the way others have, especially his brother? Why aren't his sons, Biff and Happy, more successful? Willy's wife, Linda, supports and defends her husband, yet Willy kills himself, hoping the insurance money will give his children a new start. "Nobody dast blame this man," exclaims Willy's friend Charley. "A salesman has got to dream, boy. It comes with the territory." There would be no insurance money and the small confined house, any greenery having long ago disappeared, would stand empty.[9]

Other writers emerged who also challenged the staid orthodoxy of capitalist, conformist America. Together they came to be known as the beat generation—a name coined by Jack Kerouac, author of *On the Road* (1957), a defining novel of a generation that revolted against establishment norms. At Columbia University, Kerouac had met Allen Ginsberg, who became the poet of the beat generation. Ginsberg's "Howl" (1956) opens, famously, with "I saw the best minds of my generation destroyed by madness, starving hysterical naked." His poem "America" (1956) offers an indictment of an atomic nation that narcotizes citizens with television and anticommunist hysteria: "America I've given you all, and now I'm nothing." Disillusionment was everywhere, nowhere more so than in J. D. Salinger's *Catcher in the Rye* (1951), which features alienated protagonist Holden Caulfield's search for companionship and his disillusionment with the phoniness he perceives all around him.

These authors spoke to a dynamic youth culture that reshaped America after World War II. Teenagers came to the fore in the 1950s and teenage alienation and generational conflict pervaded the era, embodied by movie stars such as James Dean, featured in *Rebel Without a Cause* (1955), and Marlon Brando in *The Wild One* (1953). At one point in the film, Brando's character is asked, "What are you rebelling against?" His answer: "What have you got?" The teens speak in slang: jive, square, stay cool. And they move to a new sound roaring from a jukebox.

The music to which teenagers danced and partied was called rock 'n' roll. Alan Freed, a Cleveland disc jockey who played the music on his radio show, is credited with coining the name, though it was used previously in various contexts, including Bill Moore's song "We're Gonna Rock" in 1948. Rock 'n' roll was something new, an American invention that went everywhere. It fused the syncopated beat of rhythm and blues (a new term in the 1940s for what had been called, at least by whites, "race music") and country music. This new music featured guitars instead of saxophones, a strong backbeat, and prominent vocals led by a front man who often mirrored the incantations of a gospel minister. Boosted by transistor radios and the 45-rpm single, featured in movies, performed by black artists such as Chuck Berry and white ones such as Jerry Lee Lewis, rock shook the culture. Established institutions felt threatened. Cities tried to ban the music; ministers denounced it; journalists mocked it; Congress held hearings. Masses of integrated youth assembling in crowds, singing and dancing at events, led *Time* to warn in 1956 that the gatherings "bear passing resemblance to Hitler's mass meetings."[10]

Mass movements of any stripe require a charismatic figure and the new sound soon had one. Elvis Presley did not invent rock 'n' roll, but he did embody it. The singer and performer, who was born in 1935 in Tupelo, Mississippi, and was raised in Memphis, Tennessee, became the "King of Rock 'n' Roll" and a transformative cultural icon. Songs such as "Hound Dog," "All Shook Up," "Jailhouse Rock," and "Don't Be Cruel," stayed at the top of the charts. Equally important were Presley's live performances, where teenagers screamed and shrieked in fits of ecstasy. On September 9, 1956, he appeared for the first time on the *Ed Sullivan Show*, a popular weekly entertainment revue. More than 60 million viewers (over 80 percent of the television audience) watched as Elvis performed with his backup group, the Jordanaires. Elvis exuded sexuality. He wore makeup, he looked androgynous, his lips sneered, and hips gyrated. Rock 'n' roll, Presley style, was wild and free, sensual and sexual, a liberating experience that forced the body to move. Sexual liberation was not attributable to Presley alone: movie star Marilyn Monroe served as national seductress and *Playboy* magazine began publishing in 1953. In 1960, the Food and Drug Administration approved the first oral contraceptive, legal at first only for married couples and by 1972 for everyone. Mainstream America could take only so much. When Presley appeared on the Sullivan show for a third and final time on January 6, 1957, the camera showed him only from the waist up.

Presley was a rebel. He also quickly became a commodity, the first rock star and also a movie star. There had never been anything like him. "There was just no reference point in the culture to compare it," said singer Roy Orbison. John Lennon of the Beatles, whose appearance on the *Ed Sullivan Show* in 1963 would launch a second rock 'n' roll and social revolution, put it simply: "Before Elvis there was nothing."[11]

Cold War

Elvis Presley was inducted into the US Army and served in Germany from 1958 to 1960. He quickly became enlisted in the Cold War. Although communist nations saw Presley as a symbol of capitalist decadence, the US government exploited his popularity with German youth and used him as a symbol of freedom.[12] In April 1959, East

German Communist Party leader Walter Ulbricht told a cultural conference that it was "not enough . . . to speak out against the ecstatic 'singing' of someone like Presley. We have to offer something better."

The Cold War between the United States and the Soviet Union began in earnest at the end of World War II. Financier Bernard Baruch coined the phrase in a speech delivered to the South Carolina House of Representatives on April 16, 1947: "Let us not be deceived. We are in the midst of a cold war. Our enemies are to be found abroad and at home. Let us never forget this: our unrest is the heart of their success." A few months later, journalist Walter Lippman, a friend of Baruch's, used the term in his widely read newspaper column. The fear of the spread of communism led Truman to address a joint session of Congress on March 12, 1947, and lay out what would soon be known as the Truman Doctrine: support for democratic nations around the world that faced economic hardship and communist insurgency. He spoke specifically of Greece and Turkey, and outlined a principle of US foreign policy in stark terms that contrasted free institutions characterized by democratic government, free speech, and individual liberty with a system of political oppression based on fear, fixed elections, control over the press, and "the suppression of personal freedoms."[13]

At the same time, the United States adopted what came to be known as the Marshall Plan (officially the Foreign Assistance Act of 1948) after Secretary of State George Marshall's call to provide support for the rebuilding of Europe in the aftermath of World War II. The Soviet Union refused to participate. Under American supervision, billions of dollars over the next several years flowed into Western Europe, fostering economic growth and reducing communist influence.

The Marshall Plan was part of a policy of containment, first articulated by diplomat George F. Kennan. In an anonymous piece published in 1947 in *Foreign Affairs*, he argued for "a long-term, patient but firm and vigilant containment of Russian expansive tendencies," not through military confrontation but by promoting "tendencies which must eventually find their outlet in either the break-up or the gradual mellowing of Soviet power." A more aggressive blueprint was articulated by NSC-68, a National Security Council policy statement presented to Truman in 1950. NSC-68 called for massive military spending and a build-up of both conventional and nuclear weapons. Between 1950 and 1953, the Truman administration tripled defense spending as a percentage of gross domestic product, from 5 to 14.2 percent.[14]

The economic and political struggle between West and East, democracy and communism, became a war when North Korea (supported by communist China and the Soviet Union) invaded South Korea on June 25, 1950. Toward the end of World War II, concerned that the Soviets would occupy the Korean peninsula, the United States had suggested the division of the area along the 38th parallel, a dividing line picked almost randomly from a map. The Soviet Union accepted, and Korea was bifurcated into the communist North and noncommunist South, with the line guarded by an American occupation force. The area was of no strategic importance to the United States. Later, Secretary of State Dean Acheson would say, "If the best minds in the world had set out to find us the worst possible location in the world to fight this damnable war, politically and militarily, the unanimous choice would have been Korea."[15]

Recalling the lesson of appeasement at Munich in 1938, when Hitler was allowed to annex Czechoslovakia, Truman made it clear: "We are going to fight. By God I am not going to let them have it." With demobilization of the military after World War II, and cuts to the military budget, US forces were at first unprepared. North Korean forces, supplied with Russian tanks, initially pushed back South Korean and US troops, fighting under the United Nations umbrella. North Korean soldiers were stopped at the Battle of Pusan, and in September 1950, United Nations and South Korean forces, under the command of Douglas MacArthur, won a decisive victory and recaptured Seoul in the Battle of Inchon.

The war would take another turn with the growing presence of Chinese forces. MacArthur miscalculated by mounting a drive to the Yalu River, the border with China. The Chinese responded in October by sending massive forces across the river, routing American forces and driving them back over a hundred miles. In April 1951, Truman relieved MacArthur of command. Celebrated on his return, McArthur lamented, "Old soldiers never die; they just fade away." The war fell into a stalemate. An armistice agreement was signed on July 27, 1953, creating a Korean Demilitarized Zone, which ran northeast of the 38th parallel, and a buffer zone between North and South Korea. More than 2 million Americans served and 33,000 of them were killed in battle. Coming in the aftermath of World War II, and in a culture not yet inundated with television news, the Korean War would be remembered, when remembered at all, as the "forgotten war."[16]

Early in the Korean War, Truman acknowledged that he would consider the use of the atomic bomb. With success at Inchon through conventional warfare, that ominous possibility passed. Soon the world learned of an even more terrifying weapon: the hydrogen bomb, a thermonuclear weapon with hundreds of times the explosive power of an atom bomb. The United States tested the first H-bomb, known as Ivy Mike, on November 1, 1952, on an atoll in the Pacific. Within a short time, the Soviet Union displayed that it too had the hydrogen bomb. Anxiety over the use of the H-bomb, and its resulting mass death and destruction, cast a shadow over postwar America. Cities adopted civil defense measures, such as warning sirens and fallout shelters. In school drills, students crawled under their desks. Books such as *How to Survive an Atomic Bomb* (1950) proved popular. As the decade progressed, anxieties became more acute. Nevil Shute's novel *On the Beach* (1957) was made into a film that showed the gradual extinction of humanity in the aftermath of a nuclear explosion. In *Fail-Safe* (1964), a mistaken bombing of Moscow leaves the president no choice but to allow the Soviet Union to retaliate by bombing New York. It seemed that only black comedy could address such a sober topic as nuclear annihilation, and *Dr. Strangelove* (1964) both amused and terrified audiences with its depiction of crazed politicians, scientists, and generals leading the nation to nuclear destruction.[17]

In addition to fears of attack from above, the Cold War generated fears of subversion from within. In March 1951, Julius and Ethel Rosenberg were convicted of espionage for providing the Soviet Union with designs of atomic devices. As a Soviet agent, Julius had recruited his brother-in-law David Greenglass, who worked on the Manhattan Project building the first atomic bomb at Los Alamos National Laboratory. The Rosenbergs were sentenced to death and executed on June 19, 1953. The case led to international condemnation, as many thought the Rosenbergs had been framed. Files released decades later indicate the Julius was a spy and that his wife was only tangentially involved. FBI director J. Edgar Hoover wanted to use Ethel to compel her husband to confess. When Rosenberg did not confess, the government executed the couple, who had two young children. They are the only two people ever to be executed under the Espionage Act.

The Rosenberg case prompted and fed growing anticommunist hysteria. Fears of subversion were not new of course—a Red Scare took hold in the aftermath of World War I. In 1938, Congress created the House Un-American Activities Committee (HUAC), which became a standing committee in 1945. In 1947, the committee investigated communist influence in Hollywood and created a blacklist of writers and directors who refused to testify about their possible communist connections and influences. Through the 1950s, HUAC summoned celebrities, actors, novelists, and playwrights. Arthur Miller testified in 1956 and refused to name anyone he knew who had communist leanings. His play *The Crucible* (1953), about the Salem witch trials of the early 1690s and an allegory of HUAC investigations, had opened three years earlier.

The search for alleged communists accelerated with the election of Republican Senator Joseph McCarthy from Wisconsin. McCarthy, a working-class Irish American from Appleton, served from 1947 until his death in 1957. "McCarthyism" became a term synonymous with the use of smear tactics and witch hunts against supposed subversives. In 1950, in a speech delivered in Wheeling, West Virginia, he claimed to have a list of 205 "members of the Communist party and members of a spy ring" who had infiltrated the US State Department. McCarthy usually avoided specifics ("talking to Joe was like putting your hands in a bowl of mush," said one reporter). For the next several years his accusations and threats nurtured a climate of fear.

McCarthy's influence began to unravel with Senate hearings and the question of whether McCarthy had pressured the army to advance the career of one his aides. The hearings lasted thirty-six days and were televised. Toward the end, McCarthy responded to a question by the army's attorney, Joseph Nye Welch, about providing a list of communists in the defense industry by accusing Welch's associate of being a communist. "Have you no sense of decency, sir, at long last. Have you left no sense of decency?" asked Welch. At the same time, journalist Edwin R. Murrow aired a profile of McCarthy on his show *See It Now*. The footage portrayed McCarthy as ruthless and dishonest. Murrow made it clear that McCarthy's success depended on the backing of ordinary Americans.[18]

In December 1954, the Senate censured McCarthy for "deliberate deception and fraud." The vote was 67–22. One senator who did not vote because he was recovering from back surgery was John F. Kennedy. McCarthy, who identified as Catholic, had a close relationship with Kennedy's father, Joseph P. Kennedy, who was fervently anticommunist. Kennedy Sr. helped fund McCarthy's campaigns, and McCarthy stood aside in 1952 when the young Kennedy ran for the Senate against Republican Henry Cabot Lodge Jr. By the time Kennedy was elected president in 1960, McCarthy was in the grave. The Cold War, on the other hand, showed no signs of abating.

Kennedy was young (forty-three) and with wife Jacqueline and two young children (Caroline was three and John Jr. was born several weeks after the election), he seemed poised to lead the nation into a new decade. In his acceptance speech at the Democratic National Convention Kennedy declared, "We stand today on the edge of a New Frontier." He was the first Catholic elected president. He was in many ways the first television president. In the first of four televised debates with Richard Nixon (who had served as vice president under Eisenhower and had been a member of HUAC as a California congressman), Kennedy looked vital and vigorous. Nixon came off as pale and anxious. Those who listened on the radio thought Nixon had won; those who watched believed that Kennedy had clearly triumphed.[19]

Five months after his inauguration, Kennedy met Soviet leader Nikita Khrushchev in Vienna. Khrushchev bullied Kennedy mercilessly. "He savaged me," admitted Kennedy, who was shocked when "[I] talked about how a nuclear exchange would kill 70 million people in 10 minutes, and he just looked at me as if to say, 'So what?'" Two months later, the German Democratic Republic constructed the Berlin Wall, dividing communist East Berlin from the democratic west.[20]

Communism inched closer to American shores when, in 1959, Fidel Castro seized power in Cuba. Alarmed by Castro's Communist regime only 90 miles from the United States, Kennedy felt compelled to authorize the CIA in April 1961 to coordinate an invasion at the Bay of Pigs by anti-Castro exiles, an invasion that failed miserably. In February 1962, Kennedy signed an embargo on all Cuban goods. (Before doing so, he secured 1,200 of his favorite Cuban cigars.) In October 1962, Kennedy was informed of the discovery of Soviet medium-range and intermediate-range ballistic missiles in Cuba, placed there in part to ward off another invasion and in response to the presence of US Jupiter missiles in Turkey and Italy. Kennedy ordered a quarantine of Cuba and announced that the United States would retaliate against the Soviet Union should Cuba launch any missiles. He demanded their removal. Khrushchev denounced the American "blockade" (different from a quarantine) as an "act of aggression" and declared Soviet ships would not obey it. Tensions mounted and it seemed the United States would invade Cuba, when suddenly Khrushchev indicated a willingness to remove the missiles if the United States promised not to invade the island. Privately, the United States also agreed to remove its Jupiter missiles from Turkey. The realization of how close the world had come to nuclear war led in 1963 to a Partial Nuclear Test Ban Treaty, which prohibited tests in the atmosphere and, a decade later, led to Strategic Arms Limitation Talks.

The arms race between the United States and the Soviet Union was also a space race. In 1957, Americans were shocked when the Soviet Union launched a satellite into space. Although only the size of a beach ball, and weighing 184 pounds, Sputnik's beeping signal (one writer described it as a "cricket with a cold") could be heard at listening posts across America. When the evening news broadcast the signal, an announcer said, "Listen now for the sound which forever more separates the old from the new." In response, the United States took a variety of actions, including the creation of the National Aeronautics and Space Administration in 1958. On April 12, 1961, the Soviets put the first human in space, Yuri Gagarin; several weeks later, Alan Shepard became America's first astronaut. The United States began an Apollo space program. In a speech to a joint session of Congress on May 25, 1961, Kennedy set the goal of landing a man on the moon by the end of the decade. In September 1962, Kennedy declared that such an endeavor would "organize and measure the best of our energies and skills." The goal was reached on July 20, 1969, when Neil Armstrong became the first person to walk on the moon. As he stepped from Apollo 11 he said, "That's one small step for man, one giant leap for mankind." He thought he had said "a man," but the article was lost in transmission.[21]

Civil Rights

In 1949, HUAC summoned Jackie Robinson. Two years earlier, on April 15, 1947, Robinson had broken the color barrier in baseball when he took the field for the Brooklyn Dodgers (on that first day he went 0–3). Asked about communists stirring up blacks, he said, "Negroes were stirred up long before there was a Communist Party, and they'll stay stirred up long after the party has disappeared— unless Jim Crow has disappeared by then as well."[22]

Some of those discriminatory laws had begun to disappear. Starting in the 1930s, the NAACP had developed a strategy to challenge legalized segregation. Led by Charles Hamilton Houston, a graduate of Harvard Law School and the dean of Howard University's law school, the NAACP systematically attacked the separate but equal doctrine established by the Supreme Court in *Plessy v. Ferguson* in 1896. Houston had help from his former student Thurgood Marshall. Born in Baltimore, the grandson of slaves, Marshall attended Lincoln

University, a historically black institution in Pennsylvania. In 1930, the University of Maryland Law School denied him admission based on race. Marshall attended Howard Law School, where he studied with Houston. In 1935, he defended Donald Gaines Murray who was seeking admission to the University of Maryland Law School. Marshall argued that Murray had been denied separate but equal treatment because the State of Maryland had not provided another segregated institution for Murray to attend. The Maryland Court of Appeals agreed, and Murray was admitted. This led to a string of victories in which Marshall proved that the various facilities at issue were not equal. In 1940, Marshall headed the NAACP Legal Defense and Education Fund and continued the assault on segregation in state-supported educational institutions. The victories had mainly involved higher education and professional schools. With a new case, *Brown v. Board of Education of Topeka,* Kansas, the US Supreme Court turned its attention to public school education.

On May 17, 1954, a unanimous Court ruled in the *Brown* case that separate but equal facilities are "inherently unequal," and declared legalized segregation of public schools unconstitutional because it violated the Fourteenth Amendment guarantee of equal protection under the law. In a footnote, the Court cited psychological and sociological studies that showed the detrimental effects of segregation on the development of black children. The *New York Times* rejoiced that "the highest court in the land, the guardian of our national conscience, has reaffirmed its faith—and the undying American faith—in the equality of all men and all children before the law." As long as whites and blacks were legally segregated, the United States' claims to democracy rang hollow, and communist nations reveled in the hypocrisy. Not any longer.[23]

In 1967, Marshall would become the first African American to serve on the Supreme Court. (In 1961, Kennedy named Marshall to the US Court of Appeals for the Second Circuit and in 1965 Lyndon B. Johnson appointed him solicitor general.) "Sometimes history takes things into its own hands," he once said. Historical forces were pushing against legalized segregation. Fate, too, played a role. *Brown v. Board of Education* was first argued in 1952, and in 1953 Chief Justice Fred Vinson, a Kentuckian who doubted the authority of the Court to overturn the *Plessy* ruling, died of a heart attack. Eisenhower nominated Earl Warren, a Republican governor of California, and for the next sixteen years, the Warren court advanced civil liberties, civil rights, and federal power. Vinson's death, quipped Justice Felix

Frankfurter, who supported the *Brown* decision, "is the first indication I have ever had that there is a God."[24]

The Supreme Court ruled on the law, not the remedy. "With all deliberate speed" was their injunction in the follow-up to *Brown* for achieving desegregation. Southern states resisted the decision. A Southern Manifesto, signed by nineteen senators and seventy-seven representatives (Texas Senator Lyndon Johnson was among those who did not sign), decried, "the Supreme Court's encroachments on rights reserved to the States and to the people." The language of interposition and nullification filled public discourse, as it had at other times in American history. White citizens councils to prevent integration were formed in many communities. The *Daily News* in Jackson, Mississippi, warned of miscegenation and predicted "human blood may stain Southern soil in many places because of this decision."[25]

The battle over school desegregation erupted at Little Rock, Arkansas, in 1957. The NAACP had handpicked nine African American children (four boys and five girls) to desegregate Central High School. Segregationist mobs gathered and Governor Orval Faubus called out the National Guard to prevent the students from entering the building. Eisenhower responded by sending in federal troops, members of the 101st Airborne, to protect the students and preserve the rule of law. It was a dangerous and difficult year for the black students, who had to endure the taunts and provocations of many white protesters and students. Their ordeal also marked the emergence of network television reporting that made the events at Central High national news. Cameras captured the mob taunting Elizabeth Eckford on the first day and screaming for her to be lynched; the arrival of federal troops; and the commencement exercises at the end of the year, when Ernest Green became the first black student to graduate from Central High School.

What so many found shocking about what took place at Little Rock was that the city was considered moderate—a year before, Little Rock had voluntarily desegregated its public transportation. The movement to desegregate public transportation had helped trigger a broader civil rights movement when, on December 1, 1955, Rosa Parks refused to comply with a Montgomery, Alabama, ordinance that barred blacks from sitting at the front of the bus. Parks, a tailor's assistant and an active member of the NAACP, took her action only days after the acquittal of two white men for the brutal kidnapping and murder of fourteen-year-old Emmett Till in Mississippi several months earlier. When the bus driver ordered her to move, she remained seated and was arrested. In response, the Women's

Political Council, a civil rights organization in Montgomery, called for a bus boycott and spread the word through the black churches. The boycott lasted just over a year and ended after a court ruled segregation on buses and public transportation unconstitutional. One protester, Sister Pollard, who walked miles rather than take the bus, was asked if she was tired. Her answer was "my feets is tired, but my soul is rested."[26]

Martin Luther King Jr., who led the Montgomery bus boycott, recounted that story. Born in Atlanta in 1929, King attended Morehouse College and Crozer Theological Seminary. In 1954 he became pastor of the Dexter Avenue Baptist Church in Montgomery. The following year he earned a doctorate in theology from Boston University and headed the Montgomery Improvement Association, which led the bus boycott. In December 5, 1955, he spoke at the Holt Street Baptist Church about being tired, trampled, humiliated, and shoved from summer sunlight into winter chill. He avowed opposition to violence and reaffirmed his faith in Christian teachings. "The only weapon that we have in our hands this evening," he said, "is the weapon of protest."[27] King was only twenty-five years old at the time.

Throughout his career, King's speeches embodied in style and content the qualities he would convey to the end: remarkable oratory, characterized by rhythmic repetition of phrases delivered in a harmonic baritone, and a commitment to nonviolent protest. Following the success of the Montgomery bus boycott, in 1956 King and several fellow ministers helped found the Southern Christian Leadership Conference (SCLC), which they envisioned as a national civil rights movement based on the principle of nonviolent direct action. King served as president, and other ministers, including Montgomery's Ralph Abernathy, Birmingham's Fred Shuttlesworth, and Mobile's Joseph Lowery, played leading roles. At a Prayer Pilgrimage for Freedom held in Washington on May 17, 1957, thousands gathered and heard King deliver a speech, "Give Us the Ballot," that made him a national figure. It had been nearly ninety years since the Fifteenth Amendment giving black men the right to vote was ratified. Continuous and relentless disfranchisement measures, including intimidation and violence, had taken its toll: in 1940, for example, only 3 percent of eligible black men and women were registered to vote in the South.

Civil rights activism by the SCLC and other groups, such as the Congress of Racial Equality (CORE) and the Student Non-Violent Coordinating Committee (SNCC), expanded across the South.

Through the spring and summer of 1961, CORE organized white and black activists called Freedom Riders to ride interstate buses across the South to challenge nonenforcement of Supreme Court decisions that had ruled segregated buses unconstitutional. They also held sit-ins and mixed racially at segregated lunch counters. Mobs, in some cases aided by members of the KKK and supported by local police forces, attacked the Freedom Riders, who were beaten and arrested. Mostly students and clergy, they persisted, and images of the beatings and firebombed buses shocked the nation. Attorney General Robert Kennedy pleaded for "a cooling off period," to which James Farmer, head of CORE, responded, "We have been cooling off for 350 years. . . . If we cool off anymore, we will be in a deep freeze."[28]

Although President Kennedy may have been slow to embrace civil rights (he did not want to alienate Southern Democrats, known as Dixiecrats), in July 1963, he proposed civil rights legislation that would outlaw discrimination in places of public accommodation such as lunch counters and hotels and also give enhanced protection to the right to vote. As the bill made its way through Congress, other provisions were added, including prohibition of employment discrimination by companies with fifteen or more employees and discrimination by agencies of state and local government that received federal funding. The final bill applied to discrimination based on religion, sex, and national origin as well as race and color.

Kennedy acted a month after the assassination of NAACP activist Medgar Evers outside his home in Jackson, Mississippi. A few months later, Kennedy himself was assassinated in Dallas on November 22, 1963. Lee Harvey Oswald, a former marine and a self-declared Marxist, fired the shot from the Texas School Book Depository that overlooked Dealey Plaza and the route of Kennedy's convertible limousine. Two days later, during his transfer from Dallas police headquarters, Oswald was killed by Jack Ruby, a night club owner. A commission led by Earl Warren concluded that Oswald had acted alone. Conspiracy theories about the assassination endure. Kennedy's death shocked the nation, with a young and vital president being shot down at age forty-six. A columnist said to Assistant Secretary for Labor Daniel Patrick Moynihan, "We'll never laugh again." Moynihan responded, "We'll laugh again. It's just that we'll never be young again."[29]

Lyndon Johnson immediately called on Congress to pass civil rights legislation to honor Kennedy's memory. Southern Democrats opposed the Civil Rights Bill. In 1946, Senator Richard Russell of Georgia had declared that they would fight "intermingling and amalgamation of the races" to the "bitter end." Southerners remained true to his word. Senators Strom Thurmond of South Carolina and Robert Byrd of West Virginia, among other Southern Democrats and one Republican, used a filibuster to try and defeat the measure. In the end, Johnson's lobbying and the work of Democratic Whip Hubert Humphrey of Minnesota and Senate Minority Leader Everett Dirksen of Illinois helped defeat the filibuster and the Civil Rights Bill of 1964 was passed. Johnson recognized the political cost to the Democrats in the South as Republicans used a Southern strategy that appealed to racial anxieties. "I think we just delivered the South to the Republicans for a long time to come," he predicted.[30]

On August 28, 1963, a month after Kennedy had proposed a civil rights act, Martin Luther King Jr. headlined a march on Washington for jobs and freedom. Organized primarily by labor leader A. Philip Randolph and pacifist Bayard Rustin, the march united concern for economic opportunity with civil rights. A crowd estimated at 250,000 gathered before the Lincoln Memorial and heard numerous speakers and singers, including Roy Wilkins of the NAACP, John Lewis of SNCC, gospel singer Mahalia Jackson, and Marian Anderson. An attendee who was not invited to speak was James Baldwin, novelist and essayist whose work *The Fire Next Time*, published earlier in the year, offered a searing examination of racism. His voice earned him the cover of *Time* magazine, yet organizers may have seen him as too radical to address the crowd.

One of the performers was Bob Dylan. Born Robert Zimmerman in Duluth, Minnesota, in 1941, he left for New York and on his arrival started playing the cafés and coffeehouses in Greenwich Village. In 1962 he legally changed his name and the 1963 release of his second album, *Freewheelin' Bob Dylan*, made Dylan the folk voice of the civil rights movement. The titles of the tracks indicate why: "A Hard Rain's Gonna Fall," "Don't Think Twice, It's All Right," "Masters of War," and "Blowin' in the Wind." The following year he released "The Times They Are a-Changin'." Dylan drew on the long history of folk and gospel music and wrote songs that sounded prophetic and timeless. At the rally, he and Joan Baez performed "When the Ship Comes In" and "Only a Pawn in the Game," about Medgar Evers's assassination. Another group, Peter, Paul and Mary, sang Dylan's "Blowin' in the Wind." The song opens with a question: "How many roads must a man walk down before you call him a man?" "Blowin' in the Wind" suggests the solution is right there for the taking if only one reaches out and harnesses its power.

The program ended with a speech by Martin Luther King Jr. King had long been thinking about the American dream. A few years earlier he suggested that "in a real sense America is essentially a dream—a dream yet unfulfilled. It is the dream of a land where men of all races, colors, and creeds will live together as brothers." Now, before a statue of Lincoln "in whose symbolic shadow we stand," King brought the March on Washington to a close. In his dream, he imagined the children of slaves and the children of slaveholders joining together in brotherhood; he imagined Southern intolerance and injustice yielding to freedom and justice; he dreamed of a time when his four children would "not be judged by the color of their skin but by the content of their character." His dream, he said, "is a dream deeply rooted in the American dream" of equality and freedom, and he closed praying for a moment "when all of God's children, black men and white men, Jews and Gentiles, Protestants and Catholics, will be able to join hands and sing in the words of the old Negro spiritual: 'Free at last. Free at last. Thank God Almighty, we are free at last.'"[31]

Writing in the *New York Times,* James Reston observed that the speech was "an anguished echo from all the old American reformers." The peaceful protest and King's speech grabbed the attention of the Kennedy administration, which saw momentum toward civil rights legislation building. King was named man of the year by *Time* magazine, and in 1964 he received the Nobel Peace Prize.[32]

The following year, some 600 activists tried to march the fifty-four miles from Selma to Montgomery to protest continued denial of their constitutional rights. On March 7, 1965, they crossed the Edmund Pettus Bridge in Selma and were confronted by Alabama police who fired tear gas and used clubs. The day came to be known as Bloody Sunday. Two days later, King led a second symbolic march while awaiting a federal court order permitting a full-scale demonstration. The order came and on March 21 a growing crowd of thousands set out for Montgomery and reached their destination four days later. In August, Congress passed a Voting Rights Act that offered general protection of the right to vote and banned specific tests used to deny the franchise.

King began to expand the scope of his activism. He participated in the Chicago Freedom Movement in 1966, the main objectives of which were to rebuild the city's slums and combat housing discrimination. Just as in the South, white mobs attacked the demonstrators. King also condemned the Vietnam War and made plans for a Poor People's Campaign to end poverty. J. Edgar Hoover, head of the FBI,

Figure 9.2 Charles Moore, *Selma to Montgomery* (1965). Briscoe Center for American History.

which had been monitoring King for years, saw him as a communist subversive. At one point, they sought to blackmail him for his
marital infidelities. King persevered in his work and was in Memphis
supporting striking sanitation workers when, on April 4, 1968, he
was assassinated while standing on the balcony of the Lorraine Motel.
Two months later, Robert Kennedy, who was running for president,
was also assassinated. In his final speech, King spoke of "difficult
days ahead," and sensed he would not live to see the unconditional
triumph of freedom and justice. He assured his audience, however,
that "we, as a people, will make it to the promised land."

Counterculture

Not everyone shared King's vision of an American promised land.
Part of his influence stemmed from the fact that he was a palatable alternative to more radical, revolutionary voices both in the civil rights
movement and the student movement. Among these was Malcolm
X. Born Malcolm Little in 1925, he took the name Malcolm X after
a prison conversion led him to join the Nation of Islam. Malcolm
was Martin's antagonist. Not integration, but separation from "white
devils," not nonviolence but revolution "by any means necessary,"

not white Christian America but black Islamic nationalism. "White America must now pay for her sins. White America is doomed."[33]

Malcolm X spoke not of a Negro revolution but a black revolution. King's movement, he said, was no revolution: "whoever heard of a revolution where they lock arms . . . singing 'We Shall Overcome'?" Malcolm exemplified a growing militancy expressed as black power and symbolized by a raised fist. (In the 1968 Summer Olympics in Mexico City, Tommie Smith and John Carlos gave the black power salute on the podium as they received their medals for finishing first and third in the 200-meter track event.) Malcolm wanted no part of America: "I see America through the eyes of the victim. I don't see any American dream; I see an American nightmare."[34]

It is easy to cast the two men as antagonists. Yet in fact, the positions of King and Malcom X converged over time. Malcolm X left the Nation of Islam and began to advocate for human rights. For his opposition to leader Elijah Muhammad, he was assassinated in New York on February 21, 1965. And King came to acknowledge what Malcolm saw from the start: In 1968 he said, "Truly America is much, much sicker than I realized when I began in 1955."[35]

Taking up the call of violent resistance, Bobby Seale and Huey Newton founded the Black Panther Party in Oakland, California, in 1966. Utilizing open-carry gun laws, members organized armed community patrols to protect against police brutality. In a program called "What We Want Now," the Black Panthers called for full employment, housing, and education as well as freedom and power "to determine the destiny of our black community." In part, they were responding to the riots that had occurred in Harlem in 1964, Watts in 1965, Detroit and Newark in 1967, and in other cities. The party quickly gained a foothold across the United States.

They also received the attention of the FBI, which had been monitoring Martin Luther King Jr. and Malcolm X, and saw in the Black Panther Party an even greater threat to the nation. In 1969, J. Edgar Hoover decided to target the Panthers, using COINTELPRO, a counterintelligence program established in 1956, to infiltrate, discredit, and disrupt opposition political groups by the use of various, often illegal, tactics. By the early 1970s, violent confrontations with police and schisms within the party led to its splintering. Seale and Newton were in jail; Eldridge Cleaver, the party's minister of information and author of a wide-selling collection of essays, *Soul on Ice* (1968), had fled to Cuba after being involved in an ambush of police in Oakland. Perhaps the ultimate sign of the decline of the Black Panthers was its embrace by liberal civil rights activists. The conductor Leonard Bernstein held a fundraiser for the Panthers in his Park Avenue penthouse; the writer Tom Wolfe coined the phrase "radical chic" to describe the endorsement of radical politics by celebrities.[36]

If radical politics became chic, it was also because its message had broad appeal. This was especially the case with student activism and radicalism. In 1962, Tom Hayden, a student at the University of Michigan, drafted a political manifesto known as the Port Huron Statement and helped found Students for a Democratic Society (SDS). Hayden had participated as a Freedom Rider and he sought to broaden the scope of activism. The statement opened, "We are people of this generation, bred in at least modest comfort, housed now in universities, looking uncomfortably to the world we inherit." Complacency was partly responsible for the "common peril" of the Cold War and the "human degradation" of racial bigotry. The statement went beyond politics to the state of the soul characterized by "loneliness, estrangement, isolation." Rather than power based on possession and privilege, Hayden's generation sought power based on "love, reflectiveness, reason and creativity." Only participatory democracy could bring people "out of isolation and into community."[37]

Members of the SDS organized student protests, sit-ins, and teach-ins. The group initially favored political action and economic reform and formed a key component of the New Left, an umbrella term for activists engaged in social issues and an alternative to the older labor movements. By 1968, SDS became a household acronym after organizing a nationwide student strike and occupying campus buildings. At Columbia College in New York, they held the dean hostage for twenty-four hours as a protest against the university's building of a gymnasium in a nearby Harlem park and its ties to organizations that were aiding the war effort in Vietnam. The phenomenon of student protest and activism extended well beyond the SDS. In France, for example, millions of students and workers banded together in sometimes violent actions that for a while seemed to portend a revolution or civil war. In 1969, a faction of the SDS radicalized. Called the Weather Underground (they took their name from Bob Dylan's lyric: "you don't need a weatherman to know which way the wind blows"), the Weathermen advocated violence and organized a bombing campaign.

Other groups seized on the moment to call for change. The American Indian Movement formed in 1968 and battled for Native American sovereignty. In 1969, activists, led by Adam Fortunate Eagle, occupied abandoned Alcatraz Island for nineteen months and insisted that it be returned to Native hands under the terms of the Treaty of Fort Laramie (1868). In 1972, representatives traveled to Washington to demand a review of treaty commitments and the creation of new treaties. Those demands contributed to a siege at Wounded Knee that lasted seventy-one days in 1973 as activists Russell Means and Carter Camp organized to oppose tribal chairman Richard Wilson, under whose leadership life at the Pine Ridge Reservation had deteriorated, and to call for the United States to honor its treaties. Native American rights gained worldwide attention when, at the Academy Awards in 1973, when Marlon Brando was nominated for an Oscar for his role in *The Godfather*. Rather than attend, Brando asked Sacheen Littlefeather, a name she adopted at the Alcatraz occupation to honor her Apache heritage, to take his place. Brando won the Best Actor award and Littlefeather went to the podium and turned it down in protest of the treatment and depiction of Native Americans in the film industry.

In addition to Native American activism, an emerging Chicano movement fought for civil rights for Mexican Americans. In 1962, Cesar Chavez, who was raised in Arizona and settled in California after World War II, became interested in the plight of farm workers and founded, along with Dolores Huerta, the National Farm Workers Association (NFWA), which later became the United Farm Workers. In 1965, the NFWA launched a strike against grape growers in Delano, California. At one point, Chavez fasted for twenty-five days, living on water only. Martin Luther King Jr. wrote how moved he was by Chavez's example. In 1970, the boycott ended when grape growers signed a union contract.[38]

Chavez represented a commitment to pacifism and even some of the more radical voices of the day shared in a generational revolt expressed by the slogan "make love not war." The peace sign, designed by the British Campaign for Nuclear Disarmament in 1956, became ubiquitous. A generation of youth challenged convention and establishment norms: men grew their hair long; men and women wore tie-dyed garments, bell-bottomed jeans, and sandals; conventional sexual norms were challenged; marijuana use became widespread and some experimented with psychedelic drugs as part of a spiritual journey for fulfillment outside of organized Western religion. "Turn On, Tune In, Drop Out," was the motto of former Harvard psychologist Timothy Leary, who advocated using LSD to raise one's sense of consciousness and well-being. (Richard Nixon labeled him "the most dangerous man in America.")[39]

The Beats of the 1950s had given way to the hippies of the 1960s and the larger culture took note. In 1968, the play *Hair* opened on

Broadway. Subtitled *The American Tribal Love-Rock Musical*, the show featured an interracial group of hippies and activists living a free life in New York, taking drugs, enjoying sexual freedom, protesting the establishment, and opposing the military draft. "Beads, flowers, freedom, happiness," chanted the performers. Many of the songs became hits, including "Aquarius," "Let the Sunshine In," and the title song in praise of "long beautiful hair."

The song "Hair" name-checks the Grateful Dead, the San Francisco–based band that embodied the improvisational, psychedelic cultural turn. They were one of dozens of acts to perform at the Woodstock music festival held at Bethel, New York, in August 1969. Billed as "Three Days of Peace and Music," the festival attracted hundreds of thousands who swarmed over the 600-acre farm on which it was held. Traffic jams led to the closing of the New York State Thruway and rainy conditions created a sea of mud. Some of the preeminent performers of the day—Jimi Hendrix, perhaps most memorably—played through the night and Woodstock immediately marked a seminal cultural moment. It outstripped the Monterey Music festival held two years earlier during what was dubbed the Summer of Love, and it served as a placeholder for what *Life* magazine called an era of "sex, drugs, and rock 'n' roll."[40]

If the cultural impulses of the 1960 led to an inward turn, consciousness-raising also forced people outward and the counterculture energized any number of causes that fused the personal and the political. In 1964, students at UC Berkeley launched the Free Speech Movement. In a rousing address, civil rights activist Mario Savio warned against passivity. The only way of overcoming the "machine" was to throw your bodies "upon the gears and upon the wheels, upon the levers, upon all the apparatus." Despair over the industrial machine helped give rise to a new environmentalist consciousness, ignited in part by Rachel Carson's *Silent Spring* (1962), which exposed the destructive effects of the use of pesticides. In 1970, the first Earth Day was held, both a celebration of nature and a call for environmental protection.[41]

Women played a central role in many of these movements, and none more so than in their own. In 1963, Betty Freidan published *The Feminine Mystique*, detailing the unhappiness of the vast majority of middle-class women who felt trapped in roles of housewife and mother. In 1966, the National Organization of Women was founded and called for "true equality for all women," including economic equality in the workplace. A new era of feminism had been launched, known as second-wave feminism. Women exercised control over their bodies with the use of oral contraceptives that had been approved in 1960. They fought for the right to obtain an abortion legally, a right recognized by the Supreme Court in its 1973 decision *Roe v. Wade*. They lobbied for an amendment to the Civil Rights Act of 1964 that protected them from discrimination and sexual harassment in the workplace. In 1972, Congress passed Title IX, which states, "No person in the United States shall, on the basis of sex, be excluded from participation in, be denied the benefits of, or be subjected to discrimination under any education program or activity receiving Federal financial assistance."

Women's liberation and gay liberation emerged together. In San Francisco, activists organized groups to help fight discrimination against young gay men, and in New York protesters challenged a law that made it illegal to serve homosexuals in licensed bars. In 1969, at the Stonewall Inn in New York's Greenwich Village, a spontaneous demonstration against a police raid led to days of rioting and the formation of gay alliances. A year after Stonewall, gay pride marches took place around the country. By then even the staid *Wall Street Journal* reported, "U.S. Homosexuals Gain in Trying to Persuade Society to Accept Them."[42]

Most activists, whatever their specific concern, whether civil rights or women's rights, embraced the peace and antiwar movement. On January 15, 1968, Jeanette Rankin led a women's peace march against the Vietnam War. Rankin was an original suffragette and in 1916 became the first woman elected to Congress. Elected again in 1940, her pacifist principles forbade her from voting for war against Japan; she was the only member of Congress to vote no. Now eighty-seven years old, the Montana resident came east and led nearly 5,000 women in a group called the Jeanette Rankin Brigade. Among the signs they carried was one that read "Sisterhood Is Powerful." Within days of their march the Vietnam War would take a turn, protests would spiral, and a greater number of Americans would discredit what the government was telling them.

Vietnam War

In 1954, French colonial powers relinquished control of Vietnam after being defeated at the Battle of Dien Bien Phu. Under the terms of the Geneva Conference of 1952, Vietnam was divided into the Communist North (Democratic Republic of Vietnam), led by Ho Chi Minh, and the anti-Communist South (Republic of Vietnam), led by Ngo Dinh Diem, who had the support of the United States. Diem's ruthless and corrupt leadership did not endear him to the Americans, but incursions into the South by North Vietnamese fighters and the building of the Ho Chi Minh Trail through Cambodia and Laos to facilitate the movement of troops and supplies, led the United States under President Kennedy to increase financial support for the regime and the number of military advisors.

Kennedy feared that if the communists triumphed, American "security may be lost piece by piece, country by country." Pulling out of Vietnam would have created another Joe McCarthy. Kennedy was adhering to the domino theory first espoused by Eisenhower in 1954. Eisenhower expressed the fear that one country falling to communism would lead to another and soon all of Southeast Asia would be ruled by communist dictatorships: "You have a row of dominoes set up, you knock over the first one, and what will happen to the last one is a certainty that it will go over very quickly."[43]

Kennedy chose to increase American military involvement in Vietnam and by1962 US troops had ballooned from 600 to 15,000. Although technically advising the South Vietnamese Army (ARVN), these soldiers, made up of elite Green Beret units, also engaged in guerilla warfare against the National Liberation Front (Viet Cong). In May 1961, Vice President Lyndon Johnson visited Vietnam and voiced support for Diem, whom he called the "Churchill of Asia." Others were less sure. Journalists such as Homer Bigart and David Halberstam of the *New York Times* reported that Diem's authoritarian regime was failing and the South was falling to the Communists. The government's official position, however, remained optimistic. With Johnson as president, US involvement escalated and what was called a "credibility gap" emerged between the administration's rose-colored portrait of progress and what seemed actually to be taking place, a gap that grew over time. By the time Johnson took office, Diem had been assassinated in a coup carried out with the acquiescence of the CIA.[44]

In August 1964, following a military incident in the Gulf of Tonkin, Congress passed a joint resolution that gave Johnson the authority to send conventional combat troops to Vietnam without a formal declaration of war. The incident that led to the resolution remains controversial. The USS *Maddox* claimed to have been attacked by North Vietnamese torpedo boats on August 2 and again on August 4, but the second attack never actually happened. Privately, Johnson admitted, "For all I know, our navy was shooting at whales out there." No matter. Within a year Johnson expanded military operations. He authorized Operation Rolling Thunder, the massive carpet bombing of North Vietnam that lasted from 1965 to 1968. Troop numbers climbed from 75,000 to 125,000, and in 1965 combat troops were deployed. By the end of 1967, nearly 500,000 American troops were stationed in Vietnam.[45]

During the Gulf of Tonkin debate, Senator Ernest Gruening of Alaska, one of only two senators to vote against the resolution, warned, "All Vietnam is not worth the life of a single American boy." That view became increasingly widespread and protests against the war continued to grow. As part of the escalation, Johnson had increased the number of draftees, and in response protesters burned their draft cards. The Supreme Court held that federal law making the act of burning one's draft card illegal did not violate free speech rights. In 1967, Martin Luther King Jr. joined the antiwar movement when he publicly denounced American actions in Vietnam. Speaking at Riverside Church in New York on April 4, 1967, King foresaw the prospects of endless war: "A nation that continues year after year to spend more money on military defense than on programs of social uplift is approaching spiritual death."[46]

The protests continued to grow, and various constituencies added to the resistance. A march on the Pentagon in October 1967 drew tens of thousands led by Abbie Hoffmann and Jerry Rubin, leaders of the Youth International Party, whose members came to be known as Yippies. Their radicalism touched on anarchism. Hoffman declared, "We shall raise the flag of nothingness over the Pentagon and a mighty cheer of liberation will echo through the land." Soldiers stood guard with their rifles out and, at one point, a protester placed a dandelion in the barrel of the gun. A photograph of that gesture was one of many that helped shape public attitudes toward the war. So too Eddie Adams's photograph in 1968 of the public execution of a captured North Vietnamese officer. Perhaps no photograph was more powerful than Nick Ut's 1972 photograph of a naked nine-year-old South Vietnamese girl running and screaming in agony after a napalm attack. In addition to photographs, graphic newsreel footage of the fighting appeared nightly on the televised evening news. Media theorist Marshall McLuhan would later say that "Vietnam was lost in the living rooms of America—not the battlefields of Vietnam."[47]

Many of the various antiwar constituencies—National Mobilization Committee to End the War in Vietnam, the SDS, the Yippies, and the Black Panthers—gathered outside the Democratic National Convention in Chicago in 1968. Johnson's decision not to run for reelection had shocked the nation. Only four years earlier he had defeated Republican Barry Goldwater of Arizona with an

Figure 9.3 Nick Ut, *Napalm Girl* (1972). Nick Ut/Associated Press.

astonishing 62 percent of the popular vote. Now the unpopularity
of the Vietnam War made it questionable whether he would be
reelected. (Even in 1964 Johnson knew Vietnam posed a trap: "I don't
think it's worth fighting for and I don't think we can get out. And
it's just the biggest damned mess.") Thousands of antiwar protesters
gathered and the police, called out by Mayor Richard Daley, used tear
gas and bludgeoned many of them. Shocked Americans witnessed
the violence on television. America seemed to be unraveling, and
more people than ever came to agree with CBS news anchor Walter
Cronkite who, on February 27, 1968, commented, "To say that we
are closer to victory today is to believe, in the face of the evidence,
the optimists who have been wrong in the past. To suggest we are on
the edge of defeat is to yield to unreasonable pessimism. To say that
we are mired in stalemate seems the only realistic, yet unsatisfactory,
conclusion."[48]

Cronkite's comments came weeks after the Viet Cong launched
the Tet Offensive against South Vietnamese and American forces. At
Khe Sanh, US Marines and South Vietnamese soldiers faced massive
bombardment in a siege that lasted more than two months. General
William Westmoreland, commander of US forces, failed to see the

attack on Khe Sanh as a diversionary tactic for the coordinated attacks that followed on major cities such as Saigon and Hue, where North Vietnamese forces massacred thousands of South Vietnamese military officials and civilians. These attacks came as a surprise, and although the North Vietnamese Army and National Liberation Front suffered severe casualties and ultimately were driven back, Tet marked a shift in public support for the war. Soldiers also suffered a decline in morale, and many were radicalized. If early in the war they mocked the draft dodgers who refused to fight, these soldiers now flashed peace signs and gave black power salutes. Throughout the war, the fighting was treacherous and even nightmarish. Soldiers waded through rice paddies and slashed through jungles across the Central Highlands and Mekong Delta. US bases at Da Nang and Long Binh also came under attack during Tet. The North Vietnamese avoided engaging in large-scale battles, and although their losses dwarfed those of US forces (by as much as a 10–1 ratio), they managed to remain intact. US soldiers went from village to village in quest of the enemy. The Viet Cong used a maze of tunnels to move unmolested around the countryside, even tunneling under some American base camps.

Hundreds of thousands of civilians on both sides perished during the war, and millions were displaced. A program of "pacification" sought to win over the rural South Vietnamese from the Viet Cong. As part of it, the United States attempted to deny the enemy physical cover by spraying nearly two million gallons of Agent Orange, a toxic defoliant that caused severe illness and depopulated vast areas. Pacifying villages led to atrocities, one of the worst of which occurred at My Lai on March 16, 1968, when American soldiers massacred nearly 500 civilians. Some of the women had been raped and their bodies mutilated. The following year, when news of the massacre became public, Lieutenant William Calley, one of the platoon leaders, was convicted of premeditated murder. Sentenced to life in prison, he ended up serving several years under house arrest.

Peace talks between the United States and North Vietnam had begun in Paris in May 1968. Little progress had been made when a new president, Richard Nixon, was sworn in, and the Vietnam War continued to claim casualties both abroad and at home. Nixon, steadfastly anti-communist, intensified the war effort even as he tried to shift responsibility for fighting it to the South Vietnamese. "I will not be the first president of the United States to lose a war," he vowed. In May 1970, Nixon announced expansion of the conflict into Cambodia and Laos, a move that further intensified opposition to the war. That same month, an antiwar protest at Kent State

University turned violent when the National Guard used tear gas and then opened fire on the students, killing four and wounding nine. A photograph showed a teenage girl kneeling over the dead body of one of the students in what seemed to be a modern-day Pieta. Ten days later, on May 14, police killed two students and injured twelve others at historically black Jackson State College in Mississippi.[49]

In 1971, the *New York Times Magazine* published an article by Donald Kirk titled "Who Wants to be the Last American Killed in Vietnam." Kirk described extensive drug use, racial tensions (troops were fully integrated for the first time), and an uneasy "limbo between victory and defeat" in which soldiers tried to survive. "Far as I'm concerned," said one soldier, "they can have this whole country. There ain't no reason for us bein' here." A year later, after an Easter Offensive by North Vietnam failed, Le Duc Tho (who succeeded revolutionary leader Ho Chi Minh on his death in 1969) agreed to a peace treaty negotiated with national security advisor Henry Kissinger. On January 27, 1973, the parties signed the Paris Peace Accords.[50]

America's longest war at the time, lasting ten years, was over; its legacy reverberated for decades. More than 58,000 American soldiers were killed and more than 100,000 wounded. Some 3 million soldiers served in Vietnam. They returned home to none of the glory enjoyed by World War II veterans. Nixon had called the Paris Accords "peace with honor." It did not feel that way to Americans who would debate the question of who lost Vietnam, a question that gained purpose when communists took over Saigon in August 1975. The antiwar movement had been opposed by those who supported the president, and the conflict had opened a cultural gulf between those who chanted, "Hell no we won't go" and those who replied, "America, love it or leave it." To prevent future presidents from waging an undeclared war, in 1973 Congress passed, over Nixon's veto, the War Powers Act, which required the president to notify Congress within forty-eight hours of committing armed forces.

What was labeled the "Vietnam Syndrome" caused many Americans to oppose further US involvement in foreign affairs. Running for president in 1972, Senator George McGovern of South Dakota argued it was time to return the nation's focus to domestic concerns. "Come home," he said, "to the affirmation that we have a dream. Come home to the conviction that we can move our country forward." Despite the war's unpopularity, McGovern's entreaties gained little traction with the electorate. Nixon trounced McGovern, and for the first time Republicans swept the South, using a strategy that appealed to the prejudices of white voters who were perhaps reacting to the of extension civil rights and celebration of the counterculture. Conservatism had regained a foothold.[51]

CHAPTER 10

Government Is the Problem

ARCHIE BUNKER WAS AN URBAN, blue-collar Republican who lived in Queens, New York, and bellowed to whoever would listen about the state of America while pining for "the good old days." He was also fictional, a television character played by Carroll O'Connor on the situation comedy *All in the Family*, which ran from 1971 to 1979 and became the most watched show in America. Even President Nixon tuned in. The bigoted Bunker ranted about minorities and gays, about too much government interference, about people on welfare, and about a nation gone awry. What made it acceptable was that he did so in a way that had everyone laughing. Created by Norman Lear, a left-leaning Democrat, the show attracted legions of fans, some of whom were amused not necessarily because they thought the show was mocking Archie, but because he articulated their own beliefs and resentments. The show at first came with a disclaimer: "It seeks to throw a humorous spotlight on our frailties, prejudices and concerns. By making them a source of laughter, we hope to show—in a mature fashion—just how absurd they are." In time, other shows would push the boundaries of satire: the animated situation comedy *The Simpsons*, for example, began in December 1989 and several decades later would become the longest-running prime-time series in television history. Few others shows, however, can claim to have made as indelible a political mark: Archie Bunker received a vote for vice president at the 1972 Democratic Convention.[1]

Watergate

On June 13, 1971, the *New York Times* began publishing what came to be known as the Pentagon Papers. These were excerpts from leaked documents from a massive study of US involvement in Vietnam commissioned in June 1967 by Secretary of Defense Robert McNamara. McNamara had played a key role in expanding American involvement in Vietnam. By 1966 he had come to recognize that no amount of American military power would bring victory. He left office in February 1968. The study he commissioned, however, continued and expanded to dozens of volumes. Daniel Ellsberg was among the analysts assembled by McNamara. He worked at the Defense Department and, in 1966, served in Vietnam as a civilian on assignment to the State Department. On his return, he became increasingly dismayed by the war effort. The final report demonstrated that the American public had been lied to by four administrations and that Kennedy and Johnson, more concerned about communist China than South Vietnam, escalated the war while harboring doubts that it was winnable.

Ellsberg photocopied the report and gave copies to various members of Congress, none of whom acted. He then met with *New York Times* reporter Neil Sheehan, and after an internal discussion about whether these leaked national security documents could be published, the paper went to press. The Nixon administration obtained an injunction against the *Times*. As the case rose to the Supreme Court, the *Washington Post* also began publishing excerpts. On June 30, 1971, the Supreme Court ruled 6–3 that the government did not meet the extremely high burden for prior restraint. "Only a free and unrestrained press can effectively expose deception in government. And paramount among the responsibilities of a free press is the duty to prevent any part of the government from deceiving the people and sending them off to distant lands to die of foreign fevers and foreign shot and shell," wrote Justice Hugo Black for the majority.[2]

Although the Pentagon Papers exposed the duplicity of two previous Democratic administrations, their release enraged Richard Nixon, who imagined a treasonous left-wing conspiracy to undermine support for the government. He also feared disclosure of his own Vietnam secrets, including an effort to subvert peace talks prior to the 1968 election. Obsessed with government leaks, the White House formed a special investigation unit, known informally as the Plumbers, whose members proceeded to break into Ellsberg's psychiatrist's office in search of damning material. The break-in yielded nothing and proved pivotal in the dismissal of charges brought against Ellsberg for violating the Espionage Act of 1917. Nixon lamented, "The sonofabitching thief is made a national hero."[3]

The efforts of the Plumbers—E. Howard Hunt, a former CIA agent, G. Gordon Liddy, a former FBI agent, and others—did not cease with the Ellsberg case. Liddy turned his attention to Nixon's reelection campaign. In June 1972, as part of a plan approved by John Mitchell, former attorney general and now director of the Committee to Re-elect the President, a team of burglars broke into the headquarters of the Democratic National Committee located at the Watergate hotel complex in Washington, DC. They photographed documents and installed listening devices. An attempted second break-in failed, and police arrested five men who had in their possession radio scanners, walkie-talkies, cameras, and listening devices. A grand jury indicted the burglars, Liddy, and Hunt. Nixon probably did not know of the break-in ("Who was the asshole that did?" he asked). He nevertheless certainly understood the damage it could cause his reelection, and he acted to make certain no one could tie the break-in to his staff. (Despite his fears, Nixon won reelection with nearly 61 percent of the popular vote and took every state with the exception of Massachusetts and the District of Columbia. Governor George Wallace of Alabama, a zealous defender of segregation, ran as an independent and carried five southern states.)[4]

Journalists began to investigate the connection between the break-in and the reelection campaign. None were more tenacious than Bob Woodward and Carl Bernstein of the *Washington Post*. They cultivated a number of anonymous sources, the most important being someone they referred to as Deep Throat. (Decades later he was identified as Mark Felt, associate director of the FBI.) Meeting with the reporters in an underground garage, Felt connected the break-in to Howard Hunt, whose name was in two of the Watergate burglars' address books, and told the reporters that a cover-up originated with White House Counsel John Dean, Charles Colson, and John Ehrlichman, and Chief of Staff H. R. Haldeman. In 1974, Bernstein and Woodward published *All the President's Men*, a book *Time* magazine would include on its list of all-time best works of non-fiction. Two years later, a film version with stars Robert Redford and Dustin Hoffman would win accolades (but it would lose the best picture Oscar to *Rocky*, a movie about a small-time underdog boxer who fights for the heavyweight championship).

Following all the revelations, and the conviction of former Nixon aides G. Gordon Liddy and James W. McCord Jr., for conspiracy, burglary, and wiretapping, the US Senate authorized hearings to investigate the Watergate break-in and cover-up. Millions of Americans tuned in to follow the testimony of Nixon's aides, televised over two weeks in May 1973. Democrat Sam Ervin of North Carolina chaired the committee and Howard Baker of Tennessee was the ranking Republican member. At one point, Baker asked, "What did the President know, and when did he know it?" John Dean gave explosive testimony in which he claimed that Nixon was personally involved in the Watergate cover-up and he believed that there was a taping system in the Oval Office that recorded all conversations. A month later, the existence of taped conversations was confirmed.[5]

Simultaneous with the congressional investigation, the Justice Department had appointed Archibald Cox as a special prosecutor. Cox subpoenaed the recordings. Claiming executive privilege, Nixon refused to turn them over. Ervin declared, "There is nothing in the Constitution that authorizes or makes it the official duty of a President to have anything to do with criminal activities." "I deeply regret that this situation has arisen," he lamented, "because I think that the Watergate tragedy is the greatest tragedy this country has ever suffered." The constitutional crisis would only worsen. On October 20, 1973, in what came to be known as the "Saturday Night Massacre," Nixon ordered Attorney General Elliot Richardson to fire Cox. He resigned rather than do so, as did Deputy Attorney General William Ruckelshaus. Solicitor General Robert Bork then fired Cox, who was replaced by Leon Jaworski. Facing growing public disdain and deepening political and legal trouble, Nixon declared, "I am not a crook."[6]

Nixon finally agreed in April 1974 to release redacted versions of the White House tapes. Several months later the Supreme Court, in *United States v. Nixon*, ruled 8–0 that executive privilege did not apply to the tapes and ordered them released to the special prosecutor. (Justice Rehnquist recused himself because of his friendship with Richard Kleindienst, who was attorney general in 1973). In those tapes, John Dean could be heard explaining to Nixon that Watergate was "a cancer on the Presidency." Nixon acknowledged that the Watergate burglars "have to be paid" hush money. In a conversation with Chief of Staff Haldeman held on June 23, 1972, Nixon agreed that his office should ask the FBI to stop its investigation. Evidence of a criminal conspiracy to obstruct justice stemming from the Oval Office now seemed clear. On July 27, the House Judiciary Committee voted to submit three articles of impeachment.[7]

On August 8, 1974, in a speech to the nation, Nixon resigned from office. Acknowledging that he no longer had the support of a Republican Congressional political base, he stepped down in the nation's interest. He explained, "I regret deeply any injuries that may have been done in the course of the events that led to this decision. I would say only that if some of my judgments were wrong, and some were wrong, they were made in what I believed at the time to be the best interest of the Nation." In reviewing his accomplishments, he expressed pride in his visit to China in February 1972, a visit that thawed a bitter cold war between the two nations and led to the normalization of relations. It brought Nixon to his highest approval rating as president; four months later the Watergate break-in took place and the unraveling began. Gerald Ford, Republican House minority leader from Michigan, who had been appointed vice president when Spiro T. Agnew resigned after pleading no contest to charges of tax evasion, became president.[8]

On September 8, Ford pardoned Nixon for any crimes he might have committed. He wanted to save the nation from further political turmoil. Perhaps he also wanted to help his old friend, whom he knew "had real demons." Those demons were evident long before Watergate. Nixon was by nature distrustful and paranoid. He hated the press and saw himself as besieged by enemies. According to Secretary of State Henry Kissinger, each crisis "drove him deeper into his all-enveloping solitude." He drank too much and slept too little. His presidency might have been a great success. He appointed four Supreme Court justices, signed Title IX, a federal civil rights law that banned discrimination based on gender, ended the military draft, supported the Twenty-Sixth Amendment that lowered the voting age to eighteen, signed the Paris Peace Accords and an antiballistic missile treaty, and helped reduce cold war tensions. None of those achievements could erase the stain he had left on the presidency.[9]

Ford's pardon roiled those who believed the president was not above the law and that justice needed to be served. "A profoundly unwise, divisive and unjust act," wrote the *New York Times*. Senator Walter Mondale of Minnesota lamented, "We may never know the full dimensions of Mr. Nixon's complicity in the worst political scandal in American history."[10]

The pardon would contribute to Ford's defeat in the election of 1976. Jimmy Carter, the former governor of Georgia, was the surprise winner of the Democratic nomination. Little known outside his home state, the former peanut farmer took advantage of missteps by his better-known opponents (Henry Jackson of Washington, Morris Udall of Arizona, and Jerry Brown of California). A last-minute "Anyone But Carter" campaign failed to stop the nomination. In a close election, Carter took 297 electoral votes and Ford won 240. A shift of only thousands of voters in Hawaii and Ohio would have given the election to Ford.

The US Bicentennial in July 1976 had come at a propitious time. With Vietnam and Watergate, American patriotism and pride were in a lull and celebrations of independence momentarily lifted the nation's spirits. The feeling did not last. Riots in South Boston over the busing of students to achieve desegregation left many wondering what had happened to the cradle of liberty. A blackout in New York City in 1977 led to looting and rioting. In 1979, a nuclear accident at Three Mile Island in Pennsylvania caused a partial meltdown of the reactor. Across the decade, Americans endured an economic crisis that led to runaway inflation and an oil crisis produced rising gasoline prices that created long lines at the gas pumps. The most powerful nation on earth seemed stuck.

Figure 10.1 First Day of Gasoline Rationing (1979). Bettmann Archive/Getty Images.

The Great Inflation

Inflation skyrocketed through the 1970s. In 1973, the rate doubled to 8.8 percent. By 1980, it reached 14 percent. The causes dated back to economic policy adopted after World War II when the Federal Reserve implemented monetary policies that, under the Employment Act of 1946, required it to "promote maximum employment, production and purchasing power." Believing that there was a predictable inverse relationship between inflation and unemployment, policy makers supported rising inflation with the belief that it would curb unemployment rates. "We'll take inflation," said Nixon, but "can't take unemployment."[11]

Yet as inflation rose, so did unemployment. With the election of 1972 in view, Nixon took a series of actions to address the economy. He broke from an agreement made at Bretton Woods, New Hampshire, in 1944 when representatives from forty-four nations met and created an international monetary system that tied currencies to the price of gold in the hopes of creating a foreign exchange rate system and protecting against devaluation. The value of foreign currencies was fixed in relation to the US dollar. Over time, however, the United States did not have enough gold to cover the rising volume of US dollars in circulation. In 1970, the government's gold coverage of the dollar declined from 55 percent to 22 percent. Concerned that foreign governments would sell the currency (billions in assets were being drained), and the government would have to devalue it, thus leading to greater inflation, Nixon suspended the dollar's convertibility into gold. He also imposed wage and price controls for ninety days and levied a 10 percent tariff surcharge on the import of foreign goods. The president announced these measures, known as the "Nixon Shock," in a speech to the nation on August 15, 1971. "The time has come for a new economic policy for the United States. Its targets are unemployment, inflation, and international speculation," he announced, and he hoped Americans would believe that the nation's "best days lie ahead."[12]

The economy worsened before it recovered. Nixon's policies, although popular at the time, contributed to what came to be known as the "stagflation" of the 1970s, characterized by stagnant economic growth, high inflation, and rising unemployment. And they contributed to the recession of 1973–1975, a worldwide economic downturn that saw the stock market lose more than 45 percent of its value. An oil crisis compounded these woes. On October 19, 1973, the Organization of Petroleum Exporting Countries (OPEC) agreed to stop exporting oil to the United States. It did so because the declining value of the dollar resulted in reduced revenue for oil contracts priced in US dollars and to punish the United States for supporting Israel in its Yom Kippur War against Egypt. The embargo continued until March 1974. In that time, the price of oil rose from \$2.90/barrel to \$11.65/barrel. The price of a gallon of gas rose 42 percent.

As supplies shrank, long lines formed at gas stations and Americans were forced to wait hours to fill their tanks. Some states imposed rationing with odd/even days to purchase gas based on license plate numbers. To conserve gas, the national speed limit was set at 55 miles per hour. Americans found the situation humiliating and intolerable. A nation known for plenty and abundance had been brought to a near standstill. "The greatest country in the world," lamented one customer waiting in line for gas, "is stifled by a few sheiks."[13]

The crisis led to a search for renewable sources of energy such as solar, wind, and nuclear power. Congress passed an Energy and Policy Conservation Act in 1975 and created the Department of Energy in 1977. Meanwhile the American appetite for oil only increased. The search for domestic sources of petroleum led to the construction of the trans-Alaska pipeline built between 1974 and 1977. Running 800 miles from the Prudhoe Bay oil field to Valdez, Alaska, the pipeline, at its peak, carried more than 2 million barrels of oil per day. Native Americans opposed the pipeline as an intrusion on their land claims and a threat to their way of life. Environmentalists feared the destruction of wildlife and its effect on the landscape. One of the worst environmental disasters occurred in 1989 when the *Exxon Valdez*, an oil tanker, struck a reef and spilled more than 10 million gallons of oil into Prince William Sound. The following year, Congress passed an Oil Pollution Act that made provisions for prevention and the settlement of liability claims in the future. American dependence on oil continued. Through the 1980s and 1990s, oil imports increased dramatically, as did consumption.

The financial and energy crisis of the 1970s contributed to unprecedented federal deficits (from 1974 to 1975 they jumped from \$6 billion to \$53 billion as the government tried to spend its way out of stagflation). President Ford opposed efforts to increase spending and vetoed sixty-six bills during his brief tenure in office. His election campaign seized on the motto "Whip Inflation Now," and supporters wore WIN buttons that opponents turned upside down. They defined NIM in various ways, including Need Immediate Money. As

New York City faced bankruptcy in 1975, Ford announced that he would "veto any bill that has as its purpose a Federal bailout of New York City to prevent a default." New York's *Daily News* ran with the headline "Ford to City: Drop Dead." The following year, Jimmy Carter narrowly won New York State, and in Manhattan, he carried 73 percent of the vote.[14]

Carter made energy a centerpiece of his presidency and he sought to expand uses of solar and geothermal energy. He even had thirty-two solar panels installed at the White House. He faced political opposition from Republicans and southern Democrats who sought deregulation, opposed increased taxes on use of oil and gas, and defended the business interests of the energy industry. The idea of conservation disturbed many Americans who saw limitation as nothing less than an insult to the American way. Carter cultivated an image as a populist man of the people: he often wore a cardigan sweater and carried his own garment bag off of Air Force One. Yet he was also aloof and moralistic, perhaps never more so than in a speech on national energy goals delivered on July 15, 1979, that would come to be known as the "malaise" speech, though he never used that word.

Carter defined the greatest threat to America "a crisis of confidence." Emulating FDR and his "nothing to fear but fear itself" speech, Carter identified a "growing doubt about the meaning of our own lives and in the loss of a unity of purpose for our nation." Although the speech was well received at the time despite its call for Americans to overcome "self-indulgence and consumption," Carter lost whatever momentum it might have brought when, two days later, he fired six cabinet members. A call for civic sacrifice would soon give way to a truculent celebratory nationalism. Carter's opponent in the election of 1980, Ronald Reagan, declared, "I find no national malaise."[15]

Born in Illinois in 1911, Reagan graduated from Eureka College, went into broadcasting, and moved to Hollywood in 1937. He forged a successful film career; one of his nicknames, the "Gipper," came from him having played George Gipp in the 1940 film *Knute Rockne, All American*. (Notre Dame football player Gipp died at age twenty-five and Rockne exhorted his team to "win one for the Gipper.") From 1947 to 1952, and 1959 to 1960, Reagan served as president of the Screen Actors Guild (SAG). Fervently anti-communist, Reagan provided the FBI with names of communist sympathizers in Hollywood. He was also a New Deal Democrat. As SAG leader he won important victories for members, including payment of residuals. He became increasingly disturbed, however, by the Democrats' embrace of big government, taxation, and social welfare legislation such as Medicare, the national health insurance for Americans over age sixty-five. He said of John F. Kennedy, "Under that tousled boyish haircut is still old Karl Marx." In 1962, Reagan joined the Republican Party. "I didn't leave the Democratic Party," he said, "the Democratic Party left me."[16]

In 1966, California elected Reagan governor and reelected him four years later. He maintained a mostly conservative agenda, characterized by an emphasis on limited government, fiscal responsibility (despite his desire to lower taxes, he raised them to balance the budget), opposition to entitlement programs, and contempt for social activism. When students at Berkeley engaged in protests against the Vietnam War in 1969, he sent in California Highway Patrol officers who used force to disperse the crowd. Reagan had found a formula that would carry him to the presidency in 1980.

In a speech delivered on the eve of the election, he offered his vision of America. He called for a reordering of the relationship between government and the people and an "era of national renewal." He stressed that there was nothing wrong with America or the American people. He invoked John Winthrop's 1630 sermon, "A Model of Christian Charity," in which he declared, "We shall be as a city upon a hill." "Americans in 1980," Reagan asserted, "are every bit as committed to that vision of a shining city on a hill, as were those long-ago settlers."[17]

Two months after his inauguration, Reagan and three others were shot outside the Washington Hilton by John W. Hinckley, who acted out of obsession with Jodie Foster, who starred in the film *Taxi Driver* (1976). The movie features a character who plans to assassinate a presidential candidate. Reagan's quips after being shot endeared the Western optimist to the American people. On seeing the medical team when entering the operating room, he said to a Secret Service agent, "I hope they are all Republicans."[18]

Reagan's American vision meant controlling and limiting the federal government, its "intervention and intrusion in our lives." In his inaugural address, he proclaimed, "Government is not the solution to our problem; government is the problem." Reagan's election (he trounced Carter, carrying 44 states and winning 489 electoral votes) marked the triumph of a conservative vision based on limiting government action, enacting tax cuts, deregulating business and banking rules, and attacking welfare and abortion rights. "It is my intention," he said, "to curb the size and influence of the Federal establishment."[19]

Reagan's economic plan to combat a decade of inflation centered on what came to be called "Reaganomics." The so-called Reagan Revolution had been at least a decade in the making, and it marked the overthrow of economic thinking known as Keynesianism, after the British economist John Maynard Keynes who argued that the government must take the lead in stimulating the economy, including through deficit spending if required. Whereas Keynesian economics focused on the demand for goods and services, Reaganomics focused on supply. Lowering taxes and decreasing government regulation, argued so-called supply-side economists, would stimulate economic growth. None of this began with Reagan. Though not a supply-sider, Milton Friedman, who won the Nobel Prize in 1976 and taught at the University of Chicago, was one of the leading economists to challenge Keynesian orthodoxy. Appointed by Carter to head the Federal Reserve, Paul Volker applied some of Friedman's ideas and adopted a monetarist policy that viewed changes in the money supply, as opposed to government spending, as critical to economic growth. In 1978 voters in Reagan's home state of California passed Proposition 13, which held that property would not be taxed at more than 1 percent of its real cash value. As Reagan took office, a new conservative economic orthodoxy, one centered on free markets, took firm hold of the government that Reagan saw as an evil. The shift in thought was not America's alone and the transformation in economic ideas led to similar policy changes in countries across the globe, including nations such as Mexico and France that abandoned their statist policies.[20]

Under Reagan, the largest tax cuts in American history became law. The Economic Recovery Tax Act (ERTA) of 1981 reduced income tax rates by 25 percent over three years and also cut estate and corporate taxes. The measure did not, however, have the immediate effect proponents hoped for as the country fell into a recession and the deficit ballooned. A law passed in 1982 revised the ERTA, though signs of economic recovery and the end of the stagflation of the 1970s became evident as the inflation rate dropped from over 12 percent in 1980 to under 4 percent by decade's end. Unemployment fell from 7.2 percent to 5.3 percent between 1980 and 1988. The supply-side, free market economists insisted that Reaganomics had worked. Others contested the claim. In promoting economic growth, tax cuts did not pay for themselves—someone had to pay. Critics had a name for the idea that tax cuts for the wealthy (the highest marginal tax rate fell from 70 percent to 28 percent during the 1980s) would stimulate the economy. They derisively called it "trickle-down economics." One economist labeled it the horse-and-sparrow theory: if you feed the horse enough oats, some will pass through to the road for the sparrows. Under Reagan, income and wealth inequality in America began to soar: in 1982, the highest earning 1 percent of families received 10.8 percent of pretax income and the bottom 90 percent received 64.7 percent. By 2012, the top 1 percent received 22.5 percent of pretax income and the share for the bottom 90 percent had fallen to 49.6 percent. The film *Wall Street* (1987) summarized the spirit of the era when a character named Gordon Gekko declared, "Greed is good."[21]

New Right

Reagan's electoral victory represented the triumph of conservative politics and a broader conservative, religious vision of America that was labeled the "New Right." The core principles of the movement—individual liberty, limited government, free-market economy, anti-communism, traditional family values—had taken root decades before Reagan's rise.

Politically, Barry Goldwater's nomination as Republican candidate for president in 1964 marked the arrival of the New Right. The Arizona senator served as a Western counterbalance to more liberal Eastern establishment politicians such as New York governor Nelson Rockefeller. The consummate Westerner, Goldwater once said, "This country would be better off if we could just saw off the eastern seaboard and let it float out to sea." Time and again, Goldwater's candor would come back to haunt him, and he once admitted some of his words "floating around in the air . . . I would like to reach up and eat." In 1960 he published *The Conscience of a Conservative,* a book, Goldwater said, intended "to awaken the American people to a realization of how far we had moved from the old constitutional concepts toward the new welfare state." "The people's welfare depends on individual self-reliance rather than on state paternalism," he wrote. He believed that freedom, not government, was the desire of conservatives, and America was fundamentally a conservative nation. The book sold more than 3 million copies. Goldwater returned to the Senate where he served until 1987. It was he who went to Richard Nixon on August 7, 1974, and told the president that Republicans would not stand in the way of impeachment.[22]

Goldwater's book had been ghostwritten by L. Brent Bozell Jr., William F. Buckley's brother-in-law. No public intellectual was more important to the emergence of the New Right than Buckley.

Born in New York in 1925, Buckley's father had made a fortune as an oil tycoon and educated his children with personal tutors and at Roman Catholic schools in England and France. Following service in the US Army from 1944 to 1946, Buckley attended Yale, where he thrived as a writer and debater. In 1951, he published *God and Man at Yale*, a stinging critique of what he saw as the university's atheist and socialist tendencies. After graduation, he joined the CIA and worked in Mexico City where his case officer was none other than E. Howard Hunt.

In 1955, Buckley started *National Review*, a magazine devoted to conservative ideas. Its influence far exceeded its circulation. Buckley wrote that the magazine "stands athwart history, yelling STOP" to the liberal consensus that had reigned since the New Deal. Buckley was an intellectual's intellectual who spoke with a British-inflected patrician accent and loved nothing more than using polysyllabic words. In 1965, on a lark, he ran for mayor of New York City and won 13 percent of the vote, a result that later would be viewed as the beginning of what would become the Reagan Democrats, white working-class voters who supported conservative policies. Asked what he would do if elected, he answered, "Demand a recount."[23]

In 1950 the critic Lionel Trilling wrote that liberalism was "not only the dominant but even the sole intellectual tradition." A decade later, conservative ideas had found several incubators. In 1973, the Heritage Foundation, a conservative public policy think tank, began its work on behalf of the principles of free enterprise and limited government. Upon his election, Ronald Reagan gave each cabinet member a copy of the foundation's report *Mandate for Leadership*, a multivolume work that ran over a thousand pages and made suggestions for curtailing the size of government and implementing conservative reforms. Reagan implemented more than 60 percent of the foundation's suggestions.[24]

The Heritage Foundation called for "traditional American values," and the emergence of an evangelical Christian alliance that supported conservative ideals was critical to the advent of the New Right in the 1980s. Jerry Falwell, a Baptist fundamentalist preacher from Lynchburg, Virginia, became a potent force in electoral politics by mobilizing the religious right. In 1971 he created Liberty Baptist College, which would become Liberty University, and his "Old-Time Gospel Hour" show began to reach a national audience. "Television made me a kind of instant celebrity," he said. Although he initially rejected any political involvement for ministers, *Roe v. Wade* led Falwell to preach against abortion. In 1979, he founded the Moral

Majority, a political organization designed to "turn back the flood tide of moral permissiveness, family breakdown and general capitulation to evil and to foreign policies such as Marxism-Leninism." At its peak, the Moral Majority claimed some 4 million members and it contributed both to Reagan's election and to making moral questions, coded as support for family values, central to the conservative political agenda. It also blazed the way for the use of new tools, such as the use of direct mail and advertisements on telephone and television, including newly created cable television, to win adherents and raise funds. In 1989, Falwell disbanded the Moral Majority, in part because of growing opposition to its platform from liberals (People for the American Way, founded by Norman Lear, became a liberal rival to the organization) but more so because of rivalry with Pat Robertson, another leading televangelist.[25]

The son of a US senator from Virginia, Robertson served in the Korean War and graduated from Yale Law School before a religious conversion led him to New York's Biblical Seminary. In 1960, he created the Christian Broadcasting Network and in 1966 debuted *The 700 Club,* a show that became a vital force in evangelical politics and the emerging cultural divide in America over such as issues as abortion, homosexuality, and women's rights. He ran for president in 1988 (Falwell supported eventual winner George H. W. Bush) and afterward formed the Christian Coalition, designed to mobilize Christian voters. By offering "in pew" registration and providing "voter guides," the coalition increasingly shaped the Republican Party at the national, state, and local levels. Robertson's apocalyptic rhetoric appealed to millions of fundamentalist evangelicals: America was at a crossroads, he warned, and either it returned to its Christian roots or it would "continue to legalize sodomy, slaughter innocent babies, destroy the minds of her children, squander her resources and sink into oblivion."[26]

Any number of issues crystalized the culture wars of the 1980s. For example, pop singer Madonna, whose video for her song "Like a Prayer" appeared on MTV, a cable television channel launched in 1981 that had an outsize influence on youth culture, was denounced by conservatives for its explicit sexuality and use of religious symbols and themes. Members of the New Right made opposition to abortion central to their agenda, and Reagan repeatedly denounced it. In his 1986 State of the Union Address he claimed, "America will never be whole as long as the right to life granted by our Creator is denied to the unborn." The Republican Party had not always been prolife, the term adopted by antiabortion advocates after *Roe v. Wade* (both Rockefeller and Goldwater were pro-choice, the term favored by those who supported abortion as a woman's right to choose). In 1976, the party adopted a platform that called for an antiabortion constitutional amendment. In doing so, it won over an increasing number of evangelical Protestant and Catholic voters.[27]

The party had also once endorsed an Equal Rights Amendment (ERA), first introduced in 1921 and reintroduced in Congress in 1971, where it was quickly approved and sent to the states for ratification. It provided simply that "Equality of rights under the law shall not be denied or abridged by the United States or by any State on account of sex." In the first year, twenty-two of the thirty-eight states needed to ratify the amendment did so. Congress had set a ratification deadline of March 1979. Starting in 1972, opposition to the ERA, led by Phyllis Schlafly, a Midwestern lawyer and Republican political activist who supported Barry Goldwater in 1964, slowed the number of states to ratify. Through her movement, STOP ERA, Schlafly decried any changes in the traditional role of women as housewives and argued that the amendment would mean men no longer had a legal responsibility to support their wives and children. She argued that the ERA would make women susceptible to conscription. "We do expect men to protect us," she declared. *Newsweek* called her "the First Lady of anti-feminism." Only thirteen more states ratified the ERA by the time the deadline passed. The amendment failed, though some states went on to ratify it while others rescinded their earlier ratifications, including Kentucky and Tennessee. No Southern state ratified the amendment.[28]

Schlafly had also stoked antigay activism, arguing that the ERA would legalize gay marriage. In the 1980s, no issue was as important or galvanizing as the AIDS epidemic. Beginning in 1981, doctors identified in gay male communities in the United States and Europe a new immune system disorder, human immunodeficiency virus (HIV). Transmitted through bodily fluids, the virus in its most severe form turned into acquired immunodeficiency disease (AIDS) and led to fatal cancer and pneumonia. By the mid-1980s, tens of thousands of men had been infected. The pandemic mobilized activists who condemned what they saw as government inaction and indifference to the disease. The Gay Men's Health Crisis organization was formed in New York City in 1982 and, several years later, a more radical advocacy group, AIDS Coalition to Unleash Power (ACTUP) took more direct action. For example, in 1987, protesters chained themselves to the New York Stock Exchange balcony to protest the high price of AZT, a drug developed to treat HIV. Activists created a poster of an upright pink triangle with the words "silence = death" that became a symbol of solidarity. In 1987, an enormous AIDS quilt with nearly two thousand 3-by-6-foot panels honoring the dead was displayed on the National Mall in Washington.

Reagan's administration responded at first with apathy or hostility. The president did not publicly mention AIDS until 1985. Some evangelicals saw the disease as punishment: "AIDS is the wrath of a just God against homosexuals," declared Jerry Falwell. Many conservatives opposed policies such as sex education and the distribution of condoms, known to prevent infection. Rush Limbaugh, who began a nationally syndicated radio show in 1988 and for decades served as a lightning rod for conservative views, worked against public health policy by claiming that condoms often failed to prevent AIDS. Even after the government began funding AIDS research and treatment, senators such as Jesse Helms of North Carolina denounced the "deliberate, disgusting, revolting conduct" of homosexuals. In 1996, Bill Clinton signed the Defense of Marriage Act (1996), which

Figure 10.2 *Silence Equals Death* (1987). New York Public Library.

defined marriage as the union of a man and a woman; the federal government would not recognize same-sex marriages. The act would be ruled unconstitutional in 2013.

Many other conservatives, lamenting the increasing influence of evangelicals on politics, came to support gay rights. When a discussion of gays serving in the military emerged in the early 1990s, Barry Goldwater declared, "You don't need to be 'straight' to fight and die for your country. You just need to shoot straight." An end to the policy banning homosexuals from the military was the result of the efforts of newly elected President Bill Clinton. The policy came to be known as "Don't Ask, Don't Tell." It satisfied neither military leaders, who opposed the service of gay men, nor gay activists, who denounced the demand for secrecy. Culture wars did not lend themselves to compromise.[29]

New Democrats

By the mid-1980s, the economy had begun to recover. Inflation was below 5 percent, the gross national product grew at over 4 percent a year, unemployment fell from a high of nearly 11 percent at the end of 1982 to below 6 percent five years later. These positive developments came to a sudden halt when, on Monday, October 19, 1987, the stock market crashed—the Dow Jones average fell 22.6 percent, the largest one-day percentage decline in stock market history. "Black Monday," as it came to be known, hit markets around the world. The crash affected all financial sectors and was fueled in part by the introduction of an automated system to deliver orders. Analysts called for greater regulation and identified the use of financial derivatives—futures and options contracts—as a leading cause of the crash. The market recovered relatively quickly, and the crisis had far less effect than a recession in 1991, which saw unemployment rise to nearly 8 percent. Democratic presidential candidate Bill Clinton took advantage of the anxiety over a $300 billion deficit created by Republican administrations. James Carville, his political strategist, distilled Clinton's message into a pithy phrase: "It's the economy, stupid."[30]

Clinton hailed from Hope, Arkansas, and attended Georgetown University and Yale Law School, where he dated Hillary Rodham, who would become a partner in both marriage and politics. In high school, Clinton had met John F. Kennedy at a Rose Garden ceremony, and the experience ignited a desire for a life in politics and public service. He not only had the ambition, he also had the charisma to succeed, and in 1978 he was elected governor of Arkansas at age thirty-two. Clinton used that stage to forge a national profile. Running for the Democratic presidential nomination in 1992, he had to contend with charges of having dodged the draft, smoked pot, and been guilty of marital infidelity (he admitted to causing pain in his marriage and said while he tried marijuana he never inhaled). Invoking religious vocabulary, he described his political philosophy as a "new covenant." While the term never stuck, he believed he represented a new approach to government that offered "more empowerment and less entitlement" and focused on personal responsibility. In the election of 1992, he won only 43 percent of the popular vote, yet easily defeated George H. W. Bush who, despite foreign policy successes, was not forgiven for raising taxes after declaring in 1988 that he never would. A third-party candidate, billionaire Ross Perot, who ran on a platform that called for balancing the budget, reducing the national debt, and cutting government bureaucracy, won nearly 19 percent of the popular vote. Clinton was the first Baby Boomer to become president. His defining experience was not the Depression and World War II but civil rights and Vietnam. In his inaugural, he proclaimed, "There is nothing wrong with America that cannot be cured by what is right with America."[31]

Clinton believed health care policy was one thing wrong with America and health care reform served as a central issue of his campaign. Since 1989, when George Bush had taken office, the cost of medical care had risen 32 percent and more than 35 million Americans had no health insurance. In 1993, Clinton's administration offered a health care plan that followed recommendations made by a task force headed by First Lady Hillary Clinton. The Health Security Act proposed universal health care coverage and included an employer mandate to provide insurance. Regional health alliances would be created to provide competition and keep prices manageable and allow consumers a choice.

Opponents denounced the plan as the expansion of big government, as overly bureaucratic, and as a threat to individual choice. They called it "socialized medicine." The task force held hundreds of meetings, and Hillary Clinton testified before five congressional committees. Opponents condemned the reform effort as secretive. The press had been excluded from ongoing task force discussion, and opponents waged an effective television campaign that featured a fictional couple, "Harry and Louise," discussing the proposal and dismissing the whole idea as "another billion-dollar bureaucracy."[32]

By the time the 1,300-page plan was ready and delivered to Congress in January 1994, Clinton had lost the window of the first 100 days that presidents since Roosevelt seized upon for legislative activity. Opposition to the plan mounted, compromise measures went nowhere, and action on health care was delayed and eventually declared dead.

Except for health care reform, Clinton differed from traditional liberal democratic positions such as support for unions and welfare programs. Indeed, he now proclaimed that "the era of big Government is over." In 1981, Ronald Reagan had led an assault on unions when he fired thousands of air traffic controllers, members of the Professional Air Traffic Controllers Organization (PATCO), who walked out in demand of better working conditions and refused to return to work. By decertifying the union, Reagan essentially destroyed it. Public sector unionism had taken a blow that emboldened private employers in their battles against unions. Calling himself "a different kind of Democrat," Clinton endorsed some anti-union measures and coddled big business interests. Unions nonetheless supported his candidacy. As one union member put it, he was "the lesser of two evils." In 1993, Clinton signed into law the North American Free Trade Agreement (NAFTA), first proposed by Reagan and negotiated by Bush. NAFTA expanded investment and trade across the borders by providing for free trade between the United States, Mexico, and Canada. Allowing US corporations to relocate elsewhere cost US workers hundreds of thousands of jobs and forced them to accept lower wages and fewer benefits.[33]

Republicans had not only supported free trade, they also attacked government welfare programs, which they viewed as part of the evil of big government. Tilting toward conservatism, Clinton had promised "to end welfare as we know it." The politics of welfare reform stretched back decades and became inextricably tied to questions of race. The stereotype of the black welfare mother originated as much with liberals as conservatives. In 1965, Daniel Patrick Moynihan, who had a doctoral degree in international relations and would one day serve as a Democratic US senator from New York, issued a report, *The Negro Family*, that identified the "welfare dependency" of the single black mother as a key factor in ongoing black poverty. Republican candidates seized on this. Running for governor of California in 1966, Ronald Reagan declared that the working class should not have to subsidize the lives of " a segment of society capable of caring for itself but which prefers making welfare a way of life, freeloading at the expense of these more conscientious citizens." He later promulgated the image of the "welfare queen," a black woman manipulating the system to avoid work and living like royalty. By stigmatizing single, black mothers it became easy to overlook the reality that white parents constituted 35 percent of the caseload for Aid to Families with Dependent Children (AFDC), a federal assistance program that began during the New Deal as part of the Social Security Act.[34]

The discussion of welfare in the 1990s also became inseparable from anxiety over crime. Handgun-related homicides more than doubled between 1985 and 1990 and aggravated assault rates had been climbing since 1970. In 1991, Rodney King, a black taxi driver in Los Angeles, was pulled over and beaten by police officers. The incident was captured on film. The officers were acquitted at trial and Los Angeles erupted in six days of riots. King went on television and appealed for peace ("can we all get along?") to calm tensions in just another flashpoint in a long history of racial violence.

By the time of the riots, hip-hop and rap had emerged as powerful cultural forms emanating from black communities and serving as a voice for the oppressed. Chuck D of Public Enemy called rap "black America's CNN," a reference to the twenty-four-hour Cable News Network launched in 1980 that within a decade surpassed the three major television networks for viewership. Rapping in rhyme to rhythmic music that used a variety of techniques for manipulating records and sound (such as scratching and spinning), artists and performers soon became prominent cultural figures, praised and denounced for songs filled with social commentary—and also violence and sexism. Dr. Dre, Ice Cube, and Tupac Shakur all wrote about the Rodney King incident. In "The Day the Niggaz Took Over," Snoop Dogg sings, "I got my finger on the trigger, some niggas wonder why / But livin' in the city, it's do-or-die."

Whatever the origins of rising crime and violence (some blamed a crack cocaine epidemic in the 1980s that resulted in legislation, the Anti-Drug Abuse Acts, which established mandatory minimum sentences for possession and disproportionately affected black inner-city communities), Clinton bragged, "No one can say I'm soft on crime." In 1994 he signed the Violent Crime Control and Enforcement Act, a massive crime bill that provided billions of dollars for expansion of police forces and prisons. The bill increased the number of federal offenses and included a provision whereby anyone convicted of a felony who had twice previously been convicted of a crime received a mandatory sentence. The legislation and the ongoing war against drugs and crime contributed to rising incarceration rates in the United States, an increase of 500 percent between 1985 and 2015.[35]

Clinton and the Democratic National Committee had learned from Reagan's victory in 1984 that white working-class voters, once the cornerstone of the Democratic coalition, deserted the party because it was soft on crime and because it was "the give-away party, giving white tax money to blacks and poor people." In the midterm elections of 1994, for the first time in forty years, Republicans won control of the House (they gained fifty-two seats) and the Senate as well as a majority of governorships and state legislatures. Whatever Clinton's inclinations on welfare reform, Republicans pushed him toward more conservative positions. Newt Gingrich, a onetime history professor who served as a Georgia congressman, became Speaker of the House. Gingrich had coauthored the "Contract with America," a document consisting of ten parts (Gingrich had in mind the Ten Commandments and Bill of Rights) and signed by 367 Republican candidates for the House of Representatives. The contract called for cutting the size of the federal government, reducing taxes, offering support to families, strengthening the military, reducing crime, and slashing welfare by enacting what was called "the personal responsibility act." When Republicans took control of Congress, they proceeded on what they saw as a national mandate.[36]

In seeking welfare reform, Clinton and Congress seemed in tune with a broader public that desired some change (a *Time*/CNN survey in 1994 found 81 percent of respondents welcomed "fundamental reform"). Although Clinton vetoed the first two welfare reform bills that came to him, in 1996 he relented and signed the Personal Responsibility and Work Opportunity Act. It replaced AFDC with Temporary Assistance for Needy Families. The bill limited welfare to five years and required recipients to work. It also prohibited teenage mothers from receiving benefits. Supporters of welfare reform had argued that welfare programs such as AFDC promoted perverse incentives, such as divorce and having children out of wedlock, and made people dependent on government support. The effect of the new legislation was to reduce the number of welfare recipients as well as the number of cases, though analysts disagree as to its effects on helping families to escape poverty or improving the prospects for children. Privately, Clinton said it was "a decent welfare bill wrapped in a sack of shit." Publicly, he said he would work to change the parts of the legislation, such as limited support for child care for working mothers, that were "far from perfect," but "on balance this is a real step forward for our country, our values, and for people who are on welfare."[37]

Clinton's conservative credentials did not inhibit political opponents from coming after him. His presidency endured numerous investigations, including the Whitewater scandal, in which the Clintons were accused of participating in a fraudulent Arkansas land scheme; Travelgate, in which Clinton was accused of inappropriately firing employees in the White House Travel Office; and Filegate, in which the White House was accused of improperly gaining access to FBI files. None of the investigations found criminal culpability.

Those scandals paled in comparison to the scandal over Bill Clinton's affair with Monica Lewinsky, an unpaid White House intern. Kenneth Starr, an independent counsel who had been appointed to investigate Whitewater, began to probe whether Clinton committed perjury or obstruction of justice in testimony given in a civil case over whether he had sexual relations with another woman. In January 1998, as allegations of the affair with Lewinsky became public, Clinton announced on television, "I did not have sexual relations with that woman." In August, Clinton testified before a grand jury. After Starr delivered his report to Congress, the House Judiciary Committee launched an impeachment inquiry. At year's end, the House approved articles of impeachment, stating that Clinton perjured himself and obstructed justice. The trial lasted a month, and on February 12, 1999, the Senate acquitted Clinton. The Democrats sought to censure the president for "shameless, reckless, and indefensible behavior." No such resolution was ever passed. Despite these travails, Bill Clinton remained popular. When he left office, his approval rating stood at 65 percent and the Clintons would continue to shape American politics into the new century.[38]

New World Order

On December 16, 1998, Bill Clinton ordered air strikes against Iraq for refusing to allow United Nations inspectors to investigate whether the nation was building nuclear or chemical weapons. Many in America saw the timing of Clinton's actions as a ploy to distract from the impeachment investigation. Bob Dole, the Republican senator from Kansas, who lost to Clinton in the election on 1996, supported the action: "In matters like this, all of us think not as Republicans or Democrats, but as Americans." Clinton did not want Iraq's leader, Saddam Hussein, to think he was weakened by the political controversy at home and acted despite the opposition of many world leaders. Clinton warned, "In the next century, the community of nations may see more and more of the very kind of threat Iraq poses now—a rogue state with weapons of mass destruction."[39]

Hussein had seized power in Iraq in 1979. That same year, in Iran, fundamentalist cleric Ayatollah Ruhollah Khomeini became the Supreme Leader, following a revolution that overthrew the shah of Iran, bringing an end to more than 2,000 years of monarchical reign. The two regimes clashed, and in September 1980 Iraqi forces invaded Iran. The United States would one day go to war against Iraq, but in the Iran-Iraq War (1980–1988) the administration supported Hussein. Ironically, so did the Soviet Union, whose invasion of Afghanistan in 1979 led Jimmy Carter to announce that the United States would use military force to defend its interests in the Persian Gulf.

Under Ronald Reagan, the United States restored diplomatic relations with Iraq, provided economic aid, and even shared intelligence reports. The US Navy also patrolled the Gulf. In supporting Hussein, the United States turned a blind eye to his use of chemical weapons. Officials believed Iraq provided the best chance for regional stability as well as protection of oil interests.

There was also no way the United States could support Iran. On November 4, 1979, Iranian college students stormed the US embassy in Tehran and took more than sixty hostages, holding fifty-two of them for more than 400 days. As the days passed, and Carter's administration failed to win their release, theocratic Iran rejoiced in its triumph against democratic America. "America can't do a damn thing," declared Ayatollah Khomeini. The United States attempted two military rescue missions. Both failed. The crisis dominated the news in the United States. Every evening, Walter Cronkite, whose CBS evening news report was watched by millions, signed off by saying how many days the hostages had been held. Differences within Carter's administration over how best to approach the crisis led to the resignation of Secretary of State Cyrus Vance, who favored negotiation over confrontation. Carter's presidency suffered as the administration looked weak and vacillating. Only in the aftermath of Iraq's invasion of Iran did Khomeini offer terms for release of the hostages. An agreement was signed on January 19, 1981. The United States agreed to release $8 billion of frozen Iranian assets. The hostages were freed the next day, some twenty minutes after Ronald Reagan delivered his inaugural address. The crisis had led to Carter's defeat. Some believed that the Reagan campaign secretly made a deal with Iran not to release the hostages before the election in return for money and arms secretly funneled their way. House and Senate investigations found no credible evidence for such a plot.[40]

Reagan soon created his own foreign entanglement when he committed US Marines to Lebanon as part of a multinational peace-keeping force. Israel had invaded southern Lebanon on June 6, 1982, in an attempt to defeat the Palestine Liberation Organization (PLO), which had been launching attacks from across the border, force Syria (backed by the Soviet Union) out of Lebanon, and help establish an independent government. Less than four years earlier, Jimmy Carter had hosted Menachem Begin of Israel and Anwar Sadat of Egypt at Camp David and after twelve days of secret negotiations in September 1978 emerged with a framework for peace in the Middle East. It was perhaps the greatest triumph of Carter's pres-idency. The framework unraveled, however, as other Arab nations resented Egypt acting unilaterally and signing a peace treaty with Israel (Sadat would be assassinated in 1981) and the problem of the creation of Palestinian state remained unresolved. Although Reagan at times expressed exasperation over Israeli policies (Reagan said of Begin, "Boy that guy makes it hard for you to be his friend"), the United States remained a steadfast ally.[41]

US forces arrived in Lebanon to help enforce a ceasefire and facilitate the evacuation of PLO forces. When president-elect Bashir Gemayel was assassinated in 1982, the war worsened and the mul-tinational force became a target. On October 23, 1983, terrorists driving a yellow Mercedes truck carrying 2,000 pounds of explosives blew up the barracks that housed the multinational forces. More than 200 marines and 50 French paratroopers were killed. The Lebanese terrorist group Hezbollah, supported by Iran, declared that it was re-sponsible for the bombing. Four months later, Reagan removed US forces from Lebanon. He denounced all terrorist regimes—he named Iran, Libya, North Korea, Cuba, and Nicaragua—and declared, "We are especially not going to tolerate these attacks from outlaw states run by the strangest collection of misfits, 'Looney Tunes' and squalid criminals since the advent of the Third Reich."[42]

Yet Reagan's administration soon secretly engaged in negotiations with Iran through Israel to provide arms in order to secure the release of hostages in Lebanon, as well as to fund the Nicaraguan contras, a group of rebels who were fighting against the socialist Sandinistas who took power in 1979 when they overthrew the US-supported dictator Anastasio Somoza. Between 1982 and 1984, Congress passed three measures, collectively named the Boland Amendment after their sponsor, Massachusetts congressman

Edward Boland, to limit support to the contras. The administration found ways to circumvent Congress. At the forefront of these efforts was Oliver North, a lieutenant colonel in the Marines who, while serving on the staff of the National Security Council, helped find ways to fund the contras. When the Iran-Contra affair became public, North was dismissed, and in televised testimony before Congress in 1987 he admitted to lying to Congress and destroying evidence of his efforts on behalf of the contras, whom he praised as "freedom fighters." He also said all his actions had been authorized. North testified in uniform and, with his blunt answers and sharp looks out of central casting, won the admiration of the public at large. In an address to the nation, Reagan claimed he did not know of the diversion of funds from arms sales to support the contras. He later admitted that such an exchange had indeed taken place. At the same time, he defended American support around the world for those "who are fighting for democracy and freedom."[43]

Reagan survived the Iran-Contra affair, in part because of his relentless assault on communist regimes, particularly the Soviet Union, which he had dubbed an "evil empire" in a 1983 speech to the National Association of Evangelicals. Placing military strength at the top of his priorities, Reagan eschewed his promise to cut federal spending and instead increased military expenditures by 7 percent a year between 1981 and 1986. Although Reagan despised the Soviet regime, he developed a warm relationship with Mikhail Gorbachev, who came to power in 1985. Gorbachev was seeking to transform the Soviet Union by moving away from militarization and redirecting resources to the struggling Soviet economy. He advocated glasnost—a more open government—and perestroika—reform of the economy. In 1987, the two men signed an Intermediate-Range Nuclear Forces Treaty that reduced certain classes of ballistic missiles. Gorbachev bristled at Reagan's mantra "trust but verify" with respect to compliance inspections, and he objected to Reagan's support for a space-based missile defense program called the Strategic Defense Initiative (known generally as "Star Wars"). Still, they had in common a desire to end the threat of mutually assured destruction through nuclear weapons.[44]

Remarkably, the Soviet Union began to collapse. The Soviet economy suffered when the price of oil fell from $120 per barrel in 1980 to $24 per barrel in 1986. Russian military spending continued to increase, and the country had not recovered from a failed ten-year occupation of Afghanistan between 1979 and 1989 that left many dissatisfied. The Russian people were suffering, and

Gorbachev's policy of openness allowed them to vent in ways never before possible. Democratization led to the fragmentation of the Soviet Union into multiple republics, and the Iron Curtain, a term used by Winston Churchill in a speech in 1946 to describe how the Soviet Union sealed itself and Communist Eastern bloc allies off from the West, began to weaken. In Poland, for example, an anti-communist movement, Solidarity, triumphed and elected Lech Walesa, a labor leader, as president. No symbol of the Iron Curtain was more conspicuous than the Berlin Wall. On June 12, 1987, in a speech delivered in West Berlin, Ronald Reagan implored Soviet leaders to "tear down this wall." The line became notable when, three years later, the ninety-six-mile-long concrete wall separating East and West Germany did indeed came down. On December 25, 1991, Gorbachev resigned, and Boris Yeltsin became president of the independent republic of Russia.

President George H. W. Bush was thrilled. A cold war that had raged for more than four decades was over. A liberal world order based on democracy, free markets, and cooperation had triumphed. On Christmas Day 1991, he spoke to the nation about the demise of the Soviet Union that was "a victory for democracy and freedom. It's a victory for the moral force of our values." Although in the same speech he promised to address the nation's economic woes, foreign policy would define his presidency. On December 20, 1989, he authorized Operation Just Cause and sent troops into Panama to remove Manuel Noriega from power. Ironically, Bush had been director of the CIA in 1976 and Noriega's rise to power had been abetted by the agency. The dictator's involvement in the drug trade and support for the Sandinistas in Nicaragua made him toxic. Noriega surrendered and served seventeen years in a US prison.[45]

Bush's greatest challenge came when Saddam Hussein, in the aftermath of the Iran-Iraq war, invaded Kuwait. Hussein was seeking to rebuild his nation and re-establish economic health (Iraq owed $37 billion to foreign governments). He resented that Kuwait would not forgive a $14 billion debt and accused the nation of stealing Iraq's oil. In what he considered a preemptive attack, he invaded Kuwait on August 2, 1990, and occupied the country for seven months. The United Nations Security Council passed a resolution demanding that Iraq withdraw, and Bush began to assemble an international coalition to oppose Hussein. After diplomatic efforts failed, Congress authorized the use of military force. On January 17, 1991, Operation Desert Storm began with air strikes against Iraq. A month later, ground forces, led by half a million US troops, sped across the region and within several days reached Kuwait City. Iraqi forces, the fourth largest army in the world, surrendered, and the Gulf War quickly came to an end. American battle deaths totaled 146 men. It had been a television war, and Americans at home watched in real time as cruise missiles struck their targets. The public embraced General Norman Schwarzkopf, who led coalition forces and earned the nickname Stormin' Norman. With comparisons being made to Eisenhower, there was talk of him running for president as a Democrat. In the end, he supported the president's reelection campaign.

In a speech to Congress and the nation in the war's aftermath, Bush declared, "Until now, the world we've known has been a world divided, a world of barbed wire and concrete block, conflict and cold war. And now, we can see a new world coming into view. A world in which there is the very real prospect of a new world order . . . A world in which freedom and respect for human rights find a home among all nations."[46]

President Clinton sought to build on the opportunity to forge a new world order and called his foreign policy strategy one of "democratic enlargement," which linked economic goals with promoting democracy abroad. He intervened successfully in Haiti, Bosnia, and Kosovo, without any American combat loses. The triumph of the Gulf War, however, was not easy to replicate. A Bush-initiated mission to Somalia failed (images of dead American soldiers dragged through

Figure 10.3 Cruise Missiles, Desert Storm (1991). Associated Press.

the streets of Mogadishu shocked the nation), and Clinton would always regret his decision not to intervene in the Rwandan genocide in 1994 when Hutu death squads murdered hundreds of thousands of Tutsis. Clinton helped advance the Arab-Israel peace process when, in 1993, he hosted Israel's Prime Minister Yitzhak Rabin and PLO leader Yasser Arafat for the signing of the Oslo accords by which a process was begun to settle issues of borders and create a Palestinian home. The Oslo agreement would collapse and peace in the Middle East would remain elusive.

Americans soon discovered that the violence and terror abroad could also strike at home. On February 26, 1993, a truck bomb exploded in an underground garage beneath New York's World Trade Center. The Islamic militants who planned the bombing had hoped the explosion would lead to the collapse of the towers. Although it left a huge crater six stories down in the parking garage, it only knocked out the electrical systems and sent smoke cascading through the buildings. Six people were killed and more than 1,000 injured. Five years later, the FBI reported to Congress that extremists "pose a real and significant threat to our security" and in the future would have "an even more dizzying array of weapons and technologies available to them."[47]

By the time of those hearings in 1998, Americans had also withstood domestic attacks from antigovernment activists. The worst of these occurred on April 19, 1995, when Timothy McVeigh, a Gulf War veteran, and accomplice Terry Nichols bombed the Alfred P. Murrah Federal Building in Oklahoma City. Both men espoused antigovernment beliefs and were part of a burgeoning right-wing, survivalist paramilitary militia movement. They were energized by events at Ruby Ridge in Idaho in 1992, where resistance to an attempted arrest led to FBI involvement and deaths, and Waco, Texas, in 1993, where a raid on a religious compound resulted in a two-month siege that ended with an FBI assault. A fire that broke out during the assault killed dozens of people. The Oklahoma City bombing killed 168 people and injured hundreds more. At a ceremony called a Time for Healing, President Clinton remarked, "One thing we owe those who have sacrificed is the duty to purge ourselves of the dark forces which gave rise to this evil."[48]

The growth of international and domestic terrorism demonstrated that it was easier to proclaim a new world order than to create one, and the approaching millennium would challenge the power and security of the United States in unimagined ways.

CHAPTER 11

The Change That We Seek

I N LATE AUGUST 2005, a category five storm, Hurricane Katrina, battered New Orleans and the Gulf Coast with winds up to 175 miles per hour. When the levees failed, much of New Orleans flooded and remained underwater for weeks. More than 1,500 people died. The hurricane caused $108 billion in damage and left hundreds of thousands homeless. Evacuations were slow to occur and the government response seemed lagging and mismanaged. African Americans suffered disproportionately and felt abandoned by George W. Bush's administration. The debate over the response and plans to rebuild the area turned deeply partisan. Democrats attacked Republicans for "corruption and cronyism"; Republicans blamed Democrats for trying to "somehow shift all of this back over to the White House." One bipartisan investigation concluded, "Katrina was a national failure, an abdication of the most solemn obligation to provide for the common welfare." Hurricane Katrina also became part of an ongoing debate over climate change and global warming, an issue also polarized along partisan lines. "No challenge poses a greater threat to future generations than climate change," said President Barack Obama in 2015. By contrast, his successor, Donald Trump, once tweeted that global warming was a Chinese-fueled hoax designed to cost Americans jobs and that whatever was changing "it will change back again."[1]

War on Terror

At 8:46 a.m., on Tuesday, September 11, 2001, a sunny, cloudless morning, American Airlines Flight 11, which had taken off from Boston headed for Los Angeles, crashed into the North Tower of the World Trade Center in New York City. At 9:03, a second plane, United Flight 175, also scheduled for Boston to Los Angeles, smashed into the South Tower. The planes had been hijacked by Islamic terrorists, members of Al-Qaeda. A third hijacked plane crashed into the western façade of the Pentagon, while the passengers on a fourth tried to retake the hijacked airliner, which crashed in a field near Shanksville, Pennsylvania. By mid-morning, both towers of the World Trade Center had collapsed, killing nearly 3,000 people, those inside the buildings as well as hundreds of first responders, firefighters, and police. It was the deadliest attack ever by a foreign entity on US soil.

People around the world watched in real time as the horrific events of the day unfolded. Film crews arrived shortly after the first plane hit. Cameras were ubiquitous (though not yet on cell phones). According to one photo editor, new digital technology as well as cable and satellite transmission and the internet meant that "September 11, simply put, was the most widely observed and photographed breaking news event in world history." President George W. Bush was in Florida, visiting a second-grade classroom and listening to

Figure 11.1 September 11 Terrorist Attack (2001). Associated Press.

students read a children's book, *The Pet Goat.* He attempted to concentrate as his chief of staff whispered in his ear, "America's under attack." Footage showed shock on the president's face, though he remained in the classroom for several minutes, trying to project calm. That evening he spoke to the nation and reassured the world that Americans would not be frightened by terrorist acts, that the country's foundations remained strong. Summoning providential language, he declared that "America was targeted for attack because we're the brightest beacon for freedom and opportunity in the world. And no one will keep that light from shining."[2]

The son of George H. W. Bush, George W. Bush, a graduate of Yale and Harvard Business School, was elected governor of Texas in 1994. Espousing conservative, Christian values ("Christ . . . changed my heart," he said), Bush ran for president by portraying himself as a reformer who would restore honor to the office. He held off Senator John McCain of Arizona, whose campaign appealed to more moderate and independent voters. As his running mate, Bush chose his father's former secretary of defense, Dick Cheney (who would play an outsize role in the administration). At the Republican Convention held in Philadelphia, Bush vowed to "seize this moment of American promise."[3]

Bush's opponent was Al Gore, Bill Clinton's vice president for eight years and previously a senator from Tennessee. Gore easily won the nomination and advisors encouraged him to focus on the economic success of the Clinton administration. Gore knew he also needed to separate himself from the president to counter "Clinton fatigue." He launched his campaign talking about family life in America and offering "moral leadership." Yet Gore often seemed leaden when he spoke and in the first televised debate against Bush, he sighed loudly and displayed exasperation with Bush's answers. Afterward, the polls, which had showed Gore ahead, tightened to a near dead heat.

On election night, Gore secured 250 electoral votes and Bush 246. The winner needed 270 and all attention turned to the 25 electoral votes from Florida, which was too close to call. For the next thirty-six days, the nation awaited a winner as the Florida vote was recounted. Both campaigns filed lawsuits. Some counties began manual recounts that were halted and then restarted and produced almost existential questions as to whether a hanging chad on a punch ballot was a vote or not. Overseas absentee ballots were counted, though it was unclear whether they complied with state laws. On November 26, Florida Secretary of State Katherine Harris, who was also Bush's state campaign cochair, certified Bush as the winner by 537 votes. Gore's campaign filed suit, and on December 8, the Florida Supreme Court, by a 4–3 vote, ordered a manual recount of all votes. The US Supreme Court heard Bush's appeal and, on December 12, overturned the Florida Supreme Court and ruled 5–4 that there would be no additional vote counting. The next day, Al Gore, who had won the popular vote by 500,000 votes, conceded. "It is time for me to go."[4]

It is unknown who would have won had the Supreme Court not intervened. Some electoral studies say Gore would have triumphed; other studies suggest Bush. Some commentators argue that Ralph Nader, an environmentalist running as the nominee of the Green Party, played spoiler by taking votes away from Gore in Florida. Although the Supreme Court may have spared the nation additional months of uncertainty, its ruling smacked of partisanship and conservative judicial activism. In his dissent, Justice John Paul Stevens concluded, "Although we may never know with complete certainty the identity of the winner of this year's Presidential election, the identity of the loser is perfectly clear. It is the nation's confidence in the judge as an impartial guardian of the rule of law."[5]

In the aftermath of 9/11, the rule of law would be tested in ways not previously imagined. In an address to a joint session of Congress on September 20, Bush identified Al-Qaeda as the loosely affiliated group of Islamic terrorists responsible for the attack on America. He explained that the group was given refuge in Afghanistan, where they supported the Taliban regime. Bush spoke to Muslims throughout the world and made it clear that while we respected their faith "those who commit evil in the name of Allah blaspheme the name of Allah." (His words, however, did little to prevent hate crimes against Muslims in the United States, which continued beyond the decade). Bush announced a "war on terror" which would start with Al-Qaeda but include others. "It will not end until every terrorist group of global reach has been found, stopped and defeated."[6]

Bush knew it was easier to proclaim a war on terror than to win one. Unlike war against another country, this was a war against groups of individuals who did not fight using conventional weapons. Instead, insurgent tactics could easily offset America's military and technological advantage. Experts called it "asymmetric warfare," as terror groups targeted noncombatants in public spaces with suicide bombings and kidnappings. America's response was drone warfare, the use of unmanned, remote-controlled aircraft in lethal attacks against suspected terrorists. It will be "a lengthy campaign," warned Bush.

On September 14, three days after the attack, Bush had come to New York, to Ground Zero where the Twin Towers had stood. As he spoke through a bullhorn someone shouted, "We can't hear you!" He responded, "I can hear you. The rest of the world hears you. And the people who knocked these buildings down will hear all of us soon." Six weeks later, on October 30, Bush returned to New York, to throw out the first pitch before Game 3 of the World Series between the New York Yankees and Arizona Diamondbacks. He later recalled that standing on the mound was "by far the most nervous moment of my entire presidency." Wearing an FDNY pullover (beneath it was a bullet-proof vest no one could see), Bush gave a thumbs up and threw a strike. It was an act of defiance and an act of healing. It felt as if the nation could finally exhale.[7]

In the immediate aftermath of 9/11, Congress passed a resolution, Authorization for Use of Military Force Against Terrorists, which provided the president wide-ranging statutory authority to use "all necessary and appropriate force" in combating terrorist attacks. In time that authorization, and one passed a year later, would be used by presidents to justify all US military deployments, which, by 2018, included some nineteen countries. On October 26, President Bush signed the USA Patriot Act (which stood for Uniting and Strengthening America by Providing Appropriate Tools Required to Intercept and Obstruct Terrorism). The act gave federal authorities expanded powers of surveillance both abroad and at home and included "roving wiretaps," which allowed agencies to follow suspects across various electronic media without a warrant. The act also expanded the Foreign Intelligence Surveillance Act (1978) to permit any business records to be subpoenaed. The Patriot Act provided as well for the freezing of financial assets of suspected terrorists, increased border security, and new categories of criminal statutes. Some provisions, such as the roving wiretaps, had sunset clauses whereby they would expire in 2005 unless renewed. Congress reauthorized the bill in 2006, making some provisions permanent and requiring others to be reauthorized, which they were in 2011. In a climate of fear, the bill passed the House 357–66 and the Senate 98–1 (Democrat Russ Feingold of Minnesota was the lone dissenter), though most congressmen admitted that neither they nor their staff had read it.

In 2002, a new cabinet department was created, the Department of Homeland Security, and charged with coordinating all measures being taken to prevent future acts of terrorism. Some of those measures included illegally spying on innocent Americans. A program known as the Terrorist Surveillance Program was devised by Vice President Cheney. Succeeding programs, such as PRISM, which collected internet communications from leading companies that controlled the data, was leaked to the public in 2013 by Edward Snowden, a National Security Agency contractor who received asylum in Russia.

The Bush administration launched its war on terror in October with Operation Enduring Freedom, an invasion of Afghanistan with the goal of destroying Al-Qaeda, removing the Taliban from power, and capturing Osama Bin Laden, the mastermind behind the 9/11 attack. Aided by the United Kingdom, this initial phase of the war in Afghanistan succeeded in ending the Taliban's regime, though Bin Laden escaped from a cave complex in Tora Bora, southeast of Kabul, and made his way to Pakistan (where he would finally be tracked down and killed by Navy Seals on May 2, 2011). Although President Bush called for a major international effort to reconstruct Afghanistan, too few resources were allocated. The United States, however, remained committed to democratic reform in Afghanistan and viewed the country as the front line against terrorism. Ten years after the initial invasion, 100,000 troops had been deployed and no end was in sight to a war that had resulted in nearly 2,000 casualties and cost nearly $500 billion.

Two years into the war in Afghanistan, on March 20, 2003, the United States invaded Iraq. In his State of the Union address on January 29, 2002, Bush had included Iraq, along with Iran and North Korea, in what he termed an "axis of evil," nations that supported terrorism and sought to develop weapons of mass destruction. Iraq had at times refused to cooperate with UN inspectors who had first begun their efforts in 1991 to determine whether the Iraqi regime was developing such weapons. In 2002, Iraq agreed to the return of UN inspectors and the United States insisted on a resolution permitting military action for noncompliance. In October 2002, Congress passed a resolution, giving the president authorization to use force against Iraq. For Democrats, who in the Senate split 29–21 in favor, how one voted would later become a political litmus test. Newly elected Senator Hillary Clinton from New York voted yes; independent Representative Bernie Sanders of Vermont voted no. Barack Obama, a rising politician and member of the Illinois Senate, spoke out against it, saying he was opposed to "a dumb war. A rash war. A war based not on reason, but on passion, not on principle but on politics." On February 5, 2003, Secretary of State Colin Powell told the UN Security Council that Iraq was hiding weapons of mass destruction from inspectors. Bush had already decided on military action and the speech was intended to justify it to the international community. It turned out there were no weapons of mass destruction in Iraq; Powell had doubts even as he testified.[8]

The invasion, titled Operation Iraqi Freedom, played out on televisions around the world and began with "shock and awe," a massive bombing campaign against Baghdad and other targets. An American-led coalition committed over 170,000 troops. A month into the war Baghdad fell and a military occupation began. On May 1, standing aboard the USS *Lincoln* in the Persian Gulf, Bush announced the "end of major combat operations" before a sign that read "Mission Accomplished." The mission, however, was far from over, nor had it succeeded. The arrest of Saddam Hussein in December 2003 (he would be executed three years later) did little to stop a growing Iraqi insurgency against coalition forces, who faced suicide bombers and roadside improvised explosive devices (IEDs) that killed or dismembered thousands of US troops. A battle for Fallujah, an hour from Baghdad, was waged building by building, street by street, and is considered the bloodiest battle of the war. Dexter Filkins, a *New York Times* correspondent embedded with the Bravo Company of the First Battalion, Eighth Marines, reported that this " plunge into urban warfare" was something new for this generation of fighters: "a grinding struggle to root out guerrillas en-trenched in a city, on streets marked in a language few American soldiers could comprehend."[9]

Photographs of the abuse of Iraqi detainees at Abu Ghraib prison, located twenty miles west of Baghdad, served to fuel the in-surgency against American occupation. Guards had placed prisoners in sexually compromised positions, placed a leash around the neck of one prisoner, and had another stand shrouded on a box with elec-trical wires attached to his hands. A military report found countless instances of "sadistic, blatant, and wanton criminal abuses." Several guards received prison sentences. The larger scandal to emerge was the revelation that by executive order, US military personnel could use "enhanced interrogation techniques," a euphemism for var-ious forms of torture, including waterboarding, physical beating, and sleep deprivation. These methods extended beyond Iraq to Afghanistan and at Guantanamo Bay in Cuba, a military facility that detained hundreds of alleged terrorists without trial. As of 2019, forty detainees remained in Guantanamo, each imprisoned for more than ten years.[10]

US forces did not leave Iraq until the end of 2011. The war had lasted nearly nine years. More than 4,400 Americans died and more than 30,000 were wounded. The financial cost exceeded a trillion dollars. At least 100,000 Iraqi civilians perished. The war divided Americans and compromised the reputation of the United States abroad. Establishing democracy in Iraq proved difficult, and with the elimination of Saddam Hussein the sectarian divide between Sunni and Shia Muslims exploded. By 2014, Iraq was plunged into civil war and a splinter group of Al-Qaeda known as ISIS (Islamic State of Iraq and Syria) sought to create a caliphate across the region based on traditional Islamic Sharia law. American forces returned to Iraq in 2014 to combat ISIS, which had held Americans hostage and executed American citizens by beheading them. Religious wars know no end, and the global war on terror continued.

Figure 11.2 Hooded Man (2003). Associated Press.

Globalization

On January 31, 1990, a McDonald's opened in Moscow (the "Big Mac" was called the "Bolshoi Mac"). McDonald's had long done business abroad and would continue to expand around the globe, including opening a franchise in Baghdad in 2006. Globalization—the movement of capital, goods, information, and people around the world—had begun centuries, even millennia, earlier. The voyages of Christopher Columbus, for example, led to unprecedented exchange between Old and New Worlds. In the 1990s, "globalization" as a term took hold to characterize not only trade between nations, which was abetted by such developments as the end of the Cold War, the signing of North American Free Trade Agreement, and the establishment of the World Trade Organization, but also the belief that technological developments had made the world smaller and that national borders no longer mattered.

When media theorist Marshall McLuhan coined the phrase "global village" in 1962, he could not have imagined the innovations that would make his famous pronouncement "the medium is the message" more prescient than even he realized. In 1982, instead of naming a person of the year, *Time* magazine named a machine of the year: the personal computer (PC). By then, Apple had introduced Apple II (and in 1984 the Macintosh) and IBM the PC. Software enabled word processing and electronic spreadsheets. Modems permitted telecommunication links. Steve Jobs and Steven Wozniak had incorporated Apple in 1977. In 1983, Bill Gates of Microsoft introduced Windows, the user interface for MS-DOS, the computer operating system. Jobs, raised in California and a student at Reed College, understood the importance of design ("simplicity is the ultimate sophistication") and Apple products would in time dominate the look and feel of personal communication and entertainment devices. In 1997, however, Apple was struggling and Microsoft invested in the company, ending a legal dispute over whether Gates's company (founded along with Paul Allen) had copied Apple's operating system. Gates, born in Seattle, had dropped out of Harvard to start his own enterprise. By the time he stepped down as chairman in 2014, he was one of the wealthiest men in the world (worth at the time $81 billion), devoting most of his time to philanthropic efforts through a foundation he established in 2000.[11]

As transformative as PCs were, they were not connected until the creation of the internet and World Wide Web. The internet began in 1983 as a US government network of networks that by

1992 linked more than a million computers. The High Performance and Computing Act, passed in 1991, provided millions of dollars toward creating what Vice President Gore would call the "information superhighway." In 1990, the World Wide Web emerged from the efforts of a British physicist working at the European Organization for Nuclear Research. Web development exploded and browsers competed against one another (Microsoft created Internet Explorer in 1995). Connectivity shifted to cable-free networking known as Wi-Fi. At the end of 1996, there were 36 million web users; by 2000, 360 million; by 2010, over two billion.

Enthusiasm for the possibilities of online commerce led to exuberant investing in internet companies, known a dot-coms for the suffix that followed their name. Venture capital poured into new companies and initial public offerings raised billions of dollars as well as stock prices, though these companies had yet to earn any money, let alone show profits. In 2000, the bubble burst. The ensuing decline in the stock market continued to 2002, plunging the United States into a recession. The NASDAQ, a stock exchange heavy in tech stocks, fell 78 percent. Other companies collapsed as well. Executives at Enron, an energy and commodities company in Houston, used financial manipulation to hide corporate losses and keep stock prices artificially high. In 2001, Enron declared bankruptcy. More than 20,000 jobs and $2 billion in retirement benefits were lost, though executives had cashed out before the stock zeroed out. The CEO, Jeffrey Skilling, went to jail for fraud. As the dot. com bubble burst, dozens of companies disappeared and hundreds found their stock value drop by 80 percent or more. Despite the setback, optimism and enthusiasm for the internet did not diminish, and the emergence of a new search engine that could produce relevant results for users led to an initial public offering that set records.

In 1999 two doctoral students at Stanford, Larry Page and Sergey Brin, founded Google (the name bowdlerized from googol, a mathematical name for a vast number). They devised PageRank, an algorithm that measured the importance of web pages, and they figured out how to monetize searches by selling advertising linked to keywords in what was called "sponsored content." In 2004, Google became a public company valued at $23 billion. In 2018, Google's parent company, Alphabet, had a market value of $766 billion. (Apple's in 2018 was $927 billion.) Google expanded into multiple areas (cloud computing, Chrome browser, Gmail, Google docs, virtual assistant) and transformed the culture. "Google" became a verb, a synonym for searching on the internet (at least thirty languages have a word for Google: in Japanese it translates as *guguru* and in Polish *googlowac*). Cognitive psychologists have suggested that the search engine changed the way humans think and can manipulate a user's actions. Google mines massive amounts of private data, and some have argued that Google even has the ability to determine the outcome of an election by influencing undecided voters based on search rankings. Information is power, and Google has a near monopoly on information.[12]

Google expanded its influence by buying up other companies. Notably, in 2005, Google purchased Android, the system that runs 80 percent of the world's smartphones (Apple's iPhone, introduced in 2007, runs on a different system, IOS). These phones brought computing power into people's hands and transformed their daily lives. A proliferation of software applications (apps) made possible instantaneous modes of gathering information, being entertained, or going shopping.

Digital platforms transformed how people obtained the news (between 2000 and 2015, print newspaper advertising declined from $60 billion to $20 billion), were entertained (attendance at movie theaters reached a twenty-five-year low in 2017), and shopped (a record number of brick-and-mortar stores closed in 2017 as consumers turned to online shopping).

No business better exemplified globalization and disruption than Amazon, whose very name suggested faraway places. Founded by Jeff Bezos in 1994, Amazon began as an online bookseller and soon expanded into becoming the single largest internet retailer in the world. Bezos, who attended Princeton and opened the company in Seattle, became the wealthiest man in the world in 2018, with a personal fortune estimated at over $150 billion. The influence of his company continued to expand as it pioneered an e-book reader, called Kindle, a virtual home assistant, named Alexa, its own studio to create movies and shows, and web services that provide cloud computing.

New forms of information technology and the rise of global capitalism had profound consequences for American workers. The availability of cheaper labor overseas meant the closing of thousands of factories and loss of millions of jobs. Apple's iPhones, to take one example, say "designed by Apple in California," yet they are produced in places such as Mongolia, China, Korea, and Taiwan, where labor costs are far less than in the United States and where the phone's components are manufactured. Legacy manufacturing companies have also shifted jobs overseas. In 2017, Ford Motor Company announced plans to build its compact car in China. Of course, global manufacturing had been taking place for decades. Nonetheless, the outsourcing of some 5 million jobs to overseas production, as well as the increase in manufacturing automation, proved beneficial to companies and reshaped the labor force.

While manufacturing jobs decreased, service industry jobs increased, though real wages for American workers remained stagnant, offering employees the same purchasing power in 2018 as in 1978. What wage gains had been realized went to those who earned the most. Widening income inequality gave greater wealth and power to the top 1 percent of American households. Statistic after statistic told a similar story of average American families declining in net worth between 2000 and 2011. The situation was even worse for black and Hispanic families, whose net worth was twelve times less than that of a typical white family. Equally important, the distance between rich and poor was increasing in other ways. In the United States, the top 1 percent held 42.5 percent of national wealth, greater than in any of the other thirty-five member countries of the Organisation for Economic Co-operation and Development.

Concern over rising income inequality and wealth gained traction in American politics. In 2018, Senator Bernie Sanders of Vermont proposed legislation titled the Stop Bad Employers by Zeroing Out Subsidies Act (STOPBEZOS), aimed at taxing companies like Amazon. "The American people are tired of having to subsidize the wealthiest people in this country who are paying wages that are just so low that people can't get by," Sanders said. Perhaps in response, Amazon soon raised its minimum wage to $15, though they cut other benefits that workers had been receiving. The embrace of free markets, deregulation, the decline of unions, tax cuts that benefited corporations and the wealthy, a movement away from government support for welfare measures, and globalization itself all played a role in an economic transformation so profound that some believed it marked the end of the American Dream, whereby future generations would experience upward mobility.[13]

President Barack Obama addressed the issue of globalization and inequality. In 2016, he warned that the pace and path of globalization needed to be checked. Three years earlier, he had discussed the frustrations of Americans, a frustration "rooted in the nagging sense that no matter how hard they work, the deck is stacked against them. And it's rooted in the fear that their kids won't be better off than they were." He lamented growing inequality and the lack of upward mobility and feared that the American promise of a better life for those who worked hard had been broken. "Making sure our economy works for every working American" was the reason he gave for running for president.[14]

Vote for Change

In 2004, Illinois State Senator Barack Obama delivered the keynote address at the Democratic nominating convention in Boston. The speech electrified the delegates in the arena and catapulted him to national prominence. Addressing the shorthand code of Red States and Blue States for the divide between Republicans and Democrats, Obama declared that he had news for the pundits: "We worship an 'awesome God' in the blue states, and we don't like federal agents poking around in our libraries in the red states. We coach Little League in the blue states and yes, we've got some gay friends in the red states. There are patriots who opposed the war in Iraq and there are patriots who supported the war in Iraq. We are one people, all of us pledging allegiance to the stars and stripes, all of us defending the United States of America."[15]

John Kerry, senator from Massachusetts and the Democratic nominee, had chosen Obama, who he thought "should be one of the faces of our party." Kerry's campaign tried to reach a generation of young voters and encourage them to Vote for Change, the name given to an October tour of rock artists that included Bruce Springsteen, Pearl Jam, Neil Young, the Dixie Chicks and many others. Younger voters did indeed turn out in the election of 2004 (47 percent of Americans aged 18 to 24 voted, as compared to 36 percent in 2000). They supported Kerry 56 to 43 percent. Kerry was hurt by a smear campaign from Swift Boat Veterans for Truth, a group that challenged the Vietnam vet's record. He lost to George W. Bush, who overcame declining popularity in the aftermath of the invasion of Iraq.[16]

At his speech in 2004, Obama, whose father was born in Kenya and whose mother was born in Kansas, acknowledged that "my presence on this stage is pretty unlikely." If so, his election as president in 2008 must have seemed impossible. He ran on a campaign of hope and change. "Yes, we can," became his anthem. He warned against apathy and hopelessness, waiting for other people or other times to make change. "We are the change that we seek," he declared.[17]

Obama defeated Hillary Clinton to win the nomination. He ran against Republican Senator John McCain, who chose as his running mate Sarah Palin, governor of Alaska, a conservative populist firebrand whose inflammatory comments (she said Obama had links to terrorists) and lack of knowledge (she could not name the countries that were part of NAFTA) cost Republicans in the general election. Even without her, McCain would likely not have overcome George Bush's unpopularity (an approval rating of 31.9 percent), opposition to the Iraq War, and an economy that was entering the worst recession since the Depression. Obama received nearly 10 million more votes than McCain. "It's been a long time coming," he said to a crowd gathered in Chicago's Grant Park, "but tonight, because of what we did on this date in this election at this defining moment, change has come to America."[18]

Obama would not have long to savor the victory. He entered office with the nation in a severe economic crisis that began with a mortgage lending crisis. Banks and financial companies, in an environment with few regulations, offered subprime mortgages—loans made to customers with poor credit. Home prices continued to rise, and when the bubble burst tens of thousands of homeowners could not keep up their payments. Through 2007 and 2008, banks foreclosed on homes and many communities were left abandoned. Those mortgages had been bought by investment banks, such as Lehman Brothers, which was forced to declare bankruptcy. The firm held $600 billion in debt of which $400 billion was guaranteed by credit default swaps, contracts that guaranteed against default and were traded in unregulated markets. When the debt came due, companies such as American International Group (AIF), which sold the swaps, could not cover the contracts. To prevent AIG from going bankrupt, which would have caused a global economic collapse because of the trillions of dollars invested in the company, the Federal Reserve bailed it out in September 2008 by providing $85 billion in financing. The federal government also took over Fannie Mae and Freddie Mac, two mortgage companies that had been chartered by Congress. Fed chairman Ben Bernanke and Secretary of Treasury Henry M. Paulson Jr. testified about the imminent destruction of the world's financial system. "When you listened," admitted Senator Chuck Schumer of New York, "you gulped."[19]

On October 3, 2008, President Bush signed the Troubled Asset Relief Program (TARP) that provided $700 billion in federal bailout money. It passed only in the aftermath of the worst single-day loss in stock market history, when on September 15 the Dow lost 770 points. The decline persisted. For the week of October 6–10, the Dow fell 18 percent. The government continued to act. The Federal Reserve lowered the interest rate to zero for the first time in history.

TARP funds bailed out General Motors, Chrysler, and Ford, as well as Bank of America, Citigroup, and other financial institutions. In February 2009, President Obama signed a $787 billion stimulus package (the American Recovery and Reinvestment Act) that provided tax incentives (it cut taxes by $288 billion), set aside billions for investment in infrastructure, education, and health care, extended unemployment benefits, and allocated $275 billion to create jobs through federal contracts and loans. By most measures, the stimulus succeeded, though it took time. A month after it was passed the Dow bottomed out at 6,547, a drop of nearly 54 percent from its high in October 2007.

The Great Recession, as it came to be known, was a global financial crisis. The real gross domestic product, a measure of goods and services produced by an economy, fell in countries around the Western world: the United Kingdom, Germany, France, Italy, Japan, and Spain. Countries that relied on fiscal austerity, cutting spending rather than providing economic stimulus, took longer to recover. Regardless of the economic policies adopted, in the aftermath of the Great Recession both left-wing and right-wing populist movements proliferated around the world. Although these movements varied from country to country, they all shared an appeal to the people and a critique of governing elites. For example, in 2016, driven by nationalist feelings, economic worries, and a desire to take control of the country's policies and borders, British voters approved a referendum for the United Kingdom to leave the European Union. China alone seemed to escape the worst effects of the crisis, and in the aftermath its economy grew and its banks became the biggest in the world, although the very boom that fueled China's economic growth connected it to the vagaries of world markets.

The Great Recession of 2008 had long-lasting effects in the United States. Median household income collapsed (from $126,000 in 2007 to $97,000 in 2016); wages declined for the bottom 70 percent of all workers; consumer credit card debt rose 30 percent between 2008 and 2017; homeownership fell; and it took longer for people to find jobs and longer to graduate from college. More millennials, the generation born between 1982 and 1996, lived at home. The effects were uneven: blacks, Hispanics, and Asian Americans suffered greater losses, losing more than 50 percent of household wealth, whereas whites lost 16 percent. The top 1 percent, those who earned at least $394,000 a year, also suffered in the immediate aftermath of the recession, yet between 2009 and 2012 their income increased 31 percent and they captured 95 percent of the rise in wealth during the recovery.[20]

On September 17, 2011, protesters in New York gathered in Zuccotti Park near Wall Street to denounce rising inequality and the vast wealth of the 1 percent. Chanting "We are the 99 percent," the demonstrators, mainly young people in their twenties, encamped in the park. The movement, known as "Occupy Wall Street," had no leaders and made no specific demands. Yet it changed the conversation about wealth in America and around the world. The protesters, concluded one journalist, "ignited a national and global movement calling out the ruling class of elites by connecting the dots between corporate and political power." Mayor Michael Bloomberg had the police clear the encampment of tents and tarps. By then the movement was exerting an effect on other grassroots causes, such as protests against construction of the Keystone XL pipeline from Canada into the United States, and reshaped the political rhetoric of the Democratic Party. Hillary Clinton, far from being a radical, would announce in 2015, "The deck is stacked in favor of those at the top."[21]

If Occupy Wall Street helped launch a political movement from the left, the Tea Party became the foremost political movement on the right. Outraged by the Obama administration bailout that included help for homeowners facing foreclosure, Rick Santelli, a CNBC reporter, was reporting from the Chicago Mercantile Exchange on February 24, 2009, when he ranted, "This is America! How many of you people want to pay for your neighbor's mortgage that has an extra bathroom and can't pay their bills?" "President Obama, are you listening?" he screamed. "We're thinking of having a Chicago Tea Party in July. All you capitalists that want to show up to Lake Michigan, I'm going to start organizing." Tea Party rallies and chapters spread across the nation. Sarah Palin, speaking at the first national Tea Party Convention in Nashville, mocked President Obama's message of hope ("how's that hopey-changey stuff working out for you?") and fired up the crowd with her homespun, colloquial talk that sounded anti-elitist. Tea Party members opposed federal government interference, denounced taxes (TEA, they said, stood for "taxed enough already"), and promoted free markets. Others spoke against immigration and displayed deep racial animus in their opposition to Obama—a large part of the Tea Party's success was appealing to the racial anxiety and resentment of white Americans. The grassroots populist movement quickly politicized, and in the midterm elections of 2010 Republicans gained sixty-three seats in the House and six seats in the Senate. Rand Paul, a victorious senate candidate from Kentucky, declared it was a "Tea Party tidal wave."[22]

Republican members of Congress devoted themselves to opposing Obama's agenda. They became the Party of No, strategizing to limit Obama to one term in office and, when that failed, continuing to obstruct any initiatives issued by the White House. "If he was for it, we had to be against it," explained one Republican. In 2011, some Republicans went so far as to refuse to to raise the debt ceiling, so the Treasury could pay for already authorized spending, unless Obama approved deep spending cuts, which led to a downgrade of the government's credit rating. In 2013, the government shut down for sixteen days because Congress had not approved the appropriations bill necessary to keep it open.[23]

No measure more roiled Republicans than passage of the Affordable Care Act (ACA) on March 23, 2010. The Senate passed a version of the bill that differed from the House bill by a vote of 60–39. The House amended its bill and passed it by a vote of 219–212. Every Republican voted against it. On signing, Obama declared that the Act affirmed "the core principle that everybody should have some basic security when it comes to health care." Various elements of the ACA rolled out over time and included an attempt to lower health care costs for consumers by providing health exchanges where they could choose from health care plans. The ACA also offered protections for those with preexisting conditions as well as provisions for preventive care and extended coverage for young adults (who could stay on their parents' plans until age twenty-six) and a strengthening of Medicare. Opponents challenged the constitutionality of the act, particularly the individual mandate that required Americans to obtain insurance or face a penalty. In 2012 the Supreme Court, in a 5–4 decision, upheld the major provisions of the act. As what was referred to as Obamacare expanded, the percentage of Americans without health insurance declined from over 18 percent in 2010 to 10.5 percent by 2015, though the trend began to reverse following the 2016 election as a new Republican administration took steps to repeal the act.[24]

If the election of 2012 was a referendum on health care, the president's reelection over Mitt Romney (who, despite having supported health care reform in Massachusetts while he was governor, opposed the ACA) might have been taken as a mandate for Obamacare. Republicans never relented in their desire to repeal or modify the act. They voted against it dozens of times despite its growing popularity with citizens across the political spectrum. In

March 2017, Republicans withdrew a proposed American Health Care Act, and in July 2017 the Senate vote on a Health Care Freedom Act lost when three Republicans, including the mortally ill John McCain who gave a dramatic thumbs down, voted against it. A dejected Paul Ryan, the Speaker of the House, admitted, "Obamacare is the law of the land." As his second term came to an end, Obama spoke in Florida about the lives the law had helped and about ways to continue to improve it. The act was passed, he said, because the American people mobilized and applied pressure to get something done. "That's how change happens in America," he rhapsodied.[25]

Social Media

New ways of communicating have always reshaped history. The advent of the personal computer, the internet, and the smartphone, however, allowed for an explosion of instantaneous interaction with people anywhere in the world. In the late 1990s, for example, people began to blog, short for "weblog," and offer online any content they wished to on any topic. Some blogs were diaries, others offered advice. There were tech blogs, adventure blogs, food blogs, and political blogs. In 2005, the White House for the first time granted press credentials to a blogger. More than 32 million Americans read blogs and increasingly viewed them. YouTube, a video-sharing platform eventually purchased by Google, emerged in 2005, and a decade later it became the most popular social media platform, used by 73 percent of US adults. Video games became a mass cultural phenomenon. One game, Fortnite, achieved 200 million registered users in an online community that would make it the seventh-largest nation in the world. By 2018, gaming generated more money than any other entertainment product.

Of all the social media platforms (Twitter, Instagram, Pinterest, Snapchat, LinkedIn) none was more important than Facebook. Founded in 2004 by Mark Zuckerberg and a group of fellow students at Harvard, Facebook became the largest social network platform in the world. Users created profiles, uploaded photos and videos, updated their status, joined groups, and communicated with other users who they "friended." As of June 2018, Facebook had more than 2 billion active monthly users, more than 200 million of whom were in the United States (the entire population of the United States was 326 million). Facebook transformed the way people interacted and reshaped society, culture, and politics. It connected people, made them feel part of a community, and provided information. In the spring of 2011, for example, it played a role in uprisings that came to be known as the Arab Spring, as protesters rose up in Tunisia, Egypt, Libya, and Bahrain and used social media to inform the world of what was taking place.

Social media could do more than just inform. It allowed people to retreat into information silos of their own choosing and made them susceptible to manipulation. Following the election of 2016, Congress investigated whether the Russians used Facebook to spread disinformation and influence the election outcome. Russian intelligence, through an organization called the Internet Research Group, masqueraded as American media companies, created fake personas, and targeted specific groups (African American voters for example) with the aim of discouraging them from voting. Whether or not the disinformation campaign swung the election, the nefarious power of social media had been made evident.

In less heinous ways, social media helped mobilize people and created online activism, and was used to sway public opinion on social and political issues. For example, a gay rights advocacy group, the Human Rights Campaign, encouraged users to change their profile pictures to a pink and red logo in support of marriage equality as the Supreme Court decided the constitutionality of same-sex marriage laws that had been adopted by thirty-seven states and the District of

Figure 11.3 Social Media (2019). Associated Press.

Columbia. Millions did so. Whatever role public opinion played, in 2015 the Court ruled in *Obergefell v. Hodges* that gays could marry. Justice Anthony Kennedy wrote, "They ask for equal dignity in the eyes of the law. The Constitution grants them that right."[26]

Gay rights were part of the culture wars of the twenty-first century. So, too, were black lives. On February 26, 2012, George Zimmerman, a neighborhood watch volunteer in Sanford, Florida, shot and killed seventeen-year-old Trayvon Martin, who was unarmed. In April, Zimmerman was charged with second-degree murder, and the outcry that enveloped the nation immediately after the shooting ("If I had a son, he'd look like Trayvon," said President Obama) galvanized into a mass movement when in July 2013 a jury acquitted Zimmerman on grounds of self-defense. Users of social media regularly employed hashtags, a word or phrase following the hashtag symbol that allows followers on Twitter and other social media platforms to identify postings on a common topic. The hashtag #BlackLivesMatter led to a mass movement against systemic racism, police brutality, and violence against black communities.[27] Critics of the movement adopted the hashtag #AllLivesMatter.

Numerous incidents, many of them filmed by bystanders, deepened and extended the Black Lives Matter movement. For example, Eric Garner died after being put in a chokehold by New York Police Department officers, and his words "I can't breathe" became another shorthand for the movement. In Ferguson, Missouri, the shooting of Michael Brown on August 9, 2014, led to weeks of protests and riots. Using the internet as a device for mass mobilization, the Black Lives Matter movement had an impact on public opinion, played a role in local political elections (Florida's state attorney lost her bid for reelection), triggered investigations of police brutality and the militarization of police forces, and spurred protests around the country.

When Colin Kaepernick, a quarterback for the San Francisco 49ers, kneeled during the playing of the national anthem at a game in September 2016, he sparked a broader protest and a debate over patriotism and race. "I am not going to stand up to show pride in a flag for a country that oppresses black people and people of color." His protest led many, including President Trump, to denounce his actions as unpatriotic. Kaepernick lost his job in the NFL and sports manufacturer Nike risked a boycott of its goods when the company sponsored an ad that featured the quarterback saying, "Don't ask if your dreams are crazy. Ask if they are crazy enough."[28]

Racial violence in modern America arrived at an unthinkable moment when, on June 17, 2015, twenty-one-year-old Dylan Storm Roof, a white supremacist, walked into Charleston's Emanuel African Methodist Episcopal Church, a historic church whose congregation dated to before 1820, and opened fire on a group engaged in bible study. Nine people, ranging in age from twenty-six to eighty-seven, were killed. Governor Nikki Haley lamented, "We woke up today, and the heart and soul of South Carolina was broken." In the aftermath of the massacre, Haley signed a bill to remove of the Confederate flag from state house grounds. Elsewhere, the University of Mississippi ordered removal of the state flag, which incorporated the Confederate battle flag, the stars and bars.[29]

Across the nation, a debate over Confederate monuments and memorials intensified, some defending them as symbols of Southern pride and others denouncing them as tributes to white supremacy. In Charlottesville, Virginia, in August 2017, a group of white nationalists and neo-Nazis marched in protest of a decision to remove a statue of Robert E. Lee. Chanting "blood and soil" and "Jews will not replace us," they were met by counter-protesters, one of whom was killed when a car driven by a right-wing protester plowed into the crowd. Earlier that summer, in New Orleans, Mayor Mitch Landrieu had monuments to Confederates Jefferson Davis, Robert E. Lee, and P. G. T. Beauregard removed, as well as a memorial to the Battle of Liberty Place in 1874, when members of the paramilitary White League sought to overthrow the Reconstruction government. The statues, he said, were erected as much as acts of terrorism against blacks as a tribute to Southern heroes. Where, he asked, were the monuments to the slave trade and the slave market. "We have not erased history," he declared. "We are becoming part of the city's history by righting the wrong image these monuments represent and crafting a better, more complete future for all our children and for future generations."[30]

The mass shooting in Charleston was one of many that knew no bounds based on race, gender, age, or region. In the history of mass shootings, defined as four or more people killed by a lone gunman in a twenty-four-hour period, the United States figures prominently. According to one researcher, between 1983 and 2013, 119 mass shootings took place around the world and 78 (66 percent) occurred in the United States. Starting at the close of the twentieth century, those shootings became increasingly lethal. The five deadliest shootings took place after 2007 and included children gunned down at Sandy Hook Elementary School in Connecticut; people shot at Virginia Tech in Blacksburg, Virginia; dozens killed at a gay night-club in Orlando, Florida; and fifty-eight killed when a gunman fired from a Las Vegas hotel window on thousands of concertgoers. On October 27, 2018, a gunman opened fire in a Pittsburgh Synagogue and killed eleven congregants. Each shooting led to calls for gun control in America, which has the highest per capita ownership of firearms anywhere in the world and no nationwide prohibition on semiautomatic weapons such as the AR-15, which grew in popularity after a ten-year federal ban expired in 2004.[31]

A shooting on February 14, 2018, at Marjory Stoneman High School in Parkland, Florida, killed seventeen students and staff. Students organized and pressed for the passage of stricter gun control laws. Using the hashtag #NeverAgain, these students entreated lawmakers for change and organized a March for Our Lives to register students to vote. They vowed to fight the National Rifle Association (NRA), a powerful lobbying organization for gun rights that had successfully blocked legislation in Washington. Tanzil Philip, a sophomore at Marjorie Stoneman, addressed the NRA directly: "We are not afraid of you, we will not be silenced by anything you have to say. We are here, our voices are loud, and we're not stopping until change happens." In response to the Parkland shooting, many state legislatures acted. Generally, Democratic-controlled legislatures favored tightening restrictions and Republican-led legislatures favored looser restrictions. In the aftermath of the shooting, legislative chambers led by both sides passed various laws that included universal background checks, raising the minimum age to purchase guns, tightening concealed-carry laws, banning bump stocks and trigger activators used on semiautomatic weapons, and barring people deemed dangerous due to mental illness from owning a gun.[32]

Congress, however, did not act, in large part because of the influence of the NRA, which successfully mobilized its millions of members who were overwhelmingly white and Republican and viewed gun control as a liberal cause and themselves as protectors of the Second Amendment. Money also made a huge difference in politics and legislation. In 2010, the Supreme Court, in *Citizens United v. FEC*, removed restrictions on corporate spending in politics by ruling that corporations had the same right to political speech as individuals. An array of political action committees and social welfare groups that participated in political activity began to receive hundreds of millions of dollars in outside money. With respect to gun control, the political spending of the NRA tripled following *Citizens United* and billionaire conservatives such as Charles and David Koch gave more than $10 million to the NRA. Liberal billionaires could also give. Michael Bloomberg's Everytown for Gun Safety spent more than the NRA in state and federal races in the election of 2018. Both sides sent newly elected members to Congress. On every issue, Americans remained deeply divided along partisan lines.

American Ideals

With no incumbent running, multiple candidates jockeyed to win their party's nomination in 2016. The Democratic race came down to Hillary Clinton versus Bernie Sanders. Clinton had served as secretary of state under Obama and it was easy to make the case that given her various experiences in government—as first lady, senator, and member of a Obama's cabinet—no one was more qualified for the position of president. If nominated, she would be the first woman elected president. Various investigations, however, brought her poll numbers down. Republicans repeatedly probed an attack on the US Consulate in Benghazi, Libya, in September 2012, during Clinton's tenure as secretary of state, an attack that led to the death of the US ambassador and others. Though no wrongdoing was found, Clinton's favorability rating declined. Clinton was also investigated for using a personal e-mail account while secretary of state, perhaps in violation of federal requirements. FBI Director James Comey found her to be "extremely careless," though he did not recommend the filing of charges.[33]

Other issues plagued Clinton as well. Anderson Cooper, a popular host on CNN, challenged the candidate in a televised Democratic presidential debate about her shifts in position on various issues, including same-sex marriage, immigration policy, and trade policy. "Will you say anything to get elected?" he asked. Clinton argued that her positions were consistent and some evolved based on new information, but to many she seemed hypocritical and inauthentic.[34]

Clinton was also being pushed to the left by Bernie Sanders, whose candidacy gained unexpected momentum. Sanders was an Independent who described himself as a "democratic socialist." He denounced wealth inequality in America, favored a single-payer health care system, and advocated for free college education. He also addressed the reality of climate change as carbon dioxide, which traps heat, rose over the previous decades to unprecedented levels in the atmosphere, leading to a warming of the planet's surface temperature and rising of global sea levels as ice sheets melted. A climate change report released in 2018 led Sanders to remark, "The future of our planet is at stake." Bill McKibben, climate change journalist and activist, warned, "If we don't solve it soon, we won't solve it ever."[35]

Running for president, Sanders spoke repeatedly of "a political revolution" bringing together working people and young people. He succeeded in rousing millennials with whom he held a 54 percent favorability rating (Clinton's was 37 percent). Sanders triumphed in more than twenty primaries and gathered more than 1,800 delegates (2,383 were needed to win). The Clinton campaign had influence over the Democratic National Committee, which may have tipped the scales toward her in the primaries.[36]

Whereas the Democratic nomination came down to two candidates, the Republican field was so crowded all the candidates could not gather on one stage. They included Governor Jeb Bush of Florida, Senator Marco Rubio of Florida, Senator Ted Cruz of Texas, Governor Chris Christie of New Jersey, Governor John Kasich of Ohio, prominent neurosurgeon Dr. Ben Carson, Carly Fiorina, the former CEO of Hewlett Packard, and Donald Trump, a billionaire real estate magnate and reality TV star who promoted himself as a shrewd businessman and dealmaker. In announcing his candidacy, Trump declared, "The American dream is dead—but if I win, I will bring it back bigger and better and stronger than ever before. Together we will make America great again."[37]

In the days after his announcement, analysts gave Trump a 1 percent chance of winning the nomination. Trump, whose trademark line on his television show *The Apprentice* was "You're fired," and who spearheaded the birther movement, claiming Barack Obama was not born in the United States and hence not constitutionally eligible to be president, knew how to attract and keep an audience. He rejected the accepted standards for political decorum and instead insulted, ridiculed, derided, and denounced his opponents. He gave them mocking nicknames: "Low Energy Jeb," "Lyin' Ted," "Little Marco." He disparaged Clinton as "Crooked Hillary." He went after the media, referring to them as "the enemy of the people" and perpetuating the idea of "Fake News," that anything reported by the "liberal" media was biased and could not be trusted. The repeated accusations of news reports as fake or phony damaged the media and allowed the candidate to spread falsehoods without having to pay a political price for doing so. Untruth became a hallmark of Trump's campaign. To the surprise of many, he won the Republican nomination.

Trump made for good television, and by covering his rallies the networks provided thousands of hours of free advertising. He would rouse the crowds, encouraging them to chant "Lock her up!"

when he spoke of Clinton. The more boorishly he behaved, the more authentic he seemed. To a growing number of Republicans, he appeared like a true outsider who would "drain the swamp" of Washington, reverse political correctness, undo Obamacare, slash taxes, cut regulations, and make trade deals that profited the United States.

No issue became more identified with Trump than illegal immigration and his intention to build a wall ("a big, beautiful wall," he called it) between the United States and Mexico. Trump was not the first to raise concerns about illegal, unauthorized, or undocumented immigrants (the different names suggest different attitudes toward the problem). In fact, the number of undocumented immigrants had declined from 12.2 million in 2007 to 10.7 million in 2016. Describing these immigrants as dangerous, Trump promised to secure American borders and "get rid of the criminals." He also vacillated on the question of a path to citizenship for children brought to this country without documentation but raised here. In 2010, Congress did not pass the Dream Act, which would have created such a pathway. In 2012, President Obama announced a program of Deferred Action for Childhood Arrivals (DACA), through which some 800,000 dreamers, as they had come to be known, came forward, obtained work permits, and were protected from deportation. Trump vowed to end DACA.

Trump's campaign slogan was "Make America Great Again!" (He trademarked the phrase.) Its ambiguity helped make it resonate. It was backward looking and appealed to those who felt that the nation had regressed during Obama's two terms. Many concluded it signaled a desire for a more homogenous America, a less diverse America, a whiter America. Trump was peddling nationalism, nativism, and racism. He won over white evangelicals, despite his personal history of multiple marriages and affairs, with an appeal to cultural conservatism and antiabortion. In the election of 2016, 81 percent of white evangelicals voted for Trump. He won over the white working class, many of whom had not recovered from the economic crisis of 2008 and to whom Trump promised to bring jobs back to America. Fifty-four percent of all white voters regardless of income and 64 percent of white noncollege graduates voted for him. While women in general voted for Clinton (54 percent of all women), white women overwhelmingly supported Trump (62 percent). This despite a growing #MeToo movement in which women, following sexual abuse accusations against Harvey Weinstein, a Hollywood magnate, self-identified as victims of sexual harassment and assault.

A tape of Trump speaking lewdly about women in 2005, released a month before the election, seemed to have little effect. The results of 2016 also revealed an urban/rural divide: Clinton carried urban areas with over 72 percent of the vote whereas Trump dominated rural areas by more than 84 percent.

In the election, Hillary Clinton won the popular vote by nearly 2.9 million votes, but by carrying Pennsylvania, Wisconsin, and Michigan, Trump secured the Electoral College victory 304–227. In the aftermath, various reasons were offered for how Clinton, a 3–1 favorite on election day, lost to Trump: she was not trusted; the Democrats shed one in four of Obama's white working-class supporters from 2012; turnout decreased for black voters; Clinton failed to spend sufficient time campaigning in Michigan and Wisconsin; the Russians hacked the election in favor of Trump; James Comey sent a letter to Congress on October 28 that revived the e-mail scandal by announcing that the FBI had "learned of the existence of emails that appear to be pertinent to the investigation." This last reason may have been the most significant: pollsters claimed Comey's

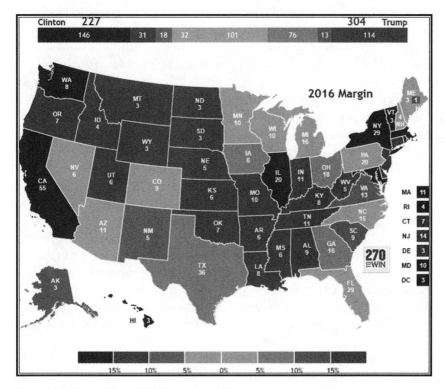

Figure 11.4 Electoral Map (2016). Associated Press.

announcement shifted the race by several percentage points. In the aftermath, Clinton, for one, believed that the Comey letter, which raised "groundless, baseless" doubts, had cost her the presidency.[38]

With Trump elected, Republicans controlled the executive and legislative branches of government. Conservatives also preserved a Supreme Court majority. When Supreme Court Justice Antonin Scalia died suddenly in February 2016, the Republican Senate refused to consider Obama's nomination to the vacant seat. Instead, Trump's nominee Neil Gorsuch was confirmed. And after Justice Anthony Kennedy announced his retirement, Brett Kavanaugh, the principal author of the Starr Report that led to Clinton's impeachment, was confirmed after an explosive confirmation hearing that aired sexual assault complaints against the nominee. Within a year, Congress passed a major tax bill, the Tax Cut and Jobs Act of 2017. It lowered individual tax rates until 2026 and corporate tax rates (from 35 to 21 percent) permanently. It also eliminated many deductions (it allowed a maximum deduction of $10,000 in property taxes) while doubling the estate tax exemption. The cuts cost nearly $1.5 trillion over ten years and added significantly to the budget deficit, thus marking a reversal of conservative policies that traditionally opposed large deficits. Under Trump, in fiscal year 2018, the federal budget deficit grew 17 percent to $779 billion and federal revenues fell short of predictions that the cuts would stimulate growth and pay for themselves.

Trump also took executive action on free trade. He continued to threaten to withdraw from NAFTA, which he belittled as "the worst trade deal ever," while negotiating a new US-Mexico-Canada Agreement. Calling himself "a tariff man," he launched a trade war with the rest of the world by imposing tariffs on steel, aluminum, and other imports. The confrontation with China, in particular, had severe consequences on American workers and farmers who suffered from retaliatory tariffs imposed by the Chinese government. For example, US soybean exports to China dropped by more than 90 percent and reached zero in November 2018. Analysts agreed that the trade war with China and the world was proving harmful to the global economy and might contribute to a sudden turn in the US economy, as signaled by a market correction at the end of 2018 when the stock market fell 6.9 percent in a week, the steepest decline since October 2008.[39]

Trump's nationalism moved the United States toward isolationism. "America First" became one of his mottoes, a phrase used by those who had opposed US entry into World War II. He threatened repeatedly to leave NATO and urged Britain to leave the European Union, which was being buffeted by the same global forces. Trump met with Kim Jong Un of North Korea in an attempt to end North Korea's nuclear program, though the summit was viewed as more of a photo op than a serious denuclearization negotiation. Trump withdrew from a nuclear deal with Iran and announced that the United States would withdraw from a nuclear arms treaty with Russia. Trump also withdrew from the Paris Climate Accord, an agreement signed by 195 nations that pledged to cut greenhouse emissions. He continued to deny global warming, undo environmental protections, and support coal mining, one of the fossil fuels responsible for heating the atmosphere. Trump's decision to withdraw US troops from Syria led Secretary of Defense James Mattis to resign, one of dozens to leave the administration in its first two years. Numerous commentators expressed dismay over the new isolationism. Some made historical comparisons to 1940, when the United States was reluctant to enter World War II. Others saw the president as not valuing alliances and established rules of the international order. One columnist argued that the United States "at its best has always stood up for the universal values of freedom and human rights."[40]

Trump's insistence on building a wall on the 2,000-mile-long border with Mexico served as an apt symbol of American isolation. Few policy experts agreed with him that a wall was necessary: some 700 miles of fencing on federal land already existed, other forms of surveillance, such as drones and thousands of agents, protected the border, and illegal crossings had dropped 82 percent from its peak in 2000. Nonetheless, Trump had promised his constituency a wall and he continued to exploit the politics of fear, calling a migrant caravan an invasion, claiming terrorists lurked among them, and sending the army to the border. His administration also authorized the separation of children from their parents and establishment of detention centers. Widespread outrage, in which critics compared the actions to those taken in Hitler's Germany, led to Trump reversing the separation order, though sporadic separations continued to occur. Trump tried as well to overturn federal law and deny asylum to migrants who illegally crossed the border. The Supreme Court, in a 5–4 decision, upheld a lower court blockage of Trump's plans. Demanding that the wall be funded, Trump refused to sign a bipartisan bill that would have extended the debt ceiling, and prior to Christmas 2018, the government shut down for thirty-five days, the longest in American history. Trump tweeted, "I am all alone."[41]

Nothing made Trump angrier than an investigation into whether Russia interfered in the 2016 election and whether his campaign colluded with the Russians and obstructed justice. On May 17, 2017, the deputy attorney general appointed Robert Mueller, a former director of the FBI, as special counsel to investigate. Mueller's probe soon led to multiple indictments and guilty pleas from Michael Flynn, former national security advisor, George Papadopoulos, former campaign advisor, and Michael Cohen, Trump's personal attorney, and a guilty verdict for Paul Manafort, Trump's campaign chairman in the summer of 2016. Trump raged that the investigation was a "witch hunt." He even questioned the conclusion of US intelligence agencies that Russia, through trolling and cyberattacks, had meddled in the election, and he instead publicly embraced Vladimir Putin, an act that led some to accuse the president of treason.

Trump wanted the Mueller probe to end. He fired Attorney General Jeff Sessions, perhaps with the plan to appoint someone who would eliminate Mueller's budget. His ally in the campaign against Mueller was Fox News. The network, built by Roger Ailes, who was forced out in 2017 because of a sexual harassment scandal, had come to have enormous public influence and had helped turn politics into entertainment and information into tribalism. In 2010, one out of every four Americans received their news from Fox. Trump watched the station religiously, changed his position in response to what commentators said, and was no doubt pleased when anchors helped disseminate #FireMueller and stoked opposition to the special counsel.[42]

Investigations into Trump promised to expand after the midterm elections. The Democrats gained forty seats to retake control of the House. Republicans, however, extended their Senate majority from 51–49 to 53–47. Turnout for the election reached a fifty-year high. There were many firsts: a record number of women elected; the first Muslim women elected; the first openly bisexual person elected to the Senate; the first black women to represent Connecticut and Massachusetts; the first Latina women from Texas; and two Native American women elected to Congress. Trump professed not be concerned by the results. After all, every sitting president lost seats in the midterm elections. Support for him remained steady. It seemed no matter what he said or did, his approval rating stood at around 40 percent.

Trump's demagoguery, authoritarianism, crudity, and flouting of democratic norms seemed to know no bounds. So, too, his assault on truth. According to the *Washington Post* Fact Checker, through

December 20, 2018, Trump made 7,546 false or misleading claims. The cumulative effect of these falsehoods was to diminish faith in the news media, in government, in expertise, in truth itself. Trump's presidency, it seemed to some, was nothing less than an assault on the meaning and history of America.

Many made this point, including John McCain. Throughout his career, McCain had remained a steadfast Republican, though he never hesitated to break with his party. He had not changed, though the political environment had, as the parties became more polarized and partisan. McCain was a war hero, a navy pilot who had been shot down and imprisoned during the Vietnam War. He endured solitary confinement and torture (for the rest of his life he could not lift his arms above his ahead). Offered a chance to be released because his father was head of the US Pacific Command, he refused because, he said, there were POWs who had been imprisoned longer. He spent more than five years in captivity. When allowed to be with other prisoners, he led a social studies class to keep sharp and engaged. The subject: "A History of the World from the Beginning."

Diagnosed with a terminal illness, McCain coordinated his funeral arrangements and made sure not to invite Trump, who had said while campaigning that McCain was not a war hero because he had been captured. George W. Bush and Barack Obama delivered eulogies on September 1, 2018, in a televised memorial that offered a tacit rebuke of the president as much as unqualified admiration for McCain's life of service. As one of his last acts, McCain composed a farewell letter to the nation in which he offered his final thoughts on America's meaning: "we are citizens of the world's greatest republic, a nation of ideals, not blood and soil. . . . Do not despair of our present difficulties but believe always in the promise and greatness of America, because nothing is inevitable here. Americans never quit. We never surrender. We never hide from history. We make history."[43]

Epilogue

"Let America Be America Again"

I N THE AFTERMATH OF DONALD TRUMP'S election, a poem by Langston Hughes started trending on social media. Perhaps it was the word "again" that drew peoples' attention. Long before Trump used the word in his 2016 campaign slogan to "Make America Great Again," Hughes published a poem, written in 1935, called "Let America Be America Again."

Sometimes referred to as the "poet laureate of Harlem," Hughes was born in 1902 in Joplin, Missouri, raised in the Midwest and, after living in Mexico for a year, arrived in New York in 1921 to study engineering at Columbia University. Drawn to the literary life, he joined other voices at the forefront of the Harlem Renaissance, writers such as Alain Locke, Zora Neale Hurston, James Weldon Johnson, Claude McKay, and Arna Bontemps. Hughes's first poem, "The Negro Speaks of Rivers," published in 1921, addressed the black experience in America: "my soul has grown deep like the rivers."[1]

Hughes left Columbia and traveled to the west coast of Africa, Rotterdam, Paris, and northern Italy. He returned to the United States in 1924. In 1926, he published his first book of poems, *The Weary Blues*. Influenced by poets such as Walt Whitman, Carl Sandburg, and Paul Lawrence Dunbar, Hughes embraced free verse. His collection included the poem "I, Too," which opens "I, too, sing America," and closes "I, too, am America." ("I hear America singing," his spiritual mentor Whitman had written).

In 1929, Hughes graduated from Lincoln University, the nation's first degree-granting historically black college. He traveled widely and, through the 1930s, he wrote poems, plays, short stories, and novels. He never joined the Communist Party, though many of his friends did. He was sympathetic to radical causes and his work across the decade displayed a socialist rhetoric common to the era. "Let America Be America Again" was published in an abbreviated version in 1936 and appeared in final form in *A New Song*, a collection issued by the International Workers Order in 1938. The work addresses the meaning of America and offers both a critique and an affirmation of the American ideal.[2]

It begins "Let America be America again / Let it be the dream it used to be," then continues "Let America be the dream the dreamers dreamed." It's a dream of freedom, democracy, equality, opportunity, and liberty of the sort that so many in this book have had and that I have tried to evoke. Yet a parenthetic voice adds "(America never was America to me)."

Knowing Hughes's work, it is tempting to read the parenthetic "me" as a victim of the long history of racial segregation and oppression. The poem anticipates our question and a new voice asks, "Say who are you that mumbles in the dark?" What follows is a list of everyday Americans: "the poor white," "the Negro," "the red man," "the immigrant," "the farmer," "the worker." All are carrying hope for a better future and all have fallen victim to "the same old stupid plan / Of dog eat dog, of mighty crush the weak." America is not America to any of them.

Given Hughes's radical sympathies, the class analysis is not surprising. The poem laments the conditions of the Depression, with millions unemployed and on relief, and asks what happened to America, the purported "homeland of the free," where so many have nothing left "except the dream that's almost dead today."

"Almost dead," but unvanquished.

For Hughes, the United States was an unrealized, perhaps unrealizable, ideal. It was a land that "never has been yet / and yet must be," a dreamland unlike any other country. Yet the nation's failure time and again to live up to its aspirations is a profound part of the story. Whatever its struggles, the United States has been a nation that has identified itself by its dreams. Dreams inspired by abstractions like democracy and rights. Dreams animated by seeking the balance between individualism and community. Dreams stirred by those making a new home in America and pursuing a better life. And dreams also driven by the desire to break free of all the dreams. Sometimes achieved, and often broken, dreams have defined the history of the United States.

Hughes believed in those dreams and his poem ends not with despair, but with an urgent plea:

> We the people, must redeem
> The land, the mines, the plants, the rivers.
> The mountains and the endless plain—
> All, all the stretch of these great green states—
> And make America again!

Hughes would continue to think about America, asking in a 1951 poem titled "Harlem," "what happens to a dream deferred?" Martin Luther King Jr. had also been contemplating dreams, long before his speech at the Lincoln Memorial. King and Hughes were friends; in 1956, King recited a Hughes poem ("Mother to Son") from the pulpit. Because of Hughes's suspected Communist sympathies (he had testified before Joseph McCarthy's Senate Permanent Subcommittee on Investigations), King publicly kept his distance. Still, in 1967, six months after Hughes died, King declared, "I am personally the victim of deferred dreams, of blasted hopes." Yet "I still have a dream."[3]

King must have appreciated the closing of "Let America Be America Again," where the people are summoned to redeem the land. In a sermon first delivered in 1954, he declared, "Instead of making history we are made by history." The line is easily misunderstood. King was not offering an argument for why history matters; rather, he was decrying passivity and insisting on agency. It was a call to action. The preacher was telling his congregation that the time for waiting on dreams was over—the time for making dreams come true had begun.[4]

ACKNOWLEDGMENTS

I N MY CAREER TEACHING AMERICAN HISTORY, I have offered surveys of US history and a course on the American Dream at Rutgers University. That experience informs this book and I am grateful to my students for pushing me to think hard about what matters and why.

I have also been lucky to interact with a very different audience. Through One Day University, I have lectured across the country to adults eager to continue their education. My thanks to Steven Schragis, Blair Erich, and Kevin Brennan for affording me this platform.

My colleagues in American Studies and History at Rutgers have been generous and supportive. I owe a special debt to Allan Isaac for helping me navigate the challenges of serving as Department Chair. I am indebted as well to Executive Dean Peter March and Dean of the Humanities Michelle Stephens.

A number of friends and colleagues read all or part of the book. Jonathan Freedman, Doug Greenberg, and Ron Spencer provided comments on the entire manuscript and challenged me to defend my choices and clarify the narrative. My deepest thanks and appreciation to them and others who read chapters in their fields of expertise: Bob Allison, Carla Cevasco, Jeff Decker, Jim Goodman, Chris Hager, Peter Mancall, Nicole Marionni, Jamie Pietruska, Aaron Sachs, Tom Slaughter, and Jimmy Sweet. My thanks as well to David Krauss. Joseph Westendorf tracked down sources and citations, and Maxine Wagenhoffer, a former student who is now in the doctoral program at Ohio State, did a remarkable job fact-checking the manuscript. The errors that remain are my responsibility alone.

This is my second book with Timothy Bent, and his editorial suggestions improved all aspects of the work. His former assistant, Mariah White, prepared the manuscript for publication. I am grateful to Amy Whitmer, senior production editor, for addressing any issues that emerged. My thanks as well to Joellyn Ausanka, with whom I first worked more than thirty years ago, for seeing the book through to publication. I am fortunate to have Zoe Pagnamenta as my agent and I offer my thanks to her and Alison Lewis.

The extended Masur and Fox clan continue to provide unconditional support and I look forward to future occasions that will bring us all together. I hope my two-year-old grandnephew, Ryan Masur, one day enjoys seeing his name here. I am thankful that I can always rely on the love and friendship of Dave Masur, Mark Richman, and Bruce Rossky.

My children, Ben and Sophie, got married while I was writing this book and it is a joy to welcome Rachel Akkerman and Garrett Jaffe into the family. I am blessed to have a daughter-in-law and son-in-law who love travel and sports and who still listen politely when I ramble on about American history.

Without Jani's encouragement, I would not have undertaken this project, nor much else for that matter. For more than forty years, we have traveled side by side and shared each other's dreams. Once more, "love is wild, love is real."

NOTES

PROLOGUE: "LAND OF HOPE AND DREAMS"

1. J. Hector St. John de Crèvecoeur, *Letters from an American Farmer* (New York: Penguin, 1981), 66–90.
2. James Truslow Adams, *The Epic of America* (Boston: Little, Brown, 1931), xx.
3. Louis P. Masur, "Bruce Springsteen and American History," *History News Network*, August 31, 2009, http://historynewsnetwork.org/article/115729; "Interview at International Press Conference in Paris," in *Talk About a Dream: The Essential Interviews of Bruce Springsteen*, ed. Christopher Phillips and Louis P. Masur (New York: Bloomsbury, 2013), 407–408.
4. "Obama's November 7, 2007, Speech on the 'American Dream,'" http://www.cnn.com/2007/POLITICS/12/21/obama.trans.americandream.
5. "Remarks by the President at the 50th Anniversary of the Selma to Montgomery Marches," March 7, 2015, https://obamawhitehouse.archives.gov/the-press-office/2015/03/07/remarks-president-50th-anniversary-selma-montgomery-marches; Abraham Lincoln, "Annual Message to Congress, December 3, 1861," in *The Collected Works of Abraham Lincoln*, ed. Roy P. Basler, 9 vols. (New Brunswick, NJ: Rutgers University Press, 1953–55), 5:53.

CHAPTER 1

1. Hakluyt quoted in Peter Mancall, ed., *Envisioning America: English Plans for the Colonization of North America, 1580–1640* (Boston: Bedford Books, 1995), 39; John Locke, "Of Property," in *Second Treatise on Government* (Mineola, NY: Dover Publications, 2002), 22.
2. John M. Thompson, ed., *The Journals of Captain John Smith: A Jamestown Biography* (Washington, DC: National Geographic, 2007), 139; Nancy Struna, *People of Prowess: Sport, Leisure, and Labor in Early Anglo-America* (Urbana: University of Illinois Press, 1996), 46.
3. James Horn, *A Land as God Made It: Jamestown and the Birth of America* (New York: Basic Books, 2006), 223.
4. William Waller Hening, *Statutes at Large; Being a Collection of all the Laws of Virginia* (Richmond, VA: Samuel Pleasants, 1809–23), 11:170, 260.
5. Robert Beverly, *The History and Present State of Virginia* (Chapel Hill: University of North Carolina Press, 2013), 216.
6. Nathaniel Bacon, "Declaration of Nathaniel Bacon in the Name of the People of Virginia, July 30, 1676," Massachusetts Historical Society Collections, 4th ser., 1871, 9:84–87, http://historymatters.gmu.edu/d/5800.
7. David Lee Russell, *Oglethorpe and Colonial History, 1733–1783* (Jefferson, NC: McFarland, 2006), 177; Adams quoted in Henry Bruce, *Life of General Oglethorpe* (New York: Dodd, Mead, 1890), 250.
8. William Bradford, *Of Plymouth Plantation, 1620–1647* (New York: Modern Library, 1981), 84, 70, 126.
9. John Winthrop, "A Modell of Christian Charity," in *The Journal of John Winthrop, 1630–1649*, ed. Richard S. Dunn and Laetitia Yeandle (Cambridge, MA: Harvard University Press, 1996), 1–12.
10. Bradford, *Of Plymouth Plantation*, 179.
11. Bradford, *Of Plymouth Plantation*, 227.

12. Eve LaPlante, *American Jezebel* (San Francisco: Harper, 2005), 12, 121.
13. Baird Tipson, *Hartford Puritanism: Thomas Hooker, Samuel Stone, and Their Terrifying Puritanism* (New York: Oxford University Press, 2015), 7.
14. Deodat Lawson, "A Brief and True Narrative," in *Salem-Village Witchcraft: A Documentary Record of Local Conflict in Colonial New England*, ed. Paul Boyer and Stephen Nissenbaum (Boston: Northeastern University Press, 1972), 113.
15. John Williams, *The Redeemed Captive Returning to Zion* (Boston: Samuel Hall, 1795), 45.
16. "The Flushing Remonstrance," Historical Society of the New York Courts, http://www.nycourts.gov/history/legal-history-new-york/legal-history-eras-03/history-era-03-flushing-remonstrance.html. Also see Kenneth T. Jackson, "A Colony with a Conscience," *New York Times*, December 27, 2007.
17. Andrew Burnaby, *Travels Through the Middle Settlements in North-America in the Years 1759 and 1760* (London: T. Payne, 1775), 158.
18. *The New York Conspiracy Trials of 1741: Daniel Horsmanden's Journal of the Proceedings*, ed. Serena R. Zabin (Boston: Bedford Books, 2004), 159.
19. Mancall, *Envisioning America*, 80.
20. Thomas Morton, *New English Canaan* (New York: DeCapo Press, 1969), 59.
21. John Martin, "The Manner How to Bring the Indians into Subjection," in *Records of the Virginia Company*, ed. Susan Myra Kingsbury (Washington, DC: Government Printing Office, 1935), 3:704.
22. Benjamin Franklin, *The Autobiography of Benjamin Franklin with Related Documents*, ed. Louis P. Masur (Boston: Bedford Books, 2016), 120.
23. New Netherland Act quoted in Peter Mancall, *Deadly Medicine: Indians and Alcohol in Early America* (Ithaca, NY: Cornell University Press, 1995), 103.
24. Amherst quoted in Colin Calloway, *The Scratch of a Pen: 1763 and the Transformation of North America* (New York: Oxford University Press, 2006), 73.
25. Cherokee Chief quoted in Colin Calloway, *First Peoples: A Documentary Survey of American Indian History*, 3rd ed. (Boston: Bedford Books, 2008), 162.
26. David Waldstreicher, ed., *A Companion to Benjamin Franklin* (London: Wiley-Blackwell, 2011), 171–172.
27. Washington quoted in Ron Chernow, *Washington: A Life* (New York: Penguin Books, 2010), 59.
28. Wolfe quoted in Fred Anderson, *Crucible of War: The Seven Years' War and the Fate of Empire in British North America, 1754–1766* (New York: Knopf, 2000), 254.
29. Franklin quoted in Gordon S. Wood, *The Americanization of Benjamin Franklin* (New York: Penguin, 2004), 91.
30. Boston protest quoted in Anderson, *Crucible of War*, 605.
31. Morris quoted in Patricia U. Bonomi, *A Factious People: Politics and Society in Colonial New York* (New York: Columbia University Press, 1971), 203.
32. John Adams to Benjamin Kent, June 22, 1776, https://founders.archives.gov/documents/Adams/06-04-02-0130. In 1818, Adams still used the metaphor in recounting the history of the American Revolution. He wrote to Hezekiah Niles, "thirteen Clocks were made to Strike together." Adams to Niles, February 13, 1818, https://founders.archives.gov/documents/Adams/99-02-02-6854.

CHAPTER 2

 1. Thomas Jefferson to John Adams, February 15, 1825, https://founders.archives.gov/documents/Jefferson/98-01-02-4962; Jefferson to John Holmes, April 22, 1820, https://founders.archives.gov/documents/Jefferson/98-01-02-1234; Jefferson quoted in Louis P. Masur, *1831: Year of Eclipse* (New York: Hill & Wang, 2001), 59.
 2. John Adams to Thomas Pickering, August 6, 1822, https://founders.archives.gov/documents/Adams/99-02-02-7674; John Adams, *Diary and Autobiography of John Adams*, ed. L. H. Butterfield (Cambridge, MA: Harvard University Press, 1961), 3:335.
 3. Edmund S. Morgan, *The Genius of George Washington* (New York: Norton, 1980), 41.

4. *Letters from a Farmer in Pennsylvania* (Philadelphia: J. Almon, 1774), 31–32.

5. *The Letters of Richard Henry Lee*, ed. James Curtis Ballagh (New York: Macmillan, 1911), 1:114.

6. Knox quoted in Ron Chernow, *Washington: A Life* (New York: Penguin, 2010), 324.

7. Thomas Paine, "Common Sense," in *The Thomas Paine Reader*, ed. Michael Foot and Isaac Kramnick (New York: Penguin, 1987), 65.

8. *Collections of the Massachusetts Historical Society*, 5th ser. (Boston, 1877), 3:436–437.

9. Adams quoted in Joseph J. Ellis, *His Excellency George Washington* (New York: Vintage, 2004), 95.

10. Wayne Bodle, *Valley Forge Winter: Civilians and Soldiers in War* (University Park: Penn State University Press, 2002), 108.

11. John Adams to Hezekiah Niles, February 13, 1818, https://founders.archives.gov/documents/Adams/99-02-02-6854.

12. James Madison to Thomas Jefferson, March 18, 1786, https://founders.archives.gov/documents/Jefferson/01-09-02-0301.

13. Alexander Hamilton to Edward Stevens, November 11, 1769, https://founders.archives.gov/documents/Hamilton/01-01-02-0002.

14. Alexander Hamilton to Robert Morris, April 30, 1781, https://founders.archives.gov/documents/Hamilton/01-02-02-1167.

15. Henry quoted in *Encyclopedia Virginia*, http://www.encyclopediavirginia.org/Henry_Patrick_1736-1799#start_entry.

16. Cecilia Kenyon, ed., *The Anti-Federalists* (Indianapolis, IN: Bobbs-Merrill, 1966), 15.

17. Madison, "Federalist 51," in *The Federalist Papers* (New York: New American Library, 1961), 322.

18. Jefferson to Madison, December 20, 1787, https://founders.archives.gov/documents/Madison/01-10-02-0210.

19. William Pierce quoted in Carl Van Doren, *Benjamin Franklin* (New York: Penguin, 1938), 744; Benjamin Franklin, *The Autobiography of Benjamin Franklin with Related Documents*, ed. Louis P. Masur (Boston: Bedford Books, 2016), 21, 77.

20. Franklin, "An Address to the Public," November 9, 1789, in *Autobiography of Benjamin Franklin*, 185–186.

21. Franklin to Jean Baptiste Leroy, November 13, 1789, in *The Writings of Benjamin Franklin*, ed. Albert Henry Smyth, 10 vols. (New Yok: Macmillan, 1907), 10:69.

22. Jefferson to Francis Hopkinson, May 13, 1789, https://founders.archives.gov/documents/Jefferson/01-14-02-0402.

23. Jefferson quoted in Ron Chernow, *Hamilton* (New York: Viking, 2004), 390; Thomas Jefferson to Abigail Adams, June 21, 1785, https://avalon.law.yale.edu/18th_century/let29.asp.

24. Jefferson, "Notes on State of Virginia," Query XIX, 175, https://docsouth.unc.edu/southlit/jefferson/jefferson.html.

25. Jefferson to Washington, September 9, 1792, https://founders.archives.gov/documents/Jefferson/01-24-02-0330; Hamilton to Edward Carrington, May 26, 1792, https://founders.archives.gov/documents/Hamilton/01-11-02-0349; Marcus Daniel, *Scandal and Civility: Journalism and the Birth of American Democracy* (New York: Oxford University Press, 2009), 50.

26. Jefferson to Madison, September 1, 1793, https://founders.archives.gov/documents/Madison/01-15-02-0063; Matthew Carey quoted in Thomas Apel, *Feverish Bodies and Enlightened Minds: Science and the Yellow Fever Controversy in the Early American Republic* (Stanford: Stanford University Press, 2016), 2.

27. Poem quoted in Thomas P. Slaughter, *The Whiskey Rebellion: Frontier Epilogue to the American Revolution* (New York: Oxford University Press, 1986), 132.

28. Jefferson to Martha Jefferson Randolph, May 17, 1798, https://founders.archives.gov/documents/Jefferson/01-30-02-0251.

29. Douglas Bradburn, "A Clamor in the Public Mind: Opposition to the Alien and Sedition Acts," *William and Mary Quarterly*, 3rd ser. (2008): 566; Jefferson to Philip Mazzei, April 24,

1796, https://founders.archives.gov/documents/Jefferson/01-29-02-0054-0002; Jefferson to John Taylor, June 4, 1798, https://founders.archives.gov/documents/Jefferson/01-30-02-0251.

30. Matthew Lyon quoted in Stanley Elkins and Eric McKitrick, *The Age of Federalism: The Early American Republic, 1788–1800* (New York: Oxford University Press, 1993), 710.

31. *Connecticut Courant* quoted in Susan Dunn, *Jefferson's Second Revolution: The Election of 1800 and the Triumph of Republicanism* (Boston: Houghton Mifflin, 2004), 1; *Letter from Alexander Hamilton, Concerning the Public Conduct and Character of John Adams, Esq. President of the United States* (New York: John Lang, 1800), 12.

32. Thomas Jefferson to Spencer Roane, September 6, 1819, https://founders.archives.gov/documents/Jefferson/98-01-02-0734.

33. Thomas Jefferson to Pierre Samuel DuPont De Nemours, July 14, 1807, https://cdn.loc.gov/service/mss/mtj//mtj1/038/038_0983_0984.pdf.

34. Madison quoted in Howard Jones, *Crucible of Power: A History of American Foreign Relations to 1913* (Lanham, MD: Scholarly Resources, 2002), 66.

35. James Madison, "War Message to Congress," June 1, 1812, https://millercenter.org/the-presidency/presidential-speeches/june-1-1812-special-message-congress-foreign-policy-crisis-war.

36. NJ Legislature, November 11, 1812, Archives Online at Indiana University Library, https://collections.libraries.indiana.edu/warof1812/exhibits/show/warof1812/the-war-1812.

37. *An Exact and Authentic Narrative of the Events that Took Place in Baltimore* (Baltimore, n.p., 1812), 27. See Paul Gilje, "The Baltimore Riots of 1812 and the Breakdown of the Anglo-American Mob Tradition," *Journal of Social History* 13 (Summer 1980): 547–564.

38. *London Times* quoted in Gordon Wood, *Empire of Liberty: A History of the Early Republic, 1789–1815* (New York: Oxford University Press, 2009), 681.

39. Elizabeth Dowling Taylor, *A Slave in the White House: Paul Jennings and the Madisons* (New York: St. Martin's Press, 2012).

40. John William Ward, *Andrew Jackson: Symbol for an Age* (New York: Oxford University Press, 1955), xii.

41. James M. Banner, *To the Hartford Convention* (New York: Knopf, 1970), 338.

42. Monroe Doctrine, December 2, 1823, Avalon Project, http://avalon.law.yale.edu/19th_century/monroe.asp.

43. *State v. Mann*, 13 N.C. 263 (1829), http://moglen.law.columbia.edu/twiki/pub/AmLegalHist/TedProject/Mann.pdf.

44. Calhoun quoted in Louis P. Masur, *The Civil War: A Concise History* (New York: Oxford University Press, 2011), 7; Hammond quoted in Drew Gilpin Faust, *James Henry Hammond and the Old South: A Design for Mastery* (Baton Rouge: Louisiana State University Press, 1982), 120.

45. Richard H. Brown, *The Missouri Compromise* (Boston: DC Heath, 1964), 26; *Annals of Congress*, Fifteenth Congress, 2nd Session, 1:1191–1193.

46. James Madison to James Monroe, February 23, 1820, https://founders.archives.gov/documents/Madison/04-02-02-0019.

47. John Eaton to Andrew Jackson, March 11, 1820, in *The Papers of Andrew Jackson*, ed. Harold D. Moser, David R. Hoth, and Geroge H. Hoemann, 10 vols. (Knoxville: University of Tennessee Press, 1994), 4:362.

48. Calhoun quoted in Clyde A. Haulman, *Virginia and the Panic of 1819* (London: Pickering and Chatto, 2008), 25.

49. Clay quoted in George Dangerfield, *The Awakening of American Nationalism, 1815–1829* (New York: Harper & Row, 1965), 119; Thomas Jefferson to John Holmes, April 22, 1820, https://founders.archives.gov/documents/Jefferson/98-01-02-1234.

CHAPTER 3

1. Morris Birkbeck, *Notes on a Journey to America* (London: Ridgeway and Sons, 1818), 30; Lyman Beecher quoted in David Brion Davis, ed., *Antebellum American Culture: An*

Interpretive Anthology (New York: D.C. Heath, 1979), 377; Robert V. Remini, *Andrew Jackson: The Course of American Empire, 1767–1821* (New York: Harper & Row, 1977), 30; Herman Melville to Gansvoort Melville, May 29, 1846, in Lynn Horth, ed., *The Writings of Herman Melville: Correspondence* (Evanston, IL: Northwestern University Press, 1993), 41. James 3:5 states, "Behold how great a matter a little fire kindleth."

2. Jackson to Robert Hayne, February 8, 1831, quoted in Richard Ellis, *The Union at Risk: Jacksonian Democracy, States' Rights, and Nullification* (New York: Oxford University Press, 1987), 47.

3. John William Ward, *Andrew Jackson: Symbol for an Age* (New York: Oxford University Press, 1955), 83–86.

4. Quoted in Louis P. Masur, *1831: Year of Eclipse* (New York: Hill & Wang, 2001), 170.

5. Alexander Hamilton to Theodore Sedgwick, July 10, 1804, https://founders.archives. gov/documents/Hamilton/01-26-02-0001-0264.

6. Thomas Jefferson to Francis Hopkinson, March 13, 1789, in Merrill Peterson, ed., *The Portable Thomas Jefferson* (New York: Penguin, 1975), 435.

7. J. P. Mayer, ed., *Alexis de Tocqueville, Journey to America* (New Haven: Yale University Press, 1962), 66, 182; Alexis de Tocqueville to Ernest de Chabrol, October 7, 1831, in Roger Boesche, ed., *Alexis de Tocqueville: Selected Letters on Politics and Society* (Berkeley: University of California Press, 1985), 59.

8. Alexis de Tocqueville, *Democracy in America*, trans. Phillip Bradley (New York: Knopf, 1945), 1:427.

9. Calhoun quoted in Merrill D. Peterson, *The Great Triumvirate: Webster, Clay, and Calhoun* (New York: Oxford University Press, 1987), 257.

10. "South Carolina Exposition and Protest," in *The Papers of John C. Calhoun*, ed. Clyde N. Wilson and W. Edwin Hemphill (Columbia: University of South Carolina Press, 1977), 10:444–539.

11. James Madison quoted in Masur, *1831: Year of Eclipse*, 148–149.

12. Jackson quoted in Robert V. Remini, *Andrew Jackson and the Bank War* (New York: W. W. Norton, 1967), 15–16; Nicholas Biddle to Henry Clay, August 1, 1831, in Reginald McGrane, ed., *Correspondence of Nicholas Biddle Dealing with National Affairs, 1807–1844* (Boston: Houghton Mifflin, 1919), 196.

13. Jackson quoted in Masur, *1831: Year of Eclipse*, 150.

14. Jackson quoted in Masur, *1831: Year of Eclipse*, 167–168.

15. Thomas Jefferson to Danbury Baptist Association, January 1, 1803, in *Portable Thomas Jefferson*, 303.

16. *Memoirs of Rev. Charles G. Finney* (New York: A. S. Barnes & Company, 1876), 24.

17. Harriet Beecher Stowe, *Uncle Tom's Cabin, or Life Among the Lowly* (New York: Penguin, 1986), 224.

18. See Amanda Clayburgh, "Temperance," in *American History through Literature, 1820–1870*, ed. Janet Gabler-Hover and Robert Sattlemeyeretroit (New York: Scribner, 2006), 1152–1158; and W. J. Rorabaugh, *The Alcoholic Republic: An American Tradition* (New York: Oxford University Press, 1981).

19. Henry W. Sams, ed., *Autobiography of Brook Farm* (Englewood Cliffs, NJ: Prentice Hall, 1958), 25.

20. Joel Porte, ed., *Emerson in His Journals* (Cambridge, MA: Harvard University Press, 1982), 221, 247–248.

21. Porte, *Emerson*, 185.

22. Jackson quoted in Michael Paul Rogin, *Fathers and Children: Andrew Jackson and the Subjugation of the Indian* (New York: Knopf, 1975), 131. See Francis P. Prucha, *American Indian Policy in the Formative Years* (Cambidge, MA: Harvard University Press, 1962), and Steve Inskeep, *Jacksonland: President Andrew Jackson, Cherokee Chief John Ross, and a Great American Land Grab* (New York: Penguin, 2015).

23. Godfrey Vigne, *Six Months in America* (London: Whitaker, Treacher, 1832), 1:216–217.

24. Jefferson used the phrase "Empire of Liberty" on multiple occasions. See, for example, his letter to George Rogers Clark, December 25, 1780, https://founders.archives.gov/documents/Jefferson/01-04-02-0295, and his letter to James Madison, April 27, 1809, https://founders.archives.gov/documents/Jefferson/03-01-02-0140.

25. Everett quoted in Masur, *1831: Year of Eclipse*, 118–119.

26. Wirt quoted in Masur, *1831: Year of Eclipse*, 120.

27. Wirt quoted in Masur, *1831: Year of Eclipse*, 122–123.

28. Richard Peters, *The Case of the Cherokee Nation Against the State of Georgia* (Philadelphia: John Grigg, 1831), 15–80; Joseph Story quoted in Masur, *1831: Year of Eclipse*, 124.

29. *Worcester v. State of Georgia*, 6 Peters 515 (1832), 243.

30. Soldier quoted in Lydia Bjornlund, *The Trail of Tears: The Relocation of the Cherokee Nation* (Detroit: Gale, 2010), 62; Missionary quoted in Vicki Rozema, ed., *Voices from the Trail of Tears* (Winston-Salem, NC: John F. Blair, 2003), 147.

31. Quoted in Amy Greenberg, *A Wicked War: Polk, Clay, Lincoln and the 1846 U.S. Invasion of Mexico* (New York: Knopf, 2012), 8.

32. Texas Declaration of Independence, March 2, 1836, Avalon Project, http://avalon.law.yale.edu/19th_century/texdec.asp.

33. *Niles' Weekly Register*, April 9, 1836, 99.

34. Inaugural Address of James Knox Polk, March 4, 1845, Avalon Project, http://avalon.law.yale.edu/19th_century/polk.asp.

35. John O'Sullivan, "Annexation," *United States Magazine and Democratic Review*, July–August, 1845, 5–10.

36. Message of President Polk, May 11, 1846, Avalon Project, https://avalon.law.yale.edu/19th_century/polk01.asp.

37. *American Whig Review*, January 1847, 1; *Whig Journal*, February 1847, 109; Ralph Waldo Emerson, *Journals and Miscellaneous Notebooks*, ed. Ralph H. Orth and Alfred R. Ferguson, 16 vols. (Cambridge, MA: Harvard University Press, 1971), 9:430–431.

38. Abraham Lincoln, *The Collected Works of Abraham Lincoln*, ed. Roy P. Basler, 9 vols. (New Brunswick, NJ: Rutgers University Press, 1953–55), 1:439–440.

39. *Charleston Mercury* quoted in Daniel Walker Howe, *What Hath God Wrought: The Transformation of America, 1815–1848* (New York: Oxford University Press, 2008), 770.

40. *New York Herald* quoted in Greenberg, *Wicked War*, 57.

41. U. S. Grant quoted in Greenberg, *Wicked War*, 274.

42. Henry David Thoreau, "Civil Disobedience," in *Walden and Civil Disobedience*, ed. Owen Thomas (New York: W. W. Norton, 1966), 224–243.

43. Thoreau, "Walking," quoted in Robert D. Richardson, *Henry Thoreau: A Life of the Mind* (Berkeley: University of California Press, 1986), 288.

44. Lansford W. Hastings, *The Emigrants' Guide to Oregon and California* (Cincinnati: G. Conclin, 1845), 6.

45. Quoted in Ray Allen Billington, *The Far Western Frontier* (New York: Harper & Row, 1956), 87–88.

46. Royce quoted in H. W. Brands, *The Age of Gold* (New York: Random House, 2002), 139.

47. John D. Unruh Jr., *The Plains Across: The Overland Emigrants and the Trans-Mississippi West, 1840–1860* (Urbana: University of Illinois Press, 1979), 156, 169.

48. Polk, "Message to Congress," December 1848, https://millercenter.org/the-presidency/presidential-speeches/december-5-1848-fourth-annual-message-congress.

49. Sherman quoted in Brands, *Age of Gold*, 46; Michael Traynor, "The Infamous Case of *People v. Hall*," *California Supreme Court Historical Society Newsletter* (Spring/Summer 2017), 4.

50. Hawthorne quoted in Robert V. Hine and John Mack Faragher, *The American West: A New Interpretive History* (New Haven: Yale University Press, 2000), 488.

CHAPTER 4

1. Annie Fields, ed., *Life and Letters of Harriet Beecher Stowe* (Boston: Houghton Mifflin, 1897), 163; Ralph Waldo Emerson, *Journals and Miscellaneous Notebooks*, ed. Ralph H. Orth and Alfred R. Ferguson, 16 vols. (Cambridge, MA: Harvard University Press, 1971), 15:28.
2. John Wentworth, *Congressional Reminiscences* (Chicago: Fergus Printing Company, 1882), 28.
3. *Congressional Globe*, Senate, 31st Congress, 1st Session, Appendix, 115–127 (hereafter *CG*).
4. Harriet Martineau, *Retrospect of Western Travel* (New York, Harper & Brothers, 1838), 1:147.
5. *CG*, Senate, 31st Congress, 1st Session, 451–456.
6. Wentworth, *Congressional Reminiscences*, 33–34.
7. *CG*, Senate, 31st Congress, 1st Session, Appendix, 269–276.
8. New Orleans *Daily Crescent*, March 16, 1850; *North American Review*, 104 (January 1867), 115.
9. *CG*, Senate, 31st Congress, 1st Session, Appendix, 260–268.
10. "The Doctrine of the Higher Law: Mr. Seward's Speech," *Southern Literary Messenger*, March 1851, 32; Seward quoted in Walter Stahr, *Seward: The Indispensible Man* (New York: Simon & Schuster, 2012), 125.
11. *Boston Slave Riot and Trial of Anthony Burns* (Boston: Fetridge & Company, 1854); Charles Emery Stevens, *Anthony Burns: A History* (Boston: John P. Jewett & Company, 1856). See Albert J. Von Frank, *The Trials of Anthony Burns* (Cambridge, MA: Harvard University Press, 1998), and Steven Lubet, *Fugitive Justice* (Cambridge, MA: Harvard University Press, 2010).
12. Amos A. Lawrence to Giles Richards, June 1, 1854, quoted in Jane J. and William H. Pease, eds., *The Fugitive Slave Law and Anthony Burns: A Problem in Law Enforcement* (Philadelphia: Lippincott, 1975), 43. In 1855, a group led by Reverend Leonard Grimes purchased Burns's freedom. He became a minister in Canada and died in 1862.
13. Louis Ruchames, ed., *The Letters of William Lloyd Garrison* (Cambridge, MA: Harvard University Press, 1975), 4:290.
14. *Liberator*, January 1, 1831.
15. Michael F. Holt, *The Rise and Fall of the American Whig Party: Jacksonian Politics and the Onset of the Civil War* (New York: Oxford University Press, 1999), 763.
16. Abraham Lincoln, *The Collected Works of Abraham Lincoln*, ed. Roy P. Basler, 9 vols. (New Brunswick, NJ: Rutgers University Press, 1953–55), 2:323 (hereafter *CW*).
17. Lydia Maria Child, *The Duty of Disobedience to the Fugitive Slave Act* (Boston: American Anti-Slavery Society, 1860), 5.
18. Charles Beecher, *The Duty of Disobedience to Wicked Laws* (New York: John A. Gray, 1851), 21.
19. Louis P. Masur, "Harriet Beecher Stowe's Powerful Mosaic of Facts," *Chronicle of Higher Education*, July 3, 2011, https://www.chronicle.com/article/Harriet-Beecher-Stowes/128069/. See David Reynolds, *Mightier Than the Sword: Uncle Tom's Cabin and the Battle for America* (New York: W. W. Norton, 2011).
20. Robert W. Johannsen, *Stephen A. Douglas* (Urbana: University of Illinois Press, 1997), 451.
21. *Appeal of the Independent Democrats to the People of the United States*, January 19, 1854, 1, https://www.loc.gov/item/mss156100212.
22. *CW*, 2:255, 266.
23. George E. Baker, ed., *William H. Seward: With Selections from His Works* (New York: J. S. Redfield, 1855), 392.
24. Atchison quoted in James M. McPherson, *Battle Cry of Freedom* (New York: Oxford University Press, 1989), 147.
25. Edward L. Pierce, ed., *Memoir and Letters of Charles Sumner* (Boston: Roberts Brothers, 1893), 4:85.
26. *The Crime against Kansas: Speech of the Honorable Charles Sumner in the Senate of the United States, 19th and 20th May, 1856* (Boston: John P. Jewett, 1856), 2, 5, 9, 13.

27. Brooks quoted in James A. Rawley, *Race and Politics: Bleeding Kansas and the Coming of the Civil War* (Lincoln: University of Nebraska Press, 1979), 128; *Charleston Mercury*, May 28, 1856; *Boston Post*, May 29, 1856.

28. *Boston Atlas*, May 23, 1856; *New York Tribune*, May 24, 1856.

29. Frederick Douglass quoted in John Stauffer and Zoe Trodd, eds., *The Tribunal: Responses to John Brown and the Harpers Ferry Raid* (Cambridge, MA: Harvard University Press, 2012), xxv.

30. Bernard C. Steiner, *Life of Roger Brooke Taney* (Baltimore: Williams & Wilkins, 1922), 87.

31. William Salter, ed., "Letters of John McLean to John Teesdale," *Bibliotecha Sacra* 56 (October 1899): 737.

32. See Don Fehrenbacher, *The Dred Scott Case: Its Significance in American Law and Politics* (New York: Oxford University Press, 1978).

33. *Richmond Enquirer*, March 13, 1857; *Cleveland Plain Dealer*, March 11, 1857.

34. *New Hampshire Patriot*, March 18, 1857.

35. *New York Tribune*, March 7, 1857.

36. *CW*, 2:401.

37. *CW*, 3:9, 28–29.

38. Frederick Douglass, *Narrative of the Life of Frederick Douglass, An American Slave* (Mineola, NY: Dover Publications, 1995), 20.

39. Frederick Douglass, "The *Dred Scott* Decision: Speech Delivered May 14, 1857," University of Rochester Frederick Douglass Project, http://rbscp.lib.rochester.edu/4399.

40. McPherson, *Battle Cry of Freedom*, 177.

41. Frederick Douglass, *Life and Times of Frederick Douglass* (Mineola, NY: Dover, 2003), 195

42. Stephen B. Oates, *To Purge This Land with Blood: A Biography of John Brown* (Amherst: University of Massachusetts Press, 1984), 351.

43. Stauffer and Trodd, *Tribunal*, 26–27.

44. *The Life, Trial and Conviction of Captain John Brown* (New York: Robert M. De Witt, 1859), 95.

45. Mary Anna Jackson, *Life and Letters of General Thomas J. Jackson* (New York: Harper & Brothers, 1892), 130.

46. Henry D. Thoreau, *A Plea for John Brown*, October 30, 1859, Avalon Project, https://avalon.law.yale.edu/19th_century/thoreau_001.asp; *Correspondence between Lydia Maria Child and Gov. Wise and Mrs. Mason* (New York: American Anti-Slavery Society, 1860), 14; Ralph Waldo Emerson, "Courage," in Stauffer and Todd, *Tribunal*, 113; George Templeton Strong, *Diary of the Civil War: George Templeton Strong*, ed. Allan Nevins (New York: Macmillan, 1962), 466, 473.

47. *Daily Herald*, December 5, 1859; *Cincinnati Inquirer*, December 3, 1859.

48. Stauffer and Trodd, *Tribunal*, 83, 200, 225.

49. *North Carolina Register*, December 21, 1859.

50. Oliver P. Anderson, *A Voice from Harper's Ferry* (Boston: n.p., 1861), 62.

CHAPTER 5

1. Don Fehrenbacher and Virginia Fehrenbacher, eds., *Recollected Words of Abraham Lincoln* (Stanford, CA: Stanford University Press, 1996), 13; Abraham Lincoln, *The Collected Works of Abraham Lincoln*, ed. Roy P. Basler, 9 vols. (New Brunswick, NJ: Rutgers University Press, 1953–55), 5:537; 4:438.

2. *CW*, 4:262–271.

3. Thomas Goode, March 28, 1861, *Proceedings of the Virginia State Convention* (Richmond: Virginia State Library, 1965), 2:518.

4. *CW*, 4:263.

5. *CW*, 3:478–479.

6. Walt Whitman to Nathaniel Bloom and John F. S. Gray, in Edwin Haviland Miller, ed., *The Correspondence of Walt Whitman* (New York: New York University Press, 1961), 1:82; *CW*, 2:459; *CW*, 1:8.

7. *CW*, 3:512.

8. *CW*, 2:461; 3:550.
9. *CW*, 4:45.
10. *CW*, 4:50.
11. *CW*, 4:150.
12. *CW*, 4:190, 193, 130.
13. *CW*, 4:270–271.
14. Toombs quoted in Maury Klein, *Days of Defiance: Sumter, Secession and the Coming of the Civil War* (New York: Knopf, 1997), 399; C. Vann Woodward, ed., *Mary Chesnut's Civil War* (New Haven: Yale University Press, 1981), 46.
15. *CW*, 5:49.
16. Grant quoted in Ronald C. White, *American Ulysses: A Life of Ulysses S. Grant* (New York: Random House, 2016), 336.
17. "Brady's Photographs," *New York Times*, October 20, 1862.
18. *Ulysses S. Grant: Memoirs and Selected Letters* (New York: Library of America, 1990), 238–239.
19. Soldier quoted in Louis P. Masur, *The Civil War: A Concise History* (New York: Oxford University Press, 2011), 35.
20. "Execution of Wirz," *New York Times*, November 11, 1865.
21. William J. Cooper, ed., *Jefferson Davis: The Essential Writings* (New York: Modern Library, 2004), 309; *CW*, 7:17–18.
22. Joan Waugh, *U.S. Grant: American Hero, American Myth* (Chapel Hill: University of North Carolina Press, 2009), 81, 201; Masur, *Civil War*, 65.
23. *CW*, 7:435.
24. Sherman quoted in Charles Royster, *The Destructive War: William Tecumseh Sherman, Stonewall Jackson, and the Americans* (New York: Vintage, 1993), 353; soldier quoted in Andrew Carroll, *War Letters: Extraordinary Correspondence from American Wars* (New York: Scribner, 2002), 107.
25. *CW*, 8:101.
26. *CW*, 8:332–333.
27. Charles Loring Brace quoted in Louis P. Masur, *Lincoln's Hundred Days: The Emancipation Proclamation and the War for the Union* (Cambridge, MA: Harvard University Press, 2012), 26.
28. *CW*, 4:532; 5:145.
29. *CW*, 2:255–256.
30. *CW*, 5:318.
31. Douglass quoted in Masur, *Civil War*, 56–57.
32. Howell Cobb quoted in Masur, *Civil War*, 75.
33. *CW*, 6:410.
34. Wills and Sawtelle quoted in Masur, *Lincoln's Hundred Days*, 229–230, 232.
35. Douglass quoted in Louis P. Masur, *Lincoln's Last Speech: Wartime Reconstruction and the Crisis of Reunion* (New York: Oxford University Press, 2015), 187.
36. Frank Key Howard, *Fourteen Months in American Bastiles* (Baltimore: Kelly, Hedian, & Piet, 1863), 3; *CW*, 6:266.
37. Buck quoted in Drew Gilpin Faust, *Mothers of Invention* (Chapel Hill: University of North Carolina Press, 2004), 249.
38. Elizabeth M. Davis to Lydia Brown, Davis, Brown, and Yale Families Correspondence, Collection No. 164, Historical Society of Pennsylvania, https://hsp.org/collections/catalogs-research-tools/subject-guides/women-during-the-civil-war.
39. *CW*, 4:259.
40. Garrison quoted in Eric Foner, *Reconstruction: America's Unfinished Revolution, 1863–1877* (New York: Harper, 1988), 90; Douglass quoted in Henry Louis Gates Jr., *The Stony Road: Reconstruction, White Supremacy, and the Rise of Jim Crow* (New York: Penguin, 2019), 29.
41. Quoted in Masur, *Civil War*, 90.
42. Leon Litwack, *Been in the Storm So Long: The Aftermath of Slavery* (New York: Vintage, 1980), 401; Stevens quoted in Hans Trefousse, *Thaddeus Stevens: Nineteenth-Century Egalitarian* (Chapel Hill: University of North Carolina Press, 2005), 172; *Report on the Joint Committee on*

Reconstruction Made during First Session of the 39th Congress (Washington, DC: Government Printing Office,1866), 1:175.

43. Philena Carkin to Ednah D. Cheney, February 28, 1875, in Lauranett Lorainne Lee, "Crucible in the Classroom: The Freedpeople and Their Teachers, Charlottesville, Virginia, 1861–1876 (PhD diss., University of Virginia, 2002), 145; Frederick Douglass, "Blessings of Liberty and Education," Speech at the Dedication of the Manassas (VA) Industrial School, September 3, 1894, http://teachingamericanhistory.org/library/document/blessings-of-liberty-and-education/.

44. Mark Twain, *The Gilded Age and Later Novels* (New York: Library of America, 2002), 134.

CHAPTER 6

1. Walt Whitman, "Democratic Vistas," in *The Portable Walt Whitman*, ed. Michael Warner (New York: Penguin, 2004), 427; "Thoughts," in Walt Whitman, *Leaves of Grass* (New York: W. W. Norton, 1965), 493; Gary Schmidgall, ed., *Intimate with Walt: Selections from Whitman's Conversations with Horace Traubel, 1888–1892* (Iowa City: University of Iowa Press, 2001), 195.

2. Henry Adams, *The Education of Henry Adams* (New York: Modern Library, 1999), 7; Henry Adams, *Democracy: An American Novel* (New York: Henry Holt, 1908), 71.

3. *The Papers of Ulysses S. Grant*, ed. John Y. Simon, 31 vols. (Carbondale: Southern Illinois University Press, 1994), 19:139–143; Henry Adams, *Historical Essays* (New York: Charles Scribner's Sons, 1891), 364.

4. *New York Tribune*, February 19, 1873.

5. Charles Sumner, *Republicanism vs. Grantism* (Boston: Lee and Shepherd, 1872), 47; Adams, *Education*, 266.

6. "Mr. Thomas Nast," *New York Times*, March 20, 1872; Tweed quoted in H. W. Brands, *American Colossus: The Triumph of Capitalism, 1865–1900* (New York: Anchor Books, 2010), 353.

7. *Memoirs of General W. T. Sherman* (New York: Charles Webster, 1891), 2:491; David Tucker, *Mugwumps: Public Moralists of the Gilded Age* (Columbia: University of Missouri Press, 1998), 79.

8. George F. Parker, ed., *The Writings and Speeches of Grover Cleveland* (New York: Cassell, 1892), 450.

9. William Graham Sumner, *What Social Classes Owe Each Other* (New York: Harper and Brothers, 1883), 12, 66.

10. This paragraph draws on Brands, *American Colossus*.

11. Abraham Lincoln, "Fragment on Free Labor, 1859," in *Collected Works of Abraham Lincoln*, ed. Roy P. Basler, 9 vols. (New Brunswick, NJ: Rutgers University Press, 1953–55), 3:464; economist quoted in Daniel T. Rodgers, *The Work Ethic in Industrial America* (Chicago: University of Chicago Press, 1978), 73.

12. Andrew Carnegie, *The Gospel of Wealth: Essays and Other Writings* (New York: Penguin, 2006), 3.

13. *New Orleans Times* quoted in Brands, *American* Colossus, 127; Thomas Scott, "The Recent Strikes," *North American Review* 125 (September 1877): 357.

14. James Green, *Death in the Haymarket* (New York: Pantheon, 2006), 203.

15. Stuart B. Kaufman, ed., *The Samuel Gompers Papers* (Urbana: University of Illinois Press, 1987), 2:308–314.

16. Quoted in Richard White, *The Republic for Which It Stands: The United States During Reconstruction and the Gilded Age, 1865–1896* (New York: Oxford University Press, 2017), 666, 670.

17. Quoted in Brands, *American Colossus*, 519.

18. Nick Salvatore, *Eugene Debs: Citizen and Socialist* (Urbana: University of Illinois, 1984), 81.

19. "Editorial Article," *New York Times*, July 9, 1894; Debs quoted in Brands, *American Colossus*, 528.

20. Edward Bellamy, *Looking Backward* (New York: Dover Publications, 1996), 20.

21. Edward Bellamy, *Principles and Purposes of Nationalism* (Boston: n.p., 1889).

22. Leonidas Polk, *Agricultural Depression: Its Causes—The Remedy* (Raleigh, NC: Edwards and Broughton, 1890), 22.

23. C. Vann Woodward, *Tom Watson: Agrarian Rebel* (New York: Oxford University Press, 1963), 220.

24. Ignatius Donnelly, *Caesar's Column* (Cambridge, MA.: Harvard University Press, 1960), 71.

25. "The Omaha Platform," July 4, 1892, http://historymatters.gmu.edu/d/5361/.

26. Adams quoted in Brands, *American Colossus*, 514.

27. Bryan's speech can be found at http://historymatters.gmu.edu/d/5354/. Also see Michael Kazin, *A Godly Hero: The Life of William Jennings Bryan* (New York: Anchor Books, 2007).

28. The paragraph draws on White, *Republic for Which It Stands*.

29. Red Cloud and Fetterman quoted in Bob Drury and Tom Clavin, *The Heart of Everything That Is: The Untold Story of Red Cloud, An American Legend* (New York: Simon & Schuster, 2014), 197, 373.

30. Sherman quoted in Matthew Carr, *Sherman's Ghosts: Soldiers, Civilians and the American Way of War* (New York: New Press, 2015), 140; Sheridan quoted in Paul Andrew Hutton, *Phil Sheridan and His Army* (Norman: University of Oklahoma Press, 1990), 180. Sheridan denied saying this.

31. Red Cloud quoted in Peter Cozzens, *The Earth is Weeping: The Epic Story of the Indian Wars for the American West* (New York: Penguin, 2016), 119–120.

32. Custer quoted in Cozzens, *Earth is Weeping*, 244.

33. The famous speech may have concluded, "I will fight no more against the white man." See discussion in Daniel J. Sharfstein, *Thunder in the Mountain: Chief Joseph, Oliver Otis Howard, and the Nez Perce War* (New York: W. W. Norton, 2017), 380.

34. Chief Joseph quoted in Sharfstein, *Thunder in the Mountain*, 397.

35. John G. Neihardt, *Black Elk Speaks* (Lincoln: University of Nebraska Press, 2014), 169.

36. Roosevelt quoted in Robert L. Di Silvestro, *Theodore Roosevelt in the Badlands* (New York: Walker, 2011), 192; Theodore Roosevelt, *The Winning of the West* (New York: Charles Scriber's Sons, 1906), 1:104.

37. Roosevelt quoted in Stephen Kinzer, *The True Flag: Theodore Roosevelt, Mark Twain, and the Birth of American Empire* (New York: Henry Holt, 2017), 22; Alfred Thayer Mahan, *From Sail to Steam: Recollections of Naval Life* (New York: Harper Brothers, 1907), 324.

38. Hearst quoted in David Nasaw, *The Chief: The Life of William Randolph Hearst* (Boston: Houghton Mifflin, 2000), 127.

39. Hay quoted in John Taliafero, *All the Great Prizes: The Life of John Hay, From Lincoln to Roosevelt* (New York: Simon & Schuster, 2013), 330.

40. Carl Schurz, *The Policy of Imperialism* (Chicago: Anti-Imperialist League, 1899); Andrew Carnegie, "Distant Possessions: The Parting of the Ways," *North American Review* 167 (August 1898): 239–249; Samuel Gompers, "Imperialism: Its Dangers and Wrongs." Speech delivered October 18, 1898, Thirteen.org., https://www.thirteen.org/wnet/historyofus/web09/features/source/C14.html; Mark Twain, *New York Herald*, October 15, 1900, Library of Congress, https://www.loc.gov/rr/hispanic/1898/twain.html.

41. Hoar and Nelson quoted in Kinzer, *True Flag*, 82, 113. Lodge in *Congressional Record*, 55th Congress, 3rd session, 959; Beveridge in *Congressional Record*, 56th Congress, 1st session, 704.

42. Twain quoted in Joe B. Fulton, *The Reconstruction of Mark Twain* (Baton Rouge: Louisiana State University Press, 2010), 167; Lowell quoted in *The Philanthropic Work of Josephine Shaw Lowell* (New York: Macmillan, 1911), 466; Addams in *Jane Addams: Writings on Peace* (New York: Continuum, 2005), 4; Elting Morison, ed., *The Letters of Theodore Roosevelt, Volume 5: The Big Stick* (Cambridge, MA: Harvard University Press, 1951), 792.

43. Theodore Roosevelt, *The Strenuous Life: Essays and Addresses* (New York: Century Co., 1902), 1.

44. Editor quoted in Edmund Morris, *The Rise of Theodore Roosevelt* (New York: Random House, 1979), 740.

CHAPTER 7

1. DeMille quoted in Kenneth Lynn, *Charlie Chaplin and His Times* (New York: Simon & Schuster, 1997), 221.

2. Frederick Hale, ed., *Their Own Saga: Letters from the Norweigian Global Migration* (Minneapolis: University of Minnesota Press, 1986), 183; Mary Antin, *The Promised Land* (New York: Penguin, 1997), 1.

3. Joseph Wtulich, ed. and trans., *Writing Home: Immigrants in Brazil and the United States, 1890–1891* (New York: Columbia University Press, 1986), 312.

4. Kearney quoted in John Soennichsen, *The Chinese Exclusion Act of 1882* (Santa Barbara, CA: Greenwood, 2011), 128; Henry George, "The Chinese in California," *New York Tribune,* May 1, 1869, in *Major Problems in Asian American History,* ed. Lon Kurashige and Alice Yang Murray (Boston: Houghton Mifflin, 2003), 99; Hoar quoted in Roger Daniels, *Asian America: Chinese and Japanese in the United States Since 1850* (Seattle: University of Washington Press, 1988), 54.

5. Roger Daniels, *Guarding the Golden Door: American Immigration Policy and Immigrants Since 1882* (New York: Hill & Wang, 2004), 32; Prescott Hall quoted in Daniel J. Tichenor, *Dividing Lines: The Politics of Immigration Control in America* (Princeton, NJ: Princeton University Press, 2002), 144.

6. Matthew Frye Jacobson, *Barbarians Virtues: The United States Encounters Foreign People at Home and Abroad, 1876–1917* (New York: Hill & Wang, 2001), 193–194.

7. Israel Zangwell, *The Melting Pot* (New York: Macmillan, 1917), 184.

8. "Roosevelt Bars the Hyphenated," *New York Times,* October 13, 1915.

9. Horace Kallen, "Democracy versus the Melting Pot: A Study of American Nationality," *The Nation,* February 25, 1915, 217–218.

10. Jacob Riis, *How the Other Half Lives* (New York: Dover, 1971), 88; Theodore Roosevelt, "Reform Through Social Work," *McClure's Magazine,* March 1901, 453.

11. William James, *Pragmatism and Other Essays* (New York: Washington Square Press, 1963), 26.

12. Upton Sinclair, *The Jungle* (New York: Bantam, 1981), 96.

13. Roosevelt and Sinclair quoted in Anthony Arthur, *Radical Innocent: Upton Sinclair* (New York: Random House, 2006), 82–83.

14. Jane Addams, *Twenty Years at Hull-House* (New York: Signet, 1981), xii; Rivka Shpak Lissak, *Pluralism and Progressives: Hull House and the New Immigrants, 1890–1919* (Chicago: University of Chicago Press, 1989), 67.

15. Theodore Roosevelt, Special Message, January 22, 1909, in Gerhard Peters and John T. Woolley, eds., The American Presidency Project, University of California–Santa Barbara, http://www.presidency.ucsb.edu/ws/index.php?pid=69658.

16. Quoted in Louis P. Masur, *Autumn Glory: Baseball's First World Series* (New York: Hill & Wang, 2003), 198.

17. Frederic Clemson Howe, *The City, the Hope of Democracy* (New York: Scribner's Sons, 1906), 291.

18. Robert LaFollette, "Danger Threatening Representative Government," Robert LaFollette Papers, Wisconsin Historical Society, https://www.wisconsinhistory.org/pdfs/lessons/EDU-Speech-SpeechesLaFollette-DangerThreatening.pdf.

19. *New York Herald* quoted in Jo Freeman, *We Will Be Heard: Women's Struggles for Political Power in the United States* (Lanham, MD: Rowan & Littlefield, 2008), 49.

20. Karen L. Stanford, ed., *If We Must Die: African American Voices in War and Peace* (Lanham, MD: Rowman & Littlefield, 2008), 106.

21. *Plessy v. Ferguson,* 163 U.S. 537 (1896), https://supreme.justia.com/cases/federal/us/163/537/#tab-opinion-1917401.

22. Louis R. Harlan, ed., *The Booker T. Washington Papers* (Urbana: University of Illinois Press, 1974), 3:583–587.

23. W. E. B. DuBois, *The Souls of Black Folk* (New York: Pocket Books, 2005), 58.

24. DuBois, *Souls of Black Folk,* 6–7.

25. Trudier Harris, ed., *Selected Works of Ida B. Wells-Barnett* (New York: Oxford University Press, 1991), 39.

26. Roberta Senechal, *In Lincoln's Shadow: The 1908 Race Riot in Springfield, Illinois* (Carbondale: Southern Illinois University Press, 1990), 2; Scott Ellsworth, *Death in a Promised Land: The Tulsa Race Riot of 1921* (Baton Rouge: Louisiana State University Press, 1992).

27. Eric Arnesen, ed., *Black Protest and the Great Migration: A Brief History with Documents* (Boston: Bedford Books, 2003), 11, 48.

28. On Wilson's quote see Mark E. Benbow, "Birth of a Quotation: Woodrow Wilson and 'Like Writing History with Lightning,'" *Journal of the Gilded Age and Progressive Era* 9 (October 2010): 509–533.

29. Dick Lehr, *The Birth of a Nation: How a Legendary Filmmaker and a Crusading Editor Reignited America's Civil War* (New York: Public Affairs, 2014), 189.

30. Eugene V. Debs, "The Socialist Party and the Working Class, Speech Delivered in Indianapolis, September 1, 1904," https://www.marxists.org/archive/debs/works/1904/sp_wkingclss.htm.

31. Eugene Debs, "A Letter on Immigration," *International Socialist Review* 11 (1910): 16–17.

32. *Bill Haywood's Book: The Autobiography of William D. Haywood* (Westport, CT: Greenwood Press, 1929), 171; J. Anthony Lukas, *Big Trouble: A Murder in a Small Western Town Sets off a Struggle for the Soul of America* (New York: Simon & Schuster, 1997), 221.

33. Lukas, *Big Trouble*, 145.

34. "Darrow's Speech in the Haywood Case," *Wayland's Monthly*, (October 1907, 29–30.

35. William D. Haywood and Frank Bohn, *Industrial Socialism* (Chicago: Charles Kerr, 1911), 4.

36. Werner Sombert, *Why Is There No Socialism in the United States?* (New York: Palgrave, 1976); Seymour Martin Lipset and Gary Marks, *It Didn't Happen Here: Why Socialism Failed in the United States* (New York: W. W. Norton, 2001); Eric Foner, "Why Is There No Socialism in America?" *History Workshop* 17 (Spring 1984): 57–80.

37. Woodrow Wilson, "An Annual Message on the State of the Union," December 7, 1915, in *The Papers of Woodrow Wilson*, ed. Arthur S. Link, 69 vols. (Princeton, NJ: Princeton University Press, 1980), 35:293–310.

38. Eugene V. Debs, Speech at Canton Ohio, June 16, 1918, https://www.marxists.org/archive/debs/works/1918/canton.htm.

39. *American Legion Weekly* quoted in Stanley Coben, "A Study in Nativism: The American Red Scare of 1919–20," *Political Science Quarterly* 79 (March 1964): 70, 72, 73.

40. "Roosevelt at Film of American Valor," *New York Times*, September 24, 1916.

41. Woodrow Wilson, "An Appeal to the American People," August 18, 1914, *Papers*, 30:393–394.

42. Woodrow Wilson, "An Address in Philadelphia to Newly Naturalized Citizens," May 10, 1915, *Papers*, 33:147–150.

43. Woodrow Wilson, "An Address to a Joint Session of Congress," April 2, 1917, *Papers*, 41:519–527; W. E. B. DuBois, "Close Ranks," *The Crisis*, July 1918, 111.

44. Quoted in David Kennedy, *Over Here: The First World War and American Society* (New York: Oxford University Press, 1980), 17–18.

45. George Creel, *Rebel at Large: Recollections of Fifty Crowded Years* (New York: G. P. Putnam's, 1947), 158; George Creel, *How We Advertised America* (New York: Harper & Brothers, 1920), xv.

46. Lloyd Staley to Mary Gray, May 28, 1918, "Letters Home from the War," http://www.u.arizona.edu/~rstaley/wwlettr1.htm; Truman quoted in Andrew Carroll, *My Fellow Soldiers: General John Pershing and the Americans Who Helped Win the Great War* (New York: Penguin, 2017), 261; S. E. Avery, March 13, 1918, "Soldier's Mail: Letters Home from a Yankee Doughboy, 1916–19," https://worldwar1letters.wordpress.com/2009/03/.

47. Woodrow Wilson, "A Flag Day Address," June 14, 1917, *Papers*, 42:498–504.

48. Quoted in Kennedy, *Over Here*, 68.

49. Woodrow Wilson, "An Address to a Joint Session of Congress," January 8, 1918, *Papers*, 45:534–539; Clemenceau quoted in Kennedy, *Over Here*, 385.

50. Warren G. Harding, "Speech at Boston, Massachusetts, May 14, 1920," in *Rededicating America: Life and Recent Speeches of Warren G. Harding* (Indianapolis: Bobbs-Merrill, 1920), 223.

CHAPTER 8

1. Jonathan Alter, *The Defining Moment: FDR's Hundred Days and the Triumph of Hope* (New York: Simon & Schuster, 2006), 327.

2. Willard quoted in Lisa McGirr, *The War on Alcohol: Prohibition and the Rise of the American State* (New York: W. W. Norton, 2016), 17.

3. William McLoughlin, *Billy Sunday Was His Real Name* (Chicago: University of Chicago Press, 1955), 154.

4. William Ashley Sunday, *Get On the Water Wagon* (n.p., 1915), 4.

5. McGirr, *War on Alcohol*, 138.

6. McGirr, *War on Alcohol*, 62, 90–91; "Prohibition Bad, Says Busch," *New York Times*, May 31, 1908.

7. Daniel Okrent, *Last Call: The Rise and Fall of Prohibition* (New York: Scribner, 2010), 252, 274.

8. Samuel Harden Church, "Paradise of the Ostrich," *North American Review* 221 (June–August 1925): 625–631; Charles L. Dana, "Nervous and Mental Diseases and the Volstead Law," *North American Review* 221 (June–August 1925): 615–620.

9. Charles Rappleye, *Herbert Hoover in the White House: The Ordeal of the Presidency* (New York: Simon & Schuster, 2016), 352; Okrent, *Last Call*, 305.

10. Calvin Coolidge: "Address to the American Society of Newspaper Editors, Washington, D.C.," January 17, 1925, in Gerhard Peters and John T. Woolley, eds., American Presidency Project, University of California–Santa Barbara, https://www.presidency.ucsb.edu/node/269410; Langston Hughes "The Negro Artist and the Racial Mountain," *The Nation*, June 23, 1926, 692–694, https://www.thenation.com/article/negro-artist-and-racial-mountain/.

11. Okrent, *Last Call*, 330.

12. Arthur M. Schlesinger Jr., *The Coming of the New Deal, 1933–35* (Boston: Houghton Mifflin, 1958), 11.

13. Eric Rauchway, *The Great Depression and The New Deal: A Very Short Introduction* (New York: Oxford University Press, 2008), 15.

14. Alan Lawson, *A Commonwealth of Hope: The New Deal Response to Crisis* (Baltimore: Johns Hopkins University Press, 2006), 24; "Shouse Declares Hoover a Failure," *New York Times*, March 4, 1932.

15. Lisa Goff, *Shantytown, U.S.A.: Forgotten Landscapes of the Working Poor* (Cambridge, MA: Harvard University Press, 2016), 224.

16. Herbert Hoover, "Statement on the Justice Department Investigation of the Bonus Army," September 10, 1932, American Presidency Project, https://www.presidency.ucsb.edu/node/207472.

17. Paul Dickson and Thomas B. Allen, *The Bonus Army: An American Epic* (New York: Walker & Company, 2004), 118.

18. Nancy Joan Weiss, *Farewell to the Party of Lincoln: Black Politics in the Age of FDR* (Princeton: Princeton University Press, 1983).

19. Joe LaPointe, "The Championship Fight That Went Beyond Boxing," *New York Times*, June 19, 1988.

20. Donald Worster, *Dust Bowl: The Southern Plains in the 1930s* (New York: Oxford University Press, 1979).

21. Michael Johnson Grant, *Down and Out on the Family Farm* (Lincoln: University of Nebraska Press, 2002), 72.

22. Timothy Egan, *The Worst Hard Time* (Boston: Houghton Mifflin, 2006), 256.

23. Jack Hurley, *Portrait of a Decade: Roy Stryker and the Development of Documentary Photography in the 1930s* (Baton Rouge: Louisiana State University Press, 1973), 90.

24. John Steinbeck, *The Grapes of Wrath* (New York: Penguin, 1992), 572.

25. John Steinbeck, *Working Days: The Journals of* The Grapes of Wrath, ed. Robert DeMott (New York: Penguin, 1989), xxxix, 105; Eleanor Roosevelt in T. H. Watkins, *The Hungry Years: A Narrative History of the Great Depression in America* (New York: Henry Holt, 1999), 456; Louis Kronenberger, "Hungry Caravan," *The Nation*, April 14, 1939, 441.

26. Franklin D. Roosevelt, "Address Accepting the Presidential Nomination at the Democratic National Convention in Chicago," July 2, 1932, American Presidency Project, https://www.presidency.ucsb.edu/node/275484.

27. Franklin D. Roosevelt, "Fireside Chat on Banking," March 12, 1933, American Presidency Project, https://www.presidency.ucsb.edu/node/207762.

28. Hopkins quoted in David Kennedy, *Freedom from Fear: The American People in Depression and War, 1929–1945* (New York: Oxford University Press, 1999), 167.

29. Kennedy, *Freedom from Fear*, 205.

30. Harold Ickes, *The Secret Diary of Harold L. Ickes: The First Thousand Days, 1933–1936* (New York: Simon & Schuster, 1953), 1:195.

31. Lippmann quoted in Richard D. White Jr., *Kingfish: The Reign of Huey P. Long* (New York: Random House, 2006), 197.

32. Alan Brinkley, *Voices of Protest: Huey Long, Father Coughlin and the Great Depression* (New York: Vintage, 1982), 92.

33. Ickes, *Secret Diary*, 2:246.

34. Franklin D. Roosevelt, "Fireside Chat," September 3, 1939, American Presidency Project, https://www.presidency.ucsb.edu/node/209990.

35. "Do You Want War?" *The Survey* 74 (1938): 179.

36. Kennedy, *Freedom from Fear*, 433; Roosevelt quoted in A. J. Baime, *The Arsenal of Democracy* (Boston: Houghton Mifflin, 2014), 104.

37. Franklin D. Roosevelt, "Campaign Address at Boston, Massachusetts," October 30, 1940, American Presidency Project, https://www.presidency.ucsb.edu/node/209314; "Fireside Chat," December 29, 1940, American Presidency Project, https://www.presidency.ucsb.edu/node/209416.

38. Franklin D. Roosevelt, "Annual Message to Congress on the State of the Union," January 6, 1941, American Presidency Project, https://www.presidency.ucsb.edu/node/209473.

39. Franklin D. Roosevelt, "Address to Congress Requesting a Declaration of War with Japan," December 8, 1941, American Presidency Project, https://www.presidency.ucsb.edu/node/210408.

40. Kennedy, *Freedom From Fear*, 753.

41. John Morton Blum, *V Was for Victory: Politics and American Culture during World War II* (San Diego: Harcourt Brace, 1976), 194–195.

42. George Roeder, *The Censored War: American Visual Experience During World War II* (New Haven: Yale University Press, 1993), 14.

43. "The Pro Who Shadowed Eisenhower's Career," *New York Times*, July 19, 2014.

44. Winston S. Churchill, " 'The Iron Curtain Begins to Fall (Final Review of the War),' August 16, 1945," in Robert Rhodes James, ed., *Winston S. Churchill: His Complete Speeches 1897– 1963* (London: Chelsea House, 1974), 7:7209–7219.

CHAPTER 9

1. Jonathan Eig, *Ali: A Life* (Boston: Houghton Mifflin, 2017), xv.

2. See James T. Patterson, *Grand Expectations: The United States, 1945–1974* (New York: Oxford University Press, 1996).

3. Suzanne Mettler, *Soldiers to Citizens: The G.I. Bill and the Making of the Greatest Generation* (New York: Oxford University Press, 2005).

4. Malcolm Gladwell, "The Terrazo Jungle," *New Yorker*, March 15, 2004, 121.

5. Herbert Gans, *The Levittowners: Ways of Life and Politics in a New Suburban Community* (New York: Columbia University Press, 1982), 417.

6. Michael Bechsloss, "Eisenhower, an Unlikely Pioneer of TV Ads," *New York Times*, October 30, 2015.

7. Nancy Gibbs, *The Preacher and the Presidents: Billy Graham in the White House* (New York: Center Street, 2007); Merle Miller, *Plain Speaking: An Oral Biography of Harry Truman* (New York: Black Dog and Leventhal, 2005), 320.

8. Michael Harrington, *The Other America: Poverty in the United States* (New York: Simon & Schuster, 1993), 18.

9. Arthur Miller, *Death of a Salesman* (New York: Viking, 1977), 18.

10. Glenn C. Altschuler, *All Shook Up: How Rock 'n' Roll Changed America* (New York: Oxford University Press, 2004), 6.

11. Peter Guralnick, *Last Train to Memphis: The Rise of Elvis Presley* (New York: Little Brown, 1994), 171.

12. Jon Weiner, "Elvis Presley: America's Secret Weapon in the Cold War," *Daily Beast*, October 14, 2012, https://www.thedailybeast.com/elvis-presley-americas-secret-weapon-in-the-cold-war.

13. Baruch quoted in John J. Tierney Jr., *Conceived in Liberty: The American Worldview in Theory and Practice* (Abingdon, UK: Routledge, 2017), 105; Harry Truman, "Address Before a Joint Session of Congress," March 12, 1947, Avalon Project, http://avalon.law.yale.edu/20th_century/trudoc.asp.

14. John Lewis Gaddis, *George F. Kennan: An American Life* (New York: Penguin, 2012), 260.

15. David Halberstam, *The Coldest Winter: America and the Korean War* (New York: Hachette, 2008), 1.

16. David Halberstam, *The Fifties* (New York: Random House, 1993), 69; Douglas MacArthur, "Farewell Address to Congress, April 19, 1951," American Rhetoric, http://www.americanrhetoric.com/speeches/douglasmacarthurfarewelladdress.htm.

17. Paul Boyer, *By the Bomb's Early Light: American Thought and Culture at the Dawn of the Atomic Age* (New York: Pantheon, 1985).

18. Halberstam, *The Fifties*, 51. On McCarthy see David Oshinsky, *A Conspiracy So Immense: The World of Joseph McCarthy* (New York: Oxford University Press, 2005).

19. John F. Kennedy, "Address Accepting the Democratic Party Nomination, July 15, 1960," in Gerhard Peters and John T. Woolley, eds., American Presidency Project, University of California–Santa Barbara, https://www.presidency.ucsb.edu/node/274679.

20. Andrew Glass, "JFK and Khruschev Meet in Vienna, June 3, 1961," *Politico*, June 2, 2017, https://www.politico.com/story/2017/06/02/jfk-and-khrushchev-meet-in-vienna-june-3-1961-238979.

21. *Life*, October 7, 1954, 34; *Time*, October 14, 1954, 19; John F. Kennedy, "Speech at Houston, Texas, September 12, 1962," NASA, https://er.jsc.nasa.gov/seh/ricetalk.htm.

22. "Negroes Are Americans," *Life*, August 1, 1949, 22.

23. *New York Times*, May 18, 1954, in Waldo E. Martin Jr., ed., *Brown v. Board of Education: A Brief History with Documents* (Boston: Bedford Books, 1998), 201.

24. Frankfurter quoted in Richard Kluger, *Simple Justice: The History of Brown v. Board of Education and Black America's Struggle for Equality* (New York: Vintage, 2004), 659.

25. *Daily News* (Jackson, Mississippi) quoted in Martin, *Brown v. Board of Education*, 204.

26. Martin Luther King Jr., quoted in Clayborne Carson et al., eds., *The Eyes on the Prize Civil Rights Reader* (New York: Penguin, 1991), 224.

27. Carson, *Eyes on the Prize*, 49.

28. Farmer quoted in Raymond Arsenault, *Freedom Riders: 1961 and the Struggle for Racial Justice* (New York: Oxford University Press, 2011), 167.

29. Steven R. Weisman, ed., *Daniel Patrick Moynihan: A Portrait in Letters of an American Visionary* (New York: Public Affairs, 2010), 70.

30. Russell quoted in Lillian Smith, *Killers of the Dream* (New York: W. W. Norton, 1978), 78; Robert Dallek, *Lyndon Johnson: Portrait of a President* (New York: Oxford University Press, 2005), 170.

31. David Howard-Pitney, ed., *Martin Luther King, Jr., Malcolm X, and the Civil Rights Struggle of the 1950s and 1960s* (Boston: Bedford Books, 2004), 104–107.

32. James Reston, "I Have a Dream," *New York Times*, August 29, 1963.

33. Howard-Pitney, *Martin Luther King*, 73 and passim.

34. Howard-Pitney, *Martin Luther King*, 102.

35. Howard-Pitney, *Martin Luther King*, 126.

36. Tom Wolfe, "Radical Chic: That Party at Lenny's," *New York Magazine*, June 8, 1970.

37. "The Port Huron Statement," in *The Port Huron Statement: Sources and Legacies of the New Left's Founding Manifesto*, ed. Richard Flacks and Nelson Lichtenstein (Philadelphia: University of Pennsylvania Press, 2015), 239–294.

38. "Dr. King's Telegram to Cesar Chavez during his 1968 Fast for Nonviolence," United Farm Workers website, https://ufw.org/dr-kings-telegram-to-cesar-chavez-during-his-1968-fast-for-nonviolence/.

39. Nixon quoted in Bill Minutaglio and Steven L. Davis, *The Most Dangerous Man in America: Timothy Leary, Richard Nixon and the Hunt for the Fugitive King of LSD* (New York: Twelve, 2018).

40. *Life*, October 17, 1969, 77.

41. Savio quoted in Robert Cohen, *Freedom's Orator: Mario Savio and the Radical Legacy of the 1960s* (New York: Oxford University Press, 2009), 3.

42. Larry Gross and James D. Woods, eds., *The Columbia Reader on Lesbians and Gay Men in Media, Society, and Politics* (New York: Columbia University Press, 1999), 360.

43. John M. Newman, *JFK and Vietnam* (New York: Grand Central Publishing, 1992), 487; Dwight D. Eisenhower, News Conference, April 7, 1954, American Presidency Project, University of California–Santa Barbara, https://www.presidency.ucsb.edu/node/233655.

44. Stanley Karnow, *Vietnam: A History* (New York: Penguin, 1997), 258.

45. Robert D. Schulzinger, *A Time for War: The United States and Vietnam, 1941–1975* (New York: Oxford University Press, 1997), 151.

46. Karnow, *Vietnam*, 391; Howard-Pitney, *Martin Luther King*, 141.

47. Katie Mettler, "The Day Anti-Vietnam Protesters Tried to Levitate the Pentagon," *Washington Post*, October 19, 2017; Douglas Coupland, *Marshall McLuhan: You Know Nothing of My Work* (New York: Atlas, 2010), 159.

48. Mark K. Updegrove, "Lyndon Johnson's Vietnam," *New York Times*, February 24, 2017, https://www.nytimes.com/2017/02/24/opinion/lyndon-johnsons-vietnam.html; Mark Bowden, "When Walter Cronkite Pronounced the War a 'Stalemate,'" *New York Times*, February 26, 2018, https://www.nytimes.com/2018/02/26/opinion/walter-cronkite-war-stalemate.html.

49. Nixon quoted in Karnow, *Vietnam*, 592.

50. Donald Kirk, "Who Wants to be the Last American Killed in Vietnam," *New York Times*, September 19, 1971.

51. George McGovern, "Address Accepting Nomination, July 14, 1972," American Presidency Project, University of California–Santa Barbara, https://www.presidency.ucsb.edu/node/216662.

CHAPTER 10

1. Emily Nussbaum, "The Great Divide: Norman Lear, Archie Bunker, and the Rise of Great Fun," *New Yorker*, April 7, 2014.

2. "*New York Times v. United States*," Oyez, https://www.oyez.org/cases/1970/1873.

3. Stanley Kutler, ed., *Abuse of Power: The New Nixon Tapes* (New York: Free Press, 1997), 473.

4. "Transcript of a Recording of a Meeting between the President and H. R. Haldeman in the Oval Office on June 23, 1972 from 10:04 to 11:39 AM," nixonlibrary.gov, https://www.nixonlibrary.gov/sites/default/files/forresearchers/find/tapes/watergate/trial/exhibit_01.pdf.

5. Baker quoted in Stanley Kutler, *The Wars of Watergate: The Last Crisis of Richard Nixon* (New York: W. W. Norton, 1990), 361.

6. "President Refuses to Turn Over Tapes," *Washington Post*, July 24, 1973; John A. Farrell, *Richard Nixon: The Life* (New York: Doubleday, 2017), 524.

7. Douglas Brinkley and Luke Nichter, eds., *The Nixon Tapes: 1973* (New York: Houghton Mifflin 2015), 275.

8. Richard Nixon's Resignation Speech, August 8, 1974, PBS, https://www.pbs.org/newshour/spc/character/links/nixon_speech.html.

9. Kissinger quoted in Farrell, *Richard Nixon*, 407.

10. "The Failure of Mr. Ford," *New York Times*, September 9, 1974.

11. Nixon quoted in Robert M. Collins, *More: The Politics of Economic Growth in Postwar America* (New York: Oxford University Press, 2000), 112.

12. Rick Perlstein, ed., *Richard Nixon: Speeches, Writings, Documents* (Princeton, NJ: Princeton University Press, 2008), 217–223.

13. Meg Jacobs, *Panic at the Pump: The Energy Crisis and the Transformation of American Politics in the 1970s* (New York: Hill & Wang, 2016), 221.

14. Edward Berkowitz, *Something Happened: A Political and Cultural Overview of the 1970s* (New York: Columbia University Press, 2006), 100.

15. Jimmy Carter, Speech on Energy and National Goals, July 15, 1979, Jimmy Carter Library, https://www.jimmycarterlibrary.gov/assets/documents/speeches/energy-crisis.phtml; Lou Cannon, *Governor Reagan: His Rise to Power* (New York: Public Affairs, 2003), 509.

16. Kiron K. Skinner, Annalise Anderson, and Martin Anderson, eds., *Reagan: A Life in Letters* (New York: Free Press, 2003), 705; Henry Olsen, "How the Right Gets Reagan Wrong," *Politico*, June 26, 2017.

17. Ronald Reagan, "A Vision for America, Speech Delivered November 3, 1980," Ronald Reagan Library, https://www.reaganlibrary.gov/11-3-80.

18. Reagan quoted in Del Quentin Wilbur, *Rawhide Down: The Near Assassination of Ronald Reagan* (New York: Henry Holt, 2011), 120.

19. Ronald Reagan, Inaugural Address, January 20, 1981, Ronald Reagan Library, https://www.reaganlibrary.gov/research/speeches/inaugural-address-january-20-1981.

20. Godfrey Hodgson, *The World Turned Right Side Up: A History of the Conservative Ascendency in America* (Boston: Houghton Mifflin, 1996), 186–215.

21. John Kenneth Galbraith, "Recession Economics," *New York Review of Books*, February 4, 1982.

22. David Kurtz, "Goldwater's 'Eastern Seaboard' Comment," Talking Points Memo, posted September 19, 2012, https://talkingpointsmemo.com/edblog/goldwater-s-eastern-seaboard-comment; "Barry Goldwater, GOP Hero, Dies," *Washington Post*, May 30, 1998; Barry Goldwater, *The Conscience of a Conservative* (Shepherdsville, KY: Victor, 1960), 3.

23. Carl T. Bogus, *Buckley: William F. Buckley and the Rise of American Conservatism* (New York: Bloomsbury, 2011), 141.

24. Lionel Trilling, *The Liberal Imagination* (New York: New York Review of Books, 2008), xv.

25. Peter Applebome, "Jerry Falwell, Leading US Religious Conservative, Dies at 73," *New York Times*, May 15, 2007.

26. Robertson quoted in Frances Fitzgerald, *The Evangelicals: The Struggle to Shape America* (New York: Simon & Schuster, 2018), 424–425.

27. Ronald Reagan, "Address Before a Joint Session of Congress on the State of the Union," February 4, 1986, in Gerhard Peters and John T. Woolley, eds., The American Presidency Project, University of California–Santa Barbara, https://www.presidency.ucsb.edu/documents/address-before-joint-session-congress-the-state-the-union.

28. Clyde Haberman, "Phyllis Schlafly's Lasting Legacy in Defeating the ERA," *New York Times*, September 11, 2016.

29. Clarence Page, "The Rise and Fall of Jerry Falwell," *Chicago Tribune*, May 20, 2007. Also see Randy Shilts, *And the Band Played On: Politics, People, and the AIDS Epidemic* (New York: St. Martin's, 1987); Barry Goldwater, "The Gay Ban: Just Plain Un-American," *Washington Post*, June 10, 1993.

30. Michael Kelly, "The 1992 Campaign," *New York Times*, October 31, 1992.

31. William J. Clinton, "Address Accepting the Presidential Nomination at the Democratic National Convention in New York," July 16, 1992, American Presidency Project, https://www.presidency.ucsb.edu/documents/address-accepting-the-presidential-nomination-the-democratic-national-convention-new-york; William J. Clinton, "Inaugural Address," January 20, 1993, American Presidency Project, https://www.presidency.ucsb.edu/documents/inaugural-address-51.

32. Howard Kurtz, "Company for 'Harry and Louise' in Debate on Health Care Reform," *Washington Post*, February 13, 1994.

33. William J. Clinton, "Address Before a Joint Session of Congress on the State of the Union," January 23, 1996, American Presidency Project, https://www.presidency.ucsb.edu/documents/address-before-joint-session-the-congress-the-state-the-union-10; "Unions are Split on Backing Clinton," *New York Times*, March 15, 1992.

34. William J. Clinton, "Statement on Signing the Personal Responsibility and Work Opportunity Reconciliation Act," August 22, 1996, American Presidency Project, https://www.presidency.ucsb.edu/documents/statement-signing-the-personal-responsibility-and-work-opportunity-reconciliation-act-1996; Ronald Reagan, "Announcement on Candidacy for California Governor," January 4, 1966, American Rhetoric, https://www.americanrhetoric.com/speeches/ronaldreagancalgovcandidacy.htm.

35. Clinton quoted in Michelle Alexander, *The New Jim Crow: Mass Incarceration in the Age of Colorblindness* (New York: New Press, 2012), 56.

36. Donna Murch, "The Clintons' War on Drugs: When Black Lives Didn't Matter," *New Republic*, February 9, 2016.

37. Lily Rothman, "Why Bill Clinton Signed the Welfare Reform Bill," *Time*, August 19, 2016; "Text of President Clinton's Announcement on Welfare Legislation," *New York Times*, August 1, 1996.

38. "The Starr Report—Part Eight of Thirteen," *New York Times*, September 12, 1998; Peter Baker and Helen Dewar, "The Senate Acquits President Clinton," *Washington Post*, February 13, 1999.

39. Elaine Sciolino, "Dole's View of the World: Complex and Idiosyncratic," *New York Times*, September 21, 1996; Robert S. Litwack, "A Look At . . . Rogue States," *Washington Post*, February 20, 2000.

40. Kambiz Fattahi, "Two Weeks in January: America's Secret Engagement with Khomeini," *BBC News*, June 3, 2016, https://www.bbc.com/news/world-us-canada-36431160.

41. Reagan quoted in George C. Herring, *The American Century and Beyond: U.S. Foreign Relations, 1893–2014* (New York: Oxford University Press, 2017), 573.

42. "Reagan Blasts Terrorist States," *Chicago Tribune*, July 9, 1985.

43. "Reagan Vows Firm Backing for Contras," *Washington Post*, January 5, 1986.

44. H. W. Brands, *Reagan: The Life* (New York: Anchor, 2016), 410.

45. George H. W. Bush, "End of the Soviet Union, Text of Bush's Address to the Nation on the Resignation of Gorbachev," *New York Times*, December 26, 1991.

46. George H. W. Bush, "After the War: The President, Transcript of President Bush's Address on End of Gulf War," *New York Times*, March 7, 1991.

47. "Statement of Dale Watson," Congressional Hearings on Intelligence and Security, February 24, 1998, https://fas.org/irp/congress/1998_hr/s980224w.htm.

48. William J. Clinton, "Remarks at Time for Healing Ceremony, April 23, 1995," Miller Center, University of Virginia, https://millercenter.org/the-presidency/presidential-speeches/april-23-1995-time-healing-ceremony.

CHAPTER 11

1. "Republican Report on Katrina Assails Administration Response," *New York Times*, February 13, 2006, https://www.nytimes.com/2006/02/13/politics/republicans-report-on-katrina-assails-administration-response.html; Barack Obama, "Remarks by President in State of the Union Address, January 20, 2015," Obama White House, https://obamawhitehouse.

archives.gov/the-press-office/2015/01/20/remarks-president-state-union-address-January-20-2015; "'I Don't Know That It's Man-Made,' Trump Says of Climate Change. It Is," *New York Times*, October 15, 2018, https://www.nytimes.com/2018/10/15/climate/trump-climate-change-fact-check.html.

2. David Friend, *Watching the World Change: The Stories Behind the Images of 9/11* (New York: Farrar, Straus, & Giroux, 2006), 36; "After the Attacks," *New York Times*, September 16, 2001, https://www.nytimes.com/2001/09/16/us/after-attacks-events-four-days-national-crisis-changes-bush-s-presidency.html; "Text of Bush's Address, September 11, 2001," CNN, http://edition.cnn.com/2001/US/09/11/bush.speech.text/.

3. Hannah Rosin, "Bush's 'Christ Moment' is Put to Political Test by Christians," *Washington Post*, December 16, 1999; "Transcript of George W. Bush's Acceptance Speech," ABC News, August 3, 2000, https://abcnews.go.com/Politics/story?id=123214&page=1.

4. "Text of Gore's Concession Speech," *New York Times*, December 13, 2000, https://www.nytimes.com/2000/12/13/politics/text-of-goreacutes-concession-speech.html.

5. "*Bush v. Gore*." Oyez, December 27, 2018, www.oyez.org/cases/2000/00-949.

6. "Transcript of President Bush's Address," CNN, September 21, 2001, http://www.cnn.com/2001/US/09/20/gen.bush.transcript/.

7. "Bullhorn Address to Ground Zero Rescue Workers, September 14, 2001," American Rhetoric, https://www.americanrhetoric.com/speeches/gwbush911groundzerobullhorn.htm; Caitlin McDevitt, "Bush's Most 'Nervous Moment,'" *Politico*, September 12, 2011, https://www.politico.com/blogs/click/2011/09/bushs-most-nervous-moment-039104.

8. "Text of President Bush's 2002 State of the Union Address," *Washington Post*, January 29, 2002, http://www.washingtonpost.com/wp-srv/onpolitics/transcripts/sou012902.htm; "Transcript: Obama's Speech Against the Iraq War," NPR, January 20, 2009, https://www.npr.org/templates/story/story.php?storyId=99591469

9. Dexter Filkins, "In Falluja, Young Marines Saw the Savagery of an Urban War," *New York Times*, November 21, 2004, https://www.nytimes.com/2004/11/21/world/middleeast/in-falluja-young-marines-saw-the-savagery-of-an-urban-war.html. See Dexter Filkins, *The Forever War* (New York: Vintage, 2008).

10. Seymour M. Hersh, "Torture at Abu Ghraib," *New Yorker*, May 10, 2004, https://www.newyorker.com/magazine/2004/05/10/torture-at-abu-ghraib.

11. Walter Isaacson, *Steve Jobs* (New York: Simon & Schuster, 2011), 80.

12. Robert Epstein, "How Google Could Rig the 2016 Election," *Politico*, August 19, 2015, https://www.politico.com/magazine/story/2015/08/how-google-could-rig-the-2016-election-121548.

13. Jennifer Calfas, "Sen. Bernie Sanders Introduces 'Stop Bezos' Bill to Target Corporations with Low-Wage Employees," *Time*, September 6, 2018, http://time.com/5388085/bernie-sanders-stop-bezos-bill/.

14. Juliet Eilperin, "Obama in Athens: 'The Current Path of Globalization Needs a Course Correction,'" *Washington Post*, November 16, 2016, https://www.washingtonpost.com/news/post-politics/wp/2016/11/16/obama-in-athens-the-current-path-of-globalization-needs-a-course-correction/?utm_term=.676f975dd5f4; Zachary A. Goldfarb, "Obama Focuses Agenda on Relieving Economic Inequality," *Washington Post*, December 4, 2013, https://www.washingtonpost.com/politics/obama-focuses-agenda-on-relieving-economic-inequality/2013/12/04/bef286ac-5cfc-11e3-be07-006c776266ed_story.html?utm_term=.a769ebcad621.

15. "Transcript: Illinois Senate Candidate Barack Obama," *Washington Post*, July 27, 2004, http://www.washingtonpost.com/wp-dyn/articles/A19751-2004Jul27.html. See Mark Leibovich, "The Speech that Made Obama," *New York Times*, July 27, 2016, https://www.nytimes.com/2016/07/27/magazine/the-speech-that-made-obama.html.

16. David Bernstein, "The Speech," *Chicago Magazine*, May 29, 2007, https://www.chicagomag.com/Chicago-Magazine/June-2007/The-Speech/.

17. "Barack Obama's Feb. 5 Speech," *New York Times*, February 5, 2008, https://www.nytimes.com/2008/02/05/us/politics/05text-obama.html.

18. "Full Transcript: Sen. Barack Obama's Victory Speech," ABC News, November 4, 2008, https://abcnews.go.com/Politics/Vote2008/story?id=6181477&page=1.

19. David M. Herszenhorn, "Congressional Leaders Stunned by Warnings," *New York Times*, September 19, 2006, https://www.nytimes.com/2008/09/20/washington/19cnd-cong.html.

20. Peter Weber, "How the Rich Won the Great Recession," *The Week*, September 11, 2013, https://theweek.com/articles/460179/charts-how-rich-won-great-recession.

21. Michael Levitin, "The Triumph of Occupy Wall Street," *The Atlantic*, June 10, 2015, https://www.theatlantic.com/politics/archive/2015/06/the-triumph-of-occupy-wall-street/395408/; Anne Gearan, "Clinton to Middle Class: 'Deck is Stacked' to Favor the Top," *Washington Post*, August 19, 2015, https://www.washingtonpost.com/news/post-politics/wp/2015/08/19/clinton-to-middle-class-deck-is-stacked-to-favor-the-top/?utm_term=.8a3f565a64e1.

22. "CNBC's Rick Santelli Chicago Tea Party," Heritage Foundation, February 19, 2009, https://www.youtube.com/watch?v=zp-Jw-5Kx8k; Don Gonyea, "'How's that Hopey, Changey Stuff,' Palin Asks," NPR, February 7, 2010, https://www.npr.org/templates/story/story.php?storyId=123462728; "Was It Really a Tea Party Tidal Wave?" *The Week*, November 3, 2010, https://theweek.com/articles/489660/really-tea-party-tidal-wave. See Robb Willer, Matthew Feinberg, and Rachel Wetts, "Threats to Racial Status Promote Tea Party Support Among White Americans," Working Paper no. 3422, Stanford Graduate School of Business, May 4, 2016, https://www.gsb.stanford.edu/faculty-research/working-papers/threats-racial-status-promote-tea-party-support-among-white.

23. Michael Grunwald, "The Victory of No," *Politico*, December 4, 2016, https://www.politico.com/magazine/story/2016/12/republican-party-obstructionism-victory-trump-214498.

24. Sheryl Gay Stolberg and Robert Pear, "Obama Signs Health Care Overhaul Bill, With a Flourish," *New York Times*, March 23, 2010, https://www.nytimes.com/2010/03/24/health/policy/24health.html.

25. "Remarks by the President on the Affordable Care Act," Miami, Florida, October 20, 2016, Obama White House, https://obamawhitehouse.archives.gov/the-press-office/2016/10/20/remarks-president-affordable-care-act.

26. "*Obergefell v. Hodges*," Oyez, December 27, 2018, www.oyez.org/cases/2014/14-556.

27. Krissah Thompson and Scott Wilson, "Obama on Trayvon Martin: 'If I had a son, he'd look like Trayvon," *Washington Post*, March 23, 2012, https://www.washingtonpost.com/politics/obama-if-i-had-a-son-hed-look-like-trayvon/2012/03/23/gIQApKPpVS_story.html?utm_term=.bc25e41d27d9.

28. Amy B. Wang and Rachel Siegel, "Trump: Nike 'Getting Absolutely Killed' with Boycotts over Colin Kaepernick's 'Just Do It' Campaign," *Washington Post*, September 5, 2018, https://www.washingtonpost.com/business/2018/09/04/people-are-destroying-their-nike-gear-protest-colin-kaepernicks-just-do-it-campaign/?utm_term=.c7a531cafbac.

29. Nick Corasaniti, Richard Perez-Pena, and Lizette Alvarez, "Church Massacre Suspect Held as Charleston Grieves," *New York Times*, June 18, 2015, https://www.nytimes.com/2015/06/19/us/charleston-church-shooting.html.

30. "Mitch Landrieu's Speech on the Removal of Confederate Monuments," *New York Times*, May 23, 2017, https://www.nytimes.com/2017/05/23/opinion/mitch-landrieus-speech-transcript.html.

31. Frederic Lemieux, "6 Things to Know about Mass Shootings in America," *Scientific American*, June 13, 2016, https://www.scientificamerican.com/article/6-things-to-know-about-mass-shootings-in-america/.

32. Sarah Todd, "The Astonishing Power of Stoneman Douglas Students, in their own words," *Quartz*, February 21, 2018, https://qz.com/1212712/florida-shooting-stoneman-douglas-student-quotes-after-the-high-school-attack/.

33. "Statement by FBI Director James B. Comey on the Investigation of Secretary Hillary Clinton's Use of a Personal E-Mail System," Federal Bureau of Investigation, July 5, 2016, https://www.fbi.gov/news/pressrel/press-releases/statement-by-fbi-director-

james-b-comey-on-the-investigation-of-secretary-hillary-clinton2019s-use-of-a-personal-e-mail-system.

34. Ian Schwartz, "Anderson Cooper vs. Hillary Clinton on Flip Flops: 'Will You Say Anything to get Elected,'" *Real Clear Politics*, October 13, 2015, https://www.realclearpolitics.com/video/2015/10/13/anderson_cooper_confronts_hillary_clinton_on_flip-flops_will_you_say_anything_to_get_elected.html.

35. Veronica Srtracqualursi, "Bernie Sanders on Climate Change Report: 'The Future of the Planet is at Stake,'" CNN, November 27, 2018, https://www.cnn.com/2018/11/27/politics/bernie-sanders-climate-change-report-cnntv/index.html; Michael Berry, "Bill McKibben Talks about 'Falter,'" Sierra Club, May 9, 2019, https://www.sierraclub.org/sierra/bill-mckibben-talks-about-falter.

36. "The Transcript of Bernie Sanders' Victory Speech," *Washington Post*, February 10, 2016, https://www.washingtonpost.com/news/post-politics/wp/2016/02/10/the-transcript-of-bernie-sanderss-victory-speech/?utm_term=.0984caf37e3a.

37. "Donald Trump's Presidential Announcement Speech," *Time*, June 16, 2015, http://time.com/3923128/donald-trump-announcement-speech/.

38. Amy Chozick, "Hillary Clinton Blames F.B.I. Director for Election Loss," *New York Times*, November 12, 2016, https://www.nytimes.com/2016/11/13/us/politics/hillary-clinton-james-comey.html; Nate Silver, "The Comey Letter Probably Cost Clinton the Election," *Fivethirtyeight*, May 3, 2017, https://fivethirtyeight.com/features/the-comey-letter-probably-cost-clinton-the-election/.

39. Maggie Severns, "Trump Pins AFTA, 'Worst Trade Deal Ever,' on Clinton," *Politico*, September 26, 2016, https://www.politico.com/story/2016/09/trump-clinton-come-out-swinging-over-nafta-228712; Alan Rappeport, "Trump, Self-Styled 'Tariff Man,' Issues China a Warning," *New York Times*, December 4, 2018, https://www.nytimes.com/2018/12/04/us/politics/trump-tariff-man-china-trade.html.

40. Thomas L. Friedman, "Time for G.O.P. to Threaten to Fire Trump," *New York Times*, December 26, 2018, https://www.nytimes.com/2018/12/24/opinion/impeach-fire-president-trump.html.

41. Philip Rucker, "'I Am All Alone': An Isolated Trump Unleashes a Storm of Yuletide Gloom," *Washington Post*, December 24, 2018, https://www.washingtonpost.com/politics/i-am-all-alone-an-isolated-trump-unleashes-a-storm-of-yuletide-gloom/2018/12/24/382fdd88-07a4-11e9-a3f0-71c95106d96a_story.html?utm_term=.3abd9307e2cc.

42. See Gabriel Sherman, *The Loudest Voice in the Room* (New York: Random House, 2017).

43. Todd Purdum, "Prisoner of Conscience," *Vanity Fair*, January 3, 2007, https://www.vanityfair.com/news/2007/02/mccain200702; "Read Senator John McCain's Farewell Statement," *New York Times*, August 27, 2018, https://www.nytimes.com/2018/08/27/us/politics/john-mccain-farewell-statement.html.

EPILOGUE

1. Arnold Rampersand, ed., *The Collected Poems of Langston Hughes* (New York: Vintage, 1995), 23. See Arnold Rampersand, *The Life of Langston Hughes: I, Too, Sing America, Volume 1: 1902–1941* (New York: Oxford University Press, 2002).

2. Rampersand, *Collected Poems*, 189–191. See, for example, Roger Cohen, "America Never Was, Yet Will Be," *New York Times*, July 6, 2018, and Paul Rosenberg, "Langston Hughes Saw Donald Trump Coming: 'Let America Be America Again' vs. MAGA," *Salon*, February 12, 2017, https://www.salon.com/2017/02/12/langston-hughes-saw-donald-trump-coming-let-america-be-america-again-vs-maga/. In 2004, John Kerry's presidential campaign used Hughes's slogan, which led one writer to offer a critique of the poem. See Timothy Noah, "America Already Is America: The Stalinist Roots of John Kerry's New Slogan," *Slate*, June 1, 2004, https://slate.com/news-and-politics/2004/06/america-already-is-america.html.

3. Rampersand, *Collected Poems*, 426; "Martin Luther King, Jr.'s 'A Christmas Sermon on Peace' Still Prophetic Fifty Years Later," Beacon Broadside, https://www.beaconbroadside.com/broadside/2017/12/martin-luther-king-jrs-christmas-sermon-

peace-still-prophetic-50-years-later.html. Also see King's sermon "Shattered Dreams," first preached in 1959, and draft from 1962–63 in the Martin Luther King Jr. Papers Project, http://okra.stanford.edu/transcription/document_images/Vol06Scans/July1962-March1963DraftofChapterX,ShatteredDreams.pdf. On King's relationship with Hughes see Jason Miller, "In His Speeches, MLK Carefully Evoked the Poetry of Langston Hughes," *Smithsonian*, April 3, 2018, https://www.smithsonianmag.com/history/in-his-speeches-MLK-carefully-evoked-poetry-langston-hughes-180968655/.

4. Martin Luther King Jr., "Transformed Noncomformist," Martin Luther King Jr. Papers Project, November 1954, http://okra.stanford.edu/transcription/document_images/Vol06Scans/Nov1954TransformedNonconformist.pdf.

FURTHER READING

CHAPTER 1

Anderson, Fred. *The Crucible of War: The Seven Years' War and the Fate of Empire in British North America, 1754–1766*. New York: Vintage, 2001.

Berlin, Ira. *Many Thousands Gone: The First Two Centuries of Slavery in North America*. Cambridge, MA: Harvard University Press, 1998.

Brooks, Lisa. *Our Beloved Kin: A New History of King Phillip's War*. New Haven: Yale University Press, 2018.

Cronon, William. *Changes in the Land: Indians, Colonists, and the Ecology of New England*. New York: Hill & Wang, 2003.

Demos, John. *Entertaining Satan: Witchcraft and the Culture of Early New England*. New York: Oxford University Press, 2004.

Demos, John. *The Unredeemed Captive: A Family Story from Early America*. New York: Vintage, 1995.

Freeman Hawke, David. *Everyday Life in Early America*. New York: Harper & Row, 1988.

Horn, James. *A Land as God Made It: Jamestown and the Birth of America*. New York: Basic Books, 2006.

Kammen, Michael. *Colonial New York: A History*. New York: Oxford University Press, 1996.

Kupperman, Karen Ordahl. *Indians and English: Facing Off in Early America*. Ithaca, NY: Cornell University Press, 2000.

Lepore, Jill. *The Name of War: King Phillip's War and the Origins of American Identity*. New York: Vintage, 1999.

Morgan, Edmund S. *American Slavery, American Freedom*. New York: W. W. Norton, 2003.

Morgan, Edmund S. *The Puritan Dilemma: The Story of John Winthrop*. Boston: Little, Brown, 1958.

Price, David A. *Love and Hate in Jamestown: John Smith, Pocahontas, and the Start of a New Nation*. New York: Vintage, 2005.

Richter, Daniel K. *Facing East from Indian Country: A Native History of Early America*. Cambridge, MA: Harvard University Press, 2003.

Shorto, Russell. *The Island at the Center of the World: The Epic Story of Dutch Manhattan and the Forgotten Colony That Shaped America*. New York: Vintage, 2005.

Taylor, Alan. *The American Colonies: The Settling of North America*. New York: Penguin, 2002.

Warren, Wendy. *New England Bound: Slavery and Colonization in Early America*. New York: W. W. Norton, 2016.

White, Richard. *The Middle Ground: Indians, Empires, and Republics in the Great Lakes Region*. Cambridge, UK: Cambridge University Press, 1991.

CHAPTER 2

Bailyn, Bernard. *The Ideological Origins of the American Revolution* Cambridge, MA: Harvard University Press, 1967.

Borneman, Walter. *1812: The War that Forged a Nation*. New York: Harper, 2005.

Chernow, Ron. *Washington: A Life*. New York: Penguin, 2010.

Davis, David Brion. *The Problem of Slavery in the Age of Revolution, 1770–1823*. New York: Oxford University Press, 1999.

Ferling, John. *Almost a Miracle: The American Victory in the War of Independence.* New York: Oxford University Press, 2009.

Forbes, Robert Pierce. *The Missouri Compromise and Its Aftermath.* Chapel Hill: University of North Carolina Press, 2007.

Freeman, Joanne. *Affairs of Honor: National Politics in the New Republic.* New Haven: Yale University Press, 2001.

Gordon-Reed, Annette. *The Hemingses of Monticello: An American Family.* New York: W. W. Norton, 2008.

Hickey, Donald R. *The War of 1812: A Forgotten Conflict.* Champaign: University of Illinois Press, 2012.

Klarman, Michael J. *The Framer's Coup: The Making of the United States Constitution.* New York: Oxford University Press, 2014.

Maier, Pauline. *Ratification: The People Debate the Constitution, 1787–1788.* New York: Simon & Schuster, 2011.

Middlekauff, Robert. *The Glorious Cause: The American Revolution, 1763–1769.* New York: Oxford University Press, 2005.

Slaughter, Thomas P. *Independence: The Tangled Roots of the American Revolution.* New York: Hill & Wang, 2014.

Slaughter, Thomas P. *The Whiskey Rebellion: Frontier Epilogue to the American Revolution.* New York: Oxford University Press, 1986.

Taylor, Alan. *American Revolutions: A Continental History, 1750–1804.* New York: W. W. Norton, 2016.

Thatcher Ulrich, Laura. *A Midwife's Tale: The Life of Martha Ballard, Based on Her Diary, 1785–1812.* New York: Vintage, 1991.

Wood, Gordon. *Empire of Liberty: A History of the Early Republic, 1789–1815.* New York: Oxford University Press, 2009.

CHAPTER 3

Billington, Ray Allen. *The Far Western Frontier, 1830–60.* New York: Harper, 1956.

Brands, H. W. *Age of Gold: The California Gold Rush and the New American Dream.* New York: Doubleday, 2002.

Brands, H. W. *Andrew Jackson: His Life and Times.* New York: Doubleday, 2005.

Ehle, John. *Trail of Tears: The Rise and Fall of the Cherokee Nation.* New York: Anchor, 1988.

Freehling, William W. *Prelude to Civil War: The Nullification Controversy in South Carolina, 1816–1836.* New York: Oxford University Press, 1965.

Greenberg, Amy S. *A Wicked War: Polk, Clay, Lincoln and the 1846 U.S. Invasion of Mexico.* New York: Vintage, 2013.

Gura, Philip. *American Transcendentalism: A History.* New York: Hill & Wang, 2007.

Hatch, Nathan O. *The Democratization of American Christianity.* New Haven: Yale University Press, 1991.

Howe, Daniel Walker. *What Hath God Wrought: The Transformation of America, 1815–1848.* New York: Oxford University Press, 2007.

Johnson, Paul. *A Shopkeeper's Millennium: Society and Revivals in Rochester, New York, 1815–1837.* New York: Hill & Wang, 1978.

Limerick, Patricia. *The Legacy of Conquest: The Unbroken Past of the American West.* New York: W. W. Norton, 1987.

Masur, Louis P. *1831: Year of Eclipse.* New York: Hill & Wang, 2001.

McLoughlin, William. *Cherokee Renascence in the New Republic.* Princeton, NJ: Princeton University Press, 1992.

Remini, Robert V. *The Life of Andrew Jackson.* New York: Harper, 2010.

Smith, Henry Nash. *Virgin Land: The American West as Symbol and Myth.* Cambridge, MA: Harvard University Press, 1950.

Unruh, John D. Jr., *The Plains Across: The Overland Emigrants and the Trans-Mississippi West, 1840–1860.* Urbana: University of Illinois Press, 1979.

Wilentz, Sean. *The Rise of American Democracy: From Jefferson to Lincoln.* New York: W. W. Norton, 2005.

CHAPTER 4

Baptist, Edward. *The Half Has Never Been Told: Slavery and the Making of American Capitalism.* New York: Basic Books, 2014.

Blight, David. *Frederick Douglass: Prophet of Freedom.* New York: Penguin, 2018.

Bordewich, Fergus M. *America's Great Debate: Henry Clay, Stephen A. Douglas and the Compromise that Saved the Union.* New York: Simon & Schuster, 2012.

Brands, H. W. *Heirs of the Founders: The Epic Rivalry of Henry Clay, John Calhoun, and Daniel Webster, the Second Generation of American Giants.* New York: Doubleday, 2018.

Delbanco, Andrew. *The War Before the War: Fugitive Slaves and the Struggle for America's Soul from the Revolution to the Civil War.* New York: Penguin, 2018.

Etcheson, Nicole. *Bleeding Kansas: Contested Liberty in the Civil War Era.* Lawrence: University Press of Kansas, 2004.

Fehrenbacher, Don E. *The Dred Scott Case: Its Significance in American Law and Politics.* New York: Oxford University Press, 1978.

Foner, Eric. *Free Soil, Free Labor, Free Men: The Ideology of the Republican Party Before the Civil War.* New York: Oxford University Press, 1972.

Horwitz, Tony. *Midnight Rising: John Brown and the Raid that Sparked the Civil War.* New York: Henry Holt, 2011.

Johnson, Walter. *Soul by Soul: Life Inside the Antebellum Slave Market.* Cambridge, MA: Harvard University Press, 1999.

Karp, Matthew. *This Vast Southern Empire: Slaveholders at the Helm of American Foreign Policy.* Cambridge, MA: Harvard University Press, 2016.

Kolchin, Peter. *American Slavery, 1619–1877.* New York: Hill & Wang, 1993.

Potter, David. *The Impending Crisis, 1848–1861.* New York: Harper, 1976.

Reynolds, David S. *John Brown, Abolitionist: The Man Who Killed Slavery, Sparked the Civil War, and Seeded Civil Rights.* New York: Knopf, 2005.

Sinha, Manisha. *The Slave's Cause: A History of Abolition.* New Haven, CT: Yale University Press, 2016.

CHAPTER 5

Blight, David. *Race and Reunion: The Civil War in American History.* Cambridge, MA: Harvard University Press, 2002.

Curry, Stephanie. *Confederate Reckoning: Power and Politics in the Civil War South.* Cambridge, MA: Harvard University Press, 2012.

Davis, William C. *Look Away! A History of the Confederate States of America.* New York: Free Press, 2002.

Faust, Drew Gilpin. *The Republic of Suffering: Death and the American Civil War.* New York: Vintage, 2009.

Foner, Eric. *The Fiery Trial: Abraham Lincoln and American Slavery.* New York: W. W. Norton, 2011.

Foner, Eric. *Reconstruction: America's Unfinished Revolution, 1863–1877.* New York: Harper, 1988.

Goodwin, Doris Kearns. *Team of Rivals: The Political Genius of Abraham Lincoln.* New York: Simon & Schuster, 2006.

Guelzo, Allen C. *Fateful Lightning: A New History of the Civil War and Reconstruction.* New York: Oxford University Press, 2012.

Levine, Bruce. *The Fall of the House of Dixie: The Civil War and the Social Revolution that Transformed the South.* New York: Random House, 2014.

Masur, Louis P. *The Civil War: A Concise History.* New York: Oxford University Press, 2011.

McPherson, James. *Battle Cry of Freedom: The Civil War Era.* New York: Oxford University Press, 1988.

Murray, Williamson, and Wayne Wei-Siang Hseih. *A Savage War: A Military History of the Civil War.* Princeton, NJ: Princeton University Press, 2016.

Oakes, James. *Freedom National: The Destruction of Slavery in the United States, 1861–1865.* New York: W. W. Norton, 2012.

Richardson, Heather Cox. *West from Appomattox: The Reconstruction of America After the Civil War.* New Haven, CT: Yale University Press, 2008.

Varon, Elizabeth. *Armies of Deliverance: A New History of the Civil War.* New York: Oxford University Press, 2019.

White, Ronald C. *A. Lincoln: A Biography.* New York: Random House, 2010.

CHAPTER 6

Brands, H. W. *American Colossus: The Age of Capitalism, 1865–1900.* New York: Anchor, 2011.

Cozzens, Peter. *The Earth Is Weeping: The Epic Story of the Indian Wars for the American West.* New York: Vintage, 2017.

Cronon, William. *Nature's Metropolis: Chicago and the Great West.* New York: W. W. Norton, 1992.

Green, James. *Death in the Haymarket.* New York: Anchor, 2007.

Jacobson, Matthew Frye. *Barbarian Virtues: The United States Encounters Foreign Peoples at Home and Abroad.* New York: Hill & Wang, 2001.

Kinzer, Stephen. *The True Flag: Theodore Roosevelt, Mark Twain, and the Birth of American Empire.* New York: St. Martin's, 2017.

Lears, T. J. Jackson. *Rebirth of a Nation: The Making of Modern America, 1877–1920.* New York: Harper, 2009.

Litwack, Leon. *Been in the Storm So Long: The Aftermath of Slavery.* New York: Vintage, 1980.

McMath, Robert C. *American Populism: A Social History, 1877–1898.* New York: Hill & Wang, 1993.

Morris, Charles R. *The Tycoons.* New York: Holt, 2006.

Painter, Nell Irvin. *Standing at Armageddon: A Grassroots History of the Progressive Era.* New York: W. W. Norton, 2008.

Postal, Charles. *The Populist Vision.* New York: Oxford University Press, 2009.

Sides, Hampton. *Blood and Thunder, The Epic Story of Kit Carson and the Conquest of the American West.* New York: Anchor, 2007.

Trachtenberg, Alan. *The Incorporation of America: Culture and Society in the Gilded Age.* New York: Hill & Wang, 1982.

White, Richard. *The Republic for Which It Stands: The United States during Reconstruction and the Gilded Age, 1865–1896.* New York: Oxford University Press, 2017.

CHAPTER 7

Anbinder, Tyler. *City of Dreams: The 400-Year Epic History of Immigrant New York.* New York: Mariner, 2017.

Baker, Jean. *Sisters: The Lives of American Suffragists.* New York: Hill & Wang, 2006.

Cappozola, Christopher. *Uncle Sam Wants You: World War I and the Making of the Modern American Citizen.* New York: Oxford University Press, 2010.

Cooper, John Milton. *Pivotal Decades: The United States, 1900–1920.* New York: W. W. Norton, 1990.

Daniels, Roger. *Guarding the Golden Door: American Immigration Policy and Immigrants Since 1882.* New York: Hill & Wang, 2004.

Dray, Philip. *There Is Power in a Union: The Epic Story of Labor in America.* New York: Anchor, 2011.

Gates, Henry Louis. *Stony the Road: Reconstruction, White Supremacy, and the Rise of Jim Crow.* New York: Penguin, 2019.

Gerber, David A. *American Immigration: A Very Short Introduction.* New York: Oxford University Press, 2011.

Hofstadter, Richard. *The Age of Reform.* New York: Vintage, 1960.

Kennedy, David. *Over Here: The First World War and American Society.* New York: Oxford University Press, 2004.

Lukas, J. Anthony. *Big Trouble.* New York: Simon & Schuster, 1997.

McGerr, Michael. *A Fierce Discontent: The Rise and Fall of the Progressive Movement in America, 1870–1920.* New York: Oxford University Press, 2005.

Rodgers, Daniel T. *Atlantic Crossings: Social Politics in a Progressive Age.* Cambridge, MA: Harvard University Press, 2000.

Weiss, Elaine. *The Woman's Hour: The Great Fight to Win the Vote.* New York: Viking, 2018.

Wilkerson, Isabel. *The Warmth of Other Suns: The Epic Story of America's Great Migration.* New York: Vintage, 2011.

CHAPTER 8

Blum, John Morton. *V Was for Victory: Politics and American Culture during World War II.* New York: Mariner, 1977.

Brinkley, Alan. *Voices of Protest: Huey Long, Father Coughlin and the Great Depression.* New York: Vintage, 1983.

Egan, Timothy. *The Worst Hard Time: The Untold Story of Those Who Survived the Great American Dust Bowl.* New York: Mariner, 2006.

Gordon, Linda. *Dorothea Lange: A Life Beyond Limits.* New York: Norton, 2010.

Gregory, James. *American Exodus: The Dust Bowl Migration and Okie Culture in California.* New York: Oxford University Press, 1991.

Hanson, Victor David. *The Second World Wars: How the First Global Conflict Was Fought and Won.* New York: Basic Books, 2017.

Katznelson, Ira. *Fear Itself: The New Deal and the Origins of Our Time.* New York: Liveright, 2014.

Kennedy, David M. *Freedom from Fear: The American People in Depression and War.* New York: Oxford University Press, 2001.

McGirr, Lisa. *The War on Alcohol: Prohibition and the Rise of the American State.* New York: W. W. Norton, 2016.

Okrent, Daniel. *Last Call: The Rise and Fall of Prohibition.* New York: Scribner, 2011.

Parrish, Michael E. *Anxious Decades: America in Prosperity and Depression, 1920–1941.* New York: W. W. Norton, 1994.

Rauchway, Eric. *The Great Depression and the New Deal: A Very Short Introduction.* New York: Oxford University Press, 2008.

Schlaes, Amity. *The Forgotten Man: A New History of the Great Depression.* New York: Harper, 2008.

Smith, Jean Edward. *FDR.* New York: Random House, 2008.

Worster, Donald. *Dust Bowl: The Southern Plains in the 1930s.* New York: Oxford University Press, 1979.

CHAPTER 9

Altschuler, Glenn C. *All Shook Up: How Rock 'n' Roll Changed America.* New York: Oxford University Press, 2004.

Branch, Taylor. *Parting the Waters: America in the King Years, 1954–63.* New York: Simon & Schuster, 1989.

Cohen, Lizabeth. *A Consumer's Republic: The Politics of Mass Consumption in Postwar America.* New York: Vintage, 2003.

Dobbs, Michael. *One Minute to Midnight: Kennedy, Khrushchev, and Castro on the Brink of Nuclear War.* New York: Vintage, 2009.

Dudziak, Mary. *Cold War Civil Rights: Race and the Image of American Democracy.* Princeton, NJ: Princeton University Press, 2011.

Gaddis, John Lewis. *The Cold War: A New History.* New York: Penguin, 2006.

Gitlin, Todd. *The Sixties: Years of Hope, Days of Rage.* New York: Bantam, 1993.

Halberstam, David. *The Fifties.* New York: Ballantine, 1994.

Hastings, Max. *Vietnam: An Epic Tragedy, 1945–1975.* New York: Harper, 2018.

Hitchcock, William I. *Age of Eisenhower: America and the World in the 1950s.* New York: Simon & Schuster, 2018.

Karnow, Stanley. *Vietnam: A History.* New York: Penguin, 1997.

Klarman, Michael J. *From Jim Crow to Civil Rights: The Supreme Court and the Struggle for Racial Equality.* New York: Oxford University Press, 2006.

Lawrence, Mark Atwood. *The Vietnam War: A Concise International History.* New York: Oxford University Press, 2010.

May, Elaine Tyler. *Homeward Bound: American Families in the Cold War Era.* New York: Basic Books, 1988.

Oshinsky, David. *A Conspiracy So Immense: The World of Joe McCarthy.* New York: Oxford University Press, 2005.

Patterson, James T. *Grand Expectations: The United States, 1945–1974.* New York: Oxford University Press, 1997.

Toland, John. *In Mortal Combat: Korea, 1950–1953.* New York: William Morrow, 1991.

CHAPTER 10

Brands, H. W. *Reagan: The Life.* New York: Anchor, 2016.

Cowie, Jefferson. *Stayin' Alive: The 1970s and the Last Days of the Working Class.* New York: New Press, 2012.

Farrell, John A. *Richard Nixon: The Life.* New York: Doubleday, 2017.

Fitzgerald, Frances. *The Evangelicals: The Struggle to Shape America.* New York: Simon & Schuster, 2018.

Freeman, Joshua. *American Empire: The Rise of a Global Power, the Democratic Revolution at Home, 1945–2000.* New York: Penguin, 2013.

Hodgson, Godfrey. *The World Turned Right Side Up: A History of the Conservative Ascendency in America.* New York: Houghton Mifflin, 1996.

Herring, George C. *The American Century and Beyond: U.S. Foreign Relations, 1893–2014.* New York: Oxford University Press, 2017.

Kornacki, Steve. *The Red and the Blue: The 1990s and the Birth of Political Tribalism.* New York: Ecco, 2018.

Kutler, Stanley I. *Wars of Watergate: The Last Crisis of Richard Nixon.* New York: W. W. Norton, 1992.

Patterson, James T. *Restless Giant: The United States from Watergate to Bush v. Gore.* New York: Oxford University Press, 2007.

Perlstein, Rick. *The Invisible Bridge: The Fall of Nixon and the Rise of Reagan.* New York: Simon & Schuster, 2015.

Schulman, Bruce. *The Seventies: The Great Shift in American Culture, Society, and Politics.* New York: DeCapo Press, 2002.

Troy, Gil. *The Age of Clinton: America in the 1990s.* New York: Thomas Dunne, 2015.

Wilentz, Sean. *Age of Reagan: A History, 1974–2008.* New York: Harper, 2009.

CHAPTER 11

Bacevich, Andrew. *America's War for the Greater Middle East: A Military History.* New York: Random House, 2017.

Farrow, Ronan. *War on Peace: The End of Diplomacy and the Decline of American Influence.* New York: W. W. Norton, 2018.

Filkins, Dexter. *The Forever War.* New York: Vintage, 2008.

Finkel, David. *The Good Soldiers.* New York: Picador, 2009.

Fountain, Ben. *Beautiful Country Burn Again: Democracy, Rebellion, and Revolution.* New York: Ecco, 2018.

Frieden, Jeffrey A. *Global Capitalism: Its Fall and Rise in the Twentieth Century.* New York: W. W. Norton, 2007.

Friend, David. *Watching the World Change: The Stories Behind the Images of 9/11.* New York: Picador, 2007.

Gordon, Robert J. *The Rise and Fall of American Growth: The U.S. Standard of Living Since the Civil War.* Princeton, NJ: Princeton University Press, 2017.

Judis, John B. *The Populist Explosion: How the Great Recession Transformed American and European Politics.* New York: Columbia Global Reports, 2016.

Meyer, Jane. *The Dark Side: The Inside Story of How the War on Terror Turned into a War on American Ideals.* New York: Anchor, 2009.

Packer, George. *The Unwinding: An Inner History of the New America.* New York: Farrar, Straus, & Giroux, 2014.

Picketty, Thomas. *Capital in the Twenty-First Century.* Cambridge, MA: Harvard University Press, 2017.

Tooze, Adam. *Crashed: How a Decade of Financial Crisis Changed the World.* New York: Viking, 2018.

Wright, Lawrence. *Looming Tower: Al-Qaeda and the Road to 9/11.* New York: Vintage, 2007.

INDEX